THE
CANADIAN
INTERNET
ADVANTAGE

OPPORTUNITIES
FOR BUSINESS
AND OTHER
ORGANIZATIONS

Jim Carroll

Rick Broadhead

Prentice Hall Canada Inc., Scarborough, Ontario

Canadian Cataloguing in Publication Data

Carroll, Jim, 1959–   .
    The Canadian Internet advantage: opportunities for business
and other organizations

ISBN 0-13-226598-2

1. Business enterprises – Canada – Communication
systems. 2. Internet (Computer network).
3. Information networks. I. Broadhead, Rick. II. Title.

HD30.335.C37 1995 650'.0285'467 C95-930723-0

Prentice-Hall, Inc., Englewood Cliffs, New Jersey
Prentice-Hall International (UK) Limited, London
Prentice-Hall of Australia, Pty. Limited, Sydney
Prentice-Hall Hispanoamericana, S.A., Mexico City
Prentice-Hall of India Private Limited, New Delhi
Prentice-Hall of Japan, Inc., Tokyo
Simon & Schuster Asia Private Limited, Singapore
Editora Prentice-Hall do Brasil, Ltda., Rio de Janeiro

ISBN 0-13-226598-2

Production Editor: Kelly Dickson
Copy Editor: Betty Robinson
Production Coordinator: Anita Boyle-Evans
Cover and Interior Design: Monica Kompter
Cover Images: Tony Stone Images Canada/Lonnie Duka; First Light/Lightscapes
Page Layout: Steve Lewis

1 2 3 4 5 W 99 98 97 96 95

Printed and bound in Canada.

Every reasonable effort has been made to obtain permissions for all
articles and data used in this edition. If errors or omissions have
occurred, they will be corrected in future editions provided written
notification has been received by the publisher.

Table of Contents

Acknowledgments

Many people deserve thanks for their assistance with this book. First and foremost, John Isley, President of Prentice Hall Canada, deserves special mention for guiding the project successfully through its early stages shortly after the 1995 edition of the *Canadian Internet Handbook* was released. We are also indebted to the rest of the *Internet Advantage* team at Prentice Hall Canada: Andrea Aris and Eric Jones for sales and marketing support; Kelly Dickson and David Jolliffe for production and editorial coordination; and finally, Sharon Sawyer and Judy Bunting, the unsung heroes at Prentice Hall, who cheerfully responded to our calls for couriers and assistance.

Betty Robinson, our editor, did an absolutely marvelous job, and was a joy to work with.

Mike Martineau of NSTN Inc. performed an independent review of the book while it was in progress. Since he has been involved in both editions of our *Canadian Internet Handbook*, he seems to be almost a member of the team. Thanks once again for useful guidance, feedback and criticism!

We are grateful to NSTN, Vaxxine Computer Systems Inc. and Inforamp Inc. for the provision of Internet services used while researching this book. Inforamp also implemented our mail robot and sponsored World Wide Web pages for us. We also want to acknowledge e-Commerce Inc., a Mississauga-based company that specializes in hosting on-line sites, for sponsoring Web pages for us. Thank you! Dale Edgar and Tim Smith of Cybersmith Inc. in New Brunswick are the Internet whizzes who created the World Wide Web site for this book and for the *Canadian Internet Handbook*. Their continued support for our books is much appreciated.

Finally, we must thank our families who have given us their unwavering support through four successive book projects. Richard, Violet, and Kristin Broadhead and Ya-Ya provided much-needed support and encouragement while Rick was writing. On Jim's side, Christa Carroll deserves a special award for putting up with a husband who decided to write a book during the latter half of her pregnancy, and for an outstanding effort at helping to pull the book together right up to her delivery date. Thanks to Willie (William Carroll) for his patience while his Daddy was writing, and to Thomas James for holding off his arrival on this earth until Daddy had the book done! Thanks also go to Oma and Opa for the use of their basement when a quiet place was much needed to write, and for their outstanding assistance and support shown while the book was in progress.

Jim Carroll
Rick Broadhead

About the Authors

....

Jim Carroll, C.A., is principal owner of J.A. Carroll Consulting, a Mississauga-based firm which assists organizations with the strategic use of telecommunications technology. Through J.A. Carroll Consulting, Mr. Carroll has assisted many organizations with the strategic use of the Internet to support global marketing and customer-based activities. Mr. Carroll is a prolific writer with a regular monthly column on electronic mail in *Computing Canada* and the *Toronto Star*, as well as a number of other publications (copies of many articles are available on his World Wide Web site, **http://www.e-commerce.com/jacc.html**). Mr. Carroll is a popular speaker and seminar leader with respect to the Internet and is in particular demand by companies and organizations seeking advice and strategies with respect to the global information highway and the Internet. Mr. Carroll is represented nationally and internationally by the National Speakers Bureau of Vancouver, British Columbia, which can be reached at 1-800-661-4110 or 1-604-224-2384, or by sending a message to **jcarroll@jacc.com** or **tgill@nsb.com**.

Rick Broadhead, B.B.A., is the principal owner of Intervex Consulting, a Toronto-based Internet consulting firm. He is recognized as a clear articulator of the Internet's benefits for business, and he is skilled at speaking about the Internet in non-technical language. He has made presentations about the Internet at business, professional, and government conferences across Canada. Mr. Broadhead has also made presentations to the senior management of a number of Canadian organizations to help them understand the strategic opportunities available on the Internet. He can be reached on the Internet at **rickb@hookup.net**, or by visiting his World Wide Web home page at **http://www.handbook.com/intervex**.

Contacting Us

We want to hear from you about this book. We welcome comments, criticisms, and suggestions. We do try to respond directly to all e-mail sent to us. Feedback is most appreciated. If your organization is launching a new Internet service, or if you are involved in an Internet initiative that you think we should know about, please drop us a line. If you think your organization is a good illustration of a strategy that we have discussed in this book, please let us know as well.

Contacting the Authors Directly

Here is how to contact us on the Internet:

handbook@uunet.ca	To reach both Jim Carroll and Rick Broadhead
jcarroll@jacc.com	To reach Jim Carroll
rickb@hookup.net	To reach Rick Broadhead

Our Mail Robot

We have established a mail robot (an automated e-mail response system) that provides information about our books by e-mail. To obtain current information about this book or our *Canadian Internet Handbook*, send a message to **info@handbook.com**. You will be sent back a message that provides information on how you can find out more about our Internet books and our on-line resources.

Our World Wide Web Sites

You can access our World Wide Web home page at **http://lydian.csi.nb.ca/handbook/handbook.html**. There you will find information about this book and the *Canadian Internet Handbook*.

Jim Carroll maintains a World Wide Web site at **http://www.e-commerce.com/jacc.html**. He posts to this site, on a regular basis, articles that he writes about the Internet and the information superhighway for *Computing Canada*, the *Toronto Star*, and other publications. Rick Broadhead maintains a World Wide Web site at **http://www.handbook.com/intervex**, which includes pointers to major corporations and businesses that have a presence on the World Wide Web. The listing is updated on a regular basis.

Foreword

Over the last couple of years there has been a sea change in Canada.

Business, government, community groups, the press have discovered the information highway and its exemplar, the Internet. The initial silence, followed by a blizzard of competing hype and cynicism, has now been eclipsed by action. There are amazing implementations, important debates, big investments underway, government advisory committees, new alliances, pilot implementations—and quietly hundreds of thousands of Canadians have come onto the Net.

The way things are going a majority of Canadians will be wired well before the end of this decade. There has never been a technology in our country which has proliferated so fast or held such a huge potential. The Net is coming into our lives.

And none too soon. I am convinced that the Internet is the foundation of a new infrastructure for a new economy. This unparalleled communications medium will change the way we create wealth and sustain social development. And any society which does not embrace this new paradigm will quickly fall behind. Punishment for laggards is already proving to be swift.

This view is still not widely held. Many see the highway as simply a way of delivering movies on demand, configuring a pizza on the screen or shopping for zirconium. For media critic Neil Postman the highway is an extension of television, taking us further down the road to couch potatodom. "Information has become a new form of garbage," he says, enabling us to "amuse ourselves to death."

But something very different and far-reaching is happening here. The developed world is changing from an Industrial Economy based on steel, automobiles and roads to a Digital Economy built on silicon, computers and networks. In this new economy, digital networks and human knowledge are transforming just about everything we produce and do. In the old economy, information, communications and transactions were physical—represented by cash, cheques, invoices, bills of lading, reports, face-to-face meetings, analog telephone calls or radio and television transmissions, receipts, drawings, blueprints, maps, photographs, records, books, newspapers, magazines, musical scores and direct mail advertisements, to name a few. In the new economy, increasingly, information in all its forms, transactions and human communications become digital—reduced to bits stored in computers and racing at the speed of light across networks.

The digitization and networking of information and knowledge has far reaching implications beyond entertainment. Call them "The Big Five."

1. Wealth Creation

For years, effective use of information technology has been central to competitiveness and success in business. Federal Express and Wal-Mart embraced networks and succeeded. The U.S. Postal Service and Sears did not and fell behind.

But as commerce moves onto the highway the whole concept of the firm is changing. Larger companies are shifting from hierarchical to networked organizations. Smaller companies use networks to acquire the benefits of size and scale without the disadvantages of deadening bureaucracy. Clusters of firms join together in new kinds of structures and relationships for mutual success. Markets are becoming electronic. We are changing the way we create, market and distribute products and services—the first fundamental change in the way business is done in over a century.

The evidence is already strong that businesses and societies which can transition to new models of wealth creation have a chance of succeeding in the new volatile, global marketplace.

2. Electronic Government

Around the world the public sector is under siege. Taxpayers everywhere want better, cheaper government. The message is simple: tinkering with the system is not good enough. What's needed is a complete reinvention of government.

Layering technology on a dysfunctional body politic will not fix the problem. But if properly conceived, networks can be central to improving the business of government. Government programs can be delivered electronically on the Net, improving quality and reducing costs. Government information can be made accessible, creating more open government. Virtual departments can combine the work of many agencies to deliver a single window to the public. Bureaucracies can be flattened by networking.

3. Learning

The digital economy is requiring a rethinking of education and, more broadly, learning and the relationship between working, learning and daily life as a consumer. Learning has become a life-long challenge. By the time you graduate from university, much of what you learned in first year is obsolete. Modern factories in Canada, like AlliedSignal's Toronto plant, are brimming with computers, robots and networks; and the workers there are continually learning sophisticated new techniques. Because the new economy is a knowledge economy and learning is part of day-to-day economic activity and life, both companies and individuals have found they need to take responsibility for learning simply to be effective.

The Net is the new infrastructure for learning, delivering everything from encyclopedias to university courses, interactive training programs about welding, scholarly discussion groups, access to the world's libraries, or information about how to care for your sick dog. While many schools and other formal institutions have been slow to respond to the challenge, there are centres of innovation springing up across the country. For example, schools in West Vancouver, Oakville, Ontario, North Toronto, Ottawa-Carleton and St. John's have become wired and their students have set out on a new learning adventure. Kids in grade four work on the Net with colleagues in Tokyo on a spiders project: The new technology for learning and learning for the new technology and economy.

4. Health Care

Can networks change the delivery of health care and in doing so save Canada's enviable health care system from the centrifugal pressures of growing costs and changing demographics? Recent evidence suggests yes. Scores of pilot projects underway in Canada and the US lend support to this prediction of better and cheaper health care. Experimental high-capacity communications systems are already enabling health care professionals to make much better use of their time, and allow an individual's expertise to be made available over a much wider geographical area.

In Quebec a test program enables doctors at the Montreal Cardiology Institute to share EKGs, ultrasounds, X-rays and mammograms via a network. Doctors save time and the need for patient revisits is being reduced. Plans call for other hospitals to join the network. In Alberta, medical specialists at the University of Calgary are helping rural health care providers through a trial system of responding to inquiries through audio, video, imaging, and data transmission. In BC, hospitals in different cities are using an advanced high-capacity communications system to conduct video training seminars. The system can send high-resolution images of microscopic tissue slides for simultaneous observation and discussion. Medical staff in fields such as pathology are cutting travel time between hospitals, using interactive voice, video and data instead.

And these are just the beginning. Secure health care cards and the computer-based patient record can cut massive costs from the system and improve the quality of health care.

5. Social Development and Nation Building

Beyond these, there are growing opportunities to improve the social fabric in this vast geographical space called Canada. For example, could networks with instant simultaneous translation help break down Canada's two solitudes?

If we do it right, the smaller country our kids inherit will be a better one. As the chair of the Ontario government's advisory committee on the information highway, I was struck by native Chief Lawrence Martin's impassioned arguments for the highway. He believes networks can bring native people together with each other and with Canada. Provinces, communities, first nations, others could be empowered, yet still be part of a coherent nation-state. Early implementations involving native communities are showing that he is right.

Broadcasting as we know it is ending. Rather than a one-way dump, the new media are interactive, enabling high capacity, person-to-person communications. The channels for human interaction are opening exponentially. Could the Net strengthen our families by bringing some economic activity, learning, health care and entertainment back into the home? Will we increase our capacity for comprehension, for learning from each other, for influencing each other and compromise, for new democratic processes which give people from all walks of life better control over their lives?

Or will we see the dark side? The Net was used to organize rescue and law enforcement efforts after the April 1995 Oklahoma bombing. But it was also used by members and supporters of extremist Michigan militia to coordinate their response as well. This is a time of promise and peril.

Passive observation of historic changes breeds paralysis and cynicism. Each of us has an opportunity to get involved. And if we do—by the millions—Canada will have competitive businesses in the new economy, avoiding the alternative of structural unemployment and economic decline. If we get involved we can craft better governments, education, health care, social institutions. If we get involved we will bring our values and aspirations and legitimate expectations to the table, achieving promise and avoiding the dark side.

If you haven't done so already, get on the Net. You will benefit from global e-mail and access to the World Wide Web. Your company needs an Internet strategy. Your community group needs a home page. Your kids' school needs to get wired. Your marketplace is becoming electronic and your products should be there.

If you don't know how to get started or be effective, one approach is to ask your kids. The generation gap has become a generation lap as our kids are naturally embracing the new media and passing us on the way.

It is in this context that the publication of the *Canadian Internet Advantage: Opportunities for Business and Other Organizations* is important. Three years ago Canada had fallen behind the United States and some other countries in highway progress. Jim Carroll and Rick Broadhead's first book, the *Canadian Internet Handbook*, helped achieve an awakening in this country. Their new book is another important contribution in getting us to a new infrastructure for a new economy. Enjoy it as together we seek to realize the promise and avoid the peril for our country, our organizations and ourselves.

Don Tapscott
1995

Don Tapscott is Chairman of The Alliance for Converging Technologies, which is conducting a multi-million-dollar investigation of the information highway and its impact on business. He is also the co-author of the best-selling book *Paradigm Shift: The New Promise of Information Technology*. His fourth and fifth books, to be published in the fall of 1995, are entitled *The Digital Economy: Promise and Peril in the Age of Networked Intelligence* (co-authored with Rod McQueen) and *Who Knows? Safeguarding Your Privacy in a Digital World* (co-authored with Ann Cavoukian).

Introduction

> This book is about what happens to people when they are overwhelmed by change. It is about the ways in which we adapt — or fail to adapt — to the future.
>
> Opening paragraph, *Future Shock*, by Alvin Toffler, 1970

There has been an incredible amount of hype, excitement, and skepticism about the Internet. Many believe that something significant is happening here, and that there will be opportunities for those who learn how to participate in this evolving network. This book is about the change represented by the Internet.

The Internet does represent change — substantial change — to the way that business and other organizations operate. Quite simply, people and organizations are learning new and more efficient methods of working through the Internet, the world's largest computer network, and are discovering new methods of marketing, selling, supporting customers, delivering services, and providing education.

This book does not hype the Internet; it identifies Internet opportunities in clear, non-technical language. It takes a look at what the Internet really represents to business, government, not-for-profit organizations, and health and educational organizations. It examines the Internet from a management perspective by providing clear guidance on the strategic opportunities to be found on the network. It is written for CEOs, business strategists, information technology managers, corporate planners, and other senior executives who need to guide their organizations into the future.

It is written for those who have little familiarity with the Internet. You do not have to be a user of the Internet to understand its opportunities. It is also written for those who have "surfed" the global Internet, but want a more detailed understanding of where the real opportunities are.

Organization of This Book

This book consists of three sections and twelve chapters. Each chapter includes a summary that highlights the important points made in that chapter.

Chapters 1 to 3 provide a non-technical introduction to the Internet. The chapters have been written to introduce readers to the Internet from a fundamental level, by putting into perspective the many different aspects of the network. It is a good primer for those who know that the Internet exists, but have not taken the plunge to "understand" it. And even if you are already familiar with the Internet, and you surf it daily, you still might find these chapters enlightening, for they may provide you with new ways of thinking about the Internet.

Chapters 4 to 8 form the heart of this book, and describe the strategic advantages to be found in the Internet. Each chapter has been written after a thorough and detailed review of the many different strategies currently being used by dozens of organizations on the Internet.

Chapters 9 to 11 discuss important issues that you need to think about when developing an Internet strategy for your organization. Chapter 9 provides a step-by-step guide to preparing an Internet strategy. Chapter 10 discusses the subject of corporate image and how it pertains to an organization's Internet strategy. Chapter 11 examines some issues that organizations need to think about as they deploy the Internet within their organization. These issues include security, electronic mail privacy, intellectual property, electronic commerce, and employee productivity.

Chapter 12 wraps up the book by discussing the long-term impact of the Internet on our economy and on our society.

There are three appendices that provide supplementary information. Appendix A, "Selected Useful On-Line Resources," provides Internet addresses for many useful, business-related Internet sites and tools. Appendix B, "Useful Internet-Related Publications," provides a summary of useful print resources that cover the Internet. Appendix C provides a listing of Canadian Internet access providers, organizations that sell access to the Internet across Canada.

This is not a technical book. If you feel that you need a more detailed technical overview of the many aspects of the Internet, we refer you to our *Canadian Internet Handbook*, discussed below.

Why We Wrote This Book

We wrote this book with two objectives in mind. First, we want to help Canadian organizations understand why the Internet is important and how it will affect their business activities. While there are many technical books about the Internet, there are few that examine the network from a business perspective.

Second, we want to help Canadian organizations understand how to use the Internet for competitive advantage. We accomplished the latter objective by undertaking an exhaustive review of the activities of hundreds of organizations on the Internet. From these activities we identified over 80 Internet strategies that are being employed by businesses, not-for-profit organizations, government agencies and departments, educational institutions, and organizations in the health care sector. *No other Internet book in the world has undertaken such an exhaustive and comprehensive review of Internet strategies.*

This is our second Internet book. Our first book, the *Canadian Internet Handbook*, 1994 edition, was released in early March 1994 and provided a unique Canadian perspective on the Internet for the many thousands of Canadians who were clamoring to join the network. That edition sold some 45,000 copies and became a national best-seller. At one point the *Financial Post* ranked it as the #1 selling non-fiction paperback in Canada. Eight months later, in November 1994, we released the 1995 edition of the *Canadian Internet Handbook*. The 1995 update reflected the tremendous growth in the Internet since the 1994 edition had been released: it was four times heavier and over 450 pages thicker than its predecessor. The 1995 edition sold over 60,000 copies by April 1995, proving once again that Canadians have embraced the Internet in large numbers.

The *Canadian Internet Handbook* provides technical, managerial, and general guidance to Canadians who want to join the Internet. The 1995 edition includes a chapter that discusses how to do business on the Internet. Many readers wrote to us and asked us to expand the concepts found in that chapter. The result is this book.

The Internet is an exciting technology, and it can be a complex and challenging system to understand from a technical point of view. While there are many technical books about the Internet, there are few that explore its business and *strategic* angle. Something significant is happening on the Internet, and we passionately believe that the network will have a profound and deep impact on all Canadian organizations. Our thoughts and strategies are crystallized in this book, written for the thinker, strategist, or any Canadian who wants to understand the strategic significance of the Internet for his/her organization.

We feel qualified to write this book. Jim Carroll is a Chartered Accountant, with a substantial practical business and financial background, combined with 12 years of experience with the on-line industry, four of those in his Mississauga-based firm, J.A. Carroll Consulting, through which he provides consulting services and speaking engagements about the Internet across Canada. Rick Broadhead runs a Toronto-based Internet consulting firm, Intervex Consulting, and has spoken about Internet business strategy at seminars and conferences across Canada. We have both provided consulting services with respect to the Internet and affiliated technologies to many *Fortune* 500 and smaller organizations across Canada.

Our business insight, combined with our Internet expertise, allows us to provide you with a truly unique insight into the strategic opportunities available on the Internet. Hopefully, you will find it a worthwhile read.

Conventions

This book is sprinkled with the names of popular Internet applications, primarily

➢ Internet electronic mail (e-mail);

➢ The World Wide Web (the Web);

➢ USENET.

We describe these applications in Chapter 3.

When dealing with the Internet, it is important to understand that we often describe various "information resources" on the network. Electronic mail addresses and the addresses of Internet "sites" are expressed in bold letters. Most of the Internet sites referred to in this book are World Wide Web sites. World Wide Web site addresses look like this: **http://location_of_site**. For example, the World Wide Web address for the Goodyear Tire Company is **http://www.goodyear.com**. The address **http://www.goodyear.com** is known as the URL, or *Uniform Resource Locator*, of the Goodyear site on the Internet. Internet users need to know this address in order to travel to the Goodyear site.

You should think of a World Wide Web address as the Internet equivalent of a telephone number. Just as every telephone number uniquely identifies a residence or business somewhere in the world, every World Wide Web address uniquely identifies a location on the Internet. If you are not yet on the Internet, you will not have much use for World Wide Web addresses. If you are on the Internet, these addresses will permit you to travel to the sites mentioned in this book so that you can examine them in greater depth.

Keep in mind that the Internet is in a state of flux and is constantly changing. The examples mentioned throughout this book existed as of April 1995. However, some locations will change, move, or disappear forever. Such is the nature of the Internet.

Examples Used in This Book

While we have written this book for Canadians, the examples used in this book are not exclusively Canadian. You will find that many American organizations are used to illustrate some of the strategies. This was done intentionally. The examples that we used were chosen based on their quality, not their country of origin. If an American organization is using a strategy in a unique or important way, then we believe that Canadian organizations can benefit by understanding what the American organization is doing.

CHAPTER 1

The Internet–A World of Opportunities

> "...new software and imaginative services are making the Internet one of the most exciting places ever for doing business."
>
> The Internet — How it will change the way you do business
>
> *BusinessWeek*, November 14, 1994

*E*ven before you bought this book, you had probably heard much about the wonders of the Internet and how it will change the world around us. While you hear a lot of talk about the Internet, you still may not be quite sure what it is or what it represents. You might be confused by the technology that surrounds it or overwhelmed by the hype that seems to envelope it.

You might be intimidated by the computer technology that makes up the Internet. You want to understand it without listening to computer geeks speak of the wonders of high-speed broadband internetworking or the joys of multitasking. You might want to understand the Internet without getting lost in talk about bits and bytes and RAM and ROM and FTP and Telnet.

You might even be using the Internet already, on a day-to-day basis, but you want a better understanding of what it is really all about. Having ventured into the Internet, you can tell that something important is going on, but you are not quite sure what. You need a clearer picture of where all this *stuff* is headed.

You have an interest in the network known as the Internet — but to your frustration, no one has been able to explain the *strategic potential* of the Internet to you. So, you want to understand the business opportunities that can be found through use of the Internet. You want to know how it can be used in an educational or government setting. You want to understand its

THE INTERNET — A WORLD OF OPPORTUNITIES

(1) The Internet is the leading trend that is linking all of the world's computers together.

(2) The Internet allows anyone to become a global publisher and turns personal computers into "information appliances."

(3) The Internet's benefits are primarily long-term.

(4) The Internet is used by people in all professions and in all walks of life.

(5) The popular press plays up the issue that the Internet is full of computer nerds, that it is full of sex, and that it is full of hackers. Media hype is not a good introduction to the reality of the Internet as a significant business and organizational communication network.

(6) You join the Internet by contracting with an Internet access provider. A list of Canadian Internet service providers is in Appendix C.

(7) There are no restrictions on business use of the Internet, but businesses should follow proper Internet etiquette when participating on the network.

(8) The Internet is transforming
  • Businesses
  • Educational organizations
  • Federal, provincial, and municipal governments
  • Not-for-profit organizations and associations
  • Medicine and science

(9) Other emerging technologies to watch include electronic data interchange (EDI), asynchronous transfer mode (ATM), commercial information databases, and the information highway.

(10) The technology is not important — the opportunities are.

role in not-for-profit organizations. You want to know its impact on scientific research and health care services.

You want to know how to put together an Internet strategy, and you want to know how to implement it within your organization. *You need to understand the Internet as a strategy, not just as a technology.*

Regardless of who you are and what your objectives, it is clear that you need a good, hard, and honest look at the opportunities that can be found in the network known as the Internet.

That's what this book is all about.

The Internet is important for one simple reason — it is the leading edge of a trend in which all the computers in the world are becoming wired together. The mere existence of such a trend gives pause for some thought. How will business be affected? Education? Government? Science? Our own personal lives?

No one knows for sure what will happen, but one thing is certain — the impact on our world of a trend in which all computers globally become linked together will be dramatic.

Quite frankly, many people view the development of the Internet as one of the most significant events in human history, equal in importance to the invention of the printing press and the telephone. Why? In effect, the Internet provides everyone who has a computer and modem with their own Gutenberg press through which they can become a global publisher. Anyone, anywhere in the world, who joins the Internet can publish information on any topic, at any time.

This is a major change in the source of world information. The impact of the Internet is that the entire global information paradigm is undergoing a complete and radical change. Information today just doesn't come from the media and the publishing industry — it comes from everywhere, from anyone, at any time, through the Internet.

Through the Internet everyone becomes a publisher, a journalist, a critic, a reporter, a writer, and an author. Through the Internet anyone is an information creator and an information distributor. Through the Internet anyone can contribute information to the world. This, too, is a significant change.

The Internet is also significant because it changes the role of computers for many people. Think about it — to this point in time, most of us have learned how to use personal computers (PCs) to do word processing, to use a spreadsheet, or to do personal or corporate accounting. We have learned to use PCs to do *personal* things. The Internet changes this in a significant way.

Since anyone can be a publisher on the Internet, there is an explosion of available information. The information resources that are available on the Internet today are mind-boggling — and new announcements of new information sites are continually made.

The result is that the Internet suddenly extends the reach of our lonely little personal computer to millions of other computers and millions of other people around the world, and to millions of information sources. Quite simply, our little PC is no longer just a computer — it is an "information appliance" plugged into the whole of human knowledge.

The Internet is a system that is here today — it is used by people for various purposes in 168 countries around the world. It is a relatively new system; even though it recently celebrated a twenty-fifth anniversary, for all intents and purposes the Internet that most of us know today is less than five years old. *The Internet is still an infant.*

People and organizations using the Internet *today* are getting a brief, exhilarating, and tantalizing view of what the world will look like in the future. They are obtaining first-hand experience at how the wired world of the future will work, and are gaining an understanding of the impact of global communications on our business and personal lives. People working with the Internet today are like new parents: full of wonder and delight with their new child, and in awe of the possibilities for the future.

Even though the Internet is in its infancy, there are benefits that can be obtained by getting involved with it today. Through the Internet you can already locate and support new customers around the globe. You can use it in the classroom to enhance the learning process and to establish new methods of learning. Governments can use it to provide services to constituents in new and innovative ways. It can be used by not-for-profit organizations to recruit new volunteers and to locate new sources of funding. For an infant, it sure shows a lot of promise.

For all the promise that the Internet shows, we need to keep in mind that we are still in the very early stages of a significant development.

We need to be cautious and realistic in our expectations of the Internet.

This is particularly true when it comes to the use of the Internet for strategic purposes. There has been a lot of talk of late about the significant "competitive advantage" that organizations can obtain by utilizing the Internet. In many ways, the opportunity has been overhyped, because many people have come to expect too much success too soon. Like any new technology, we need to be realistic in our expectations of what the Internet can deliver. We need an understanding of its promise without the hype.

In this book we will provide you with an overview of the Internet without that hype, in simple, human terms and not in technical terms.

The Internet is for the Long Term

As a first step, we'll be quite frank with you on the benefits of the Internet.

If you get involved with the Internet, you need to recognize that it is a system that can take some time to deliver results. The Internet won't dramatically affect your business overnight — it is not a place to "get rich quick." You won't instantly become a "knowledge expert," able to access the whole of human knowledge merely by pressing a key. It will take some time to learn how to navigate the Internet's massive information sources. Using the Internet for a week or a month won't dramatically change your skill set such that you are more likely to find a job or an opportunity — it will change your skills in more subtle ways.

The Internet promises a lot, but in approaching it, you need to be real in your expectations. The reality is that the Internet won't change your life in the short term, but it will change it dramatically in the longer term. Perhaps it will take months, or a year, or maybe five years. But have no doubt — it will happen. Slowly, you will learn how to use the Internet within your organization. Slowly, you will discover its richness, its diversity, and its opportunity. Then one day you will sit back and marvel at its power and be in awe by what it offers you. You will have mastered the Internet, and it will forever change your view of the world.

Key Internet Trends

If you think that the Internet is hype, that it is this year's hula hoop, or that it is a management fad, think again!

Yes, the Internet is overhyped, and there is a bit of faddishness to it. There are too many people who would like to oversell what the Internet can do. There are too many optimistic projections about its capabilities. Yet, the reality is that we are at a very early stage with this thing called the Internet.

If we keep in mind that slowly and inevitably all the computers around the world will plug together, then we can appreciate that the Internet is not going to go away. Quite simply, it is evident to many that the Internet is clearly paving the foundation for the much-hyped information highway, and that it will become as fundamental to our working and personal lives as our global telephone system.

Carefully observe some of the reality of the Internet today, and you will see some critical trends.

> There is continued corporate growth and an increase in commercial registrations in the Internet, indicating a continuing trend for use of the Internet for business purposes.

The number of commercial organizations with registered Internet domains[1] is growing by about 10% per month.[2] As of January 1995, there were over 31,000 organizations in the United States and Canada that had registered domains on the Internet. Organizations of all types, from multinational Fortune 500s to small, one-person consulting firms, are registering

---

[1] A domain is the name that uniquely identifies a site (business, government, not-for-profit, education; etc.) on the Internet. When organizations connect to the Internet, they often register a domain name for their organization. For example, pepsi.com is the domain name for the Pepsi-Cola Company.

[2] *New on the Net*, Internet Info, Falls Church, Virginia, January 15, 1995.

on the Internet and establishing links to the network in order to support some type of business or commercial activity. If you have any doubt about the fact that the corporate world has discovered the Internet, examine the box below, which shows some of the household names that are beginning to build a presence on the Internet.

SOME OF THE ORGANIZATIONS REGISTERING INTERNET DOMAINS IN 1994/1995[3]

Burger King
Calvin Klein
Cannon Inc.
Coca-Cola Foods
Embassy Suites Hotels
J. Walter Thompson
Hasbro, Inc.
Holt, Rinehart & Winston
Kellogg Company
L.L. Bean Inc.
Maytag Corporation
National Basketball Association
Nike Inc.
Nintendo
Ocean Spray Cranberries
Price Waterhouse
Ralston Purina Company
Roto Rooter
Sara Lee Corporation
Southwest Airlines
The Gap
TV Guide Magazine
Warner Bros. Records

In 1994, the number of commercial (i.e., business) organizations registered on the Internet increased by 150% over the previous year. The number of government and educational registrations increased by 64% and 33%, respectively, over the same time period.[4]

---

[3] *New on the Net*, Internet Info, Falls Church, Virginia, December 15, 1994; *New on the Net*, Internet Info, Falls Church, Virginia, January 15, 1995.

[4] **ftp.cdnnet.ca/ca-domain/statistics**

➤ An Internet information service known as the World Wide Web continues to explode in terms of the number of information locations (or servers), the number of users, and the volume of information accessed.

Use of the World Wide Web is growing at the rate of 25% per month, according to the international Internet Society, an organization that sponsors the use of the Internet around the globe. The growth in the volume of information sent through the World Wide Web from September to October 1994 actually exceeded the total usage of March 1994. It is now estimated that some 100 – 400 new information sites are established on the World Wide Web each week — new sites that contain information that can be accessed by virtually anyone in the world who is directly connected to the Internet.

➤ The number of computers connected to the Internet is growing exponentially. There are over 5 million computers physically linked to the Internet, as illustrated by the following graphs. Current projections indicate that if the current growth rate continues, there will be over 100 million computers connected to the Internet by the year 2000. Any computer linked to the Internet might support one individual or thousands of individuals.

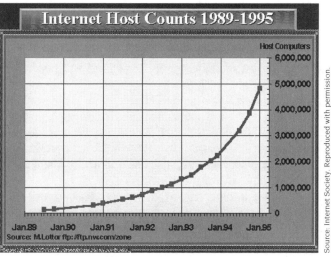

Source: Internet Society. Reproduced with permission.

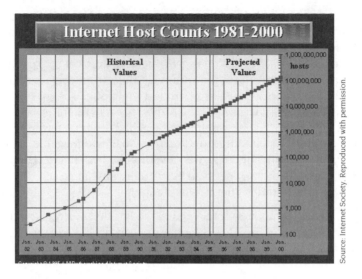

The Internet growth rates are impressive and are often used to hype the significance of the network. Even if we ignore the hype, however, we can appreciate that there is something fundamental occurring through the Internet — an explosion in the number of interlinked computers around the globe.

The significance of the Internet is also revealed by the involvement of new organizations in the business of selling access to the network — including major communication companies such as BCTEL, ED TEL, AGT, SaskTel, NBTel, Rogers Communications, AT&T, and MCI.

Major software organizations such as Microsoft and IBM are building access to the Internet into their operating system software (Windows/95 and OS/2), extending the reach of the Internet to many tens of millions more people around the globe.

Quite simply, many large organizations have come to realize that the Internet represents a substantial and significant business opportunity, and they are getting involved in the business of providing access to it.

The mere existence and continued growth of this network on a global basis gives us pause for thought. But even before we consider what is happening with the Internet, we want to take a moment to debunk some of the common myths that surround the network.

Internet Myths and Common Questions

The Internet seemed to spring out of nowhere in early 1994 and was soon featured prominently in many newscasts, magazines, and newspapers. Unfortunately, in many cases this early press coverage managed to confuse a lot of people, many of whom still aren't clear about what the Internet is all about. Hence we'll take a look at some of the common myths and common questions about the Internet.

Isn't the Internet Used Primarily by High-Tech Companies and Computer People?

Some people would lead you to believe that the Internet is dominated by computer and high-tech companies like Digital Equipment, Microsoft, and NASA, and that the only people who use it are computer geeks. This couldn't be further from the truth.

Consider some of the people whom we have recently encountered on the Internet — accountants, actors, advertising executives, archaeologists, beekeepers, bankers, chemists, chiropractors, dentists, doctors, firefighters, helicopter pilots, interior decorators, journalists, lawyers, librarians, managers, musicians, photographers, politicians, radio broadcasters, real estate agents, and veterinarians. People from all walks of life are discovering the benefits of using the Internet in their professions.

The important point to understand is that the Internet is being used by your friends, relatives, co-workers, and business partners. *The Internet is being used by mainstream society.*

Isn't the Internet Full of Sex? Nazis? Hate Literature?

If you listen to the press, the Internet would appear to be some dark, terrible place, full of terrible people and terrible information. Unfortunately, many members of the media, people who have a need for sensationalistic reporting, find that the Internet offers the perfect focus for the shocking story of the day. "The Internet carries pornography!" they report. "Nazis distribute hate literature on the Internet!" scream the headlines. It would seem that the media can't quite figure out the Internet, and they have to resort to the two-minute "sound bite" when covering it.

Their "reality" is far from the truth. Millions of people sign onto the Internet every day to research information and communicate with their business partners and co-workers. Global knowledge access and global networking through the Internet have become fundamental to the regular working lives of many millions of people. Research and knowledge exchange through the Internet is transforming science, business, education, and government. People who have discovered that the Internet provides them with new and significant global knowledge capabilities are insulted by this silly focus in the media on the Internet's "dark side."

Yes, the Internet is used for the distribution of information that is of questionable taste. Some of the material you come across on the Internet runs against current accepted community standards and could be considered to be in violation of the laws of Canada. There is no doubt that the Internet poses some extremely challenging issues to society in the areas of information access and freedom of information, and that it presents some difficult moral and legal issues. As a society we have to learn to deal with technologies such as the Internet that transcend moral and national borders.

However, given all the positive aspects of the Internet, the media's preoccupation with the Internet's dark side is disturbing.

I Heard that the Internet is Full of Computer Crackers. Won't They Invade my Computer?

This is another common story reported in the press about the Internet. Think about it. How many articles have you read that indicate that a computer "cracker" has again cracked NORAD, has compromised security at the Pentagon, or has traded secret information concerning sensitive military installations?

Perhaps all of us have seen the movie *War Games* too many times, where a youngster attacks the U.S. Department of Defense computer system by using a PC and a modem. We are led to believe that we live in a world in which a hacker-induced nuclear holocaust is just around the corner.

The reality is that the Internet does present security issues, and on occasion there are security compromises. But often the risk is overstated or overhyped by the media. Let's be realistic about the hacker threat on the Internet: if you ignore security issues, you are at risk, but if you pay proper attention to them, you can minimize many of the potential risks to an acceptable degree, although no computer risk can be removed entirely. Organizations can spend the time and effort to minimize computer security risks, and many thousands on the Internet have.

Can I Get a Computer Virus by Taking a File off the Internet?

Absolutely. Any *executable* file (i.e., software, such as a game) that you get from the Internet may contain a computer virus. Any computer programs taken off the Internet should be run through a virus program to ensure that they contain no viruses.

But the risk of getting a computer virus off the Internet should not be overstated. The risk is no higher than that of getting a computer virus from a computer bulletin board service or other on-line service.

Ok, So Who Controls It? Who Owns It? Who Runs It?

The Internet is not controlled by anyone, nor is it owned by anyone — it is a worldwide system consisting of millions of people and millions of computers, connected by all kinds of different telecommunications technologies. There is no Internet Company Inc., nor is there a central authority that sets the rules on the Internet. There is no big computer somewhere with the word "Internet" printed on it. Given the lack of control, some people have called the Internet the largest functioning anarchy in the world.

The Internet doesn't exist in a physical form, other than through the telecommunications lines on which it is built and the computers through which it runs. You don't need to know how the Internet works to use it.

So How Do I Get On It?

To get on the Internet, you need to contact a company called an "Internet access provider." Internet access providers are organizations that are in the business of selling access to the Internet. Appendix C contains a directory of companies in Canada that sell access to the Internet.

For a more technical discussion of what's involved in getting connected to the Internet, we invite you to take a look at our *Canadian Internet Handbook*, a book that explains in detail how to join the network as well as the technicalities of how to use it.

I Heard that you can't do Business on the Internet. Is this True?

The Internet has become a business network. It is also used by academic organizations, not-for-profit organizations, and the government. Many different people from many walks of life use the Internet on a daily basis.

At one time there were "acceptable use policies" on the Internet, which prohibited use of the Internet for anything but academic and research purposes. But by late 1994, most, if not all, such policies had been nullified, thus removing any restriction on the use of the Internet for business purposes.

This is not to say that any business can charge forth and use the Internet for any business purpose whatsoever. The Internet is its own society and community, albeit a wired one, which has evolved over time. And like any society, it has its own "rules" and "culture," which define what is and what is not acceptable behavior.

Your Internet neighbors expect you to function and to live in this society as a good neighbor according to current cultural norms. And one of the key norms of the Internet is that "junk mail" and "unsolicited information" are unacceptable. Hence, while it is entirely possible to do business on the Internet, it has to be done in certain ways, within the currently accepted cultural attitude of the network. We discuss this topic in greater depth in Chapter 4.

Ok, So What is It Good For?

The Internet is already defining how businesses will operate in the future. Imagine that as a small businessperson, you have the ability to market your products and support your customers and clients around the world on a 24-hour basis, no matter where you might be. Imagine new methods of reaching out to existing customers and finding new potential customers.

The Internet is reshaping education, since it offers unparalleled opportunities for educators and students alike to change the way we learn in our schools. Quite simply, the Internet is the world's largest on-line library system. Imagine a classroom that can travel to the Louvre museum in Paris to view the Mona Lisa one minute, and then the next minute communicate directly with an environmental scientist in Europe to talk about the impact of a recent Russian arctic oil spill.

The Internet is changing global research. Imagine significant scientific discoveries being shared between global experts as soon as they become known. Imagine scientific and research databases of such scope and breathtaking diversity that traditional books and publications pale in comparison. In the scientific field we are seeing the instantaneous exchange of human knowledge around the world, resulting in a complete and profound change in the way that science and research are conducted.

The Internet is changing government. Imagine being able to easily find the information that you need from a government department. Several leading politicians in Canada are discovering the benefits of the Internet, and several governments realize that services can be delivered in new and innovative ways through the Internet.

The Internet is important to everyone, because it is defining the way that people and organizations, whether they be in business, government, education, or research communities, will exchange and publish information today and in the future.

Internet Opportunities

There are many genuine opportunities for business, education, and government through use of the Internet. Although we'll focus more on these issues later in this book, we'll take a brief look at the opportunities here.

Business and the Internet

For business, the opportunities are substantial. The Internet

> offers business new methods of providing customer support and has become an invaluable tool for obtaining customer feedback;

> provides new methods of marketing goods and services and finding new customers, not just locally, but globally;

> helps to support the increasing number of joint ventures, partnerships, and team efforts occurring between companies in various industries around the world;

> offers new opportunities for cost savings, both on internal communications through technologies such as e-mail, and on external communications by making it cheaper to reach and talk with customers, suppliers, trading partners, business associates, and the general public;

> supports inexpensive research and development by providing staff with access to information on thousands of topics and subjects;

> provides a new method for corporate communications at a very low cost, including the publishing of annual reports, press releases, brochures, and other corporate information;

> provides an inexpensive and effective trend-tracking mechanism to observe industry, customer, and market developments.

Businesses that have incorporated the Internet into their strategic plan and treat the network not as a technology but as a fundamental operational tool, have discovered that the Internet represents an unparalleled opportunity for innovative and effective activities, in all areas of their business.

An example of a company making tentative efforts using the Internet for corporate communications is Fundy Cable (**http://www.discribe.ca/Fundy/opening. htm**), located in New Brunswick. Through their on-line World Wide Web server, you can access a company profile, read information about their services, access their 1994 annual report, access up-to-date press releases, or read about their information highway initiatives.

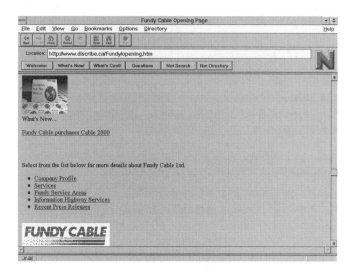

By choosing any of these options, you can access additional levels of detail about the company. For example, choosing "Company Profile" from the listing above provides you with the following screen, which gives you access to more detailed information about the company.

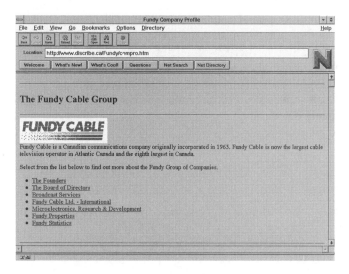

Through this technology companies are establishing on-line brochures, catalogues, price lists, product summaries, and a variety of other information. The technology is sophisticated enough that virtually anything that a company might make available in paper form can be made available to the world via the Internet.

Education and the Internet

The Internet represents a tremendous opportunity in the field of education by helping

➤ to provide access to fresh information that is not as out-of-date as print sources;

➤ to provide access to new, interactive multimedia systems (particularly through the area of the Internet known as the World Wide Web), which permit more innovative learning methods;

➤ to establish telelearning initiatives that allow the development of educational programs in which distance or location is not an issue;

➤ to add some excitement to the learning process; for many, access to the Internet and the information and capabilities it represents is a mind-boggling activity;

➤ to provide access to global information at very cost-effective rates, an issue that is crucial in these days of cost-conscious educational cutbacks;

➤ to enable children and young people to learn about computers as a tool, rather than just having them learn about computers;

➤ to encourage self-learning. The Internet is an activity that can be undertaken in a classroom setting or on its own.

One organization that is helping to sponsor use of the Internet in Canada in primary, elementary, and secondary schools is the federally and provincially sponsored SchoolNet initiative (**http://schoolnet.carleton.ca**).

Through its information service, a teacher can access some of the wealth of information available on the Internet, contact other teachers, or access lesson plans. The following screen illustrates some of the Internet resources that SchoolNet makes available to teachers.

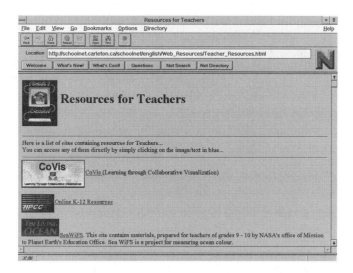

SchoolNet assists teachers who choose to plug their classroom into the Internet by providing them with pointers to valuable educational information sources on the Internet.

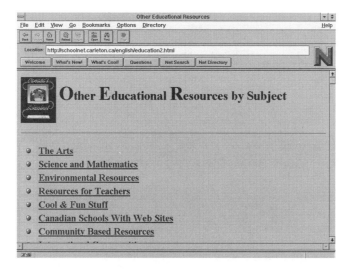

Government and the Internet

The technology emerging in the Internet, particularly through the World Wide Web, offers a new opportunity for the delivery of government services. Certainly, by making it easier to access government information, the Internet could ease a lot of the frustrations that Canadians have when it comes to dealing with the government.

And as more and more Canadians plug into the network, the Internet will offer unparalleled opportunities for the reshaping of government services. In addition to the electronic publishing and communication benefits emphasized earlier, the opportunities include

- electronic service delivery, by permitting communications between the government and its suppliers, business associates, and trading partners;

- use of the Internet as a means to achieve policy objectives, i.e., encouraging industrial relocation;

- open bidding projects, i.e., open up bidding on government contracts and tenders through an electronic bidding process;

- advertising of services such as tourism and heritage programs;

- making committee papers, legislative agendas, and other legal information available in electronic form;

- intergovernment coordination between federal, provincial, municipal and international government bodies.

Statistics Canada (**http://www.statcan.ca**) is one example of a government department launching an initiative on the Internet.

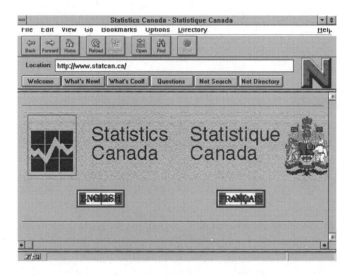

Statistics Canada is delivering an impressive array of services over the Internet, including press releases, information about Statistics Canada products and services, on-line discussion groups, and the *Statistics Canada Daily*, a daily publication of statistical information that is freely made available on the Internet.

Providing this information over the Internet improves access to the information and ensures that it receives the widest possible distribution. Government Internet services benefit not only the general public, but also other government departments that use the information for research purposes.

Not-For-Profit Organizations and Associations on the Internet

The sheer diversity and size of the Internet population make it an attractive medium for organizations that are trying to expand their base of support or are trying to get a particular message out to the public.

Organizations in the non-profit sector and clubs and associations of all types have found the Internet to be a valuable tool that supports their day-to-day activities. In the not-for-profit sector the Internet can be used

➤ to solicit volunteers and new members through on-line recruitment programs;

➤ to advance a cause or campaign by engaging in on-line public education programs;

➤ to raise awareness and understanding of an organization's purpose and mission by becoming an active information provider on the Internet;

➤ to facilitate communications and appeals for aid in the event of a natural disaster;

➤ to seek donations and to identify and to research new potential sources of funding;

➤ to exchange information with other non-profit and membership organizations around the world to maximize the sharing of resources, ideas, and experiences.

An excellent example of a Canadian not-for-profit organization that recognizes the enormous potential of the Internet is the Easter Seal Society of Ontario (**http://www.cyberplex.com/CyberPlex/EasterSeals.html**). Easter Seals has launched an Internet service to disseminate information about the organization and its activities.

Included on the site is general information about Easter Seals, program and service listings, a calendar of events, information on how to volunteer and make a donation, a directory of provincial offices and telephone numbers, and an on-line feedback form that allows Internet users to send comments directly to the Easter Seal Society by electronic mail.

Health Care

The last decade has seen incredible advances in medicine and science as a direct result of technology. It should come as no surprise, then, that the Internet is re-defining how patients, scientists, and medical specialists interact with one another. Listed below are just some of the ways in which the Internet is having a significant impact on the health care field. The Internet

➤ allows patients to have access to vast medical resources and experts;

➤ provides patients with access to on-line support groups;

> permits scientists and doctors to disseminate research results worldwide in seconds;

> provides doctors with virtually instant access to medical specialists around the world for purposes of verifying diagnoses, obtaining feedback and advice, sharing treatment information, and comparing notes, regardless of their geographical location.

The University Hospital in London, Ontario (**http://www.uh.london.on.ca**) is one of a growing number of Canadian hospitals that have joined the Internet to tap into its vast medical and scientific resources. In addition to using the Internet as a research tool, the University Hospital provides information to the Internet community via the World Wide Web service, as shown below.

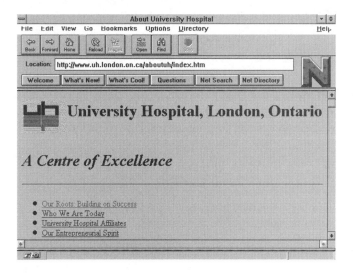

The Internet Today

The Internet presents many opportunities to organizations and people of all types. Yet, as we stressed in the introduction to this chapter, the Internet, while significant, will still take time to mature and to develop. It is important to keep a couple of issues in mind as you begin to think about use of the Internet within your organization.

Experimental Initiatives

In a nutshell, the Internet is a tool that provides efficient communications between people and organizations and instant access to virtually any Internet-connected computer in the world. In time, it will become the standard means of computer-based communication.

However, much of what is occurring in Canada on the Internet is experimental in nature. The Internet's potential is just beginning to be realized by organizations across Canada. It will take some time before the many Internet initiatives underway across Canada are relevant to and within the reach of the majority of Canadians.

Since it is still growing and developing, the Internet is not an instant panacea for business, government, or education. There is a lot of information out there, but it can be difficult and challenging to find. There are a lot of people and organizations making use of the network, but there are many more who are still trying to understand it. And don't forget that there are many people and organizations that are not even on the Internet yet.

Keep in mind, though, that the Internet is a worthwhile investment: it will be at the core of many of the information network developments of the future. Those organizations that invest now in understanding the Internet's potential will be one step ahead of their competitors.

Many Technologies

The examples in the previous pages illustrated an Internet service known as the World Wide Web. We accessed the World Wide Web using a program called Netscape. The World Wide Web, while one of the most exciting developments on the Internet, is not the only Internet tool. Other popular Internet tools include

> *Electronic mail.* Internet e-mail addresses are already becoming as recognizable as fax numbers on business cards, and over time the use of Internet e-mail will become as common as the use of fax machines.

> *Gopher.* Gopher is used by many organizations as an alternative means of electronic publishing.

> *Electronic discussion forums* (called "electronic mailing lists" or "USENET") that facilitate discussions between people around the world who share common interests.

> *Telnet.* Telnet is used to connect to other computers on the Internet.

> *FTP.* FTP is a way of accessing and distributing documents and programs on the Internet.

We'll take a look at some of these fundamental tools in Chapter 3.

There are Other Technologies

The Internet is but one important technology when it comes to electronic commerce and communication. Certainly, many others warrant attention from anyone considering an electronic communications strategy. These include

> EDI, or electronic data interchange. EDI is already in massive use throughout Canada within the manufacturing and retail sector. Organizations

such as Eaton's, Canadian Tire, and Wal-Mart are demanding that their suppliers be EDI-capable, with the ability to receive electronic purchase orders and other information related to electronic commerce.

➤ Commercial on-line services — systems such as Prodigy, America Online and CompuServe. These services boast millions of users and have become a "test-bed" of sorts for many companies exploring the concepts of electronic commerce. Yet, even they are being influenced by the Internet and have provided access to the Internet for their members.

➤ ATM, or asynchronous transfer mode. ATM is an emerging technology that will bring together voice, data, and other forms of information traffic. Many of the major communication companies in Canada are placing their bets that ATM will help to define a global information structure, while many realists in the Internet community believe that ATM will combine with the infrastructure established in the Internet to result in a global Internet that just runs faster.

➤ Commercial information databases, such as InfoGlobe and Infomart/Dialog, which offer access to incredibly rich information sources that are not available on the Internet. Certainly, anyone interested in serious on-line research must consider use of these research tools.

➤ The "information highway." No one knows what the information highway will look like in the future. Some people believe it is the Internet. Others believe that it is a system we will access through our televisions. Others believe that it is all about video-on-demand and a 500-channel universe. Still others believe it is about using computers to access the whole of human knowledge. When it comes to the much-hyped information highway, one thing is clear: given its massive and continuing growth, the Internet will have a profound effect on the future of all telecommunication systems.

The Technology Isn't Important — The Opportunities Are

As we put the opportunities of the Internet into perspective, we will talk a little about the technology. But, it isn't the technology that is important here — it is what the technology is used for.

What is important are the strategic and business objectives that can be met through use of the Internet, and the benefits that use of the Internet can provide to a person or an organization. It is the business planning and strategic view that is so critical to success in the use of the Internet within an organization. And that's what we'll focus on throughout this book.

The Significance of the Internet

Why is the Internet Important?

The Internet is important to anyone in business, government, or education, because it is the leading technology candidate to link all the computers in the world. As that happens, the Internet will provide access to an incredible range of information, a massive number of organizations, and a huge number of people. It is said that some 100 to 200 million people will be on the network by the end of the century.

The Internet is growing at fascinating rates and affecting the strategic activities of many different organizations. As it continues to grow, it is providing, in many ways, "access to the whole of human knowledge" — and becoming, for many, the foundation to the much-hyped "information highway."

The Importance of Standards

Even if you don't get involved with the technical issues of computers and related technologies, some knowledge of computer standards is important. Standards define how different organizations, people, and technologies agree to work together, through the use of a common set of rules — whether these be technical in nature or not.

We see the use of standards every day: in bar codes, in compact discs, in videotape recorders, in the size of a bathtub drain, and in the size of the

WHY IS THE INTERNET IMPORTANT?

(1) Standards define how different organizations, people, and technologies agree to work together.

(2) *De facto* standards are standards that emerge informally through widespread use.

(3) The Internet is defining a number of *de facto* standards:
- how all the computers in the world will plug together;
- how people and organizations communicate with one another by computer;
- how individuals and organizations can become global publishers;
- how organizations conduct business using tools of electronic commerce.

(4) The Internet is emerging as the preferred method of information access and retrieval since it is not proprietary.

(5) The Internet is the foundation for the information highway.

screws used in light fixtures. Standards make the world go around, because they ensure that a lot of different people, organizations, and technologies can work together in relative harmony.

There are many examples of industries and situations in which the adoption of standards has led to the rapid adoption of a particular technology. For example, the global telephone system works well, because shortly after telephones were invented, all the participants involved with the technology ensured that they had a common method of recognizing a dial tone, a commonly recognized method of dialing, and a common telephone numbering scheme (known as the North American Numbering Plan, or NANP). The result is that, today, you can pick up a telephone and dial any one of several hundred million telephones around the world.

A Lack of Standards

Imagine if there weren't any telephone standards — your telephone would only be able to reach telephones on the same phone system and wouldn't be able to reach many others. The telephone would be a rather useless technology to you.

When standards don't emerge quickly, we often see rather silly results. In the early days of the North American railroad system, there was little agreement between competing railroads concerning the width of their tracks (known as the "gauge"). Since most of the railroads had started as small, regional lines, many used slightly different gauges (or in some cases, grossly different gauges.)

Efforts at standardization were often viewed as something that was "helping the competition" (i.e., making it easier for customers to switch cargo to a competitor while in transit), and so there was little incentive for the railroads to solve the problem of the lack of standardization. This led to a rather remarkable situation in which trains had to have several sets of wheels, or very unique interchangeable wheels, to cope with the different gauges, as cargo moved from railroad to railroad.

Inevitably, this led to delays in the shipment of goods and products across North America, leading to demands for a common gauge. Eventually, those in the railroad industry realized the futility of "proprietary standards" and adopted a common rail gauge throughout North America. Remarkably, however, it took some 20 years for all railroads to participate.

Computer-Based Standards

In the same way that railroads and telephones are based upon standards, computer technologies are increasingly being built upon a variety of emerging standards. Yet, this hasn't always been true. In the early days of computer technology (i.e., as recently as the late 1980s) most computer systems were closed and proprietary. An IBM system couldn't link to a UNISYS system, which couldn't communicate with an Apple Macintosh, which couldn't link to a Digital Equipment computer. To some extent this is still true today, meaning that a computer technology from one vendor might not necessarily link to that from another vendor.

However, the last decade has seen an increasing trend, partly as the result of customer pressure but also as a result of initiatives throughout the computer industry, toward the adoption of standards. This means that it is increasingly possible for one particular computer technology to "work" with another.

De Facto Standards

Standards are critical to the computer industry. The problem is that it sometimes takes a long time for the computer industry to agree on a standard, in the same way that it took railroads a long time to adopt a common track width. Standards in any industry around the world are defined in one of two ways: by global standard-setting bodies or they emerge quickly from the grass roots.

Formal standards usually evolve over a long and complicated process, since they involve the coordination of many competing interests. But, it is this slow speed of development and adoption that often leads to *de facto* standards — the sudden and rapid adoption of a certain technology by a lot of people who are tired of waiting for formal standards.

The result is that in many cases, while the formal standard-setting bodies are still discussing their agendas and plans, a particular computer technology is adopted so widely and so quickly by so many people, that it quickly becomes known as a *de facto* standard. This is the case with the Internet. It has been adopted by so many people, so many organizations in so many countries around the globe, and by so many computer vendors that it is now a *de facto* standard for global, computer-based communication.

De Facto Internet Standards

Many have now realized that the Internet has quickly defined a number of important *de facto* standards, which are defining the very nature of interpersonal, interorganization, interenterprise computer-based communications for the future. The Internet is defining

➣ how all the computers around the world will plug together, based upon a computer technology known as TCP/IP;

➣ how people and organizations will communicate with their computers through a massive global electronic mail service and through on-line "discussion groups";

➣ how people and organizations can become "global publishers," by publishing documents on the Internet, incorporating sound, images, and text, which are instantly available to an international community of thousands upon thousands of Internet users across the globe;

➣ how people and organizations will conduct business in the future. Electronic commerce tools in use on the Internet today, such as those permitting on-line transactions and credit card orders, are rapidly becoming more powerful, more sophisticated, and more secure.

The Internet clearly isn't simply a "network of networks" or the "world's biggest network." The Internet represents the emergence of a computer-based equivalent of the global phone system that will forever change the way we interact around the planet. The Internet is a system that provides computer-based access to the whole of human knowledge, and is a system that is changing the way business, government, and educational services are conducted and delivered.

The Internet is the foundation of the global information superhighway.

Understanding These Trends

Although Internet standards are considered *de facto* standards, we should note that they have emerged over time in a unique, open environment in which many people around the world have shared their input on how a global network can work. The result has been massive acceptance of the Internet within the computer industry and within business, science, education, and government.

Let's put these *de facto* Internet standards into more perspective:

Computers around the world are plugging together through the Internet
The Internet is leading the trend in which all the computers in the world will plug together. It is doing so through a "networking protocol" known as TCP/IP. The adoption of TCP/IP by organizations around the world for networking purposes, particularly when connecting to the Internet, is resulting in the emergence of the equivalent of a global "telephone book" of computers and information resources around the world.

TCP/IP as an adopted standard is gaining significant momentum. Microsoft is supporting it in its new Windows /95 technology, and it is supported in IBM's OS/2 operating system. Computer technology companies as diverse as Hewlett Packard, Digital Equipment, and Sun Microsystems support it. Even telephone companies around the world are recognizing that TCP/IP is becoming a generally accepted standard for linking computer systems around the world, and more and more of them are or will be offering TCP/IP-based services.

Why is TCP/IP important? For two reasons. First, it links together different computer technologies from different vendors. The result is that an Apple computer can link to an IBM computer, which can link to a computer running Microsoft Windows, which can link to a Sun UNIX workstation. Through the Internet, barriers between different computer systems are broken down.

Second, organizations that link their corporate networks to the Internet are provided with what is known as an IP address (e.g., **142.1.7.1**) and a domain name (e.g., **bell.ca**, for Bell Canada). The "IP address" and "domain name" define the organization and its computers uniquely throughout the global computer world. This makes it easy for anyone to access the information that they choose to make available on their computer system. Think of the significance of this by comparing it to the global telephone system. Today, using your telephone, you can dial a unique telephone number and reach any telephone in the world.

The Internet uses the same concept for the computer world — a unique, numerical address and a unique name that can be used to reach any computer or information resource anywhere in the world — a profound development in the history of computer technology.

People and organizations are communicating with each other through the Internet   The second key trend with the Internet is that it is defining how information will flow between organizations through the emergence of a massive global electronic mail service and through the emergence of on-line "discussion groups." Internet e-mail addresses are already becoming as recognized as fax numbers on business cards. Over time, the use of Internet e-mail will become as common as the use of fax machines and as ubiquitous as the telephone.

Yet, the Internet has gone one step beyond simple e-mail. Through Internet electronic mail systems, and through another area of the Internet known as USENET, people are learning to collaborate globally and exchange knowledge. The world is segmenting itself into tens of thousands of communities on the Internet, where people share information, trade knowledge, seek answers to questions, debate topics, and report on leading-edge research.

As you read this page, hundreds of thousands of people, if not millions, are at their keyboards, participating in thousands of "global discussions" on a variety of topics. In the scientific community, Internet "electronic mailing lists" are being used to link space researchers, biomedical professionals, and anesthesiologists. In education, teachers are trading lesson plans from around the globe, while students in a classroom are discussing a topic with another classroom on the other side of the world. Staff from business and not-for-profit organizations are seeking support, assistance, information, and guidance on everything from investment strategy to computer technology to consumer trends.

We are seeing through the Internet the emergence of a unique process and standard method of global "collaboration" as people throughout the Internet learn to "network for knowledge," expanding their capabilities by participating in these unique knowledge communities. It is a fascinating development in the history of human communication.

People and organizations are publishing information in electronic form through the Internet   Perhaps an even more profound development is found through a part of the Internet known as the World Wide Web, where we are witnessing the emergence of a global information access standard.

The diversity of Canadian organizations providing information services on the Internet is striking. For example, the roster includes organizations such as Brandon University, the Yukon Department of Tourism, the Ontario Milk Marketing Board, the Royal Bank of Canada, Greenpeace, Lockheed Canada, and the Atlantic Canada Opportunities Agency.

Breathtaking types and quantities of information are appearing on the World Wide Web on a regular basis. The information can consist of text, pictures, sound, and, for those with a high-speed link, moving pictures. The Rolling Stones even performed a concert through the World Wide Web in November 1994.

Consider the World Wide Web site for a British Columbia-based record label called Nettwerk (**http://www.wimsey.com/ nettwerk**).

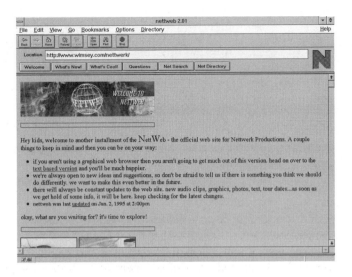

Through its Web site, it is possible to obtain information about artists represented by the label, review a catalogue, obtain information about tours and presentations, and obtain other information that Nettwerk wishes to "publish."

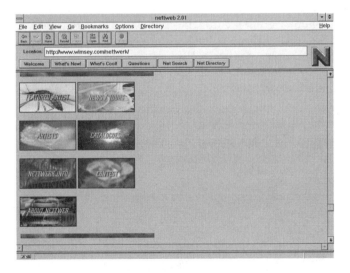

The key point to be made here is that once information has been "published" on the World Wide Web, anyone can access that information resource, from any Internet-connected computer in the world, and expect it to operate in a reliable, consistent manner. Since the World Wide Web incorporates not only text but graphics, pictures, sounds, and even moving pictures, it has become a global "multimedia" standard.

The net result for Nettwerk is that it can suddenly make itself and its line of products available to its customers, wherever they might be around the world. Not surprisingly, Nettwerk is not the only record company taking advantage of the Internet's multimedia capabilities. A few of the larger record labels, most notably Sony and Warner Bros., have established World Wide Web sites on the Internet to promote their musical artists.

The benefits don't only extend to record companies. Any organization that chooses to distribute information through the Internet can take advantage of its rich multimedia capabilities. General Electric, for example, is distributing one of its radio commercials via the Internet, and MCA/Universal uses the Internet to distribute video clips of its feature films. The possibilities are endless and will only continue to grow as we see the emergence of high-speed communications to the home and office.

Tools of electronic commerce are emerging on the Internet   People and organizations need tools that will ensure that the business and research they conduct on the network occurs in a secure and reliable environment. The result is the emergence of standards that are defining the tools of electronic commerce. Standards involving electronic commerce, including message/data encryption, security, on-line transactions and credit card ordering, are already being adopted on the Internet. As these standards are adopted, they will change business in ways that we can only begin to dream of.

Instrumental in the development of electronic tools is CommerceNet (**http://www.commerce.net**). Through CommerceNet, major computer companies such as IBM, Apple, and Hewlett Packard are coming together with major banks and commercial concerns, such as the Bank of America and MasterCard, to define the tools of future Internet-based networked commerce. The goals of CommerceNet can be seen in the following screen.

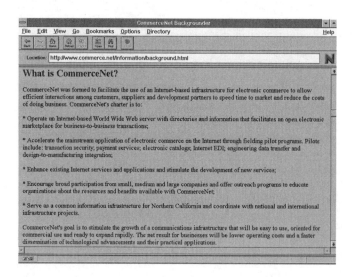

The results of these standards are massive growth and acceptance of the Internet throughout business, government, education, and research communities.

A Standard Method of Access to Information

One of the key benefits of the standards emerging on the Internet is the ability to quickly reach a number of people with your information with a minimum of fuss and effort. Just as it is no longer necessary for you to build your own railroad based on your own track width, it is no longer necessary for you to build your own information access method. Instead you can build it on the global standard for information access as found within the Internet.

Electronic Catalogues

Let's take a look at an example of this concept, in terms of an electronic catalogue. Let's say your business wants to provide the ability for your existing customers and potential customers to browse your catalogue, *electronically*. Many organizations have thought about doing this for years, and some have done it.

It's part of the whole concept of the strategic use of telecommunications: put a terminal directly in the office of the customers so they can browse your electronic catalogue, and it is bound to have a positive impact on sales. Hopefully, by making it easy for your customers to do business with you, they will purchase more of your product.

In the past, any company wanting to provide access to an electronic catalogue had to do so using proprietary technology and proprietary access methods. In the last ten years we've seen a lot of proprietary, closed attempts to establish such a strategic telecommunication link — some have worked and many have failed, but in all cases the cost of establishing such a *proprietary* communications link has been extremely high. But, with the massive adoption of the World Wide Web as an information access tool, the Internet provides nothing less than a common, standard method of accessing information from another company.

Electronic Queries

A perfect example of the power of the Internet to suddenly reach a massive customer base is Federal Express. The international courier company has established a World Wide Web information site (**http://www.fedex.com**) through which a customer can query a courier shipment.

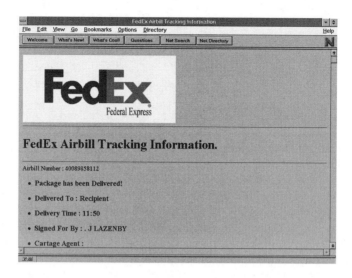

Once the customer keys in the waybill number, the FedEx system queries the parcel-tracking system to indicate the status of the parcel.

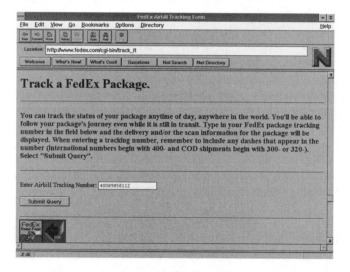

Why is this significant? FedEx has built an Internet-based information query system that can suddenly be accessed by millions of its customers around the globe. It didn't have to build a closed, expensive, proprietary information access system — it is using a globally adopted standard on the Internet, the World Wide Web.

Anyone on the Internet who can access the World Wide Web (which is by far the fastest-growing area of the Internet today) can now access the FedEx site. Since many consumers already know how to use the World Wide Web, no special training, technology, or clumsy manuals are required. The cost savings are tremendous.

Now consider it from the perspective of FedEx: it can provide a new, strategic service to millions of its customers for a fraction of the cost the company would have had had it chosen to build a closed, proprietary system. It also enhances the level of customer service for FedEx users on the Internet, because executing a parcel search using the Internet is sometimes more convenient than picking up the telephone and calling FedEx directly. It's a "win-win" situation. FedEx benefits, and so does the customer.

It's not just business that has this type of opportunity with the Internet — consider it from the angle of government, education, and not-for-profit organizations and associations. All sectors need to make information available to their "customers" and associates. Doing so through the Internet avoids the complexity of having to build unique methods of communicating and computer-based publishing.

With the existence of the Internet we are seeing the emergence, for the first time ever, of a standard, computer-based *information access appliance.* The Internet changes the capabilities of our personal computers so that they become global information tools, able to travel the globe to access an information base that, over time, will allow us to access the whole of human knowledge.

Given the growth of the Internet, its adoption by so many people and its growing critical mass, getting involved with it is one of the best computer investments any individual or organization can make.

Is the Internet the Information Highway?

Telephone and cable companies are building their own private networks, and their own "information highways," to let people do home banking, home shopping, and to access video-on-demand. This means that instead of one information highway in Canada, there might be several competing information highways, each providing its own set of services and its own access methods — some through a television instead of a computer. This "information highway" as envisioned by mainstream communication telephone and cable companies is at a very early stage.

From the perspective of many people, these companies are focusing less on building an information highway and more on an "entertainment highway." Discussions focus not on the strategic benefits of business-to-business communications as found through the Internet, but on permitting the user of the highway to access 500 TV channels, to order up a movie on demand, to play games, and to perform other "important" tasks — all through your television. Discussions focus not on allowing for global collaboration, knowledge networking, and information research, but on how these companies can build a credit card device for the television set so that the consumer will "buy lots of stuff." It is almost as if these mainstream companies want to provide us consumers with the ultimate "home-zirconium-couch-potato-shopping-network-information-highway-system."

Quite rightly, many people are skeptical about this "vision" of the information highway as touted by major communication firms and believe that the Internet, because of its massive growth and acceptance, is showing that people want more than entertainment. Patrick Bloomfield, a *Financial Post* senior editor, wrote in a column on January 18, 1995, that "the true information highway runs along our phone lines. For starters, any competent Internet server can open the door to dozens and dozens of Internet sites providing financial information — varying from U.S. interest rates over past years to the daily bulletin from Statistics Canada," and that "the information highway is no technological pipe dream. It is up and running — and used by millions of Canadians."

Not only that — the Internet is a global standard. Standards have not yet emerged for the television-based highway, and thus we face the risk of having many distinct information highways in Canada that are not compatible with one another. The information highway in Quebec sponsored by the cable company La Group Videotron might not link to Fundy Cable Highway in New Brunswick, which might not link to the Bell Beacon information highway, which might not link to an information highway built by Time Warner. It's like the early days of the railroad, all over again.

The question for you is this: If an organization chooses to publish information for the global information highway, will it do so through the global standard, the Internet? Or will it do so once through one company, again through another company, and again through another, for the television-based information highway? Will it choose to get involved with a network that is clearly becoming the backbone to the global economy, or will it choose to get involved with an "information highway" that seems to have the sole goal of permitting people to order a movie and fried chicken through their television?

Will Sony Music or the Canadian Museum of Heritage and Civilization (both of which provide information services on the Internet) develop a special access method for each of ten different Canadian information highways, or will they provide information through the global standard, the Internet?

The reality is that an "information highway" implies "information," which implies some type of information content. Clearly, the content for the information highway is rapidly emerging all around us through the part of the Internet known as the World Wide Web, a standard that is so widely adopted that you can travel from the White House to a research centre in the Antarctica to the Australian Aboriginal Centre for Research Studies to *Vancouver Magazine*, all in a matter of seconds.

No doubt, the cable and telephone companies will do all they can to develop proprietary communication highways, and no doubt they will lose billions of dollars as they try to do so. For some reason, unknown to many people, they seem to have an overwhelming passion for putting video stores out of business. In the meantime, the global Internet continues its relentless march, defining the very nature of future computer-based communications.

In the global evolution of the information highway, the telephone and cable companies are like the Soviet Politburo — slow, cumbersome, and unable to recognize the way the world is evolving around them. The Internet is free-wheeling, high-flying Russian capitalism — developments everywhere, occurring at a breathtaking pace, and progress moving forward at an amazing speed.

Is the Internet the information highway? The answer should be obvious.

CHAPTER 3

Internet Fundamentals

> "Most of our top management team really don't have a clue what to do about IT. They are at the mercy of the techies. They just nod their head and hope they don't show their ignorance."
>
> *Shaping the Future*, Peter G.W. Keen

*I*f you listen to technical people talk about the Internet, you will hear a variety of terms, ranging from e-mail and USENET to Telnet, FTP, Gopher, TCP/IP addresses, the World Wide Web, the domain name system, SLIP accounts, shell accounts, Free-Nets, Internet access providers, and even something called the amazing Fishcam. To some, the Internet is an alphabet soup of technical terms — with its own unique acronyms and language.

Yet, many people can be intimidated by Internet technology, and merely want to understand

➤ What can I use it for?

➤ How does it work?

➤ How do I join and what does it cost?

➤ How do I put information up on the Internet?

In this chapter we'll take a look at these questions without getting lost in the technology or getting buried in the complexities of the network.

INTERNET FUNDAMENTALS

(1) The Internet is used for four fundamental activities:
   - electronic mail;
   - global collaboration through Internet discussion groups;
   - information access and retrieval;
   - publishing and information dissemination.

(2) Seven key benefits to using Internet electronic mail are
   - its reach;
   - its simple method of addressing;
   - its ability to incorporate documents created in other applications;
   - its direct delivery;
   - its cost savings and the absence of long distance charges;
   - its efficiency;
   - its convenience.

(3) The Internet brings together people from around the world who share common interests or who are experts in their respective fields.

(4) The Internet allows people in geographically dispersed locations to collaborate on projects together.

(5) Knowledge networking on the Internet occurs in
   - electronic mailing lists;
   - USENET.

(6) The Internet contains thousands of information sites that are sponsored and maintained by businesses, academic institutions, not-for-profit organizations, and government departments.

(7) The World Wide Web is the most popular information access tool on the Internet because of its simplicity and its incorporation of sound, images, graphics, and text.

(8) The Internet is causing an explosion in home-based electronic publishing.

(9) Finding information on the Internet has been made easier by volunteers who have built
   - directories of sites (e.g., Yahoo);
   - directories of users (e.g., Four 11);
   - search engines (e.g., Lycos).

(10) The two primary methods of getting connected to the Internet are
   - dial-up connections;
   - dedicated connections.

(11) Internet "presence providers" can be an attractive option for organizations that wish to "outsource" their Internet publishing requirements.

What is the Internet Used For?

The Internet can be broken down into four fundamental activities:

> sending and receiving global electronic mail (Internet e-mail);

> discussing topics and sharing information with peers (global collaboration);

> accessing and searching for files and documents (information access and retrieval);

> publishing and providing information to Internet users — newsletters, reports, brochures, photographs, articles, product literature, price lists, etc. (information dissemination).

Internet e-mail

As the use of computers expands in business, education, and government, and as the personal computer becomes a standard piece of equipment in many homes, the use of electronic mail is growing by leaps and bounds. One publication estimated that the Internet carried some 4 billion electronic mail messages during 1994, and that its use grew by an astounding 220% over the prior year.

There are two primary ways that people "plug into" Internet e-mail:

> Directly via an "Internet access provider." Individuals plug into the Internet directly via a company that sells access to the Internet (companies that sell access to the Internet are known as "Internet access providers").

> Indirectly via an office e-mail system. Organizations with internal e-mail systems link to the Internet in order for their staff to communicate with people outside the organization, such as suppliers, government departments, customers, and industry and trade associations. In Canada, we have seen major organizations such as the University of Western Ontario, the TD Bank, George Weston's, the Ontario government, and Unilever Canada link internal e-mail systems to the Internet.

Electronic mail, or e-mail, is becoming an increasingly common method of communicating between people and organizations. And, with the arrival of the Internet, we are seeing the emergence of a global e-mail system that links millions of individuals and hundreds of thousands of corporate and organizational e-mail systems.

There are thousands of ways that people access Internet e-mail around the world. Regardless of the computer and the software used, everyone has an "inbox" of new messages received from people on the Internet. In the sample Inbox depicted in the screen below (which belongs to one of the authors of this book), there are 320 unread messages.[1]

---

[1] Authors of best-selling books about the Internet tend to get a lot of e-mail!

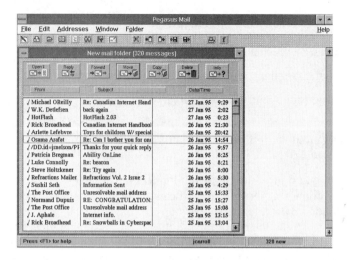

It is possible to reply to messages, as seen in this screen:

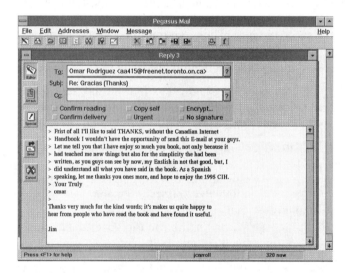

It is also possible to create new messages, to forward messages to other people, and to file messages in folders — in essence, to do with an e-mail message what you might do with a paper letter (which might include throwing the message in the trash).

Seven key reasons why Internet e-mail is important are

➤ Its *reach*. Since many e-mail systems around the world link to the Internet, the Internet's e-mail system lets you reach the greatest number of people. Through the Internet it is estimated that you can reach some

60 to 70 million people in about 160 countries. If you are not yet connected to the Internet, you may be pleasantly surprised at how many of the people that you regularly do business with are using the Internet for communication purposes.

➢ Its *simple method of "addressing."* Just as we recognize fax numbers and telephone numbers, people recognize Internet e-mail addresses. They usually look like this: **someone@somwhere.something**, for example, **jcarroll@jacc.com** or **rickb@hookup.net**, which means Jim Carroll at the company J.A. Carroll Consulting, which is part of the **.com** domain (more on that later), and Rick Broadhead, who is on the HookUp Communications network.

➢ Its ability to *incorporate documents created in other applications,* including non-text files. You can attach word processing files, spreadsheet files, graphics, and sound files to your e-mail messages. If your Internet e-mail software supports a standard called MIME, it will automatically recognize many different kinds of computer files, making it easier for you to send and receive files created in other programs by other people. The ability to include special documents in e-mail messages allows people in different locations to work jointly on spreadsheet files or reports.

➢ Its *direct delivery.* When you send an e-mail message to someone on the Internet, the message goes right to his/her "inbox," which is generally right on his/her desktop computer. There is less chance of a message getting lost or not being delivered, since there is no "intermediary" (such as a receptionist) who has to pass the message along. And because e-mail can usually be forwarded and/or retrieved remotely (just like voice mail), people can pick up their e-mail messages even when traveling.

➢ Its *cost savings* and the absence of long distance charges. The benefit of "no long distance charges" is often one of the most difficult aspects of Internet e-mail to grasp because people find it so difficult to believe. Once you have connected to an Internet provider, there are no long distance charges to send or to receive an electronic mail message, regardless of the message's destination or origin. This means that it will cost you as much to send an e-mail message to Zimbabwe as it will to send a message to your neighbor. Most Internet providers will provide unlimited e-mail capability for a few hundred dollars per year. There are a few exceptions to this rule (i.e., there are still a few Internet providers where the charge for electronic mail is based on the size of the message), but such situations are rare. Using Internet e-mail reduces paper consumption and costly fax transmissions, and the absence of long-distance charges makes e-mail extremely cost-effective for global communications.

➤ Its *efficiency.* It is estimated that as many as 50% to 70% of all telephone calls do not reach their recipient because the person is away or busy.[2] With e-mail, you don't have this problem, because the message is delivered directly to the recipient, who can access the message and respond at his/her convenience. The response, similarly, will come directly to you. Because e-mail eliminates telephone tag, it improves productivity, cuts calling expenses, and improves response times.

➤ Its *convenience.* For all the reasons noted above, Internet e-mail is a convenient way of communicating with customers, suppliers, co-workers, and other people and organizations. Electronic mail allows easy forwarding and copying of messages to people. The same message can be forwarded to a dozen or more people with only a few extra keystrokes. Electronic mail is particularly useful when communicating with people in different time zones, since messages can be left at any time of the day or night.

Suffice it to say, as all the computers around the world begin to plug together, Internet e-mail is becoming the common and standard method for communication between people and organizations. In many ways, it is becoming the fax machine of the 1990s.

Global Collaboration

Another exciting application on the Internet is the ability to correspond with people around the world who share your research interests and/or hobbies. Because the Internet is populated by millions of people with very diverse interests, there are thousands of topics being discussed on the Internet at any given moment.

On the Internet we are seeing the emergence of small on-line "communities," where people converge to discuss and to debate topics of mutual interest and to exchange and to share information. These on-line communities go by different names, such as "mailing lists," "discussion groups," "listservs," and "USENET."

Don't be confused by the terminology. While there are subtle differences between these terms, all refer to places on the Internet where people with similar interests gather and share information or discuss things. Because each of these on-line communities contains people who are experts or hobbyists in a given subject area, you can see why the Internet is such a powerful medium. *The Internet brings together people from around the world who are experts in their respective fields.*

On the Internet, getting an answer to a very specialized question is often simply a matter of locating a spot on the Internet where people are discussing the relevant subject matter, and then asking your question. Internet discussion groups allow groups of people in geographically dispersed or isolated locations to collaborate on

---

[2] Phillip Robinson, *Delivering Electronic Mail* (M&T Books, 1992), p. 6.

projects together. Time zone differences and the physical distances separating the participants become almost irrelevant. In essence, the Internet's power lies in its ability to put participants in touch with expertise on almost any imaginable topic.

What is perhaps even more wonderful about the Internet is that you can create your own "on-line" community of experts if your hobby, research interest, or line of business is not currently being discussed on the Internet. For example, suppose you are in the shoe retail business and you want to use the Internet to correspond with other shoe retailers and industry experts around the globe. You can create your own discussion group on the Internet, and by announcing it in designated places on the Internet, you can attract people who are interested in talking about the shoe industry.

(It should be pointed out that setting up a discussion group requires some technical knowledge, which is beyond the scope of this book. However, most Internet providers will assist you.)

Global collaboration, which we also call "knowledge networking," was described in our 1994 *Canadian Internet Handbook* as follows:

KNOWLEDGE NETWORKING

From the *Canadian Internet Handbook*, 1994

It used to be, that if you had a question, you went to the library to find the answer. Today, you can still go to the library, you can look up the answer in an on-line database or CD-ROM — or, you can ask the world.

Through areas of the Internet known as USENET newsgroups and electronic mailing lists, you can send questions to people with common areas of interest. With USENET or mailing lists, you can participate in local or global "electronic conversations" over a period of days or weeks. With literally thousands of topics available, you choose to belong only to those topics that interest you. You can knowledge network by sending a question to a particular group. You will find that you can usually receive an answer fairly quickly.

Many people use these Internet groups for *global knowledge networking*. By linking yourself to the globe, you establish a new method of obtaining knowledge: whether for your employer, your company, or your friends and associates.

In USENET, people can discuss and debate some 10,000 or more topics. The following screen shows an example of a few USENET discussion groups. The left side of the screen shows that the individual has joined areas in which psychology, the sport of running, the TV show Beverly Hills 90210, and Soviet politics are being discussed.[3] The right area shows some of the current items being discussed in the running discussion group, while the bottom part of the screen shows one of the current questions and answers in the running discussion group.

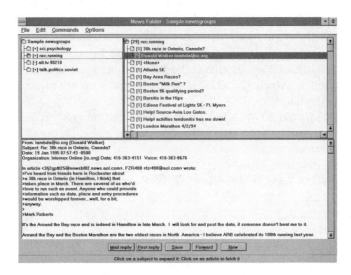

The other area of the Internet for collaboration and discussion is electronic mailing lists. Because the number of Internet mailing lists is constantly growing, it is impossible to keep a complete list of all the Internet mailing lists in existence. However, there are people on the Internet who volunteer their time to maintain directories of these lists. In the screen below we have reproduced an index page from one of those directories to give you a sense of the variety of topics being discussed on the Internet. There are thousands and thousands of Internet mailing lists, covering thousands and thousands of topics. Since any individual on the Internet can join any one of these lists, the ability to access global knowledge by topic is a straightforward experience.

---

[3] This person must have rather eclectic tastes.

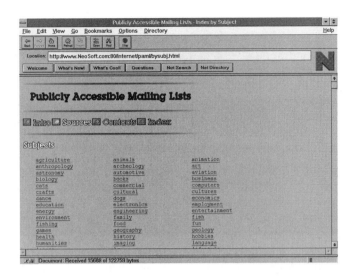

Within the area of health care, we can see that there are a variety of health-related topics that people are discussing.

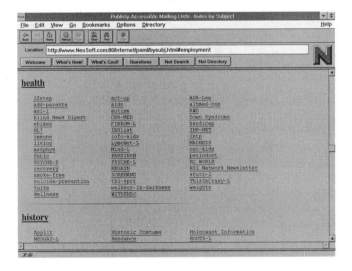

The ability to knowledge network through the Internet is significant and is one of the key reasons for participating in the network.

Information Access

The Internet is quickly becoming a standard way of accessing information provided by organizations in Canada and over 160 countries around the world. Just as the Internet features thousands of discussion groups and mailing lists on almost every conceivable subject, it is full of thousands of information sites that are sponsored and maintained by businesses, academic institutions, not-for-profit organizations, and government agencies and departments.

Many of these sites are available to you around the clock, seven days a week, at no additional charge beyond the cost of your Internet connection. Other sites (like the site we are going to show you below) charge a fee for access to their on-line services. However, at this time this is the exception rather than the rule.

There are a variety of Internet tools that can be used to access these information sites on the Internet, including Internet programs such as FTP, Telnet, Gopher, and Archie. However, the World Wide Web has quickly become the most popular information access tool on the Internet, primarily because of its simplicity, but also because it combines sound, images, graphics, and text.

The World Wide Web is a large, global system within the Internet that allows you to quickly travel from one information source to another. On the World Wide Web, and the Internet in general, national borders are invisible. You can rapidly travel from one country to another in seconds. This is part of the magic of the Internet — it makes the world a much smaller place. The World Wide Web is browsed or "searched" with a navigator — a piece of software designed to access "Web sites." The most popular World Wide Web navigators are programs called Mosaic and Netscape, but additional ones exist — IBM's popular OS/2 software includes an excellent World Wide Web navigator called WebCruiser.

Let's take a look at an example of how the World Wide Web might be used. Let's say we want to find a site on the Internet that provides stock quotes. Since the Internet is a combination of many thousands of computers worldwide, no one index of Internet information is available. Yet, just as individuals volunteer their time to maintain directories of Internet mailing lists, many individuals volunteer their time to build Internet indices that allow you to search for Internet sites by subject. One of the best World Wide Web indices we have found on the Internet is one based at Stanford University called "Yahoo" (**http://www.yahoo.com**). Yahoo provides access to the World Wide Web by category. Each category includes a number of sub-categories, thus making it very easy to find information on the Internet.

The following screen is a picture of Yahoo, taken using the Netscape navigator software:

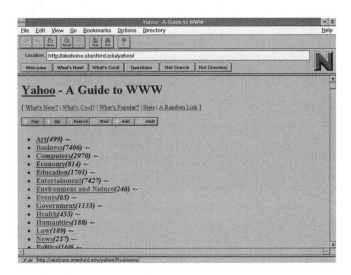

Since we want to find stock quotes, we move our mouse pointer to "Business" and double click with the mouse. Yahoo responds with a listing of business categories. Eventually we find a category called "Finance."

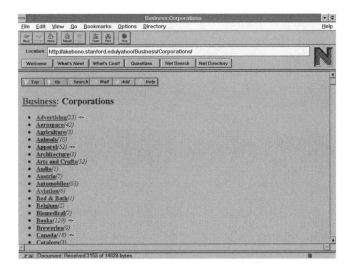

Clicking with our mouse on the word "Finance" brings us to a listing of investment-related information available through the Internet.

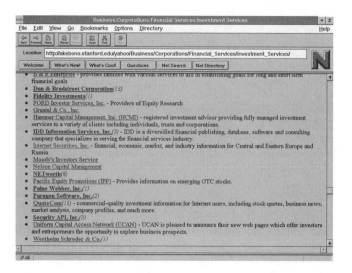

We see something called "Quote.Com." This is where the Internet gets interesting, for if we select "Quote.Com" we are immediately transported from Stanford University to the computer system at Quote.Com, which is located in the state of Nevada. From here we can access stock prices and other investment information. Quote.Com is an Internet-based financial service that provides up to 5 free stock quotes per day and also offers a basic membership package at U.S. $9.95 per month, which allows up to 100 quotes a day from U.S. exchanges with Canadian information available for an additional $9.95 per month. Other packages provide access to news wires, market reports, and historical data, as seen below:

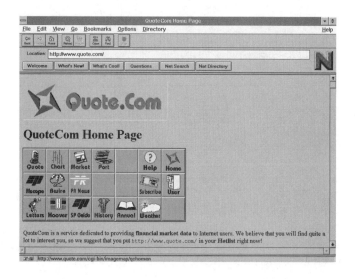

The key concept of the World Wide Web is that you can move quickly around the world — from location to location, site to site, and from country to country. With just a few clicks of your mouse you can access incredibly complex, diverse, and rich sources of information from all over the world.

Quote.Com is an example of a fee-based commercial service on the Internet, since you have to pay a fee (in addition to the cost of your Internet connection) to access all of Quote.Com's Internet services. However, most of the Internet's information resources are provided free of charge by businesses and government agencies. Hundreds of businesses and government departments all over the world have established information sites on the Internet where they provide press releases, reports, technical documents, and other interactive services to Internet users for free.

When should you expect to have to pay to access a specific Internet resource? A good rule of thumb is this: If an organization normally charges you to access a document or service *off* the Internet, then it will likely charge you to access the same document or service *on* the Internet (although the cost may be lower on the Internet as an incentive for you to access the product or service that way).

Information Dissemination

In the previous section, we explained that the Internet provides you with the ability to access thousands of information sites all over the world. These thousands of sites exist because anyone can provide information on the Internet. If you limit yourself to accessing information that other people and organizations are providing, you are not harnessing the Internet's full potential. As we pointed out in Chapter 1, anyone can be a publisher on the Internet and provide information to the world.

Organizations all over the world are finding that the Internet provides an inexpensive and cost-effective way to distribute information. Once an organization places information on the Internet, it is available to all the Internet-connected organizations with which the company does business. It can also be read by potential customers and sponsors, prospective employees, and members of the general public.

There are no limits to the type of information that an organization can provide on the Internet. Common uses include the distribution of product and service information, company newsletters, corporate profiles, employee directories, and press releases.

Consider what the Canadian Consulate in San Jose, California (**http://www. globalx.net/ccto**), is doing on the Internet. They publish a monthly newsletter to help Canadian firms that wish to do business in the Silicon Valley area. To maximize the potential readership of their newsletter, they have placed it on the Internet's World Wide Web service, where it can be accessed by organizations across the country.

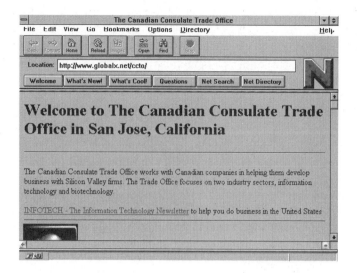

An Explosion in Home-Based Publishing

It is not just organizations that are engaging in publishing on the Internet. Individuals of all ages are establishing their own personal "kiosks" on the Internet called "home pages," where they place résumés, self-profiles, information about their hobbies and jobs, or whatever suits their fancy. It is increasingly common for Internet access providers to provide their customers with their own home pages as part of an Internet access package.

The following home page (**http://www.interlog.com:80/~shatz**) is just one example of the thousands of Internet home pages that are springing up all over Canada and the world.

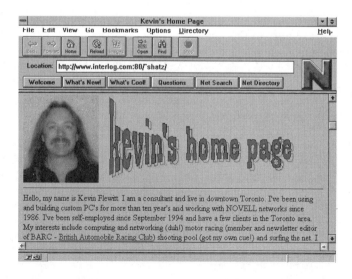

The World Wide Web's multimedia capabilities make it possible for users to include pictures of themselves on their home pages, as this individual has done.

Because users can include résumés, career histories, and skill profiles on their home pages, they provide new opportunities for Canadians to market themselves to potential employers. You can also use your home page to market yourself to potential customers, as this Winnipeg-based real estate agent has done (**http://www.mbnet.mb.ca/leblanc**):

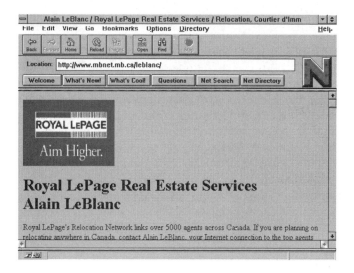

How Does It Work?

The Internet is not one large computer system somewhere: it consists of millions of computer systems, linked together via low- and high-speed communication lines. In fact, as we pointed out in Chapter 1, no one owns the Internet, no one runs it, and no one controls it. For this reason, anyone can join it (through an Internet access provider), and anyone can contribute information to it. (This is why it can sometimes be so difficult to find information on the Internet.)

TCP/IP

The millions of computers that make up the Internet are linked together using a networking technology known as TCP/IP, discussed in Chapter 2. Access is usually sold by an Internet provider, a company that buys high-speed communication access from telephone, satellite, computer, and other telecommunication companies and resells it to people or organizations that want to buy a connection to the Internet.

Obviously, once an organization joins the Internet and publishes information on its Internet site, other computers throughout the Internet have to know how to connect to it.

When you pick up your telephone and dial a telephone number, the telephone system knows how to route your call to the correct home or office. The Internet works in the same way; at the heart of the global Internet is something called the "domain name system," which keeps track of how to connect to all the computers on the Internet. The Internet's domain name system works behind the scenes to connect you to a site on the Internet, *once you have the address of a site to which you want to go.*

Finding Companies and Information

The domain name system is of limited use when you want to *find* the address of a site or person on the Internet. On the telephone system we can call directory assistance or consult the telephone book when we are looking for someone's telephone number. On the Internet things aren't that simple! Because no one controls the Internet, and since there are hundreds of different companies around the world that sell access to it, no single organization has the ability to produce a comprehensive directory of Internet users.

With the Internet growing so quickly, trying to keep an up-to-date list of Internet users and information resources would be an impossible task, even if you were to limit the scope of the directory to a smaller geographic area such as a city. Thus, finding a person or site on the Internet can be a challenge. Generally, the best recourse is to call the person or organization that you are looking for and ask for their Internet address over the telephone. Keep in mind, too, that many organizations are trying to build, on the World Wide Web, useful Internet indices that summarize companies and information on the Internet, many of which are very effective in helping you find your way around the Internet. For example, some people, recognizing the need for directory services on the Internet, have voluntarily created directories of people and sites. For example, an initiative on the Internet called Four 11 Directory Services (**http://www.four11.com**) maintains a database of Internet users and their e-mail addresses. Internet users can add themselves to the database for free and can search the directory without charge.

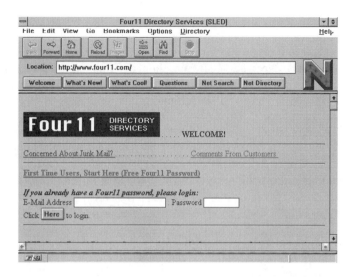

As for finding Internet sites (i.e., sites that organizations put up on the Internet), there are hundreds of subject-oriented directory initiatives all over the Internet that are maintained by people with interests in specific subject areas. One of the most popular multisubject Internet indexing services is called Yahoo (**http://www.yahoo.com**), which was developed by two Stanford University graduate students. Yahoo provides an index to the Internet by category, as depicted in the illustration below. Yahoo contains over 35,000 entries and is growing by 200 new sites every day.

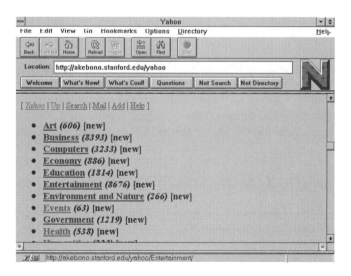

While directories such as Yahoo are extremely useful, they are never 100% comprehensive or up-to-date.

Another place to look on the Internet when you are trying to find the address of a site is an Internet "search engine." A number of people on the Internet have built programs that regularly scour the Internet for new sites. These programs create site databases that Internet users can search using powerful search engines. For example, one of the more popular search engines on the Internet is Lycos (**http://lycos.cs.cmu.edu/**), maintained at Carnegie Mellon University, which contains, as of March 1995, a database of over *1.89 million* Internet documents from around the world. Through Lycos (and similar systems) you can quickly find information on a particular topic or company, anywhere in the global Internet.

This is a very simplistic view of how the Internet functions. A detailed explanation of how the Internet works can be quite complex and is beyond the scope of this book. However, as an Internet user you don't need to know how the domain name system works to use the Internet and connect to places all over the world, just as you don't need to know how the telephone system works to make a telephone call.

Ok, So How Do I Join, and What Does It Cost?

There are two ways to access the Internet: as an individual "dialup" user or as a "dedicated" user on a corporate network.

Dialup Access

As a dialup user you access the Internet through a personal computer and a modem. Special software provides a connection from your computer through a device known as a modem to an Internet access provider. There are over 150 companies that sell access to the Internet in Canada. Providers can be categorized into three distinct groups based on the geographic area that they serve. These are

➤ National providers. National providers are companies that serve multiple provinces in Canada. This includes companies such as IBM.

➤ Regional providers. Regional providers serve an entire province or multiple cities within a province. This includes, for example, NBTel in New Brunswick, NSTN in Nova Scotia, and SaskTel in Saskatchewan.

➤ Local providers. Local providers serve a single city, town, or metropolitan area. Examples include Wimsey in Vancouver, Inforamp in Toronto, and ISIS in Halifax.

The cost for a dialup account varies across the country, but is normally in the range of $20.00 – $40.00 a month, which includes a certain number of hours of use, with additional hours costing from $0.25 to $3.00 per hour.

There are different types of dialup accounts. Three of the most popular types of dialup accounts are UUCP accounts, shell accounts, and SLIP/PPP accounts. The issue of what type of Internet account to buy is complex — and is clearly beyond the scope of this book.

But in most cases, as a dialup user you would want to buy a SLIP/PPP account, since it offers the most power, flexibility, and ease of use. Of the three types of accounts mentioned above, the SLIP/PPP account is the only one that will allow you to use programs such as Netscape, a graphical interface to the Internet's World Wide Web. The SLIP/PPP software is often provided by the Internet service provider or is bundled with "operating system software" provided by computer vendors. IBM, for example, sells OS/2, an operating system similar to (and which many people now consider to be superior to) Microsoft Windows, which includes SLIP software as well as WebCruiser, their software to access the World Wide Web. Other companies offer similar capabilities in their operating systems.

Most of the World Wide Web sites that you see throughout this book were accessed using the Netscape program, through a SLIP account. Throughout this book we will be showing you pictures of sites, as viewed through the Netscape program, in order to give you an idea of how the Internet works.

Dedicated Connection

Dialup access is appropriate for an individual user, but less appropriate for an organization that wants to provide many of its employees with access to the Internet.

Many organizations decide to go to the next level of access and provide a full-time dedicated connection from their organizational network to the Internet. This provides employees with instant access to the Internet from their desktop computers. With a dedicated connection, employees do not have to dial out to an Internet access provider using a modem.

The cost for such a connection varies depending on the company you choose to deal with, but pricing generally starts at about $600.00 a month plus the cost of the computer equipment. Prices for dedicated connections are usually flat rate, with no hourly charges. The cost of a dedicated connection increases depending on the speed of the connection that you select. In general, the more users you want to support, the faster your connection should be. Some of the more common connection speeds are 56 Kbps, 128 Kbps, and T1 speed (1.544 Mbps).

How Do I Publish On the Internet?

Earlier, we discussed how anyone can publish information on the Internet. Anyone with e-mail access to the Internet can publish his/her own newsletter, or electronic magazine, and send it out to discussion groups and mailing lists on the Internet.

Establishing a World Wide Web site is a bit more complicated, since it requires that your computer network be directly linked to the Internet, or that you utilize the services of a third party company (known as an "Internet presence provider") that will host your World Wide Web site on your behalf. Internet presence providers are an attractive alternative to organizations that want to publish on the Internet but do not want to purchase their own Internet connection.

In Chapter 10, in which we discuss how to develop an Internet strategy, we outline some of the decisions you have to make with respect to determining how to publish on the Internet.

Where Do We Go From Here?

This chapter provides a very preliminary and high-level overview of some of the key Internet technologies. We have deliberately chosen not to delve too deeply into the technology.

In subsequent chapters we will focus on how the Internet is being used within specific sectors, including business, education, government, not-for-profit organizations, and health care.

Should you require a more in-depth examination of the technology behind the Internet and how it works, we recommend you consult our *Canadian Internet Handbook*.

CHAPTER 4

Business on the Internet

Consumers will increasingly be able to buy anything they want directly from manufacturers and service providers without going through retailers — or advertisers.

Toward the new millennium:
Living, learning, and working

Futurist, November/December 1994

*T*he Internet has certainly managed to attract a lot of attention lately, but one of the consequences is that it is overhyped by too many people in too many ways. Too often this hype focuses on how the Internet will help businesses discover new markets and increase sales.

Now many have fallen into the trap of thinking that the Internet is a magical solution to business problems, or that it is a wonderful marketplace full of people just waiting to buy one's products.

The reality is that businesspeople who venture into the Internet with short-term expectations will be disappointed. Those who think they can make a quick fortune on the Internet will also be disappointed. Promises that the Internet will offer instant riches are neither realistic nor reasonable, and statements such as "if you aren't doing business on the Internet in ten years, you won't be in business," aren't helpful to business executives trying to understand the strategic impact of this network.

In many ways the Internet is more than just a means of selling goods and services on-line — it has become a basic business communications tool, as fundamental to our day-to-day activities as the telephone and fax machine. However, just as the telephone and fax took some time to change the way that business operates, the Internet will also take time to change the way we do business. And just as a business can survive without a fax machine, businesses

STRATEGIC USES OF THE INTERNET WITHIN BUSINESS

(1) Selling

(2) Marketing
- Finding new customers
- Educating consumers
- Building credibility with potential customers
- Building goodwill
- Improving brand loyalty
- Encouraging brand trial
- Building customer loyalty: membership programs
- Building customer loyalty: ongoing communications
- Building a customer mailing list

(3) Customer Relations
- Providing product information repositories
- Providing customer support
- Obtaining customer feedback
- Providing directory services

(4) Market Intelligence
- Monitoring customer discussions and attitudes
- Monitoring customer-developed World Wide Web sites
- Monitoring competitor activities
- Conducting market research

(5) Corporate Activities
- Gathering corporate intelligence
- Enhancing corporate communications
- Improving public relations
- Providing new avenues for recruitment activities
- Developing electronic publishing and new information services
- Achieving cost savings and efficiencies
- Reducing distribution costs

will survive without using the Internet. However, most will agree that a business that does not have a fax machine today is at a *strategic disadvantage*, given its predominance as a means of communication. Because the Internet is becoming the standard means for intercompany communication and electronic publishing, businesses that do not have Internet access are at a strategic disadvantage.

Is the Internet Real?

The Internet will dramatically change the business landscape through the next decade and beyond and will have a profound impact on both large and small businesses around the world. This isn't hype; this is an observation of what seems to be occurring through the Internet. Think about what is happening — the Internet is the technology that is linking all the computers in the world.

The significance of this trend cannot be overstated. The Internet is defining how all the computers in the world will be connected. Somehow, this will change the way that business is conducted.

The Internet and the whole concept of doing business "electronically" are still very new to many businesses and consumers. As the world becomes wired through the Internet, people will learn to work in new ways and become accustomed to doing business electronically. We can't expect any "revolutionary" change in accepted business practices to occur overnight, but we can expect "evolutionary" change to occur over a period of time. Slowly, the world will learn to do business through the Internet.

The Internet also provides a new vehicle for consumer activism, since consumers can use the Internet to instantly communicate their dissatisfaction with a particular product to thousands of people around the world. Anthony J.F. O'Reilly, the Chief Executive Officer of H.J. Heinz, recently stated that "tomorrow's CEO also must master a rapidly swelling revolution in communications technology. Consumer expectations and brand loyalties can be aroused throughout the world via satellite and cable television, yet the smallest media complaint anywhere can magnify in a flash, and pressure groups can mobilize with lightning speed on the information highway." Intel discovered the consumer power of the Internet when a flaw with its Pentium chip was exposed on the Internet — it took a $500 million charge to its earnings when the defect was made public. One does not trifle with the Internet.

The Internet will also redefine the nature of a company's competition. Since the Internet is borderless, companies in other provinces and countries suddenly become competitors. The Internet will force organizations to compete globally, with companies that had never previously been considered their competition. As noted in an article entitled "Avoiding the corporate dinosaur syndrome," in *Organizational Dynamics* (Autumn 1994), "With the innovations that are taking place in information technology, the globalization of business, and the creation of network organizations and partnering, it is quite likely that corporations will compete with those organizations they once had cooperative relationships with, or that they saw as irrelevant. Because of new forms of organizations, the barriers to market entry are lower. As a result, new and very different competition can appear very quickly. Established corporations must constantly reanalyze the competitive environment with an eye toward identifying nontraditional competitors who may suddenly become strong competitors."

The Internet shows no signs of slowing down. With every hour that passes, it gains more momentum. But in many ways the Internet is still in its infancy; the majority of businesses and consumers are not yet using it. But as it grows and expands, opportunities to do business through the Internet will also increase.

In this chapter we will examine the issues of doing business on the Internet and describe some of the opportunities that lie therein, such as how the Internet provides new ways for consumers to communicate directly with retailers, how it provides customer support, and how it can be used as a public relations tool.

The Cultural Landscape of the Internet

The first step in understanding how to do business on the Internet is understanding its culture. In the same way that you cannot expect to go to a foreign country and succeed in business there if you don't understand the culture, you can't expect to learn how to do business on the Internet unless you spend the time learning its unique culture.

Those who spend time on the Internet do so because they like to use it as a tool. They enjoy being able to retrieve information when they wish through the World Wide Web. They like being able to debate topics and issues in USENET newsgroups and mailing lists. They like the convenience and efficiency of electronic mail. These people have taken the time to discover how a personal computer can become an information appliance.

In many ways the culture of the Internet is that its citizens are masters of information — and they pride themselves on the fact that information does not master them. When this pride is tampered with, the citizens of the Internet rebel. People on the Internet live by one cardinal rule: *unsolicited information (or junk mail) sent through the Internet is evil, and will not be tolerated.* This point cannot be overemphasized. Just as people do not like to be disturbed at home by a telemarketer, Internet users do not like to receive unsolicited commercial e-mail messages.

And on the Internet they can fight back.

Junk Mail on the Internet

The culture of the Internet is such that users will *never* willingly accept unsolicited information. Of course, this is in complete opposition to the role of information and advertising in our society today. We are bombarded with advertisements on TV and radio, our mailboxes are stuffed with flyers and junk mail, and our streets are littered with billboards. Our senses are continuously assaulted by marketing and advertising information — much of it information that we do not want. But these are considered to be perfectly acceptable methods of doing business.

However, those who try to use the Internet to distribute junk mail will find themselves on the receiving end of the wrath of a great number of very upset people. If you try sending junk mail over the Internet, clever computer programmers may decide to use their skill and knowledge to try and shut down your computer connection to the Internet. You will find yourself the target of "hackers" who will certainly teach you a lesson. You may wake up one morning to find your electronic mailbox overflowing to such a degree that it will be unusable. Your might find that your staff are being verbally abused over the telephone, and your fax machine is full of letters of complaint. You could receive angry phone calls from Internet users at all hours of the day and night, since you could find your home phone number posted throughout the global Internet. On the Internet, people can and do fight back.

There are many people who believe that the Internet simply needs to be opened up to junk mail. The infamous Canter & Siegal case, in which two American lawyers bombarded the Internet with junk mail and subsequently encountered the wrath of the network, brought this issue to the forefront in 1994. Canter and Siegal took to the press, castigating Internet users for refusing to accept that the age of 'advertising' on the Internet was now at hand. But rather than being "commercial saviors" of the Internet (as they made themselves out to be), they failed miserably in every attempt to advertise on-line. They always will. The methods advocated by Canter and Siegal — junk mail — will always be doomed to failure, because the Internet will fight back.

Elementary marketing courses teach one fundamental rule: it does not make good business sense to upset a potential customer. And with that in mind, we have one simple piece of advice: junk mail on the Internet does not work, nor will it ever work.

Respect Internet Culture

The right way to do business through the Internet is to respect its unique culture and understand that while junk mail will never be tolerated, establishing a "site" of information that people can *choose to come to* is perfectly acceptable. Establishing an information site, and then announcing it in appropriate places, is the right way to do business on the Internet, and will succeed because it makes it possible for a business to forge a closer and more direct relationship with the customer. In Chapter 10 we discuss some of the "appropriate" places to announce your site on the Internet. In this chapter we will examine the many business activities that can be supported through the Internet.

Business on the Internet

Businesses are on the Internet for five fundamental purposes:

➤ selling goods and services;

➤ marketing goods and services;

➤ customer relations;

➤ market intelligence;

➤ corporate activities.

Selling on the Internet

The Internet is accelerating the trend toward "disintermediation," that is, the elimination of the middleman. What the Internet represents is the opportunity for the customer and seller to have a more direct relationship. Why have a record store when you can order directly from Sony? Why have a bookstore when you can browse an electronic catalogue of books and purchase them directly from the publisher? Why have a travel agent when you can book with an airline directly?

The middleman will never completely disappear, however. Going to a store to shop is simply a part of our everyday lives. But the Internet *will* have an impact on distributors, wholesalers, and retailers, since the Internet makes it possible for organizations to deal directly with the consumer.

A number of organizations selling goods and services on the Internet do so directly through their World Wide Web sites. Many organizations accept credit card numbers on-line to ease the ordering process. The World Wide Web supports the use of electronic forms, which permit people to place orders directly on the Internet through an easy, simple-to-use interface. An Internet user can pull an order form up on the screen, key in the appropriate shipping and credit card information, and the order will be transmitted directly to the retailer or manufacturer.[1]

Sony Music, for example, has established an extremely impressive World Wide Web site to promote its artists and their music (**http://www.sony.com**):

---

[1] At this time, there are still concerns over the security of credit card information provided through many Internet sites, but the concerns are quickly being alleviated through "encryption" and the emergence of other standards. This issue is discussed in greater depth in Chapter 11.

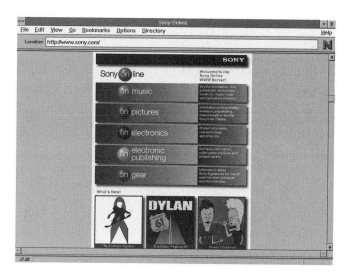

In addition to supplying artist profiles and information about new releases, Sony has provided an on-line order form so that users can place an order, for example, Bob Dylan's "Highway 61 Interactive" music CD-ROM (**http://www.sony.com/Music/ forms/BobDylan_H61.html**). Accompanying the order form is a press release and album fact sheet. Once the consumer has read about the CD-ROM and decides to buy it, Sony provides a simple order form that customers can fill out:

The form asks the user for a name, shipping address, telephone number, credit card number, the type of credit card, and the card's expiry date:

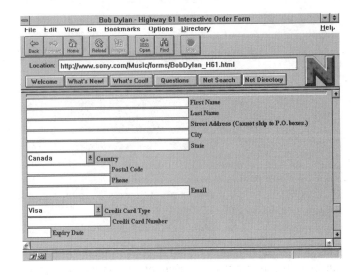

Customers who do not wish to send credit card information over the Internet can phone in their order or fax it to Sony.

The Seattle Mariners, the first major league baseball team on the Internet, is an example of an organization that has placed a merchandise catalogue on the Internet. On their official World Wide Web site (**http://www.mariners.org**), the Mariners provide pictures of team apparel and team publications. Internet users can browse the products on the Internet and then fax or mail in their order:

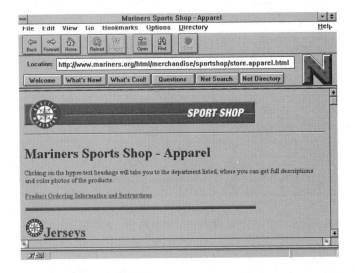

The ability of the World Wide Web to support on-line forms has made it easier for organizations to accept orders over the Internet. Since thousands already know how to use the World Wide Web, no special training, technology, or clumsy manuals are required to establish new customer relationships. The result is that for a very low cost, organizations can establish a new service for thousands of their customers — for a fraction of the cost of reaching them using other methods.

Are these organizations selling a lot of merchandise on-line? Likely not. It will take some time for a real Internet marketplace to emerge. Many of the organizations selling goods and services on the Internet have been disappointed with the lack of on-line sales to date. Many people thought that they merely had to establish a World Wide Web site where they could sell products and sit back and watch the orders roll in. Customers visited their sites, but the orders did not necessarily follow. The result was that a number of these people and the media began to criticize the Internet's potential for "on-line shopping." A January 1995 article in *ComputerWorld* questioned the Internet's sales potential:

> Dozens of electronic malls have made splashy appearances in recent months, offering Internet surfers the ultimate convenience of popping into a widening assortment of stores to buy goods on-line or via 800 numbers.
>
> But retailers and virtual mall owners acknowledge they have yet to witness any rush of new sales through this electronic channel. Some merchandisers have withdrawn from the Internet entirely after what seemed an encouraging start.
>
> Consider The Vermont Teddy Bear Co. in Shelburne, Vt., which set up a World Wide Web page last summer with Digital Equipment Corp. Within four hours of public availability, the page received 13,000 visits. Six months later, the page is gone, and the toy maker is concentrating on more traditional marketing.
>
> Cybershoppers Cruise Past Internet Retailers
> *ComputerWorld*, January 23, 1995

Disintermediation is a reality through the Internet, but we need to keep in mind that the change to a business marketplace in which the middleman plays a reduced role will be more gradual than instant. People are still learning how to use the Internet, and companies on it are still trying to learn how to do business on-line. The result is an ever-increasing march toward a world where business on the Internet is a matter of everyday routine.

The early experiences with on-line shopping do not indicate that "on-line shopping" is destined to be a failure on the Internet. We must learn to temper our expectations of how long it takes for a particular technology to change the behavior and actions of a society. On-line ordering on the Internet will take some time to be accepted and used by people, just as automatic teller machines took time to be accepted by mainstream society. Five factors limit the widespread acceptance and use of Internet-based order mechanisms:

➤ The majority of consumers are not on the Internet, which limits the potential number of users of such an ordering mechanism. This will change as more and more people and businesses around the world connect to the Internet.

➤ Concerns about the security risks of electronic transactions discourage Internet users from providing credit card numbers on-line. This is a transitional issue; once we are able to conduct secure transaction methods on the Internet, this will change. The emerging standards on this issue are discussed in Chapter 11. (While the risk of fraud is quickly being minimized with the introduction of secure order mechanisms, some people will never be convinced that the technology is 100% secure and hence will not participate in on-line ordering.)

➤ Old habits are difficult to change. People are comfortable shopping through traditional channels (e.g., stores, catalogues), and many have no desire to change. (People also said this about banking machines.)

➤ Many items are not conducive to on-line ordering since they require prepurchase trial or examination — for example, clothes and high-price items like jewelry, cars, and furniture.

➤ Many consumers are not comfortable ordering products on-line if the retailer is one with whom they have no experience. In a 1993 study the International Mass Retail Association found that consumers, when shopping electronically, preferred to deal with organizations with recognizable brand names.[2]

Consider these comments from a focus group on the subject of on-line ordering:

> - A big part of whether or not I will buy something now or in the future through these channels is the reputation of the company.
> - I would buy anything from a retailer or catalog company that I've had good experience with. I want to know that a retailer is reputable, has a name, and doesn't give me a hassle to return something.

---

[2] "Changing Channels," *Datamation*, February 1994, p. 14. The International Mass Retail Association can be reached at (202) 861-0774.

The result? The Internet supports on-line shopping, but an on-line shopping mindset is still emerging. There is no magic formula to selling on the Internet. In essence, we are still a society of consumers learning about electronic shopping in a world of suppliers still learning how to sell electronically.

Marketing on the Internet

Selling is by no means the only reason businesses use the Internet. An even more important use of the Internet is for marketing activities that *support* a company's core business objectives. For example, a business may wish to increase its market share, improve sales, revitalize its image, improve customer service, or increase consumer awareness of its products. The Internet can help organizations meet these objectives. Marketing opportunities on the Internet include

- finding new customers;
- educating consumers;
- building credibility with potential customers;
- building goodwill;
- improving brand loyalty;
- encouraging brand trial;
- building customer loyalty: membership programs;
- building customer loyalty: ongoing communications;
- building a customer mailing list.

Each of these strategies will be discussed below.

New Customers

With thousands of people using the Internet every day, it can be an excellent place to market products and services, increase brand awareness, and build recognition of your brand name. The Internet's global reach means that organizations can market their products and services worldwide from a single location on the network. For example, Saturn has a site on the Internet where it promotes its cars (**http://www.saturncars.com**).

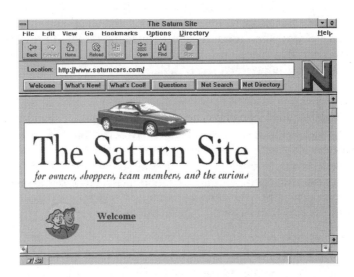

By clicking on the desired model, consumers can obtain detailed information such as color, fabric, pricing, standard features, and specifications:

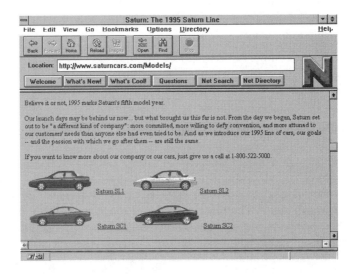

By establishing such an on-line brochure, Saturn can find potential customers.

Consumer Education

An educated consumer is a potential customer, so many organizations use the Internet to help consumers understand the goods and services offered by the company. Organizations that provide helpful advice to consumers are likely to be remembered when consumers are ready to make a purchase.

An excellent example of an organization that has taken this approach on the Internet is the Toronto Dominion Bank (**http://www.tdbank.ca/tdbank**), which has established a site full of useful financial information, including a section to help guide the new homeowner. This section includes answers to questions such as, How Do I Buy a Home? and What Kinds of Mortgages are There? There is also a document called "Everything You Wanted to Know About Buying a Home But Were Afraid to Ask," which includes a checklist of items to remember when applying for a mortgage. These information resources are similar to the many brochures available in the bank.

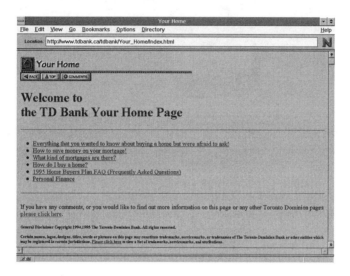

Another good example is Goodyear Tires (**http://www.goodyear.com**):

To help educate the public about tires, Goodyear has established a "tire school" on the Internet with helpful advice about good tire care and explanations of tire terminology such as "alignment", "balance" and "traction."

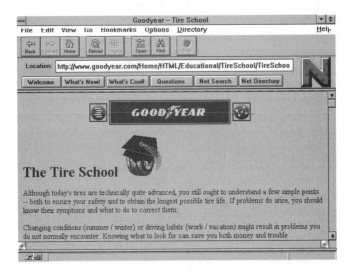

The Goodyear site provides an invaluable section on how to "read" your tires, which includes a labeled diagram of a tire.

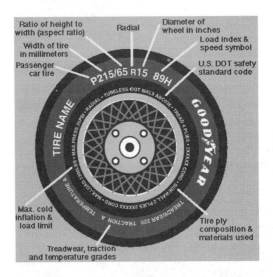

Both the Toronto Dominion Bank and Goodyear understand the importance of building a good relationship with current and potential customers, and they have extended their educational activities to the Internet. In the future there will be more commercial Internet sites that "educate," rather than just sell.

Credibility

The Internet can help businesses build credibility among consumers. This can be done by publishing a mission statement or statement of operating philosophy on the Internet to help consumers understand what the organization represents.

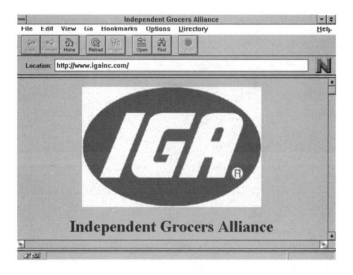

IGA, the sixth largest supermarket chain in the world, is a perfect example of this particular use of the Internet. IGA's World Wide Web site (**http://www.igainc.com**) describes the company's rich history and remarkable growth and highlights milestones and major achievements in the company's 69-year history.

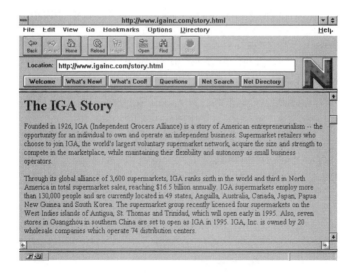

Another way for an organization to build credibility among consumers is to show how its products have been used successfully by others. For example, to prove the durability and reliability of its products, DuPont, a world leader in the lubricant products market, uses its World Wide Web site (**http://www.lubricants. dupont.com**) to show how its products are being used by racing celebrities and in prestigious racing events.

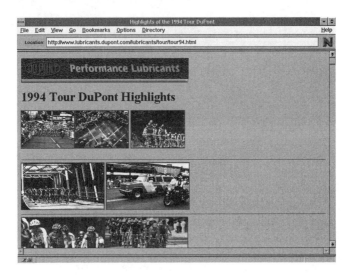

Goodwill

Many organizations use the Internet to demonstrate that their organizations are good corporate citizens. They do this by highlighting community events in which they are involved and by describing how the organization is active in the community. For example, IGA's World Wide Web site (**http://www.igainc.com**) describes the company's "Hometown Proud" philosophy and its commitment to community involvement.

> "Hometown Proud" Means Community Involvement
>
> In 1987, a committee composed of five IGA advertising executives set out to develop a means of effectively leveraging the goodwill that IGA retailers generate through their involvement in the local communities they serve. Although IGA grocers vary in the way they operate their supermarkets, they are alike in the impressive support they give to their cities, towns and neighborhoods. From helping the local school district to purchase new computers to

sponsoring fun runs to benefit charity, IGA retailers are known for being active and involved. To help communicate this impressive commitment to the community, the advertising committee devised a marketing campaign centered around the phrase "Hometown Proud." The slogan has since evolved into a guiding philosophy for IGA and differentiates its retailers from the competition.

To further help IGA retailers give back to their communities, IGA, with the help of Louisiana-Pacific Corp. and Coca-Cola USA, launched the successful hometown Trees program in 1992. The project encourages IGA retailers to work with local community groups to plant seedling trees and care for them in the coming years.

The IGA Story
http://www.igainc.com

On a larger scale, companies can set up special sites on the Internet to promote fund-raising events and other corporate sponsorship activities as a means of building goodwill toward their organizations. For example, companies like *Time Magazine* and Cadillac benefit by having their names associated with charity events such as the Cadillac NFL Classic Golf Tournament, which is promoted on the Internet on a special World Wide Web site (**http://www.nfl-golf.com/classic**):

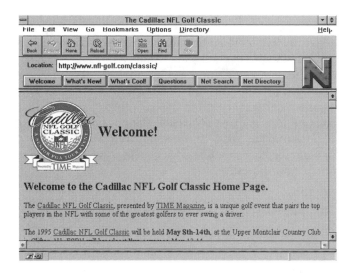

The names of the sponsors are clearly identified, and if sponsors have their own sites on the World Wide Web, they can create links back to their own home pages. In this way Internet users have the option of visiting the sponsors' own sites should they wish to obtain additional information about any of the sponsors.

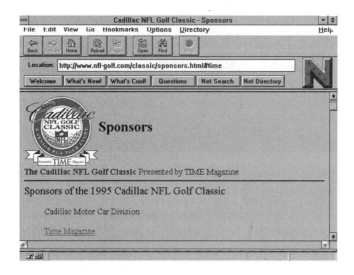

Brand Loyalty

Over the last few years the concept of "brand equity" has gained considerable attention within the business community. With an increasing move to private label products and the threat of competition from "no-name" brands, many companies are struggling to ensure that there is still value in the brand names that they own. This concept is referred to as "brand equity."

The Internet helps many companies improve the likelihood of a customer purchase of a branded product through ongoing efforts to build awareness of the product and its brand name. Most often this is done by establishing a site with information of general interest that relates to the core product being sold and by providing information that will encourage purchase of the product. Godiva Chocolates, for example, has established a site (**http://www.godiva.com**) featuring information on its products:

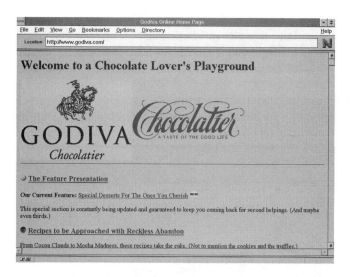

To help build brand loyalty, the site includes a number of chocolate recipes that require the use of Godiva chocolate. The concept is similar to magazine advertisements that feature a recipe and include a specific product in the list of ingredients.

To encourage consumers to keep returning to the site, new recipes are introduced on a regular basis, and the products change depending on the time of year. For example, in the weeks leading up to Valentine's Day, the site featured an assortment of chocolate gift ideas. During the Easter season, an entire section of the site was devoted to Easter chocolates, including chocolate Easter bunnies, chocolate Easter eggs, and Easter baskets.

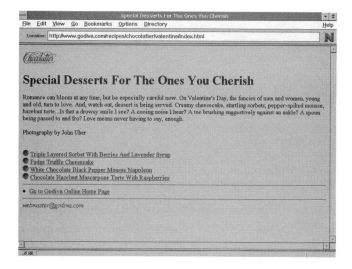

Through on-line marketing and traditional advertising, Godiva can let "choco-holics" know that there is a site on the Internet that contains chocolate recipes. People visit the site to retrieve the recipes, and, in doing so, obtain information about Godiva chocolate. In this way, Godiva builds brand awareness of its high-quality chocolate products.

Ragú, a popular brand of pasta sauces, employs the same strategy used by Godiva. Ragú promotes its line of pasta sauces on the Internet (**http://www.eat.com**). In addition to providing pictures of its pasta products, Ragu supplies ingredient lists and nutritional information to consumers.

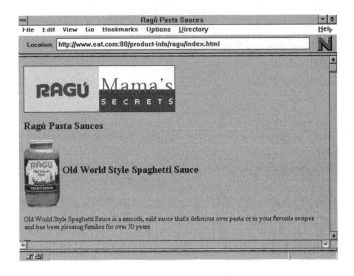

To encourage the purchase and use of its pasta sauces, Ragú provides dozens of recipes on its site, all of which require the use of a particular variety of Ragú, for example, Veal Cutlet Parmesan, Vegetable Bow Tie Pasta, and Pork Chops Creole.

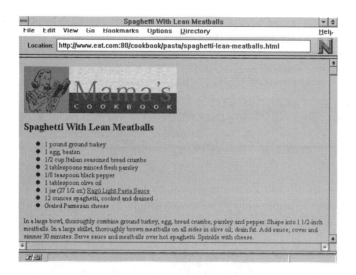

In a large bowl, thoroughly combine ground turkey, egg, bread crumbs, parsley and pepper. Shape into 1 1/2-inch meatballs. In a large skillet, thoroughly brown meatballs on all sides in olive oil; drain fat. Add sauce; cover and simmer 30 minutes. Serve sauce and meatballs over hot spaghetti. Sprinkle with cheese.

It is unlikely that these Internet marketing activities will have a dramatic impact on the sales of Godiva chocolates or Ragú in the short term. However, it is evident that many organizations are trying, through the Internet, advertising methods that work well otherwise. Will it have an impact in the long term? More than likely.

Brand Trial

Coupons and free samples of products are techniques that are regularly employed by organizations that want to encourage consumers to try out their products. Organizations hope that by removing or reducing the financial risk of a purchase, consumers will be more likely to try a product. Because these are proven methods of generating consumer trial of brands, many organizations are applying the same techniques on the Internet. Ragú, for example, has a coupon offer on their World Wide Web site (**http://www.eat.com**) worth U.S. $2.20 toward the cost of Ragú, Pizza Quick, and Chicken Tonight brands.

Internet users can fill out an on-line form on Ragú's World Wide Web site, and a coupon book will be mailed back to them through the postal system. Currently, the offer is only valid for Internet users in the United States.

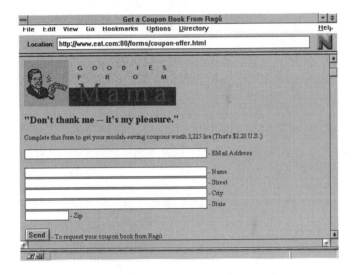

Customer Loyalty: Membership Programs

Other organizations use the Internet as a tool to build customer loyalty. "Encourage the customer to keep coming back" is the rallying cry of the "membership loyalty" approach to marketing. For instance, in recent years there has been a proliferation in the number of "frequent-buyer" or "point" programs offered by organizations such as airlines, department stores, bookstores, and credit card companies. These organizations are looking for a competitive edge in attracting and retaining customers. Many organizations are now planning similar promotions on the Internet.

Consider the opportunity for an airline, for example. Members could use the Internet to look up their point status, to request an award, to view pictures and descriptions of available prizes, and to read about program rules and conditions. Significant cost savings and new opportunities to build upon the customer relationship could result.

An example of an organization that has launched a membership program on the Internet is Cathay Pacific Airlines, which has established a CyberTraveler program exclusively for Internet users (**http://www.cathay-usa.com**). Participants can receive special travel offers and discounts from the airline. For example, Cathay Pacific CyberTraveler members can retrieve extra bonus miles on certain trips, above and beyond what they would regularly retrieve as members of the airline's frequent-flyer program.

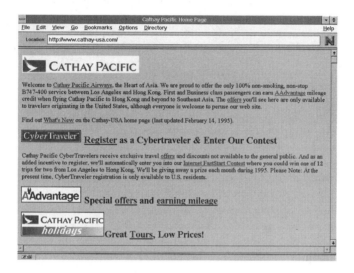

Given the cost of maintaining membership loyalty programs, organizations should recognize the potential of the Internet as a tool for supporting the communications inherent in such a program.

Customer Loyalty: Ongoing Communications

It is not just official membership programs that can be used to help build customer loyalty. Just as retailers use customer mailing lists, organizations can use Internet-based mailing lists to keep existing and prospective customers up-to-date on new products, sales, and special events. The way to do this through the Internet is through "electronic" mailing lists. A message sent to an electronic mailing list reaches all members of the list and thus becomes an effective means of reaching a targeted group of people.

While junk mail will never be acceptable on the Internet, there is nothing to prohibit an organization from establishing a *voluntary* electronic mailing list through which members can receive advertisements and update information. Since membership on the list is voluntary, distribution of advertisements to the list is acceptable.

An extremely effective example of such a list is found with Roswell Computer Books, a specialty bookstore located in Halifax, Nova Scotia. The organization has established an electronic mailing list that customers of the bookstore can choose to join. On an irregular basis, the store sends notices to its customers through the electronic mailing list, including summaries of books on sale, announcements of new products, special promotions, and other information. Since members of the Roswell mailing list know they will receive advertisements and promotions through the list, no Internet etiquette rules are broken. And by keeping its customers informed of new book arrivals and special promotions, new sales can occur.

The establishment of electronic mailing lists that anyone can choose to join fits within the unique cultural mindset of the Internet, since it makes the receipt of information voluntary. This works well for organizations, because it provides an inexpensive method of keeping customers up-to-date. Should the customer ever request it, they are immediately taken off the list. As a result, any organization intent on doing business on the Internet should consider how customer loyalty can be developed through electronic mailing lists.

Customer Mailing Lists

In the previous section we explained how an organization can build customer loyalty using Internet mailing lists. But how do you find people who want to be added to your company's distribution list? Organizations that add people to their electronic distribution list without asking them first are violating Internet etiquette. To address this problem, several organizations with Internet mailing lists have integrated automated subscription mechanisms into their World Wide Web sites. The rationale for doing this is that every person who visits an organization's Internet site is a current or potential customer. A person visiting your World Wide Web site probably has some interest in your organization's products or services. With this in mind, an organization can ask people who stop by their Internet site to subscribe to their electronic mailing list. This allows an organization to build a mailing list targeted at people interested in the organization's products and services.

Volvo is an example of an organization that uses the Internet is this way. On Volvo's World Wide Web site (**http://www.volvocars.com**), consumers have the option of adding their e-mail address to Volvo's electronic mailing list.

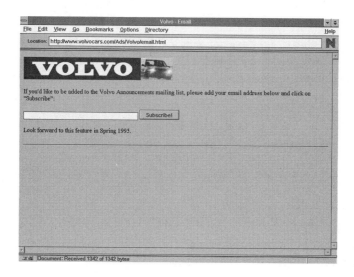

DuPont is another example of an organization that uses the Internet to build a customer mailing list. DuPont's Performance Lubricants Division has a form on their World Wide Web site (**http://www.lubricants.dupont.com**) that customers can fill out if they wish to be added to DuPont's electronic mailing list.

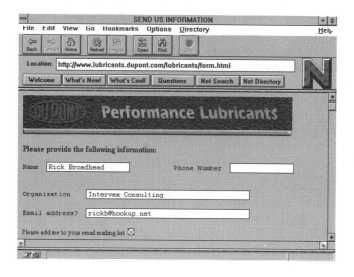

An increasing number of Internet-connected organizations are building customer databases in this way. Because customers have to explicitly request to be added to the organization's mailing list, organizations do not have to be concerned about unsolicited advertising when they send product information to members on the list.

Customer Relations

The third major area of opportunity for businesses on the Internet is in customer relations. Customer service has become a key area of competitive advantage in the 1990s. Given the high cost of providing customer support on-site or over the telephone, many organizations now look to the Internet as an opportunity to help reduce customer support costs.

The Internet excels as a customer support tool. With so many consumers becoming familiar with the concept of accessing information electronically, there are opportunities for organizations to provide access to customer support information through the Internet. Through the use of electronic forms and e-mail, organizations can provide customers with new ways of obtaining support directly from the organization.

There are four specific uses of the Internet as a customer relations tool:

➤ product information repositories;

➤ customer support;

➤ customer feedback;

➤ directory services.

Each of these strategies is discussed below.

Product Information Repositories

Many organizations make product support literature available on the Internet, which customers can retrieve seven days a week, 24 hours a day. A good example of this strategy is found with DuPont Lubricants. The organization has established a World Wide Web site (**http://www.lubricants.dupont.com**) to promote two of its lubricant products. The users of these specialty lubricant products are companies in high-tech industries, such as aerospace and semiconductor companies. These types of organizations are already very active on the Internet; hence Dupont has chosen to make over 300 pages of scientific and engineering information available on its World Wide Web site, as well as a technical overview of its products:

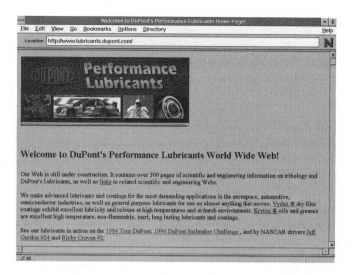

DuPont's World Wide Web site serves a dual purpose. First, DuPont uses it to promote its products. Second, DuPont supports existing customers by providing convenient and timely access to product support literature.

Another example is Compaq. Compaq maintains a World Wide Web site on the Internet (**http://www.compaq.com**) with a comprehensive customer support section:

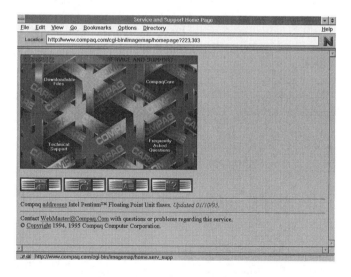

Compaq has made the following information available to Internet users:

➣ a list of frequently asked questions and answers, which is intended to help solve many of the common problems that a customer might encounter;

➢ information on how to e-mail Compaq with a technical support question;

➢ information on Compaq warranty and service programs and listings of authorized third-party repair centres;

➢ files that can be downloaded to solve specific hardware or software problems.

How does an organization benefit by providing product support information on the Internet? If customers can find the answers to their questions through the Internet before calling or contacting the company, customer satisfaction will increase. Since customers can obtain quick answers to their questions at any time of the day or night, customer support costs will decrease as customers rely less on customer support telephone lines. In addition, as customers begin to expect Internet customer support information centres, those organizations that establish such sites will build goodwill with their customer base.

Customer Support

Another method of improving customer service is to provide customers with new and improved ways of contacting an organization with product support questions. Several organizations, particularly those in the high-tech community, have connected their customer support staff to the Internet and now accept product support questions by e-mail and through the World Wide Web.

Compaq, for example, accepts questions via e-mail at **support@compaq.com**. To ensure that customers include all the necessary details in their electronic mail messages, Compaq has posted a set of instructions on their World Wide Web site (**http://www.compaq.com**) that explains how to send a support question to Compaq through the Internet:

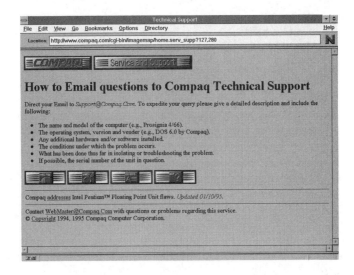

Dell Computer, a leading manufacturer of personal computers, has also established an e-mail address for technical support (**support@dell.com**) to which any type of technical question can be sent. In addition, the organization has established a World Wide Web site (**http://www.dell.com**) that provides an on-line form that customers can fill out if they have a support question:

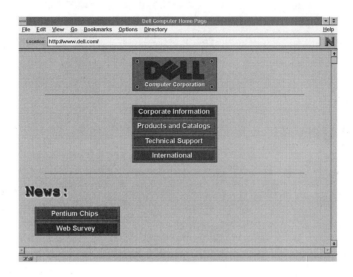

By selecting the Technical Support item from Dell's introductory World Wide Web page, a customer can discover a number of methods to obtain support from Dell through the Internet:

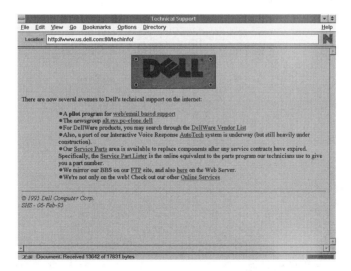

One of the options that Dell provides to its customers is a problem questionnaire that can be filled out on its World Wide Web site. The questionnaire asks the customer a series of specific questions about the problem, and the report is sent immediately to Dell's customer support centre, where it is processed by product support staff.

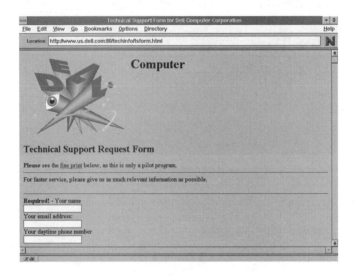

Customer Feedback

Many organizations have established mechanisms on the Internet that allow consumers to interact directly with their company. With thousands already "surfing" the World Wide Web on a daily basis, many organizations have put up a simple "comments" form on the World Wide Web which can be filled out during a visit to a company's site. For example, IGA has placed a comment form on its World Wide Web site (**http://www.igainc.com**) which allows consumers to send suggestions directly to IGA's corporate office through the Internet.

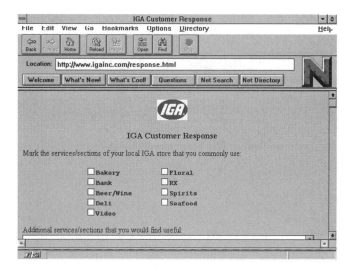

The media, in particular, make extensive use of the Internet for this purpose. Hardly a week goes by without a radio station, newspaper, or magazine announcing its Internet address. Both *Maclean's* magazine and the *Globe and Mail* accept letters to the editor via the Internet (**at letters@macleans.ca** and **letters@globeandmail.ca**, respectively).

Television networks also use the Internet to get closer to their viewers and to request feedback about their shows. The CTV Television Network has established Internet addresses for several of its shows, including Canada AM (**am@ctv.ca**) and CTV News (**news@ctv.ca**). The CBS Television Network has launched an impressive World Wide Web site (**http://www.cbs.com**) with links to many of the network's most popular shows, including the Late Show with host David Letterman and the Late Late Show with host Tom Snyder.

By selecting the Late Late Show, for example, Internet users can call up a form and send comments directly to Tom Snyder, bringing a new level of interactivity to late night TV.

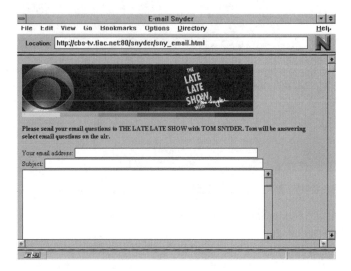

In Canada the Discovery Channel encourages viewer feedback through its World Wide Web site (**http://www.discovery.ca**). Internet users can send general comments about the station or a specific show by filling out an on-line form:

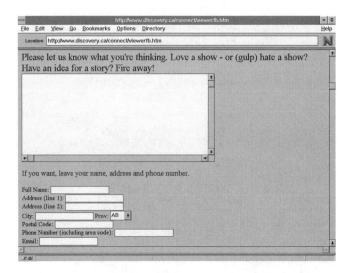

Directory Services

To do business with your organization, a customer has to know where to find your products and services, whether through a retail store, a nearby dealer, or an authorized agent. In the event that the customer needs to interact with your head office or an employee, the customer needs to know who to call with specific questions. With large organizations the difficulty of locating the right person or department can be particularly acute.

Sun Microsystems is a prime example of an organization that uses the Internet to help its customers communicate with the organization and its authorized dealers. Sun has established an area on its World Wide Web site (**http://www.sun.com**) called *Doing Business with Sun* with answers to questions such as

➤ how to place an order with Sun Microsystems, Inc.;

➤ how to contact Sun's worldwide sales offices;

➤ who to call for service, sales, training, and Sun integration services;

➤ how to locate a Sun value-added reseller.

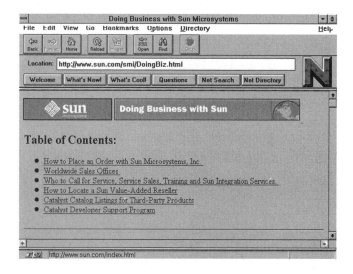

Xerox has established a similar section on its World Wide Web server (**http://www.xerox.com**) called *How to Reach Xerox*. It includes a listing of Xerox's World Wide Web servers, telephone numbers, e-mail addresses, bulletin board numbers, fax information services, and 800 numbers.

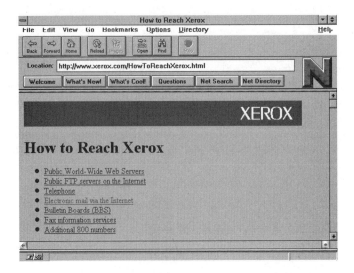

Citibank has included a directory of its branches on its World Wide Web site (**http://www.tti.com**) to help its customers find their nearest Citibank location.

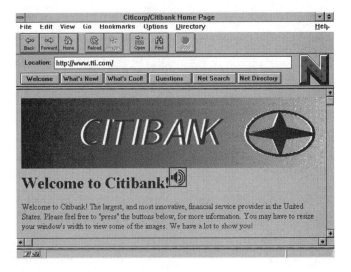

By making a series of menu choices, Internet users can locate a branch near them. For example, the following information was available on Citibank's branch in Toronto's Chinatown:

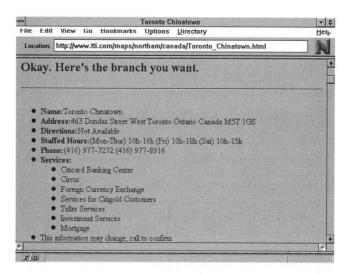

On Volvo's World Wide Web site (**http://www.volvocars.com**) consumers can use an on-line database to locate their closest Volvo dealer. For example, suppose we wish to locate a Volvo dealer in Nova Scotia. We input "Nova Scotia" on the form:

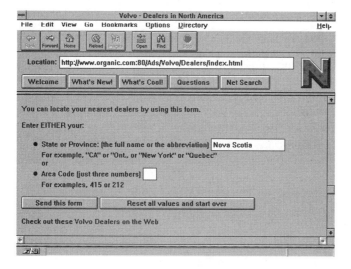

Seconds later the database returns the names and addresses of three Nova Scotia Volvo dealers in Stellarton, Halifax, and Kentville.

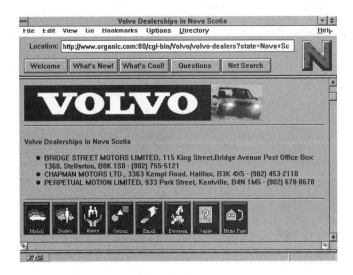

Using the Internet to let your customer know how to contact you or where to find your organization's products and/or services is a strategy that is being employed by many organizations on their World Wide Web sites. It is certainly an area that any organization involved with the Internet should explore.

Market Intelligence

Regardless of the nature of your business, it is likely that your customers and competitors are on the Internet, setting up World Wide Web sites and participating in some of the 15,000 plus different discussion groups that exist on the network. Monitoring these activities can provide organizations with valuable market intelligence information. There are four specific market intelligence activities that organizations can engage in on the Internet:

➤ monitoring customer discussions and attitudes;

➤ monitoring customer-developed World Wide Web sites;

➤ monitoring competitor activities;

➤ conducting market research.

We will address each of these activities separately.

Customer Discussions and Attitudes

Beyond providing the best possible customer support, an important part of the customer relationship is ensuring that the company is actually listening to its customers. Some organizations find that the Internet is an invaluable source of customer feedback. This is particularly true if current or potential customers are talking about the company or its products in a public area of the Internet. Product reviews and comments and opinions on particular products and services circulate on the various discussion areas throughout the global Internet on an ongoing basis. Companies can monitor these discussions to see what their customers have to say about their products and services.

For example, consider the following message from an area of the Internet called **alt.beer**. This is an area of the Internet where people exchange opinions on different brands of beer. The following message was posted in response to someone who asked if anyone had tried Red Baron beer:

> Red Baron is, of course, made by Brick Brewery in Waterloo, Ontario. It is available in bottles around South Western Ontario. I love it! I'm horrible at describing beer tasting, but I found it smooth and easy to drink but with a distinctively different taste than the mainstream Labbat Blue and Molson Canadian and EX, although I'll be damned if I could describe what that different taste is. Brick also makes an amber ale which I forget what it is called (never tried anyway), Premium Brick Lager, which I find is too bitter with a bad aftertaste, and they also brew a dark beer titled Waterloo Dark. It is only available on tap in the local area and I think it is the god of domestic dark beers, much better (and different) than Rickard's Red, Toby, Carling Dark. Upper Canada Dark Ale is almost as good though.

This message was followed up by another Internet user.

> Personally, I found Waterloo Dark to be extremely disappointing. It is just rather bland lager brewed somewhat darker; possibly it is what Labatt Copper is copying, albeit not as dark. Red Baron and Amber are targeted at the Labatt and Molson crowd wanting to take a small step toward better beer. I like the Premium Lager and their Henninger Kaiser Pils that they brew under licence.

In this case, we have potential customers trading messages about the merits of particular products, in a forum that anyone can see. The Internet represents a new era of customer feedback.

Consumers around the world use the Internet to exchange information that has a direct influence on their purchasing decisions. Internet users regularly ask other Internet users for advice and opinions on particular brands of products.

For example, the following message was posted in an Internet discussion forum called **rec.autos.makers.saturn**, where people exchange information about Saturn, the car manufacturer:

> I am currently looking at several types of cars (saturns among them) as my first. I am a student so I don't have a lot of money to blow on gas and repairs. Any opinions on Saturn would be appreciated.

Most of these discussion forums are "unofficial" in that they are not run by the companies that are under discussion. They are started by ordinary people on the Internet who want to share opinions and experiences with certain companies and their products. However, because forums like these are often full of valuable customer feedback, organizations like Saturn are well-advised to monitor them. In the Saturn discussion group at least one participant believes that Saturn *is* watching, and he sent out the following message:

> Here is my wish list for changes on the 1996 Saturns:
>
> 1. The rear window defroster can be turned off by pressing the button.
> 2. Keep the black rubber faced bumpers on the SL and SL1.
> 3. Bigger, better seats on the SL and SL1 in front.
> 4. Don't change the drivetrain.
> 5. Offer traction control with stick shift.
>
> I've bought a 1992 and 1995 and would like to go for a 1996. I won't unless at least some of the above gets done. The cheap garbage seats are a must for improvement or they've lost my family as customers.
>
> Thanks Saturn. I know you're reading even if you won't raise your hand.

Given the large number of users on the Internet, these discussion groups give the consumer a considerable degree of power. Every message posted to the discussion group is distributed to thousands around the world. People who have complaints with products will often voice their dissatisfaction on the Internet, where they can relieve their anger and seek advice from others who may have experienced the same problems. For example, the following message was posted in the Saturn cars discussion group (**rec.autos.makers.saturn**) by a Saturn owner:

> From the day that I drove my Saturn home, I have had front end vibration and an annoying pull to the right. There has been plenty of work done; none of it has resolved the situation, and I have learned to deal with it. However, recently (January) my rotors seemed to "warp" overnight. It has been in the shop, has been repaired, and is now doing this again. They tell me it is because I brake too hard. I have braked the same since day 1 and this only started this January. Feedback anyone??

When people feel slighted by a company or experience problems with a product, the Internet gives them the ability to make their complaint known to thousands around the world. With most major media outlets now monitoring the Internet, a single message can quickly turn into a public relations nightmare for an organization. Recall that Intel had to recall their defective Pentium chip in late 1994. The flaw that led to the recall was first exposed on the Internet. The incident quickly gained worldwide attention as word of the defect spread throughout the Internet. The Internet ensured that the issue could not be swept under the table.

The Internet should scare the heck out of any corporation, for it helps to tip the scale in favor of the consumer. Because of this wide-open, global communication, we are seeing the emergence of a new era of consumer activism. Organizations who ignore the Internet's discussion forums do so at their own peril.

Many organizations are surprised to discover that there are places on the Internet where people discuss the goods and services that they sell. Not all the comments in these forums are positive. For example, at the time of writing of this book, one of the authors observed a frank (and often brutal) discussion in a public area of USENET known as **can.general** (for the discussion of Canadian issues) about the relative pros and cons of Canada's two leading airlines. Some unflattering remarks with respect to the service levels of one of the airlines were made in this public forum by a number of people. These are clearly statements that could influence the attitudes of a great number of people.

Hence smart organizations now monitor some of these ongoing discussions throughout the Internet to obtain customer feedback and publicly respond to their critics. Determining which discussion areas to monitor is a challenging undertaking, considering the thousands of USENET newsgroups and mailing lists that exist. Yet, in other ways it can be simple. For example, if you are a manufacturer of running equipment, you definitely want to track what is said in the USENET newsgroup on running, **rec.sports.running**. If you are a fish aquarium wholesaler you might want to follow the **alt.aquaria** discussion group, where all aspects of aquarium keeping are discussed.

For many companies the Internet is a true gold mine of customer information. The **rec.sport.running** discussion group is an example of a "general" running discussion group. Discussion is not focused on any one product or service, but is about running in general. As a result, people might be talking about competitive products, issues in the running industry, upcoming events, or any other topics that might prove to be useful to a running shoe manufacturer. In addition to these general discussion forums, the Internet is full of product or company-specific discussion forums where consumers discuss the merits of particular organizations and their products. The Saturn discussion group referred to earlier is one example.

LEGO, the manufacturer of children's toys, woke up one day and realized that several thousand LEGO users throughout the world had carved out their own little community on the Internet. LEGO users and collectors from around the world share their thoughts on LEGO products within an Internet discussion group called **rec.toys.lego**. When informed of the LEGO discussions on the Internet, a representative from LEGO stated: "we were surprised and gratified to learn that an international network of LEGO product enthusiasts were communicating and exchanging ideas about our products. We hadn't realized that our products had entered 'cyberspace.' We have now had a chance to log onto the network and see the many creative ideas that have been shared among the participants."[3]

For LEGO the Internet discussion group is a valuable source of customer feedback, and even free advertising! Consider the following message which was posted on the Internet LEGO discussion group by one LEGO user:

> To all Legomaniacs near Vancouver BC:
>
> Eaton's Downtown (Pacific Centre) is having a big Lego display! It starts March 13th, and goes till the 26th. Sounds similar to the World Tour events Woodward's used to host. There are a couple of contests, and an area for building.
>
> Located on the 6th floor.
>
> See you there!

In a telephone call to one of the authors, Peter Arakas, a representative from LEGO headquarters in the United States, explained that the company doesn't have the resources to monitor the discussions on a regular basis. Mr. Arakas also pointed out that the people participating in the LEGO discussion group are young adults and older adults — not the typical LEGO customer. However, he did acknowledge that LEGO's advertising agency occasionally monitors LEGO activities on the Internet for trademark and copyright misuses, adding that the marketing department may give more consideration to the Internet "down the road."

---

[3] Source: **http//legowww.homepages.com/sets/lego-letter.html**

Contrast LEGO with the attitude taken by Snapple Beverage Corporation of East Meadow, New York. Snapple, of course, is known across North America for its line of natural fruit juice beverages and iced teas. In the summer of 1994, a Snapple discussion group (**alt.drinks.snapple**) was formed on the Internet by a loyal Snapple drinker to "discuss and share in the fun that Snapple is." The discussion group is used to discuss both the Snapple organization and its products. Here is one sample message from the discussion group, requesting that Snapple sell more flavors in the larger bottle sizes:

```
Subject: Snapple Big Bottles
Message-ID: <D3GA4B.1w1@rci.ripco.com>
Summary: Want more Snapple Big Bottles
Keywords: Snapple Big Bottles Want
Sender: usenet@rci.ripco.com (Net News Admin)
Organization: Ripco Internet BBS, Chicago
X-Newsreader: TIN [version 1.2 PL2]
Date: Sat, 4 Feb 1995 00:45:45 GMT
Lines: 12

I would like to see more flavors incorporated into the big-
ger bottles. Everyone has their favorite flavors, but maybe
Snapple's research department can find a few more fla-
vors that could be easily sold in the larger bottles.
```

Snapple's New York advertising agency, Kirshenbaum Bond and Partners, recognizes that the Internet provides a valuable form of customer feedback, so staff at the agency monitor the Internet discussions on a daily basis. They have also registered an Internet domain (**snapple.com**) on behalf of the company.

Steve Klein, the agency's Media Director and a partner in the firm, says the Snapple discussion group is "further evidence of the way our consumers talk to each other and talk to us about their love for the brand." Klein explained that the agency's research has revealed that Snapple is not the company's brand — "it's the consumer's brand." To see proof of this, look no further than Snapple's East Meadow headquarters, where over 1,000 pieces of "fan" mail arrive every week from Snapple drinkers around the world.

When asked why the company hasn't yet responded to any of the comments (both positive and negative) in the Snapple discussion group, Klein said his agency is being cautious with their approach to the Internet. "The whole marketing process for Snapple is organic," says Klein, explaining the brand has succeeded on customer word-of-mouth — what he calls "100% natural marketing" — without a lot of interference from the company.

There are many organizations like Snapple that have deemed it worthwhile to track public discussions on the Internet that mention their products or services. These discussions can be an excellent source of market intelligence. Put another way, if you're not watching what your customers are saying on the Internet, your competitors probably are.

Customer-Developed World Wide Web Sites

Because anyone can be a publisher on the Internet, many consumers have decided to build World Wide Web sites devoted to their favorite products and/or services. In our discussion of Snapple in the previous section, Steve Klein, the Media Director for Snapple's advertising agency, referred to the notion of "100% natural marketing." This is the process whereby a loyal customer, through word-of-mouth and other avenues, informally promotes a company's products. To see what Klein means by "100% natural marketing," one needs to look no further than some of the customer-developed World Wide Web sites on the Internet.

At Stanford University several loyal Snapple drinkers have created their own Snapple pages on the World Wide Web (**http://pcd.stanford.edu/~mogens/lickme.html**). Talk about customer feedback!

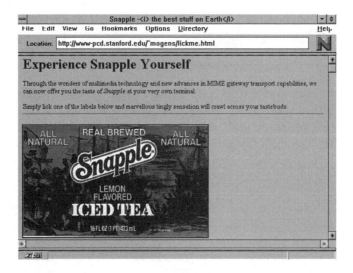

Examples like this abound on the Internet. Many of these sites are a marketer's dream come true, since the promotion is initiated by the customer. It's the ultimate opportunity for a company to reduce its advertising budget — let the customer create the ad.

LEGO, like Snapple, is fortunate to have many loyal customers on the Internet. An unofficial LEGO World Wide Web site (**http://legowww.homepages.com**) has been created by LEGO enthusiasts worldwide:

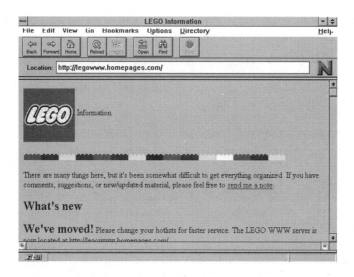

The site includes pictures of home-built LEGO constructions, information on the LEGO product line, a LEGO theme song, and some LEGO-related games and project ideas. *The site is maintained entirely by volunteers who have no affiliation with LEGO.*

Earlier in the chapter we showed you Saturn's "official" World Wide Web site. An "unofficial" Saturn World Wide Web site has been created by three enthusiastic Saturn car owners. The site provides Internet users with Saturn car reviews, general information about the company, a list of frequently asked questions about Saturn, and information on old and new Saturn models (**http://insti.physics.sunysb.edu/Saturn**).

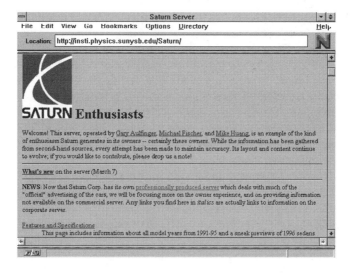

The following Web site (**http://bronze.ucs.indiana.edu/~jkonrath/coke/ coca-cola.html**), devoted to Coca-Cola, includes a list of frequently asked questions about Cola-Cola, a chronology of Coca-Cola ad campaigns dating back to 1886, audio files of some memorable Coke jingles, and links to other Coca-Cola sites on the World Wide Web. The creator has no affiliation with the company and is simply a loyal Coca-Cola fan.

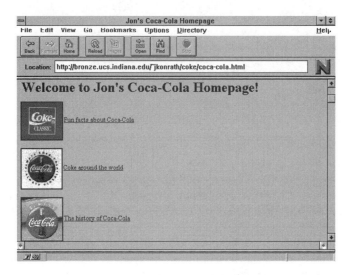

Organizations should be aware of customer-created World Wide Web sites where their products and/or services are being unofficially promoted. Organizations may want to consider acknowledging the customer's efforts or even provide funding or sponsorship to help keep the service going. It is advisable to monitor these sites for copyright and trademark infringements, since it is common for Internet users to reproduce logos and other organizational material without attributing copyright or ownership. On the other hand, organizations may wonder if they should risk causing public relations damage by worrying that a few people have posted their logo.

All the customer-created sites we have shown you in this section were created by satisfied customers. However, companies must also keep in mind that it is just as easy for anyone to establish a World Wide Web site that talks about the *negative* aspects of a particular product or organization. In the same way that the Internet can cause euphoria, it can cause a chill.

Unions, for example, have taken to the Internet in great numbers. The National Association of Broadcast Employees has set up a World Wide Web server under the domain **turnoffnbc.org**, which advocates the boycott of the NBC Television Network because of unfair negotiating practices (**http://www.turnoffnbc.org**).

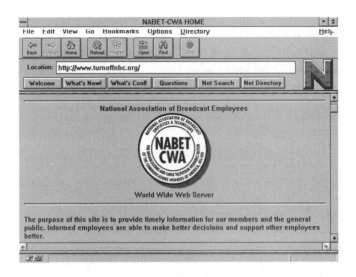

The site includes copies of the union's "mobilization newsletter," which describes the union's actions against NBC, an on-line pledge form that allows Internet users to send letters of protest to NBC's President, and a list of advertisers that support NBC. To build support for its position, the union even placed a copy of NBC's proposed contract on the World Wide Web site for the world to scrutinize.

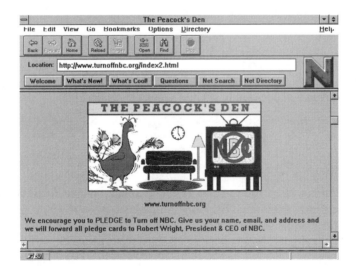

National consumer groups also use the Internet to turn consumers against organizations. A U.S. national consumer group called INFACT has launched an on-line offensive against Philip Morris and RJR-Nabisco, two manufacturers of cigarettes, in an effort to get the organizations to stop marketing tobacco to youth. INFACT has a World Wide Web site which encourages consumers to boycott products made by Philip Morris and RJR-Nabisco (**http://sunsite.unc.edu/boutell/infact/infact.html**).

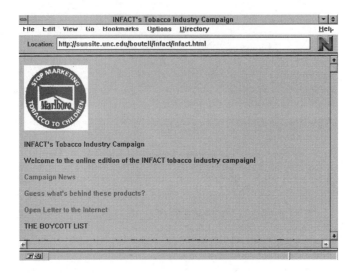

Monitoring Competitor Activities

Another important reason to be on the Internet is to monitor what your competitors are up to. This can be done in several ways:

➤ Monitoring your competitors' World Wide Web sites and public mailing lists will help you keep track of your competitors' activities, especially if they distribute press releases and other corporate information through those channels.

➤ If your company is planning on developing its own World Wide Web site, spending time examining your competitors' World Wide Web sites will help identify areas where you can improve on what they have done.

➤ Monitoring unofficial discussion forums where your competitors' products are being discussed will help you assess how consumers feel about your competitors' products. By following these discussions, you may be able to gather valuable information that will help you market your products better. For example, you might learn that one of your competitors has a poor customer service record. This knowledge could be helpful to you when you are developing an advertising campaign for your organization.

If your competitors participate in Internet discussion groups, *how* they respond to questions and comments can provide you with insight into their future plans or their attitudes on certain issues.

Market Research

Many organizations view the Internet, and the World Wide Web in particular, as an excellent vehicle for market research. As people pass through an Internet site, why not ask them a few voluntary questions? These questions can be about your organization, its products, or even about your World Wide Web site. The Sega video game company (**http://www.segaoa.com**) has put a questionnaire on their World Wide Web site entitled "Tell Us Who You Are." The questionnaire asks Internet users to list their favorite Sega products, their three favorite video games, and their favorite types of games.

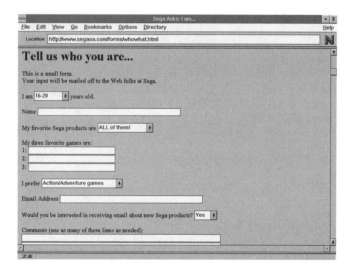

Sony Music has established a *Dear Sony Music* page on its World Wide Web site (**http://www.sony.com**), which asks users a number of questions such as: "What is your favorite type of music?" "How often do you use the Internet?" and "What is your age?" Users can also make general comments and direct them to any one of eight Sony divisions. The intent of the survey is to generate feedback on Sony's Internet services and help Sony determine what type of people visit their World Wide Web site.

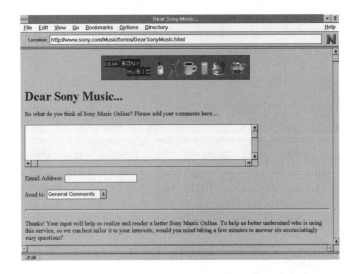

Volvo's Internet site (**http://www.volvocars.com**) features an elaborate questionnaire that visitors can fill out, including questions such as: "What is the make and model of the car you currently drive?" "When do you expect to buy a new car?" and "What is your occupation?" Users can also make general comments about Volvo and its Internet presence. Volvo, like Sony, is trying to determine the demographics of the people visiting their World Wide Web site. This information will help Volvo tailor its Internet services to the needs of the typical visitor.

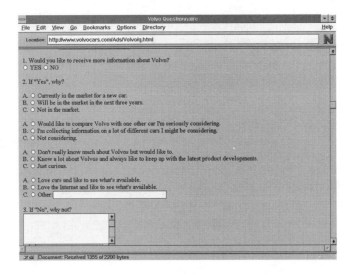

Corporate Activities

The Internet isn't just about marketing, sales, and customer support opportunities. There are a number of areas where the Internet can provide efficiencies in corporate communications and can help achieve certain corporate goals. At the corporate level the Internet has seven principal benefits:

➤ gathering corporate intelligence;

➤ enhancing corporate communications;

➤ improving public relations;

➤ providing new avenues for recruitment activities;

➤ developing electronic publishing and new information services;

➤ achieving cost savings and efficiencies;

➤ reducing distribution costs.

Each of these strategies will be discussed separately.

Corporate Intelligence

The Internet has quickly become the world's largest electronic repository of knowledge, and many organizations are learning to use it to gather intelligence and other information necessary to their operations. Research sources on the Internet include thousands of organizational and government World Wide Web sites as well as the thousands of discussion groups covering almost every topic under the sun.

Henry Demone, President of Nova Scotia-based National Sea Products, one of Canada's largest fish processing firms, uses the Internet as a means of gathering information. He says that the Internet removes most of the disadvantages of being headquartered in Lunenburg, Nova Scotia, while still permitting him to enjoy the advantages of his location. He uses the Internet in several ways, including the following activities:

➤ accessing the Securities and Exchange Commission EDGAR database for tracking customers and competitors. (The EDGAR database includes the full financial statements of any company publicly traded on an exchange in the United States);

➤ accessing a stock quote server to track stock prices of customers, competitors, and other companies;

➤ accessing the U.S. Department of Commerce Import/Export service for statistics on seafood products;

➤ gathering information from OMRI-L, an Internet mailing list that produces a daily report on events in Russia and eastern Europe;

➤ following developments in the field of aquaculture by participating in several aquaculture discussion groups on the Internet;

➤ accessing the United States National Marine Fisheries Service World Wide Web site for industry news and statistics.

Mr. Demone believes that he gets information through the Internet that is not easily accessible through other channels of communication. To illustrate the Internet's resourcefulness, he says that he sometimes hears about events in Russia before the Russians do. "We sometimes inform suppliers of events before they hear it locally. The information comes out of Russia (an important supplier of product), is picked up by us, and is communicated back to the Russians by phone or fax before they hear it!"

Corporate Communications

Organizations need to communicate information not only to potential customers, but also to the public at large, potential investors, government bodies, suppliers, community organizations, and numerous other stakeholders. The Internet makes it possible for organizations to make their information available for immediate worldwide consumption. For example, Northern Telecom includes a "press release" area within its Internet site (**http://www.nortel.com**) that includes an archive of recent press releases.

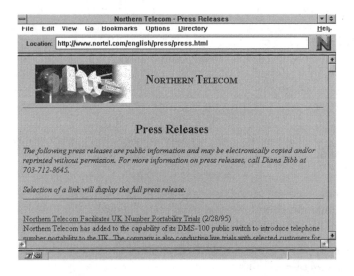

The public accounting firm Ernst and Young has also placed its press releases on its Internet site (**http://tax.ey.ca/ey**) as well as many of its tax publications that it has prepared for public distribution.

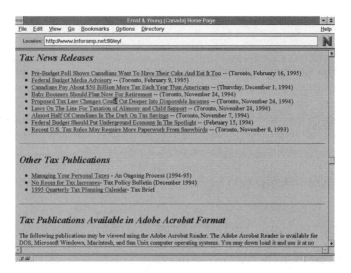

In addition, Ernst and Young made its analysis of the 1995 federal budget available through the Internet. Other Canadian organizations, including KPMG and the Toronto Dominion Bank, also made their federal budget commentaries available on their Internet sites. KPMG distributes its provincial budget commentaries via the Internet as well (**http://www.kpmg.ca**).

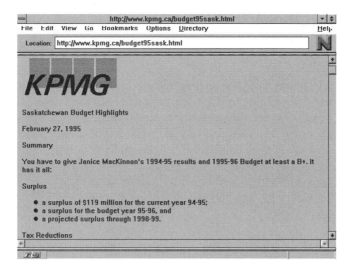

In many ways the Internet is becoming the standard for business communication. It is now the preferred method for businesses to make information available to business partners, the media, and the general public. Given the momentum that the Internet is gaining in the corporate sector, we can only expect to see more of this type of information on the Internet.

Public Relations

Public relations departments now view the Internet as a vehicle by which they can answer questions from the public. General Electric, for example, has established an Internet Business Information Centre that will handle virtually any question you have about General Electric's products and services. As can be seen on the following screen, any question that you e-mail to GE's Business Information Center (**geinfo@www.ge.com**) will be processed by a business information centre representative, who will direct your question or comment to the appropriate group within the company (**http://www.ge.com**).

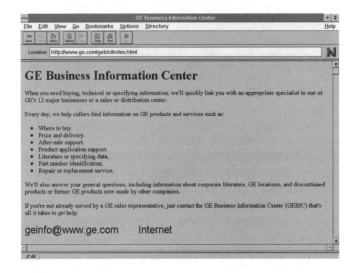

Northern Telecom also uses the Internet to accept public inquiries. Northern Telecom's World Wide Web site (**http://www.nortel.com**) contains a form that users can fill out if they have comments or questions about Northern Telecom's products and services, or if they want to be contacted by a Northern Telecom customer service representative. Users have the option of selecting whether they want their query answered by telephone, fax, e-mail, or postal mail. (To test the reliability of this service, one of the authors filled out the form and requested a return phone call. A customer service representative called back the following morning. Now that's public relations!)

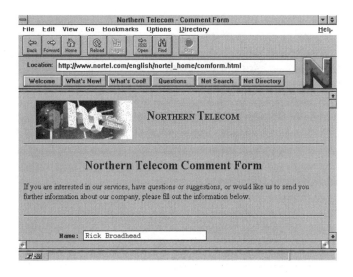

Recruitment

Recruitment is another area where there is increased corporate activity on the Internet. Businesses can advertise job openings and career opportunities in places where such postings are appropriate, such as specialized discussion groups and job-related forums. For example, the USENET newsgroup **can.jobs** is used by recruiters and corporate organizations in Canada to find job candidates. While a high proportion of the job postings at this time are for computer and high-tech companies, this is slowly changing, as the Internet's user base becomes more mainstream. For example, Kellogg recently posted a job advertisement in **can.jobs**:

Newsgroups: can.jobs
Subject: Business Analyst, Kellogg, Toronto
Date: 3 Feb 1995 22:53:52 GMT
Organization: Kellogg Canada Inc. - Etobicoke, Ontario
Lines: 24
Message-ID: <3guc60$4su$1@mhadf.production.
compuserve.com>
X-status: R

BUSINESS ANALYST

Located at Kellogg Canada corporate head office in Toronto, Ont.

Kellogg Canada is the leader in the ready-to-eat breakfast cereal market and committed to being the best food company. Our Business Analysts collaborate with the

Marketing/Sales departments to design and develop "business solutions."

To join our Information Services department, you must have a university degree in business or computer science, experience as a Systems Analyst, and proficiency with relational databases and CASE tools, preferably Oracle. Exceptionally strong communication and interpersonal skills are critical, as are high energy, a results-oriented attitude, and the ability to travel extensively to the U.S.

We offer opportunity for advancement, a competitive salary, and a comprehensive benefits package. If you are qualified and interested, please send your resume (ASCII only) to brian.skupin@kellogg.com.

Resumes may also be faxed to (416) 675-5222, or mailed to Administrator Human Resources, Kellogg Canada Inc., 6700 Finch Ave., W., Etobicoke, Ontario, M9W 5P2.

Many companies choose to advertise job openings directly through the Internet to reduce the costs of advertising in the press. Because the Internet comprises thousands of subject-specific discussion groups, it is also an effective way of targeting job advertisements at groups of people with specific skills and backgrounds.

In addition to posting job advertisements in discussion groups, companies can build their own World Wide Web sites to promote employment opportunities within their organizations. For example, Andersen Consulting, one of the world's largest consulting firms, has a World Wide Web site that describes career opportunities within the firm (**http://www.ac.com**):

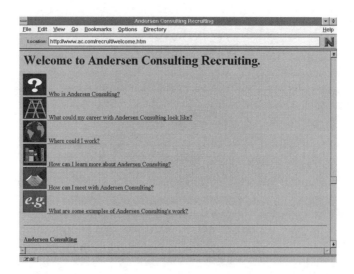

There are also several commercial career-oriented sites emerging throughout the Internet that support corporate recruitment activities. One of the most notable is CareerMosaic, a site dedicated to the provision of career-related information on the Internet (**http://www.careermosaic.com**):

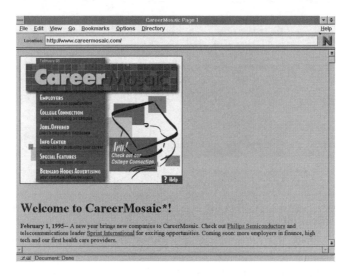

CareerMosaic is intended to be a clearinghouse for the recruitment activities of many organizations and seeks to encourage job seekers to use the site's resources, which include career-related documents and articles. It has gained the attention of a number of companies operating in the high-tech sector and hence is already influencing the recruiting activities of several organizations.

Electronic Publishing and New Information Services

As the standard for electronic publishing, many businesses have chosen the Internet as the platform of choice for their electronic publishing initiatives. For example, Time Warner has established a World Wide Web site (**http://www.pathfinder.com**) that includes electronic versions of several of its publications, including *Time Magazine*, *People Magazine*, and *Entertainment Weekly*. Time Warner's Internet service, called PathFinder, includes features from the print version of its magazine as well as new content available only on the Internet.

Efforts such as electronic publishing on the Internet are clearly preliminary and experimental, as Time Warner acknowledges. As of March 1995 the PathFinder service was free, although Time is considering how to include advertisements to fund the service and how to charge for access. As Time Warner indicated, "we're constantly analyzing response to the service. We want to see how it evolves and how the Internet evolves before we make any additional decisions in that area."[4]

Newspapers are also experimenting with electronic publishing on the Internet. *The Kamloops Daily News* in Kamloops, British Columbia (**http://www.netshop.bc.ca/dailynews/daily_news.html**), and the *Halifax Daily News* in Halifax, Nova Scotia (**http://www.cfn.cs.dal.ca/GreenPages/DailyNews.html**), both publish information on the Internet. While both newspapers make their information freely available as a community service, they hope that their on-line presence will generate increased interest in their newspapers and hence lead to more advertising commitments.

---

[4] *Internet Business Report*, February 1995.

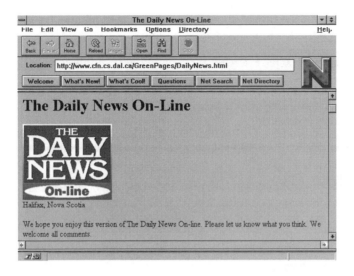

There is no question that the Internet can support electronic publishing. What remains to be seen is whether the customer will pay to access electronic versions of popular magazines such as *Time* and *People* and whether organizations will advertise in on-line magazines and newspapers.

Cost Savings and Efficiencies

Of all the Internet tools, e-mail is perhaps the most valuable to organizations, since it provides efficient and cost-effective communication between an organization and its business partners. As we explained in Chapter 3, Internet e-mail is emerging as the standard for company-to-company communication because of seven key factors:

➤ its reach;

➤ its simple method of addressing;

➤ its ability to incorporate documents created in other applications;

➤ its direct delivery;

➤ its cost savings and lack of long distance charges;

➤ its efficiency;

➤ its convenience.

Internet e-mail offers significant savings and efficiencies over fax, courier, postage, and long distance telephone costs. Consider the following:

➤ Usage of the Internet is often billed at an hourly rate with no additional surcharges for message length or destination. With rates as low as $0.50 to $1.00 an hour in many areas of Canada, and since messages can be sent at the rate of about five messages per minute, the cost to get a message to Moscow is less than a penny.

➤ Internet e-mail messages can be sent to many people simultaneously. Send a message to ten people in Moscow, and for good measure send "carbon copies" to five business associates in the United Kingdom, and your cost is still *less than a penny*.

➤ If you create an Internet mailing list, and if 2,000 customers join your list, you could send all 2,000 customers a two-page announcement for less than a penny.

Because Internet e-mail messages are not tariffed on size or destination, using Internet e-mail for intercompany communication provides substantial cost savings.

Distribution Costs

Not only can companies save on communication costs, they can save on distribution costs as well. For example, the Toronto Dominion Bank distributes its Business Planner Software for Windows through its World Wide Web site (**http://www. td-bank.ca/tdbank**). Since users can retrieve the software on-line, TD Bank does not incur the cost of packaging and mailing a diskette, thus saving over $1.00 in distribution costs *each* time a customer retrieves the software on the Internet.

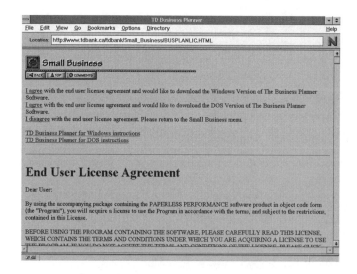

Kodak is another example. Kodak has established a World Wide Web site that provides, among other features, detailed specification sheets for its line of imaging products (**http://www.kodak.com**):

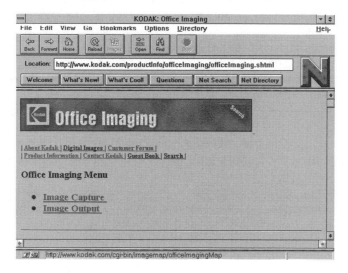

Because the specification sheets are available on the Internet (including color pictures of the products), Kodak incurs virtually no distribution cost if the organization requesting them is connected to the Internet. Because the documents are stored electronically, any changes to the specifications or other information can be made quite effortlessly.

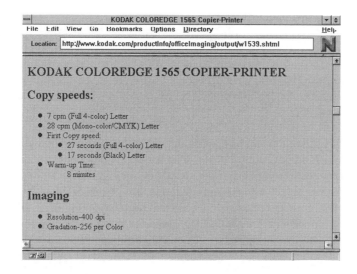

Isn't it all Hype?

As we noted at the beginning of this chapter, the Internet will significantly change the way business is conducted, but it will also take some time for this to occur. Unfortunately, many in the business community expect the change to occur dramatically, overnight. Many believed that the Internet would open vast new sales opportunities immediately, but for most this did not happen.

In an interview in the February 1995 issue of *Wired* magazine, Barry Diller, the chairman of the U.S.-based media giant QVC, observed that society's expectations of technology are too high. He observed that "there used to be a cadence, a rhythm to things. It would take time not only for an event to get known, but for it to play out — for the consequences and the analysis and the understanding to incubate. Today it takes no time at all. The most relevant example of the rush to judgment involves those dreaded words 'the information superhighway': the 500-channel universe. Surfing the Internet. The dawn of a new era. Two trillion words juiced up to define, describe, trump up all the developments, the possibilities. And then the inevitable thud. Since it wasn't going to take place in an hour and a half, the new conventional wisdom is that it's overhyped, it's not really that exciting, it's off-track, delayed, not meeting expectations. Our impatience creates an impulse to spin a subject to unsustainable heights and then let it fall."

It is true that peoples' expectations of new technology are often too high. With the incredible hype that first surrounded the Internet in early 1994, expectations for a "fast buck" from the network were common among businesspeople. For example, in a quote reported widely throughout the business press, Patricia Seybold, a respected U.S. consultant, stated: "If you're not an active Internet citizen by the mid-1990s, you're likely to be out of business by the year 2000." Unrealistic expectations result from statements such as these. When the Internet didn't revolutionize business practices as expected, the business press began to report on the "failure of the Internet."

In a January 30, 1995 article in *Forbes* entitled Where's the Money, a writer stated: "Of course, any business that ignores cyberspace ignores the future, but the smart ones aren't yet putting big bets on it. As a way to move merchandise, it has not proven itself and probably won't for a long time." Later, quoting a media analyst, it was observed that "no one needs this stuff yet. Billions of dollars will be lost in this market."

The Internet has not proven itself as a way to sell a lot of merchandise. The Internet hasn't yet had a tremendous impact on the bottom line of any organization. The quote from *Forbes* is right — many of the Internet's benefits are overhyped. Many have expectations of the Internet that cannot possibly be met in the short term. Many early Internet experiments will fail, and efforts to learn how to use it to make money will continue. Some ventures will be successful. Many will fail.

Yet, we cannot deny that something powerful is happening on the Internet. An entire global culture is emerging where people are learning to work with and use electronic information. Customers are emerging on the Internet, and disintermediation is a trend that is gaining momentum, particularly as the network continues to grow. Customers and suppliers will learn how to do business electronically, and significant opportunities will emerge on the Internet. *It's all a matter of time.* Many of the Internet's opportunities will not materialize fully in the next hour and a half, in the next day, week, month, or even in the next year. As *Forbes* indicated in its January 1995 article, "Humans have a stubborn habit of not doing things when the technologists say they ought to. The real revenue shows up a decade or two later." But the Internet *will* dramatically transform business in such a forceful way that ten years from now we will look back and marvel at the change that has occurred.

Any businesspeople thinking about the Internet as a business strategy must keep their wits and common sense about them. Don't get lost in the hype, but at the same time, don't lose sight of the opportunity.

Government on the Internet

*I*n 1992 a book was released that immediately rocketed to the top of many international bestseller lists, including those throughout Canada. *Reinventing Government, How the entrepreneurial spirit is transforming the public sector*, by David Osborne and Ted Gaebler, captured the imagination of politicians, bureaucrats, and the corporate sector worldwide.

Reinventing Government encouraged a line of thinking that governments must become more *effective, efficient* and *responsive* in the delivery of services to their "customers"—the constituents, or citizens. The book discussed how government could "re-engineer," or "change itself," to accomplish this.

The biggest fans of the trend that ensued to "reinvent government" have been U.S. President Bill Clinton and Vice-President Al Gore, who implemented the National Performance Review (NPR), a program designed to streamline the delivery of government services within the United States. Al Gore remains a huge fan of the role of the Internet in government, so some of the activities for the NPR were built around the use of the Internet.

STRATEGIC USES OF THE INTERNET WITHIN GOVERNMENT

(1) Improved Service Delivery
- reduces distribution costs
- easier access to government information
- links government databases to the Internet
- facilitates the marketing of government programs and services
- improves procurement practices
- builds partnerships between government and business
- improves intergovernmental coordination

(2) Consensus Building
- cultivates interest and support for government activities
- justifies government activities, mandates, roles, and functions
- opens the lines of communication with the general public

(3) Policy Shaping
- encourages investment
- encourages tourism
- encourages immigration
- promotes business linkages with foreign firms
- encourages infrastructure development

In these days of government cutbacks, anger within the populace at governments that appear to be unresponsive to citizen demands, and growing public cynicism with politics, the concept of "reinventing government" offered a way for
government organizations to reshape the way they deliver services to more adequately meet the needs of their constituents. New approaches to dealing with the spi-
raling cost of government services must also be found. The reinvention of
government services offers that opportunity.

In its own small way the Internet presents an opportunity for the government
to reinvent some of its activities, particularly those in which it communicates with
members of the public. However, the Internet is not a solution to all of the government's problems. "Reinventing government" is a mammoth, and to many people,
somewhat impossible task. Yet, the technology emerging on the Internet, particularly through the World Wide Web, offers new opportunities for the delivery of
government services to the public, whether from large federal or provincial government departments or small municipal governments.

In this chapter we'll take a look at the ways in which a variety of government departments are using the Internet for a variety of strategic purposes.

Why the Internet?

By making it easier to access government information, the Internet can help ease some of the frustrations Canadians have when it comes to dealing with bureaucracy. As more and more Canadians plug into the network, the Internet will offer unparalleled opportunities for the reshaping of government services.

We are already seeing some tentative efforts across the country in this regard. Many federal departments, from Health Canada to the Department of Finance to Natural Resources Canada, are experimenting with the Internet as a service delivery tool. The federal government currently supports an Internet initiative called the "Open Government Pilot," which is meant to provide a "one-stop shopping method" of accessing federal government information on the Internet.

The government of British Columbia has taken it one step further with legislation that makes it mandatory for certain records of the legislature, including committee reports, parliamentary proceedings and other information, to be made available to all citizens through the Internet.

It is not just federal and provincial governments that are getting in on the act. The Town of Slave Lake in Alberta uses the Internet's World Wide Web to make available a variety of information about the city, including tourism information and town statistics.

Certainly, the Internet is gaining momentum in government departments across the country, and like everything else on the Internet, the number of government "sites" is growing by leaps and bounds. Not a week goes by where some new Internet initiative isn't announced by some government somewhere in Canada. Yet, we are at a very early stage using the Internet as a means of communication between government and the governed. We must stress that the Internet is not a panacea. It is a communications tool that helps with some government activities but will be useless with other activities. Nonetheless, the Internet will be at the core of many of the government information network developments of the future.

Anyone responsible for strategic planning in any government body, no matter how large or small, must have an understanding of how the Internet can be used in the delivery of government services, to shape public policy, and to advance certain strategic government objectives.

What Does the Internet Offer Government?

The Internet offers several key opportunities to the Canadian government:

➤ it can help to improve and to provide efficiencies in the delivery of government services to the general public;

> it can open new channels of communication with the general public;

> it can provide a communication medium for coordinating government initiatives across various departments;

> it can improve interdepartmental and interministry communication;

> it can help a government with the sometimes tricky and difficult process of establishing a consensus towards new legislative initiatives and plans;

> it can provide new ways of monitoring public opinion on the issues of the day;

> it can improve access to local, provincial, federal, and foreign government databases of interest to Canadian government researchers, scientists, policy professionals, and economists.

Improved Service Delivery

If the objective of "reinventing government" is to provide for more effective, efficient, and responsive government, then the Internet offers a number of opportunities by which this can occur. These include

> reduced distribution costs;

> easier access to government information;

> government databases linked to the Internet;

> marketing of government programs and services;

> improved procurement practices;

> partnerships between government and business;

> improved intergovernmental coordination.

Each of these benefits will be addressed separately.

Reduced Distribution Costs

In many ways governments are in the business of delivering information: research reports, statistical summaries, books, documents—all kinds of information is produced by the government on a regular basis for distribution to the public.

There are costs associated with making such information available in paper form—the costs of production and distribution. In recognition of the opportunity that computer technology presents as an information distribution tool, some government departments have in the past established methods of permitting the "customer" to access this information electronically. Most often, these electronic access methods were built on closed, proprietary systems such as "bulletin boards," meaning that the attempts were never quite successful in reaching a large segment of the population or were overly expensive in their implementation and complicated to use.

Yet, through the Internet we are seeing the emergence of the first standard "information access tool." The fact that the Internet has become a standard means of accessing information is a trend that the government cannot afford to ignore, and, indeed, government departments at all levels are now getting involved in the Internet. Many Canadian government departments are actively publishing information on the Internet, and in the following pages you will see examples of some of these initiatives.

It is estimated that there are from one half to one million Canadians with access to the Internet in some way, either at work or at home. This includes individuals who have only an electronic mail link to the Internet as well as those who have an account that lets them use the most popular Internet application, the World Wide Web.

While the majority of Canadians are not on the Internet, the number of Canadian Internet users is growing steadily, and many government departments have begun to supplement their paper publishing with electronic publishing on the Internet. Over time, this electronic method of information distribution, while it will not reach all Canadians, will reach a sufficient number such that printing and distribution costs will decrease.

Consider this example: the Supreme Court of Canada is involved in a project with the University of Montreal, where all Supreme Court rulings from 1993 are available on the Internet for public viewing (**http://www.droit.umontreal.ca/ CSC.html**). Internet users can search the rulings database by word or phrase. Electronic distribution of Supreme Court rulings not only improves access to the information, but reduces the need for the Supreme Court to distribute its rulings in paper form to the legal community at large.

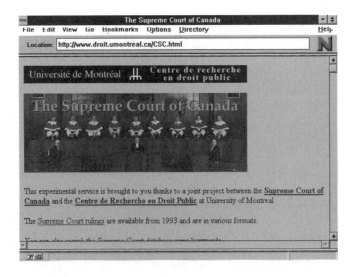

Easier Access to Government Information

The popular press is rampant with stories of people frustrated by government bureaucracy. Horror stories are told of individuals calling one department, only to be told to call another, only to be told "that's not our responsibility," only to find themselves caught in a vicious circle. The problem has become worse with the arrival of voice mail. Frankly, rightly or wrongly, government in general has an image problem when it comes to good "customer service," and we all imagine tired, surly government clerks, ready to snap at us as soon as we say hello.

There is much talk of the need for government to focus on providing better service to the public. One of the government's key objectives in this regard should be to make it *easier and more convenient* for the public to access government information. This is easily done through the Internet.

A good example can be found within the Department of Finance (**http://www.fin.gc.ca**), which is making federal budget information available on the Internet as well as electronic copies of some of their publications.

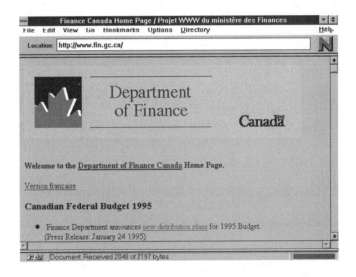

Related to the information access problem is the difficulty of trying to locate someone within a government department. Many people express frustration when trying to determine which department they should call for a particular issue. With more and more Canadian government departments establishing information sites on the Internet, this process is becoming easier as government departments place their staff telephone directories on their Internet sites. Some government departments, such as the Atlantic Region of Environment Canada, have taken the on-line telephone directory concept one step further. Instead of simply providing an alphabetical list of employees, Environment Canada's Atlantic Region (**http://atlenv.bed.ns.doe.ca**) has assembled a phone contact list of their key experts, organized by topic, and placed it on the Internet, to make it easier for Internet users to locate staff with specific areas of expertise.

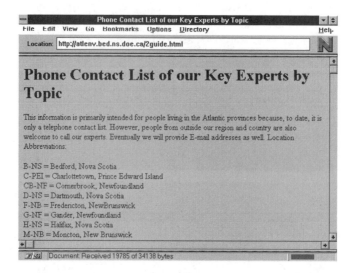

The Government of New Brunswick (**http://www.gov.nb.ca**) has also gone beyond the provision of a simple telephone directory. They have placed a *searchable* government-wide telephone book on their Internet site from which you can perform a search for the e-mail address and phone number of a particular government employee.

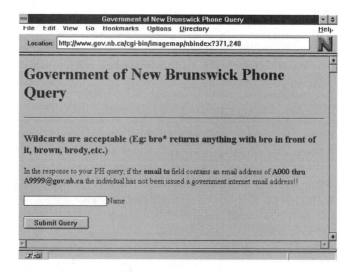

Perhaps the most significant development in improving access to government information, however, might be in the concept of using the Internet to provide "one-stop shopping" for government information. The Province of New Brunswick's World Wide Web site (**http://www.gov.nb.ca**), depicted in the screen below, is an excellent example of the "one-stop shopping" concept. The Government of New Brunswick's Internet site provides a convenient "entry point" for all New Brunswick government information on the Internet. From the main screen Internet users can choose from a menu of provincial government departments.

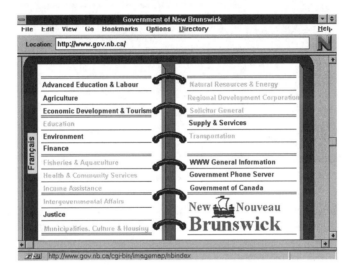

By building this type of Internet "roadmap" to provincial government services, the province of New Brunswick is making it easier and more convenient for the general public to access government information.

The Atlantic Canada Opportunities Agency (**http://www.acoa.ca**) provides an impressive example of how an organization can harness the Internet's power and improve the delivery of government information. The ACOA has established a "mail-back" server on their Internet site that allows Internet users to select ACOA documents that they want to receive. Seconds later, the documents are delivered over the Internet to the user's electronic mailbox. Since the mail-back server operates 24 hours a day, seven days a week, Internet users can request and receive ACOA documents at any time of the day or night.

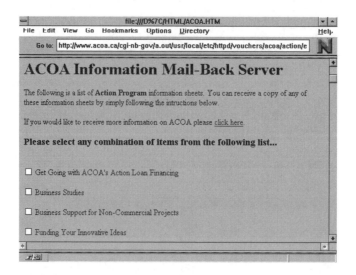

Internal Databases Linked to Internet

One of the most useful trends now emerging on the Internet is the linking of internal government databases into the World Wide Web. This means that the general public can search selected government databases on the Internet through a simple, easy-to-use interface, providing yet another method by which the public can access government information.

This trend ties into the fact that many government departments have been in the information business for a long time. They have built large, sophisticated databases for internal use and in many cases have made these databases available to the public through a proprietary method. The Internet now presents these government departments with the opportunity to link their established internal databases into the Internet. By doing so, they dramatically extend the reach and accessibility of their databases, as these databases suddenly become available to millions of Internet users around the world.

A good example of the integration of government databases with the Internet is found at Natural Resources Canada, where a database known as the Canadian Geographical Names Database (**http://www-nais.ccm.emr.ca/cgndb/geonames.html**) has been linked to the Internet. Used by cartographers, researchers, genealogists, academics, and those with an interest in the names of cities, towns and other locations across Canada, the database has existed for many years, but was unknown to most Canadians. Yet, when it was linked to the Internet, its reach and use were dramatically expanded. The database is searchable by key-word, contains some 500,000 entries, and is updated daily.

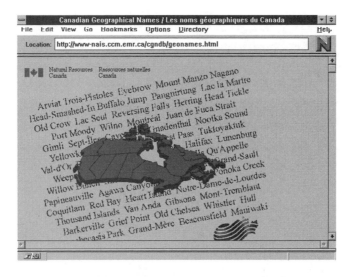

Marketing of Government Products and Services

Many government departments are in the business of selling products and services. In the same way that the Internet provides new marketing opportunities to business, it also provides new marketing opportunities to government. For example, the Geological Survey of Canada has established a site (**http://www.emr.ca:80/gsc**) where it provides details on products offered for sale:

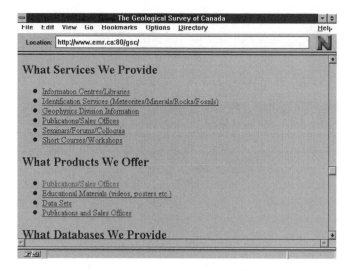

As the trend to "user-pay" services grows throughout government, and as "on-line commerce" tools continue to mature, there will be an opportunity for more government departments to "market" products and services through the Internet.

The Department of Finance (**http://www.fin.gc.ca**) sold documents related to the 1995 Federal Budget over the Internet for the first time in February 1995. The complete budget document was distributed over the Department's World Wide Web server to prepaid Internet users. The Department of Finance accepted orders over the telephone in advance of the budget's release, and passwords were issued to purchasers. Only Internet users with passwords could access the full budget document, although the full text of the Finance Minister's budget speech and other budget documents were available for free. This demonstrates how the development of on-line commercial tools within the Internet can help recoup some of the costs of government operation.[1]

---

[1] This policy of charging for the budget documents, which have previously been free, has sparked debate among many over whether or not government information should be free.

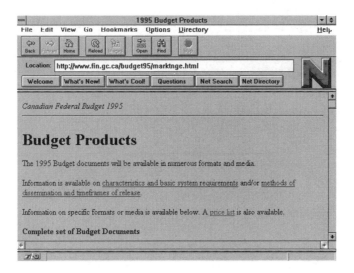

Improved Procurement Practices

Procurement refers to the solicitation of bids for government contracts. Governments are under increasing pressure to support improved procurement practices. Quite often, this begins as a policy initiative, such as a political decision by the federal government to open more federal government contracts to small business.

The Internet offers an opportunity to help open up and streamline government procurement practices by providing free and open access to information to all potential suppliers, and by providing assistance to business seeking to do business with the government.

Although this step is not yet big in Canada, we are seeing increasing use of the Internet for this purpose by the United States Government.

For example, NASA's Marshall Space Flight Center has a procurement site on the Internet (**http://procure.msfc.nasa.gov**) that offers a sophisticated procurement database with a trial underway in which companies can actually bid for government business on the Internet.

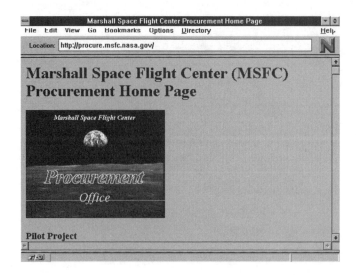

Notes the Marshall site: "we are taking steps toward implementing Electronic Commerce (EC) in the acquisition arena. This Internet on-line system is the first step! The purpose of the on-line system is to provide easy access to MSFC procurement information," including

> access to a series of "Small Business Program Coordinators," who can "assist small businesses to market their technical capabilities as well as learn about potential procurement requirements,"

> access to a list of "Major Prime Contractors which provides information to firms interested in marketing their capabilities to major prime contractors, and can be most beneficial when seeking subcontracting opportunities,"

> an "Acquisition Forecast," which "consolidates anticipated procurements at each of NASA's centers into an agency-wide report, with the aim of increasing industries' advance knowledge of NASA requirements."

The NASA procurement site on the Internet also permits electronic viewing of presolicitation notices, solicitations, solicitation amendments, and notifications of award.

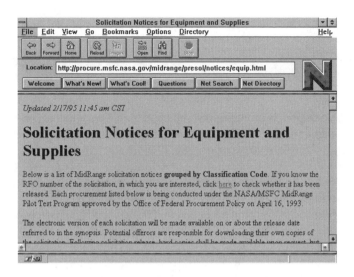

In addition to making the bidding process more equitable, the Internet is a more efficient and cost-effective way of managing the procurement process, as NASA has observed:

> One of the most frequently asked procurement questions is: "Why do procurements for $25,001 take as long as those for $10,000,000?" In answering this question, it was found that current regulations and procedures require procurements ranging from $25,001 to $500,000 to be processed in the same manner as multi-million dollar procurements. At NASA, approximately 80% of all contract actions fall in the range of $25,001 to $500,000, while accounting for approximately 11% of the contract dollars. Since procurements in this dollar range have been taking as long as the multi-million dollar procurements, the agency determined that a new procedure was needed to reduce the time, effort, and paperwork involved in processing procurements falling in the "middle range."
>
> Marshall Space Flight Center Procurement Home Page,
> **http://procure.msfc.nasa.gov**

We have seen a number of attempts to open up procurement through electronic means in Canada, but so far, these have been done through small bulletin board systems that are not easily accessible by all Canadians, meaning they have not become universally used throughout the Canadian business community. However, it is inevitable that Canadian governments will get involved in establishing Internet-based electronic procurement practices, given the strategic opportunities that this technology presents.

Partnerships Between Government and Business

One issue that has been examined in depth within the framework of "re-inventing government" is the desire to increase the focus on public/private partnerships. Since the Internet is an effective communications tool, it can succeed as a binding technology to help coordinate government and business activities.

Consider the Manitoba Economic and Innovation Technology Council. The EITC consists of up to 35 members representing business, labor, education and research communities, and other interest groups. The Council directly advises and reports to the Economic Development Board of Cabinet, which is chaired by Manitoba's premier.

The mission of the Council is "to promote and enhance a climate of entrepreneurship, innovation and technological development that spurs responsible economic growth for the benefit of all Manitobans." The organization does what it can to share success stories in the province and encourages an environment of ongoing government/private sector cooperation.

The Council has established a site on the Internet (**http://www.eitc.mb.ca/eitc.html**) that is used to summarize provincial success stories, high-tech strategies, and other information to help foster innovation and technical development in the province. One of the publications the Council has made available to Internet users is the State of Innovation Report for Manitoba, illustrated below.

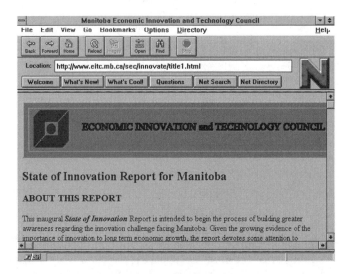

A few provinces to the east, the Atlantic Canada Opportunities Agency uses the Internet to implement its mandate, which includes promoting Atlantic Canada nationally and internationally and helping organizations in Atlantic Canada to prosper.

Like the Economic and Innovation Technology Council, the ACOA (**http://www. acoa.ca**) uses the Internet to publish information concerning regional success stories, such as that of ACOA beneficiary Sunnyland Juice, a fruit juice company based in St. John's, Newfoundland, which saw a recent quadrupling of its workforce.

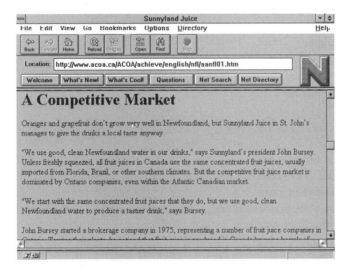

Through the Internet the ACOA hopes to raise awareness of its services and programs. The ACOA's Internet site contains information on a wide range of funding opportunities for small businesses, as well as a description of ACOA services that help small businesses sell to government.

The impact of the 1995 federal budget, which saw the start of a major shift in the role of government in Canada, had a direct impact on ACOA. The organization will now be involved less in direct funding of corporate initiatives and more in the preparation and distribution of information to the business community—the fundamental role that the Internet can play in the delivery of government services. The result is that as the federal budget begins to "reinvent government" in Canada, and as the country begins to adapt to new fiscal realities, the Internet will play a major role in the delivery of government services.

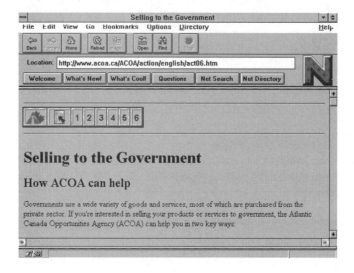

Improved Intergovernmental Coordination

Finally, there is an increasing need to coordinate activities between all levels of government in Canada. The Internet is a tool that can reduce government redundancy. With at least three levels of government (federal, provincial, and municipal) in the country and in some cases more, there is a need to share ideas, experiences, and success stories and to improve coordination across all levels of government. As a common, computer-based communication tool, the Internet represents an unparalleled opportunity for *electronic collaboration* between government departments and levels of government in the rationalization of the delivery of services.

Discussion groups, primarily through electronic mailing lists, can be used to permit people to rapidly convene a forum on-line in order to discuss a particular topic or issue. The World Wide Web can be used to establish information sites concerning particular collaborative activities or projects, and e-mail can be used to link intergovernmental committee members.

Unfortunately, in Canada we have not seen these types of initiatives pursued to any great degree. We should pressure government to adopt the Internet as a tool for open collaboration. Consider FinanceNet (**http://www.financenet.gov**) in the United States.

Through FinanceNet, the U.S. Department of Finance brings together financial officers from all over the U.S. government to participate in discussions on numerous financial topics. This is part of an overall objective of redefining the delivery of government services. As can be seen below, the initiative has the support of Vice-President Al Gore.

****
PRESS RELEASE
FINANCENET
Established by and Supported by V.P. Gore's
Office of the National Performance Review
****

FOR IMMEDIATE RELEASE

For More Information, call: Preston Rich (703) 306-1282
Linda Hoogeveen (202) 395-3812

Create Date: August 12, 1994

Attention: Public Sector Finance Professionals & Educators

Ideas are the most important ingredients in FinanceNet! FinanceNet—a terrific opportunity for you to participate in reinventing government financial management.

We invite you to join with thousands of accountants, auditors, financial managers, and others to share your ideas and information. This is a vehicle that can help you do your job better. We encourage you to join and freely participate in this project. It's free and available to anyone having

Internet access and the desire to improve government financial management. Coordination and support are provided by Vice President Gore's National Performance Review (NPR) and the National Science Foundation.

This ambitious Internet initiative links people in all Federal agencies; state, local and international communities; professional financial management organizations, and private sector support organizations. It provides a synergistic medium for sharing ideas, information, successes, news, lessons learned, best practices and experience.

SERVICES

Electronic Mailing Lists devoted to a variety of subjects related to the accountability and stewardship of public financial assets—such as Internal Controls, Audits, Financial Reporting and Policy, Payroll, Travel, Procurement, Financial Systems, Personnel and Training, Performance Measures, Audits, Accounting Standards, Cash Management, International, State and Local Issues, and many others.

Internet Gopher (**gopher.financenet.gov**) and World Wide Web Mosaic Servers (**http://www.financenet.gov/**) carry libraries of important new electronic financial management documents, news announcements, employment openings, and much more from governments all around the world. FinanceNet servers offer a "one-stop-shop" navigation of all of the Internet's extensive worldwide resources.

Usenet Newsgroup Discussion Forums on financial management topics, open to all, and an electronic online, realtime conferencing capability rounds out the service list.

WOW !!! The only thing missing is YOU.

If you have an Internet accessible e-mail address you can automatically receive complete information on the full spectrum of FinanceNet Internet services by return e-mail by simply sending a blank e-mail message to:

info@financenet.gov

Investigate FinanceNet————————your key to working smarter!

```
OFFICE OF THE VICE PRESIDENT
           WASHINGTON

September 20, 1994

Dear Members of FinanceNet:

In the spirit of "Reinventing Government," I am pleased to
congratulate you on the formation of FinanceNet. I also
want to challenge you to use your growing network to
engage government financial operations staffs and their
customers in the task of innovation in the field of finan-
cial management.

Those of you who are participants in the Federal enter-
prise—as managers or as customers of financial man-
agement services—know that we are in the midst of
massive cultural change to create a "government that
works better and costs less." Those of you who are exter-
nal stakeholders from professional associations, acade-
mia, or private sector organizations are weathering similar
changes in technologies, resources, priorities, and strate-
gies; you have much expertise to offer us.

I wish you good luck as you build a new and exciting way
of working on complex issues. I hope you will help us set
new goals in the area of financial management and create
a collaborative approach to reach them.

Sincerely,

/S/

Al Gore
AG/asc
```

FinanceNet is a true indication of the future of this type of electronic collaboration
between government departments and, indeed, the private sector.

Consensus Building

Governments of the day and, in particular, politicians, are in the business of establishing consensus by citizens and other politicians with respect to their current plans,

political or legislative agendas, or activities. The Internet represents an opportunity for "electronic consensus building" through communications with citizens. Examples abound throughout the Canadian Internet. The Internet provides opportunities to

➤ cultivate interest and support for government activities;

➤ justify government activities, mandates, roles, and functions;

➤ open the lines of communication with the general public.

We will address each of these issues below.

Interest and Support

As the political, financial, and social situation in Canada becomes more complex, governments are struggling to get their message and legislative agenda across to the public. With the number of issues facing government in Canada today, it is no surprise that politicians resort to the time-tested method of participating in high profile "question periods" and media "scrums" in order to get a nightly sound bite on the evening news. Yet, many Canadians want to examine proposed policies and legislative agendas in-depth. Clearly, through the Internet, a skillful government body can educate the public on a particular issue.

In a perfect example, the government of Alberta (**http://www.gov.ab.ca**) mounted on the Internet the full text of a recent televised address to the province by Premier Ralph Klein concerning his fight against the provincial deficit (complete with colorful graphs and charts).

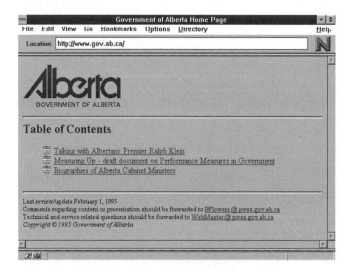

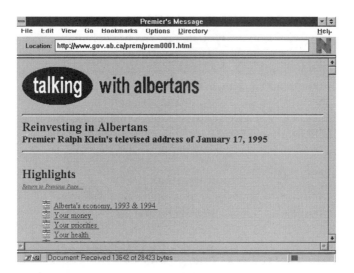

Human Resources Canada (**http://hrdc-drhc.gc.ca/**), involved in an effort to improve the delivery of social programs in Canada, has made a number of policy papers available on the Internet. Canada's Minister of Human Resources as of May 1995, Lloyd Axworthy, established an Internet address and encourages feedback from Internet users. He can be reached at **lloyd.axworthy@hrdc-drhc.gc.ca**.

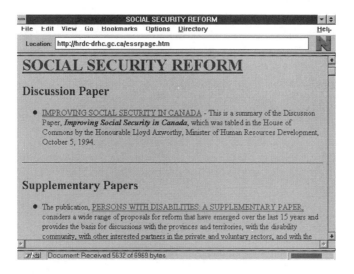

Even Canadian political parties are getting into the act. Political parties use the Internet as a vehicle to build support for their platforms. The Reform Party of Canada was the first Canadian political party to have an official presence on the World Wide Web (**http://www.reform.ca**).

> The free exchange of ideas; grassroots communication between citizens: these are essential elements of a healthy democracy. The Reform Party of Canada wholeheartedly supports these principles. That is why it is so appropriate that we now take advantage of the global Internet and the World Wide Web. The Internet is rooted in a tradition of free-spirited debate and a sense of community, values which are appreciated by Reformers.
>
> Preston Manning
> Leader, Reform Party of Canada
> **http://www.reform.ca**

The Reform Party's World Wide Web server contains the principles and policies of the party, the party's constitution, press releases, policy statements, weekly caucus updates, and pictures of all the Reform Party Members of Parliament. An Internet address (**info@reform.ca**) has been established for general queries about the party and its platform.

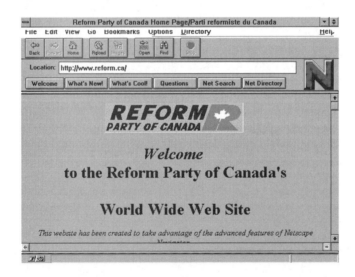

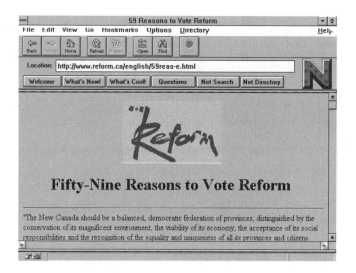

In all of these activities, the Internet is not just being used to make it easy for the public to access information—it is being used to help get a particular message or agenda across to the public. It is only a matter of time before we see more significant use of the Internet by political and government groups in Canada.

Government Activities, Mandates, Roles, and Function

As we mentioned previously, many government departments have an image problem. The public perceives government to be a great, mindless bureaucracy and believes that there is much time and effort wasted throughout all aspects of government. There is an opportunity for government to use the Internet to build public confidence and provide greater insight into the particular mandate, roles or functions of a department or government body.

Countless people "surf" the Internet on a daily basis. What better way to build an understanding of the role of any particular government body than to try to explain yourself through the network? The Canadian Radio-Television and Telecommunications Commission is attempting to do exactly that.

Of all groups with a potential image problem, perhaps the CRTC stands at the top of the list, given recent controversies in Canada over the CRTC's efforts to define what Canadians should watch.[2] Not one to shy away from controversy, the CRTC has included a section on its Internet site entitled "So, What Good is the CRTC?" (**http://www.crtc.gc.ca**). In this way, the Internet is being used as a public relations tool, in the same way that advertisements or brochures might be used.

---

[2] Since everyone can be a publisher on the Internet, bodies such as the CRTC have become largely irrelevant on the Internet, since it is impossible for them to toy with such issues as "Canadian content."

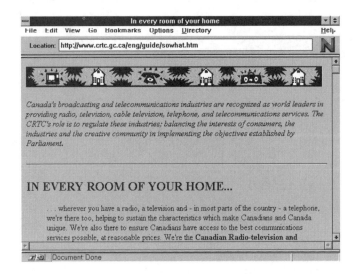

In every room of your home

File Edit View Go Bookmarks Options Directory   Help

Location: http://www.crtc.gc.ca/eng/guide/sowhat.htm

Canada's broadcasting and telecommunications industries are recognized as world leaders in providing radio, television, cable television, telephone, and telecommunications services. The CRTC's role is to regulate these industries; balancing the interests of consumers, the industries and the creative community in implementing the objectives established by Parliament.

IN EVERY ROOM OF YOUR HOME...

. . . wherever you have a radio, a television and - in most parts of the country - a telephone, we're there too, helping to sustain the characteristics which make Canadians and Canada unique. We're also there to ensure Canadians have access to the best communications services possible, at reasonable prices. We're the **Canadian Radio-television and**

Document Done

Open Lines of Communication

Many astute politicians in Canada have realized that it is to their benefit to encourage communication between themselves and the general public. At the time of preparation of this book, Premiers Bob Rae and Frank McKenna were still in power in Ontario and New Brunswick. Although the future election prospects appear slim for one and quite promising for the other, both showed political courage in 1994 by widely publicizing their Internet e-mail addresses (**premier@gov.on.ca** for Rae and **premier@gov.nb.ca** for McKenna) and by encouraging the public to communicate with them that way. A number of members of parliament and members of provincial legislative assemblies have established Internet addresses to improve communications with their constituents, and New Brunswick has provided e-mail access to all members of Cabinet. A number of civic mayors and aldermen across Canada have become involved with the Internet as well.

At the federal level, several Members of Parliament have Internet access using the addressing scheme in the box below:

PROPOSED INTERNET ADDRESSING SCHEME FOR
MEMBERS OF PARLIAMENT

first_5_letters_of_last_name+first_initial@parl.gc.ca

e.g., Don Boudria of the Liberal Party can be reached at
boudrd@parl.gc.ca

Yet, even before these formal plans to link all federal MPs to the Internet were introduced, there were many politicians across Canada who joined the Internet merely to discover what it is about and what it represents and to understand how it can be used to communicate with constituents.

Some politicians, having experienced the diversity and scope of the Internet, are profoundly changed once they observe what the Internet might mean to the political process. Senator Ray Perrault, a long-time Leader of the Senate of Canada, said the following in a private e-mail message to the authors of this book:

> Yes, I am now on the Internet. I can only say that I regret profoundly that this incredible new dimension in communications was not available many years ago when I was serving as Leader of the Government in the Senate—and even earlier in my political career.
>
> (Signed) Senator Ray Perrault, P.C.
> **perrault@direct.ca**

It is not just the politicians who realize that the Internet can open new channels of communication between the government and the general public. Several government departments and agencies with Internet sites, including the Atlantic Canada Opportunities Agency, have implemented electronic feedback capabilities that allow Internet users to submit comments and opinions electronically (**http://www.acoa.ca**).

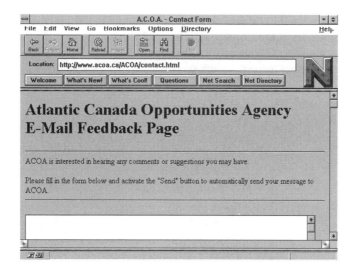

These "on-line suggestion boxes" are becoming popular throughout the Internet and will definitely continue as a trend as government bodies attempt to monitor more closely the attitudes and opinions of their citizens. So, as more politicians join the Internet, we should see more communication between citizens and their representatives. As more government bodies open themselves up to more direct interaction with their "customers," government and political service levels might improve. For many this will introduce a positive change to democracy, for it will help to ensure that politicians are in touch with their constituents and that they understand ideas and issues at the grassroots level. In doing so, the Internet will change politics forever.

Policy Shaping

Government isn't just in the business of information distribution and shaping opinion. It is also directly involved in many policy issues that encourage activities nationally, regionally, and locally. The Internet presents some exciting opportunities when it comes to shaping government policy. For example, the Internet can be used

➤ to encourage investment;

➤ to encourage tourism;

➤ to encourage immigration;

➤ to promote business linkages with foreign firms;

➤ to encourage infrastructure development.

We will discuss each of these opportunities separately.

Investment

Governments across Canada have discovered that they can use the Internet to establish information resources related to the ongoing effort to lure investors and businesses to their respective provinces. The Government of New Brunswick, for example, has been very active in this regard. On its World Wide Web site (**http://www.gov.nb.ca**), the Government of New Brunswick outlines the many reasons why a corporation might want to consider relocating to its province. The site provides extensive information on New Brunswick's labor force, educational system, recreational facilities, research facilities, tax incentives and benefits, information infrastructure, and much more.

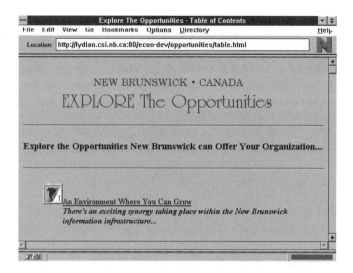

The site also provides an electronic form that can be used if a user wants to request additional information. The requests are immediately forwarded by electronic mail to New Brunswick's economic development and tourism department.

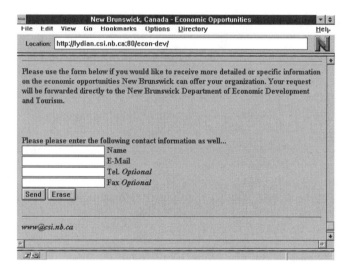

New Brunswick's Internet initiatives are noteworthy for another reason. The Department of Economic Development and Tourism has integrated its print advertising with its on-line presence so that magazine ads promoting investment in New Brunswick now carry an Internet e-mail address for enquiries. The integration of e-mail and print campaigns is a trend that will become more popular, not only in the public sector, but in the private sector as well.

Tourism

Governments are in the business of encouraging tourism, often with private sector assistance. Given the positive impact of tourism on the Canadian economy, it is an important focus. Some tourism ministries across the country have discovered the potential of the Internet as a tourism promotion tool. Not only can the Internet encourage domestic tourism, but because of its worldwide reach it can attract foreign visitors as well.

In the Yukon, the Ministry of Tourism has established a World Wide Web site (**http://yknet.yk.ca**) that provides an on-line vacation guide to the Yukon. The guide includes information about hunting, wildlife viewing, sight-seeing, a calendar of events, and lots of practical travel information about visiting the Yukon. A personal greeting from Yukon's Minister of Tourism welcomes users to the site.

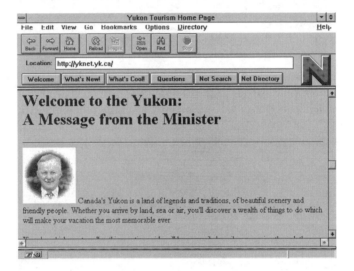

The Government of the Northwest Territories has also developed a tourism site on the Internet (**http://www.nstn.ca:80/nmd/nwt/guide**) to promote vacation opportunities in the North. The site includes information on road tours, parks, adventure travel (hiking, canoeing, camping, kayaking), naturalist tours, accommodation information, and general travel tips.

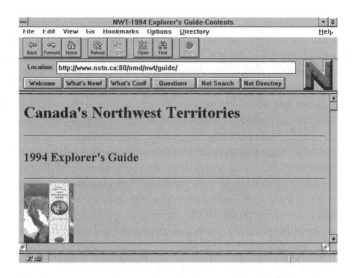

Of course, not everyone wants to read this information on-line. So, using the World Wide Web's fill-in form capabilities, the Northwest Territories government has conveniently provided Internet users with an on-line form they can fill out to receive a printed copy of a tourism guide in the mail. Once completed, the request is delivered over the Internet by e-mail to tourism department officials, who then arrange to mail the guide. In this way, the Internet becomes a method by which someone can easily request information from a government department.

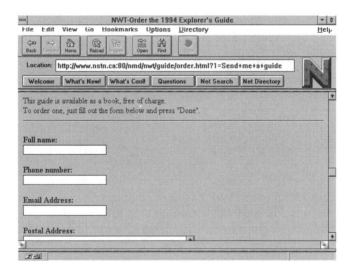

Immigration

In Canada's continuing quest to lure highly skilled immigrants to this country, the Internet is proving to be a valuable resource. With thousands upon thousands of engineers, scientists, and computer experts using the Internet every day, the Internet provides an excellent opportunity to promote Canada as a destination of choice for potential immigrants, particularly those with the high-tech skills that Canada needs.

A CTV News report called the Internet "a gateway of choice" for locating immigrants. Even Sergio Marchi, Canada's Immigration Minister, acknowledged the Internet's potential to immigration authorities, calling the Internet "the next frontier" for immigration.[3]

The Province of Manitoba, whose share of Canadian immigrants dropped 20% in the last year, is the first province in Canada to actively recruit immigrants using the Internet. Manitoba's Citizenship Division has established an Internet site (**http://www.gov.mb.ca/manitoba/chc/immsettl/project.html**) where it publishes information about the benefits of immigrating to Manitoba.

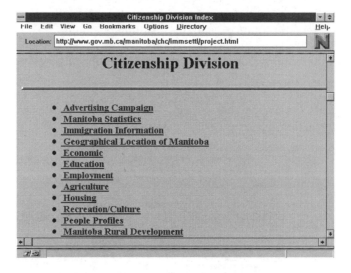

Efforts to encourage immigration are not always the result of formal departmental policy, as can be seen in the case of Donald Cameron, the Immigration Program Manager at the Canadian Consulate in Seattle, Washington. He has been advocating the use of the Internet for immigration purposes since he first realized the Internet's potential for disseminating immigration information in June 1994.

In mid-1994, he was involved in the establishment of an Internet discussion group for Canadian immigration issues called **misc.immigration.canada**. He and a number of other Canadian immigration experts now volunteer their time to answer

---

[3] CTV National News, February 7, 1995.

Canadian immigration questions from Internet users all over the world. The following screen shows some of the subjects that were under discussion in April 1995:

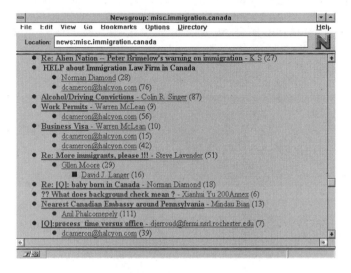

Cameron believes that the Internet is a "phenomenally effective and cheap way of disseminating information," noting that the cost of his Internet access is only $30.00 a month. "Instead of having to publish information on paper and ship it around the world," he says, "we can simply post it on the Internet, and people can download it wherever they may be." He does this, for example, by posting information on the Internet through which potential immigrants can learn about the criteria for permanent residence in Canada. The cost savings are immediate, since each time an Internet user accesses these documents, one less copy has to be printed and mailed out.

The Internet is a natural place to gain the interest of the types of immigrants that Canada wants to attract. "The number of people with PhDs and computer science and experience working for the high-tech companies…on the Internet…who are interested in moving to Canada is really quite astonishing," says Cameron.[4] (Donald Cameron can be reached on the Internet at **dcameron@halcyon.com**.)

Business Linkages With Foreign Firms

Through the Internet Canadian firms can learn of business opportunities in foreign countries. Canadian consulates in both San Diego (**http://www.cts.com:80/~cdntrade**) and San Jose (**http://www.globalx.net:80/ccto/**) have established World Wide Web sites to promote business linkages between Canadian and U.S. firms.

---

[4] CTV National News, February 7, 1995.

The San Diego Consulate's World Wide Web server, illustrated below, provides an interactive map and directory of Canadian consulates and trade offices throughout the United States as well as the Canadian Trade Officer's newsletter on the United States biotechnology marketplace. This newsletter identifies opportunities for Canadian firms to establish strategic alliances and partnerships with U.S. companies.

Infrastructure Development

Finally, we examine the role that the Internet can play in developing a national and local telecommunications infrastructure. The Internet will have a major impact on global commerce in the years to come. The result is that some government bodies have become involved in encouraging the adoption of the Internet within a community as a means of ensuring that the community participate in the information economy as it unfolds.

So far in this chapter, most of the examples discussed have focused on the use of the Internet within federal and provincial government departments. But the Internet has not escaped the reach of some of the smaller Canadian communities. For example, the mayor and town manager of the town of Slave Lake, Alberta, have determined it is necessary for the town to become involved in the Internet. As an early step, the town has established a World Wide Web site on the Internet (**http://www. supernet.ab.ca/Communities/slavelake.html**), as shown in the screen below, which contains a wealth of information about the town.

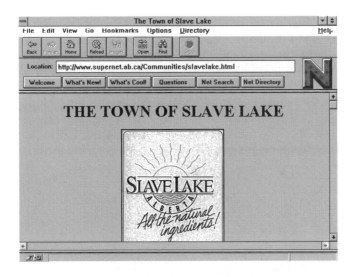

Pat Vincent, the Town Manager of Slave Lake, knows that the Internet provides Slave Lake with a number of advantages over other municipalities that aren't yet wired to the network. For example, the town's World Wide Web site is intended to be used as both an economic development tool and a device for tourism promotion. One of the central features of their site is a calendar of events, which promotes cultural and recreational events in the town.

In addition to its activities on the World Wide Web, the town uses the Internet to communicate with its twin community in Kamishihoro, Japan. Vincent says that the Internet has led to "greater frequency of communication and greater ease of communication between the two communities."[5] For example, the Internet will be used to coordinate a student exchange between the two communities, which will begin in 1995, and students in Slave Lake are already communicating with students in Kamishihoro in preparation for the exchange.

Peter Moore, the Mayor of Slave Lake, says that the Internet will open up new market opportunities for the town and enhance the provision of educational and professional services (such as medicine) to members of the community. Students will have access to a broad range of educational materials and will benefit from distance education programs and other interactive learning services that are available on the Internet.

---

[5] Electronic mail message to the authors, January 29, 1995.

> There is no doubt as people continue to rank "quality of life" as an important criterion in choosing where they live, smaller communities who are benefitting as a result of an out-migration from larger urban centres can be and will be communities of first choice. Our municipality can be on a competitive footing with any other through the use of this technology and resource, ensuring that our future is bright and will be preserved.[6]
>
> Peter Moore, Mayor
> Town of Slave Lake, Alberta

In these small ways the town of Slave Lake is exploring how the Internet can be used as a promotional vehicle—an important first step.

North Bay, Where All Road Signs Point to City Hall

Some towns have gone further. We close this chapter with the story of the City of North Bay, a bustling northern Ontario community of 56,000 people. North Bay is not your typical northern Ontario community. It has a strong telecommunications infrastructure and is home to the Canadian North American Air Defense Command (NORAD) headquarters.

A number of knowledge-based industries and high-tech companies are based in North Bay, unlike other cities and towns in the region, where the economies are largely dependent on manufacturing and/or natural resources. What also sets North Bay apart from other Northern Ontario communities is that the city has made its mark on the Internet, thanks to a collaborative effort between North Bay City Hall and Canadore College, a local community college. As a starting point, the City of North Bay has established a site on the World Wide Web (**http://www.city.north-bay.on. ca/northbay.htm**), which is depicted in the screen below, in order to provide the world with economic, tourism, and other information related to the city.

---

[6] Letter to the authors, March 8, 1995.

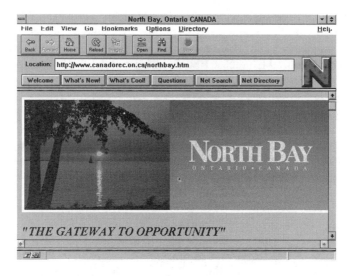

The two individuals heading up this project are Scott Bradford, a Programmer/Analyst with the Information Services Department, and Stephen Sajatovic, Director of Planning and Development for the city. The project began after Canadore College approached North Bay City Hall with the idea of building a World Wide Web site.

Canadore College had been eagerly watching what U.S. cities like San Antonio, Texas, and San Diego and Palo Alto were doing on the World Wide Web throughout 1994. As a result, two representatives from Canadore College came to North Bay City Hall in the summer of 1994 to demonstrate the potential of the World Wide Web as a means of promoting the city. Bradford and Sajatovic were immediately sold on the concept. Work began immediately on the construction of the city's World Wide Web site, using the skills of a summer school student familiar with the Internet:

> When the summer student went back to Guelph, we approached the Unemployment Insurance Program and asked them if they had anyone on the Unemployment Insurance Line who happened to know how to turn on a computer. We found a woman who came from Nova Scotia and had been involved with the establishment of Chebucto FreeNet and was also involved with the Province of Nova Scotia Library System. It was like falling into a goldmine.[7]
>
> Stephen Sajatovic, Dept. of Planning and Development, City of North Bay

---

[7] Interview with one of the authors, January 1995.

As it turned out, it was not a complicated process to build the World Wide Web site. Sajatovic rounded up about 75 to 80 of the city's best 35 mm slides, took them down to a local camera shop, and had them digitized onto a compact disc. Maps and charts were scanned from City Hall documents.

Even the cost was reasonable: about three weeks of Sajatovic and Bradford's time, $7 for a blank compact disc, $200 for digitizing, and $3000 for the summer student. The second person on the project didn't cost City Hall anything, since the Unemployment Insurance Commission picked up the cost.

North Bay then hired a second summer student to do a comparative analysis of North Bay's competitive position as a "telecommunications centre," and the results of the study were placed on the city's World Wide Web site for anyone to view. The Web site includes information on almost every facet of the city—climate, history, recreation, tourism, economic growth, labor force, education, transportation, health care, shopping and entertainment, and social services information. All this information was input from existing documents and brochures at North Bay City Hall.

Sajatovic explained that one of the benefits of the city's World Wide Web site is that the information can be updated or changed as required without any incremental cost to the city. To illustrate one of the benefits of electronic publishing, Sajatovic explained that the city has a paper brochure featuring information on the mayor and all the city councillors. A recent municipal election saw the defeat of the incumbent mayor and five of the city councillors. Sajatovic noted that the city's World Wide Web page can be updated in a few seconds to reflect the new council members, whereas the paper brochure has to be reprinted at a cost of several dollars a copy.

North Bay's World Wide Web site has been popular not only with Ontario residents, but with people around the world. The site has been visited by people in Austria, the Netherlands, Germany, Denmark, and a host of other countries. "It became very clear that the global restructuring that was going on in the economy was more than just a typical recession spike," says Sajatovic. "There was an increasing realization that the nature of business and industry was changing radically—we were migrating very quickly from the industrial age based on manufacturing to knowledge-based industries based on computer technology and telecommunications."

In recognition of the growing importance of the Internet and communication networks, City Hall has established the BayNet initiative, an ambitious program designed to create and to maintain jobs, to improve the quality of life for city residents, and to help the city improve its telecompetitiveness. North Bay is also hoping that BayNet will put North Bay on the map as a major host site for tele-computer technology.

The establishment of the North Bay pages on the World Wide Web is mandated through the BayNet program, as are a number of other telecommunications initiatives, including the establishment of a North Bay Free-Net, a local commercial Internet service, and the deployment of touch-screen "InfoBay" terminals throughout the city that will provide residents and tourists with information about the community.

While it may seem odd to some that City Hall is helping to jump-start a commercial Internet service in the city, Sajatovic sees nothing unusual about it. "My job is matchmaking," he says emphatically. Sajatovic believes that part of City Hall's mandate will be to introduce local businesses to the Internet and match them with a provider to help get them up and running. "I see it as applying the infrastructure and the technology to existing business. Instead of using a 43-cent stamp or a fax to do business with a customer, you will do it over the Internet."

Scott Bradford can be reached at **bradfords@city.north-bay.on.ca** and Steve Sajatovic can be reached at **sajatovics@city.north-bay.on.ca**.

Conclusion

Finally, we must emphasize our viewpoint on the role of government when it comes to the Internet in Canada. Not only should government everywhere take a proactive role in the use of the Internet, but it should become active in encouraging its adoption across the country.

Government leaders everywhere *must* understand that what is emerging in the Internet is a system that will affect, and indeed, shape the economy for many years to come. The Internet promises to profoundly change business. The government in Canada must shape national policy to encourage business to participate in the network so that we are not left behind.

The preamble to the business plan for CA*net, a major component of the Canadian Internet network, states quite clearly the significance of the network:

> The Canadian Internet is one of the most important developments in Canadian history, as important as the development of the trans-Canada highway system, the St. Lawrence Seaway, and the CPR. It will be used for civic discourse, commerce and delivery of government services, becoming a key component of Canadian society.

Governments have caught on—there has been much discussion in Canada on the need for governments to ensure that the country prepares itself for the twenty-first century. Much of the talk has focused on the concept of ensuring that we have an "information highway," and the word "infrastructure" is used with abandon.

There is a lot of talk about information highways in Canada, yet in many ways there is a fundamental lack of knowledge among senior politicians about what the Internet represents. As a result, the focus in Canada is on a "television-based" information highway, offering "video-on-demand," computer games, and "500 channels." "Home-shopping" dominates discussion, and technology development focuses on providing the consumer with a television-based device that reads credit cards.

Are we focusing on building the wrong type of information highway? If you listen to major communication companies, it would seem we are building some type of giant "home-zirconium-channel-shopping network," by which we will sit on our couch, watch TV, and buy stuff. The information highway will soon be responsible for a massive increase in coronary heart disease in Canada, as we turn into a nation of couch-potatoes, driving our TV-based information highway!

The global economy is changing all around us. There is fierce competition all around us, and if Canada fails to recognize the opportunities in front of her, we will fall behind. We as a nation need to recognize the strategic significance of the Internet.

Singapore, for one, plans on meeting the future head-on. In a document entitled "IT2000—A Vision of an Intelligent Island," government, industry, and education in Singapore planned for what would be necessary for the country to excel in the economy of the twenty-first century.

> The study tapped the practical and visionary expertise of more than 200 senior executives from both the public and private sectors to see how information technology can be pervasively applied to improve business performance and the quality of life.
>
> Over the past decade, Singapore has deliberately prepared herself to meet the new challenges of the information age. We have developed a substantial national IT capability. A positive environment exists for the private and public sectors to collaborate in exploiting IT for national competitive advantage. The World Competitiveness Report has, in recent years, placed Singapore among the top nations in the world in terms of strategic exploitation of IT by companies, computer literacy of workers and telecommunications infrastructure.
>
> In our vision, some 15 years from now, Singapore, the Intelligent Island, will be among the first countries in the world with an advanced nationwide information infrastructure. It *will interconnect computers in virtually every home, office, school, and factory.* The computer will evolve into an information appliance, combining the functions of the telephone, computer, TV, and more. It will provide a wide range of communication means and access to services. The vision of the IT2000 is based on the far-reaching use of IT.
>
> Singaporeans will be able to tap into vast reservoirs of electronically stored information and services to improve their business, to make their working lives easier, and to enhance their personal, social, recreational and leisure options. Text, sound, pictures, video, documents, designs and other forms of media can be transferred and shared through the high

> capacity and high speed nationwide information infra-
> structure made up of fibre optic cables reaching all homes
> and offices, and a pervasive wireless network working in
> tandem. This information infrastructure will also permeate
> our physical infrastructure making mobile telecomputing
> possible,and our homes, work places, airport, seaport and
> surface transportation systems "smarter." A wide range of
> new infrastructural services, linking government, business,
> and the people, will be created to take advantage of new
> communications and tetherless network technology.

It should not be surprising that since the release of the document, Singapore as a nation and as an economy has become *extremely* involved with the Internet.

Many believe that the global knowledge capabilities of the Internet offer far more to Canada in terms of business and economic opportunities than the "couch-potato," TV-based information highways being developed by major telecommunication companies. An information highway that will help Canadians compete in the global economy is not found in this TV-based information highway. Such a high-way does little to help Canadians access knowledge and market products and services worldwide, or provide effective customer support. Such a highway has little in the way of strategic business advantage.

We raised this question in our *Canadian Internet Handbook,* and we repeat it here again: how can we as a nation expect to compete with the city-state of Singapore, if they are concentrating on building a network that lets them participate in the world's largest knowledge network, the Internet, and we are building a highway that lets us order fried chicken with our TV remote control?

As a nation, we will fall far behind if we continue with such a focus. Hence, as a nation, we need to encourage widespread adoption of the Internet throughout the business community, in recognition of its likely impact on commerce in the twenty-first century.

Sadly, we lack senior politicians in Canada who have sufficient understanding of the Internet to form a national vision for its use. We need more leaders with an understanding of the strategic potential of the world's largest computer network.

CHAPTER 6

Education on the Internet

In the corner of 300 classrooms across Canada sits a terminal that will link children to an exciting new world of math, science and technology. It's a computer linked to SchoolNet, a national project in which students and teachers exchange ideas by computer network. Teachers may discuss ideas for science projects over the network and help students work on the projects with contemporaries in other parts of the country.

Canada gets caught up in the Internet
The Financial Post, May 21, 1994

A university or college graduate of the 1990s who cannot use a computer to create documents, analyze numeric data and communicate with people worldwide by sending electronic mail messages, is as poorly prepared for life and for earning a living in the twenty-first century as one who cannot compose a paragraph, balance a chequebook, read a book or use a library.

Computer Science in Nova Scotia
Information Technology and Economic Renewal
A Report to the Nova Scotia Council
on Higher Education
May 1994

*C*ertainly one area in which we are seeing dramatic growth in use of the Internet is within the educational sector. Over 5,000 Canadian schools are now connected to the Internet, due in large measure to a federal, provincial, and territorial initiative known as SchoolNet, which is in the process of linking all of Canada's schools to the Internet. Educators across Canada are beginning to discover the rich and diverse information that the Internet can make available to students and teachers alike.

In a February speech in Picton, Ontario, John Manley, Canada's Minister of Industry, remarked on the success of the SchoolNet project:

STRATEGIC USES OF THE INTERNET WITHIN EDUCATION

(1) Students
- Allows students to correspond with other students
- Facilitates global research
- Brings students closer to experts
- Links students with mentors
- Provides access to on-line educational resources
- Provides opportunities for tutorial-based learning
- Fosters creativity, design, critical thinking, and good writing skills
- Cultivates on-line research skills
- Provides access to job and career information

(2) Educational Organizations
- Reduces costs
- Streamlines admissions
- Promotes the institution
- Improves interdepartmental communication
- Creates virtual classrooms
- Permits distance education
- Expands student services
- Expands alumni services

(3) Educators
- Improves communication between teachers
- Supports the use of the Internet in the classroom
- Improves communication between teachers and students
- Locates lesson plans and curriculum resources
- Advances educational or policy reform
- Delivers course materials
- Keeps oneself up-to-date

(4) Parents
- Keeps parents informed of school events and activities
- Keeps parents informed of issues affecting their child's education
- Helps parents seek advice from other parents and educators
- Allows parents to keep up with their children

> The original SchoolNet program began less than two years ago as a joint federal, provincial, territorial and private sector initiative. It was designed to provide Canadian students and teachers with exciting electronic services which would develop and stimulate the skills needed in the information age. I am delighted to say that the interest in SchoolNet and its growth has been nothing short of phenomenal, surpassing all expectations. Today, over 4,500 of Canada's 16,500 schools are electronically connected, with over 700 services available to SchoolNet users across the country. Since October 1993, there have been over a million accesses to SchoolNet, representing a monthly growth rate of 65 percent.[1]

The movement to use the Internet within elementary and high schools in Canada continues to gain momentum. The Internet has caught the imagination of educators and politicians across Canada, and there is growing support for the integration of the Internet into public and high school curriculums. The federal government has announced its intention to see that all of Canada's schools, public libraries, and universities and colleges are connected to the Internet by 1998. SchoolNet will also be connecting all 417 Aboriginal schools under federal jurisdiction.

Canada is not the only country that has discovered the Internet's potential for education. Around the globe schools are plugging in, and students and teachers are learning how to use the Internet as a communication and information discovery tool. Given its roots in the university sector, the Internet is also heavily used in universities and colleges throughout Canada.

In this chapter, we will take a look at how the Internet can be used in a classroom environment by both teachers and parents as part of the educational process. We will highlight some of the changes occurring in higher education as a result of its use in that area. Finally, we will conclude the chapter by discussing some of the controversies surrounding the use of the Internet as an educational tool.

What does the Internet Offer Education?

One of the key reasons for using the Internet in the classroom is to teach computer literacy skills. With computers and computer-related technology becoming a daily part

---

[1] Speaking notes, Honorable John Manley, Minister of Industry. Announcement of the SchoolNet Community Access Project, Picton, Ontario, February 17, 1995.

of our lives, early adoption of computer literacy skills is increasingly important. Similarly, with telecommunications assuming an increasingly important role in society, using the Internet can help students to develop an appreciation and understanding of computers and computer technology at a very young age.

By using the Internet in the classroom, educators are not just teaching children how to use technology, they are teaching them *how to use technology to learn*. This is an extremely important component of the educational process and cannot be overemphasized when it comes to computer education. Children who use the Internet in the classroom will view computers in a more positive light. They will discover that computers are tools that can be used to explore, to find information, to ask questions, to probe for knowledge, to debate, and to learn.

As we enter the information age, computer literacy skills and, in particular, skills to locate, access, evaluate and analyze information, are becoming increasingly important in our workforce. Business across Canada makes the point that we need to improve computer and high-tech literacy in our schools. The Internet represents a significant opportunity to accomplish this.

In the following pages we will discuss how the Internet can be used in a classroom environment and demonstrate how it will benefit us all—students, educational organizations, educators, and parents.

Use by Students

We have identified nine key benefits of the Internet for students:

➤ it allows students to correspond with other students;

➤ it facilitates global research;

➤ it brings students closer to experts;

➤ it links students with mentors;

➤ it provides access to on-line educational resources;

➤ it provides opportunities for tutorial-based learning;

➤ it fosters creativity, design, critical thinking, and good writing skills;

➤ it cultivates on-line research skills;

➤ it allows access to job and career information.

Each of these benefits will be discussed below.

Correspondence with Other Students

One of the key attractions of the Internet for students, and educators, is the opportunity for international correspondence. Students can correspond with "e-mail pen-pals" around the world, and entire classrooms in different countries or provinces can collaborate on e-mail projects.

With 90 countries directly on the network and at least another 70 with e-mail access, students become citizens of the world. Their social experiences need no longer be limited to their classmates or their immediate environment—their knowledge and experience can come directly from their interactions with other people, no matter where they might be located around the world. In this way, the Internet helps to enhance the emotional and social growth of our children by exposing them to different ideas, different cultures, and different people.

Teachers who have used the Internet to electronically link students in different countries have discovered that the effect on children is electrifying. Suddenly, the process of learning becomes more exciting. Children look forward to opening their electronic mailboxes each morning to read their new messages, and the whole experience of communicating with distant pen pals can be turned into a classroom project. Students can share the messages they have received with the class, and teachers can use the messages as the basis for class assignments and discussion. For students, the Internet makes learning more fun, more interactive, and more challenging.

In some cases, teachers allow their students to post their own messages on the Internet, as in the following two examples:

Date: Wed, 1 Feb 1995 16:09:25 -0600
From: Debra Lynn Hopp <hopp@TENET.EDU>
Subject: seeking 3rd grade pen pal

Hi! My name is Matt and I am looking for a third grader for a pen pal. I like power rangers, jurasic park, sega, video games, computers ,etc. Please be my pen pal. I live in Texas.

From owner-k12pals@SUVM.SYR.EDU Wed Feb 1 00:11:40 1995
Date: Tue, 31 Jan 1995 19:31:33 -0800
Subject: Seeking Individual Pen Pal

I am seeking an individual pen pal aged 13-14. I am an eighth grade girl living in Canada. My interests are reading and sports, such as horseback riding, soccer, volleyball, and basketball.

Alternatively, a teacher can post a message on the Internet on behalf of an entire class, as in the following two examples:

From owner-k12pals@SUVM.SYR.EDU Sat Jan 14
16:25:54 1995
Date: Sat, 14 Jan 1995 15:25:04 -0600
From: Joan Allgier
<yuy003@MAIL.CONNECT.MORE.NET>
Subject: Seeking 2nd grade pen pals

Greetings,

Name: Joan Allgier
School: Washington/Franklin School
Location: Farmington, MO (75 miles south of St. Louis)

We are a group of 2nd grade students seeking another
2nd grade class from anywhere to correspond with from
January '95 to May '95. We are new at this but would like
to start as soon as possible. We have 27 students in our
class and would like to e-mail another class one on one at
a rate of one e-mail correspondence sent and received
per day. Hoping to hear from another class soon. We are
very eager to get started.

Joan Allgier Washington/Franklin School
Farmington R7 School District Grade 2
Farmington, Missouri 63640 USA voice:
(314) 756-5415/756-5519
yuy003@mail.connect.more.net   fax: (314) 756-0837

From owner-k12pals@SUVM.SYR.EDU Sat Jan 21
18:30:40 1995
Date: Sat, 21 Jan 1995 18:29:28 -0500
From: "Barrett T. Brickell" <barrett@HOOKUP.NET>
Subject: Seeking writers for grades 4/5 and 5/6

My name is Barrett Brickell. I teach at Riverview Alternative
School, located in Ottawa, Canada. I am seeking individual
students to correspond with two classes, one is a grade
4/5, the other a grade 5/6. There are 30 students in each
class. The correspondence can run from now until the end
of June (or further, if it works well) and should be in English.

Students should not only exchange personal letters, but
could possibly work on joint research projects together.

The concept of electronic pen pals through the Internet is perhaps the one area that is most easily understood by many people and one that offers schools an immediate return on investment.

The possibilities for global classroom communication are also quite exciting. For example, consider a classroom in Calgary that has a project on the American Civil War. If the class is linked via e-mail to a school in Virginia that is close to one of the battle sites, the Calgary students can query the Virginia students about local geography, monuments, museums and ruins in the area, and other information related to the Civil War. Or take a classroom in Charlottetown that is examining environmental issues, and link them to a school in Ukraine so that they can ask about the impact of pollution after the fall of communism in the Soviet Union.

By bringing the world to children, the Internet can make the learning process much more meaningful for students. When done on a "class project" basis, the electronic communications can become the basis for a classroom project.

The Internet is populated with teachers and educators who have discovered the Internet's usefulness as a teaching tool. Naturally, the Internet is full of requests by teachers seeking opportunities for e-mail exchanges with other classrooms. A few examples of types of requests that teachers are making on the Internet indicate the types of projects for which the network is being used:

From: KIDSPHERE Mailing List
<kidsphere@vms.cis.pitt.edu>
Subject: Acid Rain Project

Date: Mon, 30 Jan 1995 13:42:06 -0500 (EST)
From: "Marion Adams Schls. Internet Project"
<maradint@ideanet.doe.state.in.us>
Subject: Acid Rain Project

Hello!

I am a teacher who works with gifted and talented students in grades 2–5. A group of 5th graders are particularly interested in comparing our results of test acidity in snow with other parts of the US and outside the US. Indiana has a rather high concentration of acid in its precipitation, partly due to the number of manufacturing plant in the state. If your students would be interested in testing your rain, snow, or whatever with litmus paper for acidity, we would love to hear your results.

Thanks, De Carr
maradint@ideanet.doe.state.in.us

From owner-k12pals@SUVM.SYR.EDU Tue Jan 31
15:18:46 1995
Date: Tue, 31 Jan 1995 15:12:46 EST
From: <HARPELA@VM.CC.PURDUE.EDU>
Subject: seeking keypals Mexico,Canada, Gr. 5-7

Teacher : Mrs. Sandra Burkhart would like to correspond
with a class of 5th, 6th, or 7th graders from Mexico or
Canada. The class is doing research on these two countries
and the students have formulated questions. The students are from Northridge Middle School in Crawfordsville,
Indiana, USA. There are 20 students in the class and they
are currently studying Mexico and Canada. They would
like to correspond until the end of April.

From: Knappenberger Linda
<knappenb@BVSD.K12.CO.US>
Subject: 2nd grade penpals from Alaska
X-To: K12PALS@suvm.acs.syr.EDU
To: Multiple recipients of list K12PALS
<K12PALS@SUVM.SYR.EDU>

Linda Knappenberger
Ryan Elementary
Lafayette, Co
group penpals-2nd grade

We would like to correspond via e-mail with several classes
in Alaska, in English, for about two months. Small groups
of students would compose messages, and I would send
them out. Every day or so we will all come to the computer
to check our "mail." Mostly we want to find out what Alaska
is really like. We will tell you ALL about Colorado, too.

Educators getting involved in such electronic projects will find a wealth of on-
line assistance available on the Internet from groups in Canada and the United States
who provide support to educators seeking to link classrooms electronically:

➤ *The National Public Telecomputing Network* (NPTN). The NPTN has a program called Academy One that sponsors a number of projects that link classrooms together. The NPTN can be reached by electronic mail at **info@nptn.org** and via the World Wide Web at **http://www.nptn.org**. Telephone: (216) 498-4050.

➤ *SchoolNet*. SchoolNet is a Canadian project with the objective of linking all of Canada's schools to the Internet with assistance from the provincial, territorial, and federal governments, universities and colleges across Canada, and over two dozen other organizations. One of SchoolNet's primary objectives is to foster the development of electronically-based projects that link teachers and students across Canada. SchoolNet can be reached via the World Wide Web at **http://schoolnet.carleton.ca** and by e-mail at **schoolnet-admin@carleton.ca**. Telephone: (613) 788-4069 or 1-800-461-5945.

➤ *cableLINK-school*™. cableLINK-school is an initiative developed by Rogers Cablesystems, Canada's largest cable network operator, to provide schools with access to the Internet and the SchoolNet project. cableLINK-school makes use of high-speed cable modems that can transmit data up to 1,000 times faster than conventional modems. cableLINK-school can be reached at **http://www.cablelink.net**. Telephone: (416) 447-5500.

➤ *Stem~Net*. Stem~Net provides Internet access to teachers and educators in Newfoundland and Labrador and supports a number of on-going class networking projects. Stem~Net can be reached by e-mail at **staff@calvin. stemnet.nf.ca** or via the World Wide Web at **http://www.stemnet.nf.ca**. There are other provincial initiatives across Canada similar to Stem~Net. Telephone (709) 737-8836.

➤ *International Education and Resource Network* (I*EARN). I*EARN is a not-for-profit network that brings together students in over 400 schools and 23 countries. I*EARN offers an Internet "partnering" service that pairs schools in different countries for educational projects. I*EARN can be reached by e-mail at **iearn@igc.apc.org**. Telephone (914) 962-5864.

Global Research

Schools need not be restricted to communicating with other schools when it comes to using the Internet to reach other people for educational purposes. Indeed, through the Internet the world becomes a source of information from all kinds of people, from all walks of life, from all areas of the world, from all professions, and from all areas of interest. On occasion, a regular user of the Internet might be forwarded a message from someone they know that looks like the following:

From: Tracey McGee <ride0269@ride.ri.net>
To: bwcac020@llwsbe.wsbe.org Tracey McGee
Class Account
Date: Fri, 27 Jan 95 22:56:30 EDT
Subject: "Around the World in 80 days"

Hello!

You are all invited to help us travel the world without leaving our classroom.

We are a fifth grade class in Bristol, Rhode Island, USA. We are working on a project called "Around the World in 80 days". Our goal is to connect with as many people as possible within our 80 school day timeframe, through the letters/surveys returned from this request. We will be using the information we receive to learn about the different countries and places of those who respond. Weekly classroom activities will include charting responses and measuring the distance from our location to yours. This will add excitement to our writing and reading activities, as well as our technology skills.

Please help us by replying to the following survey by June 9, 1995.

Send all responses to: ride0269@ride.ri.net

Please distribute freely to any other list that will help us out.

Thank you in advance for taking time to make our project a huge success.

???

Now the journey begins!

1. What city and country do you live in?

2. What is the population of your town?

3. What special events is your area known for?

4. Where do you like to relax in town?

5. If we were to visit, what would you take us to see?

6. Do you go to school or are you a job holding citizen? Please explain.

7. What are the two most favorite forms of recreation in your area?

8. Please briefly describe your climate and local geographical features.

9. What is your native language?

10. If you live outside of the USA please briefly explain some aspects of your culture.

!!!

!!!!Thank you for traveling with us!!!!

The students of Mrs. McGee's 5th grade class

Such messages are usually sent to an Internet mailing list designed for this specific purpose. People who receive the message might forward it to a friend or acquaintance. Within a few days, the message might receive worldwide distribution, meaning that the school might suddenly find itself communicating with a wide variety of people from around the world.

The cooperative spirit and unique culture of the Internet mean that many people from around the world might take a few minutes to send a response to the note from Mrs. McGee's class above. Many people throughout the Internet are passionate in their belief that the Internet offers unique educational opportunities, so they support projects such as this.

Bringing Students Closer to Experts

Another key Internet innovation is that students and classrooms can interact, by e-mail, with experts in particular subject areas, making the learning experience more meaningful. For example, science students can interact with scientists, individuals studying weather can contact meteorologists, and physical education students can communicate with athletic experts in professional sports or at colleges and universities.

A good example of this concept is found with the Geology in the Classroom project (**http://agcwww.bio.ns.ca/schools/classrm.html**), sponsored by the Atlantic Geoscience Division of the Geological Survey of Canada, located at the Bedford Institute of Oceanography in Dartmouth, Nova Scotia. Scientists, engineers, and geology specialists involved in the study of the geology of eastern Canada voluntarily take questions by e-mail from any classroom, student, or teacher in Canada.

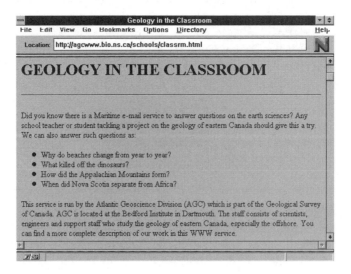

Another outstanding example of an Internet ask-an-expert program is the Ask Dr. Math program run at Swarthmore College in Pennsylvania (**http://olmo. swarthmore.edu/dr-math/dr-math.html**).

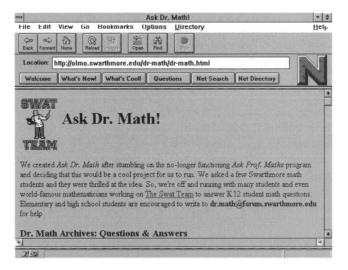

Swarthmore College has assembled a team of over a dozen mathematicians that accept questions from elementary and high school students over the Internet. The college maintains an archive of all the questions and answers, organized by school level (e.g., elementary, high school, university) and topic (e.g., addition, division, fractions and decimals, large numbers, math history, multiplication, square roots, puzzles). This site is truly a haven for math lovers.

Canada's SchoolNet project has a number of programs that link students with experts by e-mail. SchoolNet sponsors an electronic innovators program that matches students and teachers with science, technology, and engineering professionals in government, industry, and academia. SchoolNet has recruited over 400 professionals from all walks of life, and from all corners of the globe, who are available to answer questions from SchoolNet students and give advice on matters related to their area of expertise. Ask-an-expert programs can be particularly valuable for students who want to learn more about a particular career.

Some experts who find they don't have the time to answer questions personally by e-mail, have found other ways to contribute their knowledge to the Internet. One excellent example of this is *The New South Polar Times*, a newsletter that is published biweekly on the Internet and prepared by staff at the Amundsen–Scott Station in the South Pole, Antarctica. The following box explains how this Internet newsletter "came to be."

> The idea for the newsletter grew out of correspondence between several of the staff at the Amundsen–Scott Station and participants in an Internet workshop sponsored by The Virginia Space Grant Consortium during the summer of 1994. The workshop leader, Katie Wallet, and the officer in charge of operations at the station, Lt. Tom Jacobs, decided that students and teachers from around the world would be interested in learning about Antarctica, the scientific research that was taking place at the station and life at the station. Realizing that communication with individual classes was prohibitive because of the busy schedule of the staff at the station, they decided to create the newsletter which would be made available on Internet.[2]

The newsletter is freely available on the Internet at the following World Wide Web site: **http://www.deakin.edu.au/edu/MSEE/GENII/NSPT/NSPThomePage.html.**

In all of these cases, the Internet is demonstrating its potential to extend the reach of students to subject experts around the globe, providing yet another method for innovative learning in the classroom.

Linking Students with Mentors

An extension of the ask-an-expert program is linking students with mentors. "Electronic mentors" can be valuable role models for students who want to pursue a special interest or field of study. An excellent example of such a program is Hewlett

---

[2] Source: **http://www.deakin.edu.au/edu/MSEE/GENII/NSPT/NSPThomePage.html**

Packard's E-mail Mentor Program (**http://mentor.external.hp.com**), a project that uses the Internet to link students and teachers to mentors by e-mail.

One of the goals of the program is to give students more control over their education. David Neils, one of the coordinators of the project, explains how it works:

> Carol, a local 4th grader, has an interest in frogs. Now normally this interest would not be taken seriously at school or home. Carol is matched up with a mentor who treats her interest in frogs as important as o-rings on the space shuttle. Carol is pointed to places on the Internet where frogs are discussed and is now in communication with a leading scientist in Europe who is conducting acid rain research using....yes, frogs. Carol benefits in several ways from this experience. First and foremost, she realizes that her interests are important. This is a huge self-esteem builder. Second, her concept of education goes far beyond the four walls of the classroom. She also is now aware that resources, like her HP mentor, are available in the community.[3]

Access to On-Line Educational Resources

The Internet is perhaps the world's largest database of electronic information. Since everyone can be a publisher on the Internet, there is an incredibly diverse amount of

---

[3] From an e-mail message by David Neils. Posted to the KIDSPHERE mailing list (**kidsphere@vms.cis. pitt.edu**), February 28, 1995.

information on-line. Access to such information can only enrich the learning experiences of young people. Consider how the following sites, just a small sampling of what is available on the Internet, can play a direct role in the educational process:

➤ VolcanoWorld (**http://volcano.und.nodak.edu**) is a site that provides information on recent eruptions, the history and causes of volcanoes, images of various volcanoes, lesson plans for teachers involving education about volcanoes, a slide show of volcanoes, a tour of several volcanoes in Hawaii, pointers to other resource sites from around the Internet about volcanoes, and countless other sources of information about volcanoes. Enough information about volcanoes to keep a class busy for quite some time!

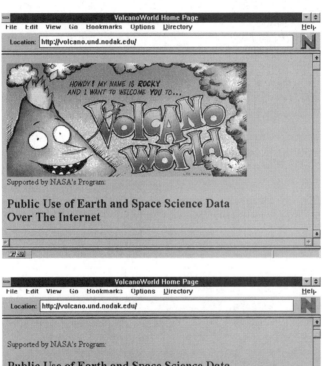

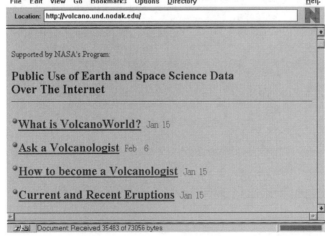

The volcano site, sponsored by NASA and the University of North Dakota, also has the support and involvement of volcano specialists at the University of Hawaii, the Mount St. Helens Volcano Monument project, and staff of the Hawaii Volcanoes National Park. In addition, the volcanologists sponsoring this site encourage Internet users to send them volcano questions by e-mail. The following message appears on the site:

> We have tried to think of all sorts of neat things to show you about volcanoes, but we aren't smart enough to think of everything. So, this is your chance to ask us anything about volcanoes that you want. The people who will answer are Scott Rowland in Hawaii, Chuck Wood in North Dakota, and if we get stumped, other volcano experts from around the world.

Some 55,000 people from around the world visited the volcano site in the month of January 1995 alone.

➤ The DNA to Dinosaurs Exhibit and Javanese Mask Collection (**http://rs6000.bvis.uic.edu:80/museum/**) is sponsored by The Field Museum of National History in Chicago, Illinois, an educational institution "concerned with the diversity and relationships in nature and among cultures." This site includes a humorous tour of the era of dinosaurs and includes, for those with a high-speed link to the Internet, sound and video.

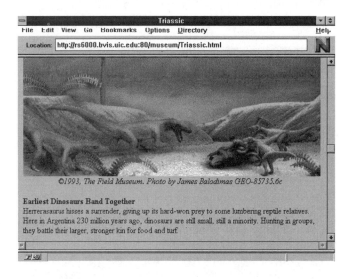

©1993, The Field Museum. Photo by James Balodimas GEO-85735.6c

Earliest Dinosaurs Band Together
Herrerasaurus hisses a surrender, giving up its hard-won prey to some lumbering reptile relatives. Here in Argentina 230 million years ago, dinosaurs are still small, still a minority. Hunting in groups, they battle their larger, stronger kin for food and turf.

The tour includes some humor that kids will appreciate, such as newspapers in which dinosaurs report their view of the world.

CityNet (**http://www.city.net**) provides quick and easy access to cities, towns, states, and countries. Want to take the classroom to Berlin? Information about the world becomes very accessible to the classroom, since it takes about 20 seconds to travel to any city or town on earth that has an Internet site available through CityNet. The listings for Europe, for example, show the following countries:

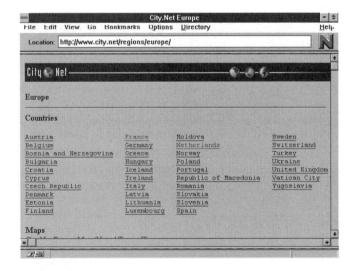

As we noted in the chapter about government involvement on the Internet, many municipalities and governments have established information sites that contain local and regional information. This is certainly the case with Berlin, as we can see below (**http://www.chemie.fu-berlin.de/adressen/berlin.html**):

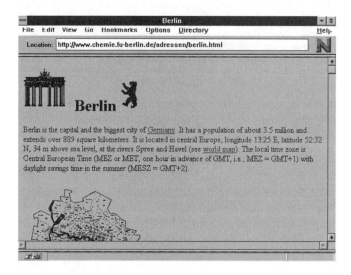

This opens up a whole new world, so to speak, for geography, history, and social study classes.

The range of information available on the Internet is stunning, and as the Internet continues to grow, it becomes even more diversified. Certainly, since the information is relevant and up-to-date, it often exceeds the utility of print information sources found in our schools.

Opportunities for Tutorial-Based Learning

Many organizations around the world are taking their Internet information sites to new heights, making them more than just a place full of information to read. Some Internet sites provide a degree of interactivity on-line, by allowing students to interactively participate in some type of activity. The Interactive Frog Dissection Tutorial (**http://curry.edschool.virginia.edu/~insttech/frog/home.html**) deserves an award for one of the most innovative projects on the Internet: at this site you can interactively dissect a frog (although we won't show you the details).

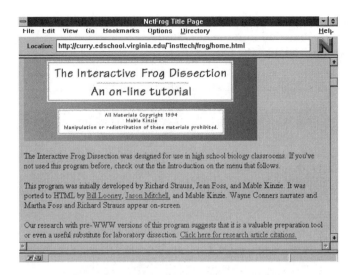

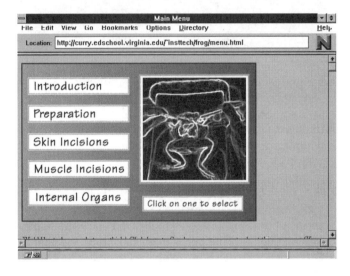

For the very young, there is the Theodore Tugboat site, maintained in Halifax, Nova Scotia, which is tied into the popular children's TV show of the same name (**http://www.cochran.com/tt.html**):

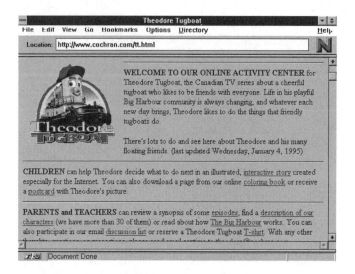

This site permits a young child to participate in an interactive "story" with Theodore Tugboat and to determine what he should do next.

Interactivity is somewhat limited on the Internet today, because many schools access the Internet over slow modem links. However, as faster access speeds become available, interactivity will become more of a reality on the Internet, providing even more innovative tools for the classroom.

Creativity, Design, Critical Thinking, and Good Writing Skills

Students can quickly become veteran publishers on the Internet. After all, the Internet is all about electronic publishing and represents a dramatic change in how we view what information is and where it has come from. Certainly, much of this change will occur within the Internet's World Wide Web service as organizations and people begin to publish information electronically.

Schools that encourage children to become directly involved in World Wide Web publishing can use the project as an opportunity to educate children about the key issues involved in creating information that is readable, accessible, and understandable. Once information is published on the World Wide Web, people from around the world can come and visit the site. These visitors can be encouraged to leave comments, suggestions, or feedback, which can then be reviewed in the classroom. Visitor feedback can be used as a basis for class discussion. Children get instant, global, and direct feedback on their efforts and can respond appropriately. What a fantastic way to get feedback on your literary and artistic skills!

We have seen a number of schools establish World Wide Web pages on the Internet. An excellent effort in Canada can be found at Rockingham School in Halifax, Nova Scotia (**http://www.cfn.cs.dal.ca/Education/RockinghamSch/ Rockingham.html**):

What is notable about Rockingham's World Wide Web site is that they are encouraging all of their students to publish their own home pages, such as this home page, created by 13-year-old student Ken Roberts:

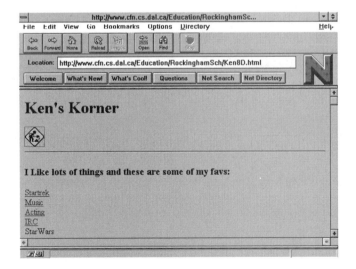

An underlying goal of any Internet project at the public or high school level is to help students understand how the technology is going to impact their lives in the future. This isn't a concept that you can teach effectively out of a textbook; this type of learning occurs best through hands-on interaction with the technology.

Student Ken Roberts, whose home page you saw above, epitomizes the type of learning that is occurring at Rockingham High School:

> I started into the world of the Internet in January of last year (94). My teacher, Michael McCormick, got me started. In the beginning, I was an IRC nut but as time went on I figured out how to use Mosaic and Netscape. A few years ago the word computer meant, to me, a thing to play games on. Now it means things that are in my future.[4]

On-Line Research Skills (Knowledge Networking)

One problem with the Internet is that there is simply too much information. Although Internet indices and searching tools are slowly emerging, anyone who gets involved with the Internet experiences frustration with the absolutely mind-boggling types of information available and the disorganized manner in which this information is presented. Yet, when someone experiences this frustration, he/she also realizes that the Internet is like the national debt—it just keeps growing and growing. There are hundreds of new information sites every day and thousands of new participants appearing on the Internet every week from around the world.

There is no doubt that the Internet is a valuable information resource. And there is no doubt that learning to navigate around this network in order to discover and find information is becoming an increasingly important skill. As business continues to get involved with the Internet, employers will increasingly look for job candidates who know how to undertake electronic research. Teaching the Internet in our schools, colleges, and universities will allow students to develop these critical on-line research skills.

Electronic research isn't just about learning to access and to navigate the World Wide Web. It is also about the ability to find and use electronic mailing lists and USENET newsgroups in order to track down experts on particular topics, to track issues related to that topic, or to participate in an on-line discussion group about the topic. It is also the ability to analyze information and to think about what the information presents in order to prepare a conclusion. The ability to synthesize *knowledge* from vast amounts of *information* will be a key skill, perhaps more important than merely learning how to navigate the network.

---

[4] Source: **http://www.cfn.cs.dal.ca/Education/RockinghamSch/Ken8D.html**

Job and Career Information

The Internet provides students with new avenues through which they can identify job opportunities and make contact with potential employers. Many organizations supplement their on-campus recruitment activities by placing job advertisements on the Internet. Because the Internet is populated with university and college students, it is an ideal place for employers to announce job openings. In addition to the many general job announcement forums on the Internet, students can follow specialized discussion groups in their field of interest, where job openings are frequently announced. For example, a student interested in working in a museum environment could monitor any museum discussion groups on the Internet for any job announcements. While many of these job postings are targeted at people with experience in the industry, they provide valuable insight into the qualifications and skills that organizations are looking for. The Internet is also an invaluable learning tool for students who have chosen a specific career path and want to learn more about their field of study. Discussion groups, for example, allow students to observe experts conversing in the "language" of their chosen discipline.

Use by Educational Organizations

At the institutional level, the Internet provides a number of advantages and opportunities, including

- cost reduction;
- streamlined admissions;
- institutional promotion;
- interdepartmental communication;
- virtual classrooms;
- distance education;
- student services;
- alumni services.

Cost Reduction

Schools, colleges, and universities across Canada are distributing academic calendars, exam schedules, telephone directories, and countless other documents via the Internet. With more and more universities providing Internet access to all their students, the electronic distribution of university documents is becoming an attractive and cost-effective way for universities to disseminate information to current and prospective students. Most universities in Canada now maintain World Wide Web servers where they distribute degree and program information. In many universities individual departments maintain their own World Wide Web servers. For example, the University of Calgary's Department of Archaeology (**http://www.ucalgary.ca/ UofC/faculties/SS/ARKY/gradprog.html**) distributes a wide variety of information about its programs and research activities via its World Wide Web server.

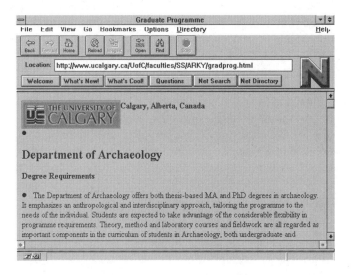

Distribution of such information via the Internet results in significant cost savings, efficiencies in the distribution process, and new methods of reaching potential students—in effect, helping the university to market its services (discussed below).

Streamlined Admissions

A number of Canadian universities now accept admission inquiries by Internet e-mail. Acadia University, for example, welcomes admissions inquiries to the e-mail address **admissions.office@acadiau.ca**. By doing so, Acadia University is making it easier and more convenient for prospective students to get information about the university and its programs. In fact, many schools across the country are moving away from paper-based registration systems. Several universities have already implemented touch-tone registration systems that permit students to register for their courses using an automated telephone system. The next step in the evolution of automated registration systems may be the Internet! Glenlawn Collegiate in Winnipeg, Manitoba (**http://www.mbnet.mb.ca:80/~bspeer/index.html**), has developed an Internet-based registration system that permits students to register for their courses.

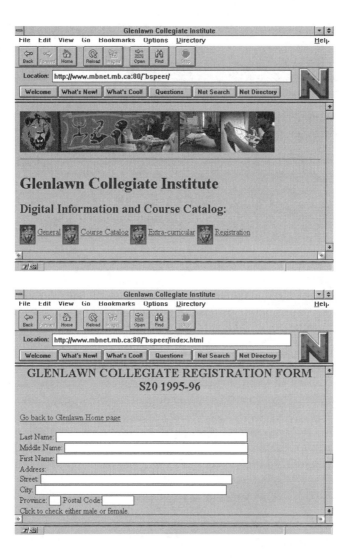

For students, speed and convenience are the primary benefits. For the school, the benefits include reduced processing costs and increased efficiency.

Institutional Promotion

With thousands of university and high school students on the Internet, universities are discovering that the Internet is a great place to market their institutions to prospective students. An excellent example is Mount Allison University in Sackville, New Brunswick (**http://www.mta.ca**). Visitors to Mount Allison's World Wide Web site can take a visual tour of the campus, read information about degree and certificate programs and study-abroad opportunities, find out about computer resources, and read about residence life, athletics, scholarships and bursaries, admissions, and university services.

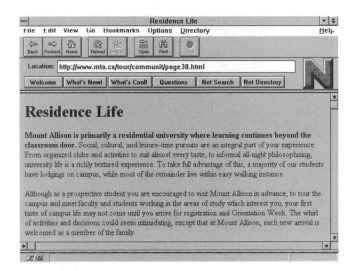

Interdepartmental Communication

Universities and colleges can be big and impersonal places, not just for students, but also for teaching assistants, researchers, professors, and other support staff. In recognition of this, several universities have turned to the Internet in an attempt to encourage more dialogue on campus.

The University of Windsor in Windsor, Ontario, is an excellent example of a university that is using the Internet to improve communications and promote the sharing of information between teaching faculty. The University sponsors an Internet-based mailing list called the teaching and learning network, which allows lecturers and professors to share teaching strategies with each other (**http://www.cs.uwindsor.ca/tlnet/welcome.html**).

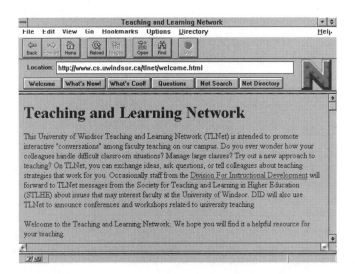

Virtual Classrooms

A number of universities are experimenting with Internet technologies known as "MUDs" (MUltiuser Dimensions), "MOOs" (Objected Oriented MUDs), and "MUSEs" (MUltiuser Simulation Environments). These technologies allow people in different locations to interact with each other in real time (i.e., "live"), using their computer keyboards. They can be used by professors to hold office hours, lectures, seminars, and to run group projects. Students can use them to hold study sessions and interact with their classmates. Pennsylvania State University, for example, is one of several universities that has set up a campus MOO for instructional and educational purposes. It can be accessed by telnet at **ccat.sas.upenn.eduport** 7777.

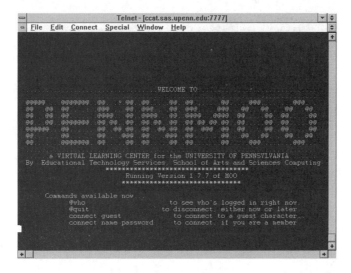

At least one class at Penn State is using the MOO to supplement lectures, and a group of Latin students uses it to practise their Latin skills with each other.

The University of Windsor in Windsor, Ontario, also runs its own MOO, called The University of MOO, and operates with the following mandate:

> The University of MOO (U-MOO for short) is a virtual world designed for the interaction of different people with different views. It is a place for meeting new people who may (or may not) share your opinion on certain issues, and discussing different issues (whether global or local) in a manner that promotes educational discussion.[5]

---

[5] Source: http://www.cs.uwindsor.ca/meta-index/general/interactive/u_of_moo.html

The University of Moo can be accessed via its World Wide Web server at **http://www.cs.uwindsor.ca/meta-index/general/interactive/u_of_moo.html**.

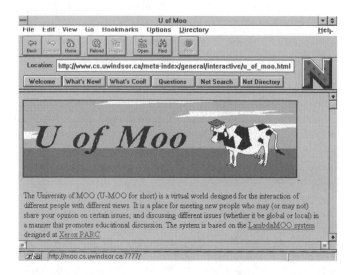

At the University College of the Cariboo in Kamloops, British Columbia, a number of philosophy courses have been taught on that college's MUD, which can be accessed by telnet at **maud.cariboo.bc.ca** port 4000.

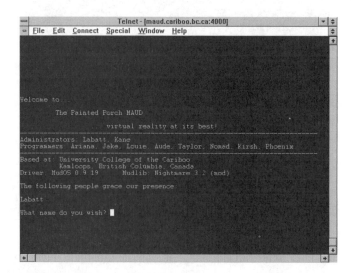

In addition to participants being able to interact with other participants, MOOs, MUSEs, and MUDs allow participants to interact with inanimate objects and build their own worlds for others to explore.

> An 8-year old student designed and built an Oz adventure based on the movie version of that classic children's story, while a 9-year-old contributor returned from his family's summer vacation and created a working model of Yellowstone National Park, complete with erupting geysers and a wandering moose. [...] The first student to earn a grade for a MUSE project was Erica Cleary, a graduate student in Environmental Studies at Boston University, who built the Amazon Rain Forest on MicroMUSE as her term project. Since then she has expanded her work to include a Mayan Temple, complete with working astronomical calendar. Elsewhere, one can find a sailing cruise to the Virgin Islands which recreates the real-life adventure of the player who created it.[6]

These virtual environments offer numerous educational benefits, some of which are summarized below.

> For younger participants, text-based virtual realities foster literacy skills: reading, writing, and composition, and technical skills such as keyboarding and spelling. For adolescent students, social interaction skills, interpersonal skills, and personality development emerge as primary activities. College students who are not computer science majors enjoy the opportunity of gaining some computer literacy and trying their hand at creating their own contributions to the cyberspace worlds, usually with the helpful guidance of friendly users with more experience.[7]

---

[6] "THE MUSE As An Educational Medium," Barry Kort, Consulting Scientist, Educational Technology Research, BBN Labs, Cambridge, Massachusetts (**http://copernicus.bbn.com:70/0/testbed/muse**).

[7] "THE MUSE As An Educational Medium," Barry Kort, Consulting Scientist, Educational Technology Research, BBN Labs, Cambridge, Massachusetts (**http://copernicus.bbn.com:70/0/testbed/muse**).

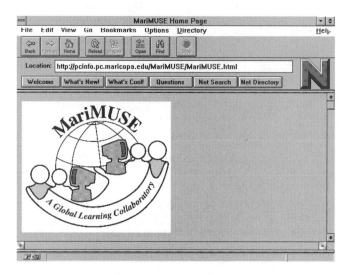

In Phoenix, Arizona, a collaboration between a local elementary school and Phoenix College provides over 300 elementary students and their teachers with access to a local MUSE based at the College (**http://pcinfo.pc.maricopa.edu/MariMUSE/ MariMUSE.html**). Jim Walters, Director of the MariMUSE program, notes that the MUSE is particularly helpful for kids who don't learn well in "traditional spaces."

> Teachers are viewing unstructured MUSE time as a learn-ing activity. As they observe the interactions that take place, they see the value of this in building reading, vo-cabulary, and writing skills. So, in addition to the cur-riculum projects, unstructured time on MUSE is a part of the daily routine in many classrooms.[8]

MariMUSE has been an invaluable personal empowerment tool for children at the local elementary school, where poverty, crime, drug abuse, and family problems are prevalent in the neighborhood. Many lack the role models and mentors that are so crit-ical to children in their elementary school years. A MUSE, therefore, can be a tremen-dous confidence builder for these children.

---

[8] Electronic mail message from Jim Walters.

[The MUSE] empowers students who have formerly been treated assecond-class citizens. Formerly powerless students:

- interact with adults as well as other children who treat them with respect and listen to their ideas;
- create friendships across generations that build a sense of worth and competence;
- create whatever they can imagine, be whomever they want to be, explore, and meet people who treat them with respect and value their thoughts and abilities;
- make something important (a computer) respond to their commands. At-risk students who have very little control over what happens to them in real life experience a virtual world where they can make things happen.
- are empowered to create and affect their environment in a way that builds perceived competence and a sense of worth.[9]

Distance Education

The Internet is making major advances in the field of distance education. Internet tools such as e-mail, discussion groups, MUDs, MUSEs, MOOs, and the World Wide Web allow students to complete courses electronically, without ever having to set foot in a classroom.

Of particular note is the Ontario Police College Distance Education Program, based at Seneca College in Ontario. Police officers access Seneca College's computer conferencing facilities through the Internet, where they complete 14-week professional development credit courses in numerous subjects, including psychology and sociology. The bulk of the course is done on-line through the Internet, with only the final exam and initial training session done in a traditional classroom setting. Sixty percent of the course mark is based on the quality of the student's on-line participation and interaction with other students.

This arrangement has worked out well for the police forces in the province, where budget cuts preclude the police colleges from taking officers off the streets for classes. Because the on-line classes have no formal meeting times, officers can complete course requirements at their convenience, as long as they meet weekly deadlines.

---

[9] Electronic mail message from Jim Walters.

This flexibility is especially important for police forces where officers are engaged in shift work. Dr. Larry Hopperton (**hopperto@phobos.senecac.on.ca**), Seneca College's Computer Conferencing Coordinator, says that computer-based conferencing forces students to become actively involved in their own learning, since "they can't sit at the back of the class and say nothing." Computer conferencing also takes the pressure out of the classroom environment, a benefit that is especially important to students where English is the second language. When they are on-line, students can take their time to formulate their thoughts and questions.

At Athabasca University in Alberta, the Internet is used extensively in the Bachelor of Science Computing and Information Systems program. Students submit their exercises through the Internet by e-mail. Tutoring also occurs by e-mail, and the university is experimenting with a MUD where students can interact with each other in real time through the Internet.

A number of other educational organizations across Canada, including the University of Quebec's Tele-université project, the Ontario Institute for Studies in Education, and British Columbia's Open University, are experimenting with the Internet as a "telelearning" course-delivery mechanism. Other universities are planning distance education courses using the Internet. For example, the University of Saskatchewan has just started developing courses for delivery on the Internet and hopes to have some courses ready for the 1996–97 school year.

Student Services

At least one Canadian university has found an innovative use for the Internet in the delivery of student services. The Counseling Centre at Acadia University in Wolfville, Nova Scotia, realized that many of the students were too embarrassed to ask personal questions in person or over the telephone. To address this problem, they set up a service called *Ask Uncle Albert* on the university's World Wide Web server. Students can fill out an on-line form and send their questions anonymously to the Counseling Centre. The answers to the questions are posted publicly so that everyone on campus can benefit from the question and the response (**http://admin.acadiau.ca/counsel/albert.html**).

Alumni Services

One of the challenges for any university, college, or high school is keeping track of alumni. After graduation many alumni move out of town, out of the province, or even out of the country. Over time, alumni lose touch with the institution *and* fellow classmates. With Internet access expanding to virtually every country on earth, universities and colleges are finding it to be an invaluable tool for keeping alumni up-to-date with programs, events, and fund-raising activities, regardless of where in the world they may be currently living. While this particular application of the Internet is not yet big in Canada, many U.S. universities and colleges have set up World Wide Web servers that are dedicated to alumni affairs.

For example, Brigham Young University has set up an Alumni Web server (**http://www.byu.edu/adm1/alumni/alumni.htm**) that includes information on class reunions, alumni activities, regional alumni chapters, alumni publications, employment opportunities, and much more.

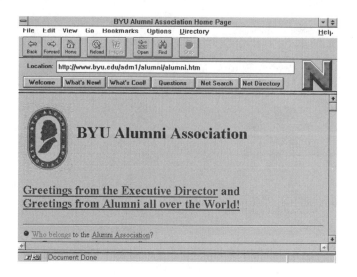

To help alumni keep in touch with one another, institutions are creating areas on their World Wide Web sites that contain the e-mail addresses of alumni or links to alumni who have World Wide Web pages elsewhere on the Internet. Princeton University (**http://www.princeton.edu:80/~alco**) is one example; it has organized its alumni Web pages by decade, thus allowing alumni to quickly locate former classmates.

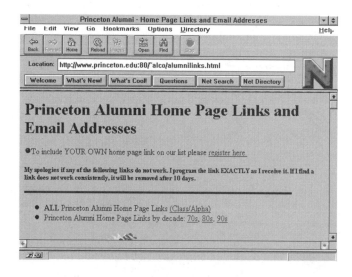

One of the more creative uses of the Internet in this area can be found at Brigham Young University (**http://www.byu.edu/adm1/alumni/alumni.htm**).

BYU's Alumni Affairs Department has a place on its World Wide Web site where alumni are encouraged to "post" their favorite memories of BYU. Here's the message that appears on their site:

> The Internet can help bring to life one of our BYU slogans, "The World is our Campus." We want to hear from you and provide a forum to communicate with other alumni, so we have this section. Alumni using browsers with forms support can leave messages for everyone to read. Use this form to
>
> • Tell about your favorite memories of BYU. This would be especially fun if you wrote of places that don't exist anymore, such as the diamond deck or food like cherry chews. Tell us what your BYU education meant over the years.
>
> • Let others know about what's new in your life. Promotion? Got married? New baby? Your baby got married?
>
> • Find someone you've lost touch with. Does anybody remember good ol' whats-'is-face? I wonder where he is now?

Proving that many alumni *are* hooked into the Internet, messages soon began to accumulate as former students discovered the BYU site on the World Wide Web. Here's a typical message:

> I have been working at Intel in Santa Clara, CA for about 3 years now as a statistician. It would be a kick to hear from any Statistics alumni or old friends who have now learned to surf the net. Send me a message and we can reminisce and exchange info on favorite Web sites to visit [.....]

In addition to the activities described above, many universities, colleges, and high schools are running Internet mailing lists that unite alumni and allow them to communicate with one another. Some educational organizations (e.g., California Institute of Technology, **http://alumni.caltech.edu**) are providing Internet accounts to their alumni as an incentive for them to create their own World Wide Web pages. Given the impact of alumni fund-raising on dwindling educational budgets, anything that encourages alumni interaction with the school community will be a positive initiative!

Use by Educators

The Internet is not just a tool for students. Indeed, some of the most active participants on the Internet are teachers and educators who use the Internet to electronically link up with other educators to share lesson plans and ideas for teaching, to pursue or advance a particular policy or political agenda, or just to discuss the experience of teaching. Specifically, the Internet can be used

- to improve communication between teachers;
- to improve the use of the Internet in the classroom;
- to improve communication between teachers and their students;
- to find lesson plans and curriculum resources;
- to advance educational or policy reform;
- to distribute course materials;
- to keep oneself up-to-date with developments in one's field of expertise.

We will look at each of these strategies below.

Improved Communication Between Teachers

In the same way that the Internet is used to link students around the world, it is also used to link teachers worldwide so that they can share experiences, ideas, success stories, and thoughts on controversial topics or special issues. An example is found on the World Wide Web, at a site called The Geometry Forum (**http://forum.swarthmore.edu**), where math teachers and educators can meet other geometry and math educators from around the world.

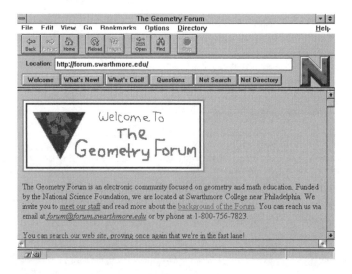

In addition to its on-line activities, The Geometry Forum sponsors conferences that explore how the Internet's resources can be used to improve math instruction. The sponsors also distribute a quarterly newsletter to keep math educators informed about developments in "on-line" math education.

Electronic mailing lists offer another opportunity for teacher-to-teacher communication. There are literally dozens of electronic mailing lists throughout the Internet that any teacher can join. By joining such a list, teachers can have close contact with their peers from around the world to discuss issues in their particular area of study or track what other teachers are doing with respect to education in a particular subject area.

The chemistry education discussion group, based at the University of West Florida, unites over 1,000 chemistry experts from over 37 countries around the world, including Australia, Belgium, Egypt, Hong Kong, Italy, Portugal, Saudi Arabia, and Venezuela. A typical question shows how the mailing list is being used.

Date: Sun, 29 Jan 1995 10:01:41 -0600
Reply-To: Chemistry Education Discussion List
<CHEMED-L@UWF.BITNET>
Sender: Chemistry Education Discussion List
<CHEMED-L@UWF.BITNET>
From: "Marcia A. Petrus" <mpetrus@NCSA.UIUC.EDU>
Subject: new course

Greetings! Briefly, here's my situation. A grant I applied for was recently funded resulting in a new science course to be offered at my high school. The course will be offered to seniors who have completed bio, chem, and physics. The focus of the course will be independent research science in which the student selects a topic and performs research (call it a science fair project, if you wish). Ethics, application of the scientific method, data analysis and the research paper will be the main points. It will be team taught by a language arts teacher, a statistics/sociology teacher, and myself. (Yes, the administration has approved all three of us in one room simultaneously!) Since the wheel has already been invented, I'm looking for blueprints. If you know of such a course offered at some high school or have some pearls of wisdom to offer, please contact me. I'm looking for tips, hints, warnings, and advice. I promise I'll mention the names of those who reply during my acceptance speech for the Nobel Prize I'll win for pulling this off. Thanks, in advance!

The Canadian SchoolNet initiative, mentioned earlier in the chapter, supports a number of discussion groups that permit ongoing interactive discussion between educators concerning the use of the Internet in the classroom and other current issues. Why do teachers use such forums? To find answers to questions, to seek ideas, or to get feedback from their peers on particular issues.

The Geometry Forum, discussed earlier, runs a number of Internet discussion lists that unite geometry educators. For example, there are discussion groups for geometry research, K-12 geometry education, college-level geometry, geometry puzzles, and geometry software. The opportunity for teachers to reach out to their peers for guidance on a difficult issue is perhaps one of the most overwhelming uses of the Internet. One recent message posted to a teacher educational mailing list is particularly telling:

> Date: Mon, 06 Feb 1995 21:53:58 -0500 (EST)
> From: KELLER004@WCSUB.CTSTATEU.EDU
> Subject: Teenage depression
>
> Am new to this list, am interested in hearing about any innovative classroom methods re. the above topic. Any input would be valued greatly..Thanks, Ken Keller

Informed teachers are better teachers, and in this way the Internet will help to improve the quality of teaching within Canada, and will help educators deal with the ongoing challenges and changes in the classroom.

Teaching The Internet In the Classroom

If you are looking for new ways of applying the Internet in the classroom, what better place to go than the Internet itself! Educators around the world are eager to share their Internet success stories with other educators through Internet discussion lists. There are several discussion lists dedicated to the discussion and/or announcement of new educational resources on the Internet. For example, the University of New Brunswick hosts an excellent discussion list called Educational Resources (**EDRES-L@unb.ca**),[10] which reviews new Internet resources of interest to educators. Here is an example of a review which appeared on the list:

> Site: KIDLINK Gopher
> Date: Sun,19 Feb 1995
> Reviewer: Peter Gadd <l8lj@unb.ca>

---

[10] To subscribe, send an e-mail message to **listserv@unb.ca** with the following message: **subscribe EDRES-L YourFirstName YourLastName**

Subject: Student use of the Internet
Audience: Middle School (10 to 15 year olds specifically)
Type: Gopher

URL: gopher://kids.duq.edu:70/
Gopher: gopher kids.ccit.duq.edu 70
Telnet: 165.190.8.35 login-gopher
WWW: http:/kidlink.ccit.duq.edu:70/

Description

The KIDLINK project is a multifaceted site that has as its objective helping youth 10 to 15 years old get involved in a global dialogue through e-mail and other telecommunication exchanges. Teachers who get involved are directed on how to help children use the Internet on a one-to-one or small group basis at a personal level. This is done through what appears to be a well thought-out manner to ensure quality, ongoing communication, using etiquette. There are a variety of activities that users can choose from: KIDLINK CAFE, where children can connect with "key-pals," join discussion groups or get information on specific questions with and from children in other countries. There are activities titled KIDLINK CHAT, KIDFORUM, KIDPROJ and KIDART. There are lesson plans on computer ethics, specifically on the importance of copyrights. KIDLINK seems to anticipate all manner of questions and problems for teachers and students. There is a myriad of means to get answers and directions; from how to get gopher client software to how to e-mail to individuals who have volunteered to help other educators get started with KIDLINK Project. There is a list of approximately 200 educators who are using KIDLINK. Each is profiled in terms of their purposes for using KIDLINK, the communications resources they have and what their personal related interests are. These personal insights and the diversity of situations should put teachers new to educational uses of the Internet at ease. There is a lot of information at this site about KIDLINK, and some of it is available in eight languages other than English. All the material seems very readable and therefore appropriate to the targeted age group. The KIDLINK Project is operated by the non-profit KIDLINK SOCIETY that anyone can join for a fee. It is controlled by an international board of directors with its headquarters in Norway.

Evaluation

This site is one that I have become very excited about. If educators are looking for justification of Internet use in education then they should look here. The stated objectives of the KIDLINK Project are educationally sound and appropriate. There is a lot of material to go through to get started, but it seems there is a choice regarding the particular use educators require. Participation in this project would mean an ongoing commitment but the first tentative steps could be small. There seems to be no end to the advice and information available. This project is emphatic about the age of the children they are targeting. They do have available, though, a list of resources on the children's use of the Internet for those who fall outside their 10-15 year old age bracket. This project has been going on for 5 years and involves presently about 40 countries. They claim a participation rate of about 30,000 students since the program started. The list of teachers using the program indicates that users in the United States out-number all other users 3-1. This might compromise the international component of the program somewhat, but international use does seem to be growing. Regardless of the apparent American domination in users, there is an obvious emphasis on communication between cultures even to the point of encouraging use of foreign languages. Educators who use the KIDLINK Project state a variety of purposes: "expanding horizons," "promoting peace," "learning about other cultures," "exchanging points of view," "opportunities for creative writing" and "students around the world can see that they are more similar than dissimilar." If these important objectives of education can be encouraged through KIDLINK, then this program would be worthwhile. I think it is.

The result of these mailing lists is that educators wanting to use the Internet in the classroom need look no further than the network itself for ideas on where to start.

In addition to mailing lists, there are many World Wide Web sites that provide support to educators who want to use the Internet as a teaching tool. One example is Cornell University's Learning Technologies Center (**http://ltc.cit.cornell.edu/InstWWW.html**).

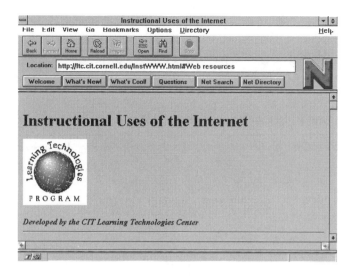

Instructional Uses of the Internet

Developed by the CIT Learning Technologies Center

Improved Communication Between Teachers and Students

For many students, trying to ask the professor a question after a lecture is an exercise in futility. Those of us who have been students in a large university or college are familiar with the scene at the end of a class—the professor is mobbed by dozens of students, all of whom are fighting to get answers to their questions. The mob spills out into the hallway, and if you're lucky, you will get 20 seconds of the professor's time. If you have another class, you don't have the time to wait around for 10 or 15 minutes, and you leave, disappointed, with your questions unanswered.

Inconvenient office hours make the situation more difficult for students to see the professor outside of class hours. If you show up, you may find there is a long lineup outside the professor's door. The experience is equally frustrating for the professor.

The Internet has proven itself to be a method of improving communication between the student and teacher. To improve the flow of information and to better manage communication with their students and classes, educators are using Internet e-mail and electronic mailing lists with great results. For example, Internet e-mail can be used to encourage discussion about course subjects outside of class hours. Entire classes or smaller tutorial groups can be placed on electronic mailing lists where students can communicate not only with their professors or teaching assistants, but with their own classmates as well.

While some educators might be hesitant about encouraging the use of a medium that allows students to send them questions at any time of the day or night, the interaction can become a rewarding experience if expectations and guidelines are established up front.

> Learning to manage e-mail relations with students is much like learning, as a junior instructor or assistant professor, how to manage relations with live students. We all work out a mix of formality/informality, intimacy/distance, seriousness/play in our personal styles. The challenge comes when the new medium seems to shift the balance toward informality, intimacy, and play. Wisdom lies in knowing how to ease gently to a new balance. Luckily, it is easy to ignore the inappropriate message, and your students will soon enough get a sense of how often you can be expected to respond, at what hours, and in what tone.
>
> James J. O'Donnell
> University of Pennsylvania
> **http://ccat.sas.upenn.edu/jod/teachdemo/badger.html**

Another use of the technology is found when the Internet is used to encourage "shy" students to interact with the class or educator. Even in a small classroom situation some students have difficulty speaking up in the presence of their peers. Many students are uncomfortable asking questions in a large lecture hall, where there can sometimes be 400–500 other people in the room.

Electronic mail can be a less intimidating environment, as Professor O'Donnell explains:

> A colleague using Internet in a secondary school course in Florida reports that in one semester's course he had 500 messages on a particular list, no fewer than 132 of them from a single student who never spoke up once in class. There's something pathological about such an extreme case, but it's a good reminder that people find their voices in different ways, and this can be one way to create a space in which the balance shifts and different voices are more clearly heard than in the liveware classroom.
>
> James J. O'Donnell
> University of Pennsylvania
> **http://ccat.sas.upenn.edu/jod/teachdemo/daunting.html**

Lesson Plans and Curriculum Resources for Teachers

Earlier we discussed how the Internet can be used by an educational institution to make available information about the school curriculum. Of course, the next logical step is to use the Internet to make available lesson plans and other classroom resources.

Some educators or parents might be concerned that using the Internet to access lesson plans means a shirking of responsibility by the teacher. But this is clearly not the case. Many organizations outside of the educational stream provide lesson plans on the Internet in order to encourage education in a particular topic or area of interest. NASA, for example, is very involved in encouraging science and space study throughout schools and has published a number of resources on the Internet (**http://spacelink.msfc.nasa.gov**) to help teachers teach space sciences in the classroom.

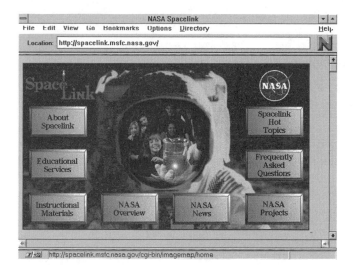

Why does NASA do this? Because NASA wants to improve the quality of space science education in schools throughout the United States and the world. With so many teachers and educators now using the Internet, it provides an excellent vehicle for distributing lesson plans and other NASA educational resources.

A Canadian example is found with the Ontario Milk Marketing Board (**http://www.milk.org**). The OMMB sponsors a program called the Dairy Education Program, which consists of a number of teaching modules related to the dairy industry, including nutrition, technology, career opportunities, and milk processing and production.

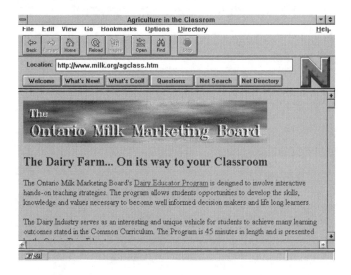

To raise awareness of its dairy education program, the OMMB promotes its education program on the Internet and provides outlines of the various teaching modules on its World Wide Web site, as illustrated below:

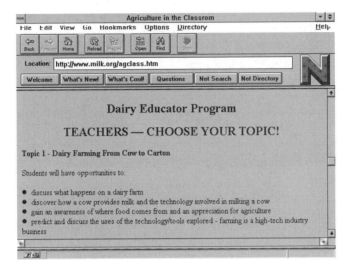

These are just two examples. The Internet is full of teaching ideas for educators to discover.

Educational Reform

Educational budgets in Canada are under stress, and because of our national financial situation, the situation is unlikely to change in the near future. As a result, educators everywhere, including teachers and school boards, are seeking new and innovative ways of dealing with cutbacks and ensuring the delivery of high quality education in a time of decreasing resources.

The Internet is being used by proactive educators around the world to raise awareness of issues related to education and its reform and to build support for their cause. One particularly good example is Engines for Education (**http://www. ils.nwu.edu/~e_for_e**), a site on the Internet at Northwestern University that discusses what is wrong with the education system and how to reform it.

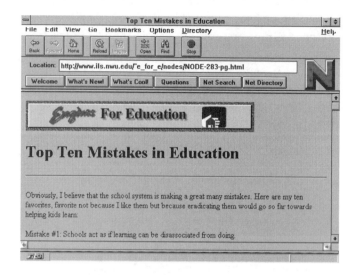

In addition to archives of policy and discussion material, there is ongoing debate within the educational community of proposed initiatives. Here is an example of a teacher seeking input on a recent matter:

From joinkids@hamlet.phyast.pitt.edu Thu Feb 2
17:32:39 1995
Date: Wed, 1 Feb 1995 17:12:06 EST
From: KIDSPHERE Mailing List
<kidsphere@vms.cis.pitt.edu>
Subject: Alternate Calendars (High School Level)

Date: Wed, 01 Feb 1995 15:26:47 -0500 (EST)
From: Jim Maines LEBANON HS
<jmaines@ideanet.doe.state.in.us>
Subject: Alternate Calendars (High School Level)

Our school board is leaning toward an alternate calendar based on 45 days on and 15 days off and wants to make this calendar a K-12 proposition. Can any of you help me find out the history of this kind of move in any of your schools at the high school level? I think we will be the only school in our state on this schedule. Let me know if you have had any experience with this calendar, good or bad.

Thank you for your time. It IS appreciated.

Jim Maines
Lebanon High School
Lebanon, IN 46052

Internet discussion groups are a popular means of stimulating discussion about educational reform. In the United States people interested in educational reform use the Internet to debate and to assess policy initiatives and share ideas and experiences. For example, in the State of Washington, the Office of the Superintendent of Public Instruction runs an Internet mailing list that brings together parents, educators, researchers, and other community members interested in discussing issues related to educational improvement.

In Canada, similar Internet initiatives are under way. Humber College in Ontario hosts an Internet discussion group on educational reform (**edref-1@admin. humberc.on.ca**),[11] with the following mandate:

> This new discussion group on education in Canada has been formed to bring together parents, teachers, administrators, trustees and others interested in educational reform across Canada. The listserv will focus discussion on educational matters at all levels (i.e., primary, secondary, and post-secondary). Topics may include liberal education, charter schools, International Baccalaureate, outcomes based education, whole language, values education, the Ontario Royal Commission on Learning, transfer payments, testing, human rights policy initiatives, education and the constitution, reform in other countries and equity policies. In addition to these topics, subscribers may want to announce to the discussion group the publication of articles and books, bibliographies and the opening of schools or centres.[12]

Delivery of Course Materials

With more and more universities and colleges providing their students with Internet access, the Internet is becoming a vehicle of choice for distributing course syllabi, assignments, lecture notes, exam answers, class calendars, and other documents to students. For example, the Internet is used for this purpose by the Financial Management class taught at the Graduate School of Business Administration, at the University of Texas. Professor Garvin places copies of all class materials on the Internet, including the course syllabus, a list of optional readings, class scores, problem sets, and exams (**http://riskweb.bus.utexas.edu/courses.html**).

---

[11] To subscribe, send an e-mail message to **listserv@admin.humberc.on.ca** with the following message: **subscribe edref-1 YourFirstName YourLastName**

[12] Electronic mail message to one of the authors from one of the owners of the discussion group.

This type of electronic distribution cuts down on paper consumption and creates a permanent depository for class documents that can be accessed by students at any time of the day or night, both on and off campus. Because the documents are electronically archived, students don't have to request additional copies of class handouts that they may have lost.

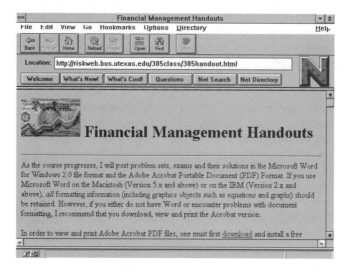

Professor Garvin also uses the Internet to encourage feedback about his classes: He has placed a form on the Internet which students fill out at the end of each lecture.

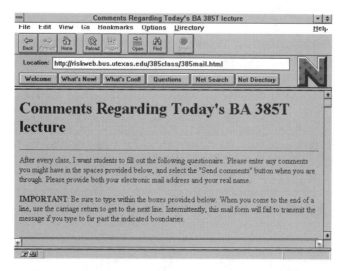

Many educators put course materials on the Internet with the understanding and hope that they will be used not just by students, but also by other educators around the world. This spirit of sharing makes the Internet a wonderful source of teaching materials. For example, the instructor of the Architectural History course at the University of Virginia has placed copies of his slides on the Internet, and he encourages their use by scholars worldwide (**http://www.lib.virginia.edu/dic/ colls/arh102/index.html**).

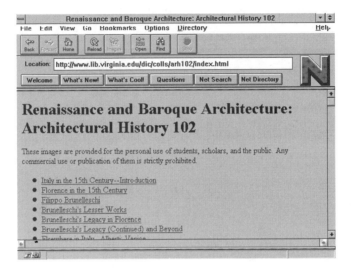

Keeping Up-to-Date

In the 1990s a challenge for every educator is keeping up-to-date with his/her field of expertise. It is crucial that educators be on top of developments in their field so that their lectures, classroom activities, and exercises reflect the most up-to-date knowledge available at that time. Internet discussion groups play a critical role in this process by allowing educators and researchers to quickly disseminate and share information with colleagues around the world. Identifying relevant discussion lists and monitoring them on a regular basis helps to keep educators in tune with developments in a particular field and is perhaps one of the key benefits of the Internet.

Use by Parents

Quite often parents decide to join the Internet because their children are on it, and they don't want to be left behind. (The authors have observed that this happens most frequently when kids go to college and automatically get an Internet account, and tell Mom and Dad to join the network. We suspect, but cannot prove, that this is done so that they can request money by e-mail!)

There are several reasons why a parent would want to use the Internet in an educational context: primarily, to help the child to learn (call it the "new math of the 1990s"), but also to be kept up-to-date on issues affecting the education of their children. Another reason why parents should be involved is to help to "streetproof their children for the information highway," an issue we discuss at the end of this chapter. First, we will address four important reasons why parents use the Internet:

- to keep informed of school events and activities;
- to keep informed of issues affecting their child's education;
- to seek advice from other parents and educators;
- to keep up with their children.

Keeping Informed of School Events and Activities

Many schools across Canada and the United States have established World Wide Web sites containing information about their schools. Saint John High School in New Brunswick (**http://www.mi.net/sjhs.html**) is one notable example. Their Internet-based information service includes information about school programs, facilities, and extracurricular activities.

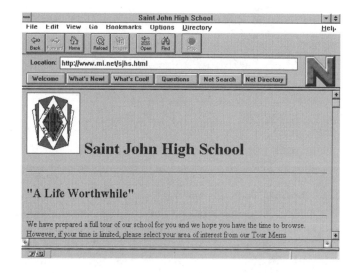

Another example is the Langley School District in British Columbia (**http:// haven.uniserve.com/~rstare/welcome.html**), which has created an Internet Info-Centre to distribute information about the school district to the community.

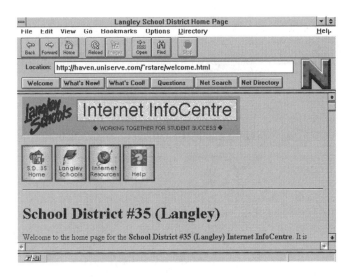

Keeping Informed of Issues Affecting Their Child's Education

In addition to school-specific resources, parents can use the Internet to access general information about parenting, education, and other related topics. For example, The National Parent Information Network (**http://www.prairienet.org/htmls/eric/npin/npinhome.html**) is an Internet-based service that offers parents information about the educational system and provides materials related to the use of the Internet in the classroom. NPIN also summarizes how parents can become more involved in their child's education.

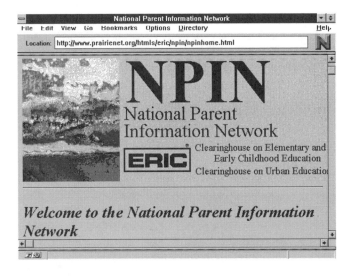

In addition, taxpayers need to be kept more informed about current activities and issues in the system. As a result, we are seeing a number of provincial ministries of education and other educational bodies establishing information resources on the Internet. An example is the British Columbia Ministry of Education (**http://www.etc.bc.ca**), which provides a number of documents on the Internet especially for parents, including reports and press releases.

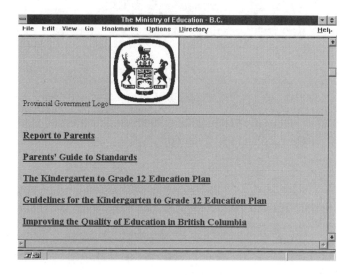

Advice From Other Parents and Educators

Some parents choose to be actively involved in debates concerning educational issues by participating in many of the Internet's mailing lists and discussion groups. In this way, parents can reach out to other parents and educators for advice and support when it is needed. For example, the following message appeared on an Internet USENET discussion group called **misc.kids**:

> I've been researching preschools for my son to attend this fall. When he starts preschool he will be 2 years 9 months.
>
> One of the preschools I'm very interested in is asking me to decide what level class to put him in—in the Bunny class, there will be 2 – 2 yr 9 month olds. This is considered the toddler class. It has a better adult-to-child ratio than the Teddy Bear class. In the Teddy Bear class there will be some 2 year 9 month olds but mostly 3 and up. This is considered the start of "real" preschool.

My question is this—what are the advantages and disadvantages of being the youngest/oldest in your class at this age? Should I build up his confidence at the risk of possible boredom by putting him in the Bunny class as the oldest kid? Or should I go for the challenge by putting him in the class with the older kids?

Any suggestions on criteria I should use to evaluate?

Just as educators use the Internet to locate lesson plans and teaching ideas, parents can use the Internet to find resources that will help their children learn. The following question appeared on an Internet service at Swarthmore College called *Ask Dr. Math* (**http://olmo.swarthmore.edu/dr-math/dr-math.html**):

Hi there. My daughter is in 3rd grade. Up until this year, math was her favorite subject. Even though she struggled with it, she enjoyed it, and we were happy with her consistent C grades. This year is awful—she can't seem to grasp the basics of subtraction and is in a panic because she's getting F's in everything, even things she could do last year. As someone who loves math, what can you suggest for someone who used to love it, but is fast developing a phobia? Any kind of fun exercises she could do, books I could get, or even computer programs. I'll try anything. Thanks for any help.

Keeping Up with Their Children

Parents will discover that even if they don't get involved in the Internet and computer-based communication technologies, their children will. Parents, dazzled by how quickly their children are becoming computer-literate, are often motivated to learn the technology for themselves. Consider this story, which isn't specifically about the Internet, but is about the use of computer-based communications:

I would like to begin by telling a simple story about computer on-line information technology and how it personally impacted my daily life. After an evening of snowfall, I, like many other Boston parents, wanted to know whether my son's school was closed or delayed. Since I am a man with certain old media habits, I turned on the radio. I then waited for the school closing announcements.

I had to wait until the announcer decided it was time to run down the school closing list. While I was waiting, my 15-year-old son went to his personal computer and logged onto his school's local area network. He read the electronic bulletin board announcement that his school was closed and went back to bed. Meanwhile, old dad was in the kitchen waiting for the radio announcer to run through the list.

One half hour later I finally had my information, and my son had that much additional sleep. My experience is a simple example of interactive computer networks providing information that the consumer wants and needs in his or her daily life. I learned my lesson.

What happened to me that snowy morning was I changed my way of getting information. I decided that I would abandon the old familiar radio channel of information, because the new interactive computer channel gave me what I needed, when I needed it.

Damn the consumers—Full speed ahead:
The electronic highway
Executive Speeches, April/May 1994

What About the Controversy?

Any educator dealing with the Internet is familiar with some of the controversial issues that surround the use of the network. First, many people within the school system express concern that use of the Internet won't help at all in the educational system, that it will do little in the ongoing effort to provide the best level of education to children.

Second, if you listen to what some of the press reports have to say about the Internet, it can seem to be a terrible, dark and dismal place. "The Internet is a hangout for cyberweebs and geeks and nerds," reports TV. "The Internet is full of computer hackers," say some radio reports. "The Internet — oh, that's the thing that's full of pornography and other terrible, terrible stuff," say newspaper and magazine articles. Both these issues are important, and it is important that each be addressed.

Isn't It All a Waste of Time?

As might be expected, negative comments about the Internet's educational potential often come from people who have never been on the network and do not understand the opportunities that it offers to the educational process. Other comments come from people who believe that exposing children to a massive information source such as the Internet does little to help them learn.

There are some valid points that are made in the controversy. Sometimes the concern is expressed by educators who actually use and understand the Internet. Consider the following message, posted to one Internet discussion group:

From ised-l-error@adler.mec.mass.edu Sun Jan 29
13:26:50 1995
Date: Sun, 29 Jan 1995 12:59:53 -0500 (EST)
From: BarrettM@cybernetics.net (CDS)
Subject: Infobahn Road Kill

"Most of the stuff on the information highway is road kill," wrote John Updike, as quoted by George Gurley of the *Kansas City Star*. Neil Postman, author of the best selling book *Amusing Ourselves To Death* has recently written a new book titled *Technopoly* in which he criticizes our current love affair with technology.

With some caveats I think Updike and Postman have legitimate concerns. Now I don't want to be misunderstood. I'm enthusiastic about technology. Our whole school is "wired" and our students love the computers. I also believe that students must be skilled in using modern technologies if they are to be prepared for the challenges of the 21st century.

Nevertheless, the biggest threat to democratic society, our civil liberties, and our economy is not technological illiteracy; its ethical, moral, cultural, and functional illiteracy. Those addicted to instantaneous bits of information, void of context and logical progression are ill equipped for rational dialog and analysis. Such rational discourse and analysis is essential for the maintenance of a civil and literate culture. Modern technology cannot substitute for a thorough understanding of the Federalist Papers, Moby Dick, Edwards, Plato, Aristotle, the Bible, William James, etc, etc...

Compounding the problem is that many teachers appear to be designing their lessons around the Internet and other computer technologies rather than determining clear objectives and then using communication technologies IF and WHERE appropriate. I wonder if seminaring, Socratic dialog, extensive writing and reading, rhetoric, classes in logic, etc would not better prepare students to be positive contributors to an advanced literate culture than surfing the Net looking for pen pals? Have you read some of the inane "communication" between Net pen pals? Could it be that the often heard complaint that pen pals do not "write" back is symptomatic of a bigger problem: students who have nothing to say? Trivia will only sustain a conversation for so long. Could it also be due to the fact that students are ill-mannered and egocentric? I see no reason to believe that surfing the Net will contribute to civility and sustainable substantive conversation.

What I'm suggesting is that viewing the Internet, or any technology, as an educational panacea is misguided. Furthermore, for teachers to devote too much time to Hypertext, multimedia activities, etc, may be to miseducate students. Rather than actually educating students, it has the potential for further addicting students to amusement and instantaneous gratification. After all, using the computer is fun; I certainly enjoy it. I wonder, though, if student time would not be better spent reading historical biographies, good literature, or engaging in well-informed conversation?

In short, after "surfing" the Net for months I've concluded that the essential value of this technology is as a retrieval system much like a library and for certain types of collaborative activities such as those provided by this Listserv and some projects like Kidlink. Beyond such limited activities, I'm concerned that time spent with Hypertext, CD ROM, etc., is a colossal waste of time.

As I prepare to teach a college course on the use of computer technologies in the classroom, I'd like your reaction to my comments. Now back to my books.......

Regards,
Barrett L. Mosbacker <BarrettM@cybernetics.net>
Headmaster
Covenant Day School
800 Fullwood Ln.
Matthews, NC 28105 USA

The points made by Mr. Mosbacker are valid, and the comment that the Internet is not a panacea is particularly important.

Educators who get involved with the Internet need to keep in mind that the Internet is just a tool. The abilities to analyze information, to think, to question, to summarize, and to debate — in effect, to learn — will continue to be critical skills. Educators need to teach children how to use the Internet as a tool and not lose sight of these key skills. This point was recognized in the same forum, by a follow-up response to the message:

From ised-l-error@adler.mec.mass.edu Sun Jan 29 22:09:45 1995
Date: Sun, 29 Jan 1995 21:55:40 -0500
From: mnelson@thayer.org (Mark Nelson)
Subject: Re: Infobahn Road Kill

To add on to Will's thought — a mediocre teacher will most likely fall into this trap. A good teacher will incorporate the material and resources that can be accessed with technology into a learning environment that develops the habits of mind in his/her students that lead to the ability to gather, synthesize, and analyze ideas — and then form reasonable conclusions.

In brief, if we wish to be worthy of the title "teacher" we must rise to the challenge of skillfully incorporating new opportunities that advances in information technologies present as we strive to develop our students' ability to think. However, we mustn't lose sight of the fact that the output from an information technology invented several centuries ago, the printing press, will continue to be a valuable tool in our bag of tricks.

Mark Nelson
Director of Information Technology
Thayer Academy
745 Washington Street
Braintree, MA. 02184

"Technophobia is far more dangerous than technology"
—Woodie Flowers

Hence, learning to use the Internet is not an end in itself but just a beginning.

What About Pornography?

If you listen to some of the news stories, you are led to believe that the Internet is being used by teenage boys, who, when they are not breaking into NORAD defence computers around the world, are staring at their Internet screens all day long looking at pictures of naked women. The media hypes the issue of "pornography on the Internet" relentlessly, and some say, without much intelligent thought and analysis.

We should put these issues into perspective. Millions of people sign onto the Internet every day to research information. Global knowledge access and global networking through the Internet have become fundamental to the regular working lives of millions of people. Research and knowledge exchange through the Internet are transforming science, business, education, and government. People have discovered that the Internet provides them with new and significant knowledge capabilities. Frankly, many of the people who have discovered the richness of the Internet are insulted by the focus in the press on the "sensationalism" angle and the fears that the media stirs up about the network.

Information Distribution and the Internet

But to be fair, educators must become familiar with certain issues related to the Internet and must understand some of the negative aspects of the network. The reality of the Internet is that it is making national borders irrelevant when it comes to the flow of information. The Internet permits millions of people around the world to communicate on any topic they like without any censorship or control. The result is that the Internet is used for the distribution of information that is of questionable taste, which could be considered to be in violation of the laws of Canada, or which may run against current accepted "community standards." But to get at this information, an individual has to consciously decide to retrieve it. It does not automatically drop into the laps of kids signing onto the Internet.

Upon hearing such things, some respond by saying that the Internet should be censored and controlled. Yet, they fail to appreciate that the reality of the design of the Internet is such that it regards "censorship" as a hardware failure, and routes the information around the point of failure. They fail to appreciate that content on the Internet is technically impossible to "control" in the same way that we can't tell people what to say and what not to say on their telephones. Censorship and control don't work on the Internet. Trying to control the flow of information on the Internet is like trying to dam a river with wire mesh. Clearly, we need to take another approach to this issue.

The Role of Educators and Parents

Parents and educators need to get involved in helping children use the Internet — if they don't, children might discover some of its more controversial aspects of the network without the benefit of parental guidance and wisdom. Kids might learn to be "awed" by the information resources found on the Internet, without learning how to analyze and interpret the information, and to question the validity of what they read. The reality is that the Internet is not going to go away, so parents and educators have to learn to deal not only with its positive aspects, but also with its darker and more critical sides.

In an article on the issue of pornography on the Internet, Howard Rheingold, author of "The Virtual Community," wrote that "sooner or later, your children will be exposed to everything you have shielded them from, and then all they will have left to deal with these shocking sights and sounds is the moral fiber you helped them cultivate." Later he says: "teach your children to be politely but firmly skeptical about anything they see or hear on the Net. Teach them to have no fear of rejecting images or communications that repel or frighten them. Teach them to have a strong sense of their own personal boundaries, of their right to defend those boundaries physically and socially."

Like it or not, the Internet is here, and it is changing the way information is distributed in our world. If we choose not to streetproof our children for the information highway, they will learn about it on their own. Would you rather that they discover the Internet's dark side on their own, without the benefit of the insight of educators and parents?

The realization that we are now in a wired world where both useful and tasteless information is available through any computer on the planet is a starting point for parents and educators. The next step is to keep in mind that, as parents, we not only need to help educate our children, but we also must shape their morals and teach them a sense of right and wrong, including the right and wrong aspects of the Internet. We can do this by monitoring and guiding the use of the Internet by our kids.

Parents and educators should teach children

> to always treat information retrieved with a critical eye and not to believe everything they read;

> to never communicate via e-mail with a stranger unless the communication has been approved by an adult;

> that just as there are some areas in society that a child shouldn't venture into, there are some areas on the Internet that are off limits;

> that the Internet, while used for extremely positive purposes by many, is also abused by some for "bad" purposes.

In all cases, parents and educators must take an active role in the use of the Internet by children. Indeed, we are beginning to see more Internet usage occur at the family level, as seen in this message sent to the authors of this book :

I use it for business and education and fun. My wife uses it for recipes and exploring women's issues. My kids log in to SchoolNet for research and fun. They use TeenTalk, KidsCafe, etc. and one of the boys actually communicates with his high school teacher from time to time. Sometimes there is a lineup to use the computer just like lining up for the bathroom in the morning (everyone is in a hurry). They play games, look for the latest news on their favorite rock bands, print stuff from the Net for other kids' school projects (graphics as well).....We will grow with the Internet as will a lot of people. I hope everyone will get on the Net and communicate. Who knows, this planet may become a better place to live. (targa@cml.com)

The Economic Impact of the Internet

Access to the Internet is probably one of the least expensive educational investments that a family or school can make. Yet, for many schools the Internet is out of reach, due to budget constraints or the lack of computer equipment in the classroom. Consider the resources that Canada's SchoolNet project makes available directly from its on-line site to any educator or student who receives access:

➤ *Platform to the Internet.* SchoolNet provides its users with a user-friendly front-end interface to Internet, the largest network in the world.

➤ *Resource manual.* The 100 best science, engineering, and technology-related resources currently available on the Internet are compiled for ease of searchability.

➤ *SchoolNet white pages.* A white pages directory of e-mail addresses of all SchoolNet participants is compiled to improve communication among users.

➤ *Electronic newsfeeds.* SchoolNet participants have access to direct, up-to-the-minute electronic newsfeeds from *The Globe and Mail* (classroom edition) and Southam News. Users are able to find out about world events, prior to watching/hearing about them on the evening news.

➤ *Announcements.* In order to keep SchoolNet users updated and in touch, announcements regarding national events and programs, revisions to the SchoolNet project, winners of SchoolNet competitions/projects, calls for participants for network projects, and new technologies are posted on SchoolNet.

➤ *Scavenger hunts.* SchoolNet participants are invited to compete in the SchoolNet scavenger hunts, searching for information on the Internet, while learning how to navigate the Net and use various Internet commands.

➤ *Government program information.* Participants have access to a wealth of government information. For example, SchoolNet carries E-STAT, the educational statistics program of Statistics Canada and the Job Futures information package of Human Resources and Labor Canada. Electronic application forms are also available for suitable government programs. Users also have access to directories compiled by the federal government for commercial/non-commercial educational resources, training services, newly released reports and newsletters.

➤ *Career selection guide.* Job Future provides students and teachers with a career selection guide listing educational requirements, salary expectations, and projected demand for a chosen field of work.

➤ *Electronic innovators.* SchoolNet has over 400 scientists and engineers on-line from around the world to provide expert advice to teachers and students through discussion news-groups, as school advisors and as in-class visitors.

➤ *Networking projects.* SchoolNet users have the opportunity to participate in collaborative projects with students across the country and around the world. Students from different classrooms can work as a team to solve problems, conduct experiments, hold e-mail debates, challenge each other in network resource hunts, etc. The projects also provide a forum for students to work with professional researchers in solving real-life problems.

➤ *Electronic libraries.* Students and teachers have access to libraries across Canada and around the globe. On-line search capabilities permit access to the most updated catalogues of published works on a wide array of topics. Some electronic systems allow books to be reserved electronically as well.

➤ *Electronic databases.* Using SchoolNet, teachers and students can access databases worldwide and obtain relevant files. Databases of software, educational resources, research work/data, worldwide Internet e-mail addresses, and Internet manuals/guides are just some of the data users will be able to access.

➤ *Links to national and international electronic educational networks.* SchoolNet provides a link to other educational networks and initiatives in other countries allowing teachers and students to go beyond the classroom walls.

➤ *Internet search facilities.* Search facilities let SchoolNet users find information on any topic on the Internet. These sophisticated search tools are important research methods at universities, and students need to be exposed to them in high school.

➤ *Discussion groups for students.* SchoolNet students can participate in discussion groups with other students from all over the world in an electronic forum—sharing information, ideas and establishing electronic pen pals.

➤ *Discussion groups for teachers.* These discussion groups will work towards ending the professional isolation that many teachers currently experience by providing them with a forum to exchange ideas and experiences with other teachers from across Canada and other countries. Discussion issues include curriculum development, teaching and learning methods, educational resources, upcoming conferences, training programs, etc.

➤ *SchoolNet archives.* A library of resources specific to Canadian SchoolNet schools and educational networking groups will be available electronically. This will include educational software, reports/manuals, pictures/graphics, and database files. New breakthroughs such as the teaching of courses on the Internet and designing "global classrooms" with voice and video interfaces over the Internet are currently being investigated as well as electronic conferencing (PARTICIPATE) and multi-user simulated environments (MOOs).

Schoolnet is a step in the right direction. However, to make real progress, educators across Canada must understand the role of the Internet in the classroom, they must take time to learn how it can be used to maximum benefit, and they must become familiar with the advantages that it offers.

In addition to SchoolNet, we are seeing many other positive developments in Canada to encourage schools to plug into the Internet. These include telephone company and cable company projects, community initiatives, efforts by volunteers, and government activities. Any teacher getting involved with the Internet faces a wealth of resources.

However, the sad reality for many schools is that the cost for a link to the Internet is often still far out of reach—a situation that we should clearly try to fix. Educators, government officials, business people—everyone—should encourage and foster an environment in Canada that makes it easier for schools to plug into the Internet. This can be done by encouraging greater government support for the Internet through tax initiatives and by creating a telecommunications environment that supports Internet investment. Business can get involved by providing funding to the educational community, by providing schools with access to the Internet through corporate networks, and by participating in ask-an-expert programs.

There is an important opportunity before all Canadians when it comes to education through the Internet, and we shouldn't lose the momentum that is already under way.

Not-for-Profit Organizations and Associations on the Internet

> Association executives need to figure out how to use technology to support members and enhance the value of their work. If members are information conduits, technology can replace them, so we need to use technology to help members expand their capacity.
>
> Almon R. "Bud" Smith,
> Executive Vice President,
> National Association of Realtors, Chicago
>
> The shape of change to come,
> *Association Management,* January 1995

> Several people involved in the network said it is not unusual at UN meetings for an official delegate to make statements in the morning and take the heat from lobbyists halfway around the world in the afternoon after the text of his or her transgressions has been posted on an electronic bulletin board.
>
> Chretien blasted for summit absence — Canadian social activists at UN meeting use alternative computer network to spread criticism of PM
>
> *Globe & Mail,* March 7, 1995

*I*n the same way that businesses use the Internet as a means of marketing goods and services, not-for-profit organizations also look to the Internet to help with ongoing public relations, to distribute information to the general public, to coordinate member activities, and to assist with fund-raising and volunteer recruitment.

In this chapter we will address several types of not-for-profit organizations, such as charities, associations of members (e.g., professional associations), activist organizations, and other not-for-profit organizations. Many of these groups find themselves under increasing strain as a result of budgetary cutbacks and other funding pressures. Charities, for example, are one group that is finding it increasingly difficult to maintain levels of service because of government and corporate cutbacks and changes in personal spending habits. Noted the *Financial Post* in an article on

STRATEGIC USES OF THE INTERNET WITHIN NON-FOR-PROFIT ORGANIZATIONS AND ASSOCIATIONS

(1) Information Research

(2) Public Relations and Marketing
- Increases awareness of objectives and activities
- Strengthens base of support
- Promotes products and services
- Promotes an activity
- Encourages advocacy

(3) Outreach Activities
- Fund-raising
- Volunteer recruitment
- Membership recruitment
- Disaster coordination

(4) Service Delivery
- External dissemination of information
- Internal dissemination of information

(5) Other Activities
- Recruitment
- Research
- Topic tracking

December 9, 1994: "it's a sign of the recent bad economic times that despite the tax advantages of being good Samaritans, charities say Canadians aren't giving as much money as they did in previous years."

Consequently, many associations and not-for-profit organizations, regardless of their function or goals, are finding it necessary to do more with less, both in the provision of services to their members and in the production and distribution of information. These economic realities are forcing not-for-profit organizations and associations to find new and innovative ways of fulfilling their organizational goals. This chapter will examine a number of ways in which not-for-profit organizations and associations can use the Internet to support their activities.

The Role of Not-For-Profit Organizations and Associations

The role of many not-for-profit organizations and associations is not necessarily the sale and distribution of goods and services. Rather, it is the distribution and communication of information related to the primary goals and objectives of the organization.

We observed in the chapter about business on the Internet that "we are still a society of consumers learning about electronic shopping in a world of suppliers still learning how to sell electronically," and that this would limit the success of marketing through the Internet for a period of time. This is not the case for not-for-profit organizations and associations, who aren't necessarily in the business of marketing products, but are in the business of providing and distributing information. Since the Internet is already very much an information culture, not-for-profit organizations and associations will find it easy to use the network to achieve many of their strategic objectives related to the communication of information; they don't need to wait for customers to appear, since the distribution of information is already possible through the Internet.

What Does the Internet Offer Not-for-Profit Organizations and Associations?

Whether a not-for-profit organization is a charity, an activist organization, or an association of members, the Internet provides a means for quick, efficient, and low-cost distribution of information, thus helping to achieve one of the primary goals of most of these types of organizations. Examine the following press release from Friends of the Earth, a large, global environmental activist group:

FRIENDS OF THE EARTH ON THE GLOBAL INTERNET

EMBARGOED UNTIL: 00:01 THURSDAY 15 DECEMBER 1994

LEADING UK ENVIRONMENTAL GROUP ON THE GLOBAL INTERNET

Friends of the Earth [1] has just launched a new public access environmental information service on the global Internet "Information Superhighway" [2].

The service — dubbed "FoEnet" — is the first on-line system of any environmental pressure group in the world to make extensive use of colour multimedia pictures, "enviro-maps" and text. Access to FoEnet is available through the Internet World Wide Web and is open to anyone with a connection to the Internet.

The FoEnet service aims to provide electronic versions of many of FoE's popular publications, as well as details of environmental campaigns across England, Wales and Northern Ireland. Environmental information available on-line right now includes: the Green Guide to Christmas, High Street Banks and Rainforest Destruction, Fighting Motorway Madness, environmental information projects and maps, information for schools, FoE press releases, FoE's trading catalogue, membership details, FoE International, how to find your nearest FoE local group using your postcode, and advice on how the public can take practical environmental action. FoEnet also provides links to other useful environmental services around the globe.

Richard Weatherley, Friends of the Earth's IT Manager, said: "The Internet is an important communications medium for the 1990s and beyond. It differs from the traditional media because it provides new opportunities for public empowerment and participation in the emerging global information culture. It offers Friends of the Earth further scope to confront government and industry with the facts about the environment — and potential solutions. Through FoEnet, we are making environmental information available in an interactive way to an important new audience."

The service is aimed at government, industry, the research community, schools and the public, in the UK and internationally. There are details of research into threats to "protected" wildlife sites, landfill sites leaking toxic chemicals to groundwater, river quality, acid rain and the dirtiest power stations in England and Wales, and the illegal mahogany trade.

FoE hopes to extend the information service in the future. New facilities may include keyword document retrieval, short video clips, and context-sensitive environmental maps which display local environmental information at the touch of a "mouse" button.

Friends of the Earth's FoEnet World Wide Web service can be found on the Internet at the following address: **http://www.foe.co.uk**

Friends of the Earth acknowledges the support of Sun Microsystems (UK) Ltd. who kindly donated a SPARCserver 20 computer for use in the FoEnet project.

…

NOTES TO EDITORS:

[1] Friends of the Earth is the largest international network of environmental groups in the world, represented in over 52 countries world-wide. Friends of the Earth (England, Wales and Northern Ireland) is one of the UK's most influential national environmental pressure groups, with more than 200,000 supporters and a network of 250 local groups. Friends of the Earth campaigns on more issues than any other environmental group in the UK. Friends of the Earth has achieved great success with the banning of CFCs, the removal of pesticides and nitrate from drinking water, the cancellation of new nuclear power stations, the exposing of health-threatening traffic pollution levels, the uncovering of secret toxic waste dumps, and reduction of trade in rainforest timber.

[2] The Internet is a vast collection of computer networks reaching into companies, governments, universities, schools and homes worldwide. It can be accessed in over 100 countries. The Internet is the "superhighway" which connects over 18,000 separate networks, 3 million computers and about 30 million regular users. Current estimates indicate that the Internet is now doubling in size every five months. The Internet provides a fast and reliable means of electronic communication with people around the world. It offers services such as electronic mail, file transfer, electronic information publishing, news and subject-oriented discussions.

Consider the types of information that Friends of the Earth is making available on the Internet:

> electronic versions of publications;

> details of environmental campaigns;

> press releases;

> membership information;

> information on how to find your nearest chapter of Friends of the Earth;

> information on how to become an environmental activist.

The benefits of placing this information on the Internet are numerous. For a relatively low cost, perhaps several hundred dollars a year for electronic mail and a little bit more to establish a World Wide Web site, Friends of the Earth has

> a global platform from which it can publish its views;

> a facility through which it can quickly and easily communicate with its members and other interested parties around the globe;

> a powerful tool for exposing any "environmentally unfriendly" government activities;

> access to a network through which it can collaborate with other activist groups around the world;

> a means of providing the general public with the tools and information it needs in order to become involved in the environmental movement.

Because many not-for-profit organizations are in the business of disseminating information, the success of a not-for-profit site on the Internet is not generally measured by how many sales or "leads" are generated. It is measured in more subtle ways. In this case, the primary goal of the Friends of the Earth Internet site is to empower the public and make them aware of the environmental crises facing the planet. Therefore, each time a person visits the Friends of the Earth site and becomes more sensitive to environmental issues as a result of what he/she reads there, the site pays for itself. With thousands of Internet users visiting the Friends of the Earth site every month, the site has paid for itself thousands of times.

Information Research Through the Internet

Many not-for-profit oganizations and associations, being in the "information business," want people to be aware of their information. The Internet represents a ready audience for electronic publishing of such information, given its use as a research tool, with so many people around the world using it to perform basic research. In fact, many users often discover information from a particular organization when conducting their research. Such information discovery can only help raise public awareness of an organization's mandate.

Consider, for example, how someone might go about using the Internet to search for articles or documents that relate second-hand smoke to cancer. One way to do this is to search the Lycos database, a massive database located at Carnegie Mellon University that provides a "keyword index" to several million World Wide Web pages on the Internet (**http://lycos.cs.cmu.edu**). To start the search, we tell Lycos that we are looking for documents that mention the words "second-hand smoke" and "cancer." (The entire phrase has been entered but can't be seen in the screen below.)

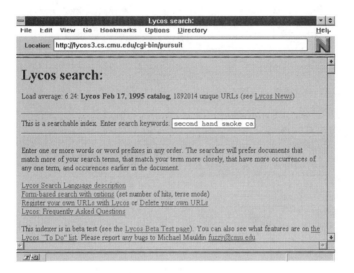

A few seconds later Lycos returns with a list of World Wide Web sites that are likely sources of information on this topic.

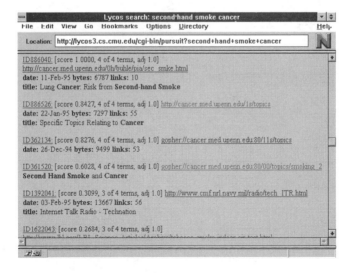

By selecting the first item, we are taken to the University of Pennsylvania, which has built a database of documents related to smoking and cancer. The database includes documents from both the federal government and the American Cancer Society.

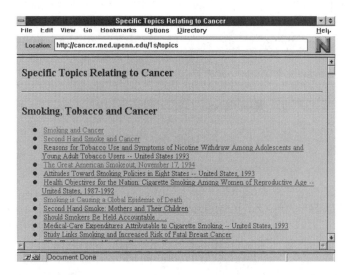

Selecting one of the items from the list, we instantly obtain a report from the American Cancer Society called the Great American Smokeout. This document includes a discussion of the risks of second-hand smoke.

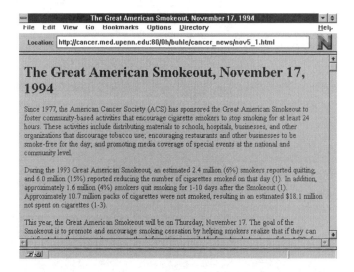

Many people perform basic research like this through the Internet. This provides not-for-profit organizations and associations with a powerful incentive to publish information through the Internet, either on their own sites or through a third party (in this case, the University of Pennsylvania).

The Internet is a true bargain for any not-for-profit organization or association, and use of it should be a cornerstone within the strategic plan of any of these organizations. In the following pages we will look at four major applications of the Internet for these types of organizations:

> public relations and marketing;

> outreach activities;

> service delivery;

> other Activities.

Public Relations and Marketing

Not-for-profit organizations, particularly smaller ones, do not have the luxury of large public relations departments, nor do they have the benefit of being able to spend a lot of money on public relations and promotional activities. Hence many look to the Internet as a cost-effective means of "getting the word out" about what they do, seeking public support for their activities, and marketing the products or services that they make available. Specifically, non-profit organizations and associations can use the Internet:

> to increase awareness of their objectives and activities;

> to strengthen their base of support;

> to promote their products and services;

> to promote an activity;

> to encourage advocacy.

Each of these strategies will be discussed below.

Awareness of Objectives and Activities

The Internet is used by many associations to spread the word about their goals, objectives, and activities. Of the literally thousands of not-for-profit organizations in Canada and the United States, many have small public profiles and are not well known to the general public. Bigger not-for-profit organizations, like the Canadian Cancer Society, obviously have more resources to carry out their missions than smaller organizations that have a much smaller budget. Yet, on the Internet all non-profit organizations have an equal voice. The Internet gives all not-for-profit organizations an equal opportunity to let the world know they exist. They can use the Internet to publish mission and vision statements, goals and objectives, and information about the activities in which they are involved.

For example, the Manitoba Animal Rights Coalition, an animal welfare group, has established an Internet site that provides on-line information about its mission and activities and summarizes information about recent efforts undertaken by the Coalition in Canada (**http://www.umanitoba.ca/arrs/marc/marc.html**). By using donated space on the World Wide Web site at the University of Manitoba, the Coalition has been able to increase public awareness of its mission.

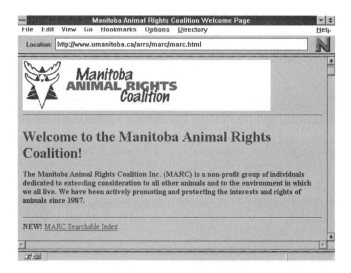

An entire section of the Coalition's World Wide Web site is devoted to public education about the organization's mandate. The site discusses MARC's contribution to the animal rights movement in key areas, such as Marine Mammal Captivity and Animal Research, as shown below:

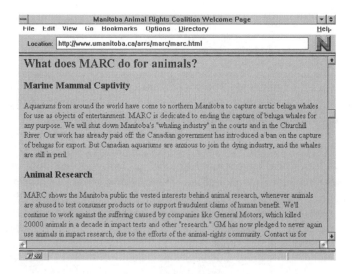

Another good example is the Canadian Centre on Substance Abuse (**http://www.ccsa.ca**), which has established a comprehensive site on the Internet with background information about the organization and an overview of the organization's purpose.

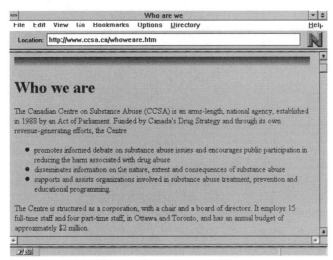

Internet users can use this site to read about specific activities in which the CCSA is involved. These range from symposiums and workshops to award ceremonies to professional development programs. Brief descriptions of each program are provided to help Internet users gain a full appreciation of the important role that CCSA plays in the prevention of substance abuse in Canada.

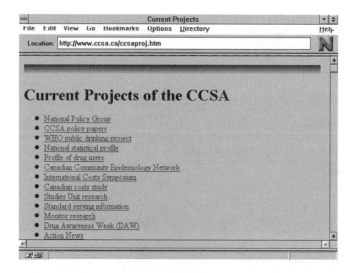

The Winnipeg-based International Institute for Sustainable Development, a not-for-profit organization sponsored with funding from the federal government and the Province of Manitoba, includes information about its mandate and programs on its World Wide Web site. For example, the following screen describes the organization's mission and its accomplishments (**http://iisd1.iisd.ca/m_about.htm**):

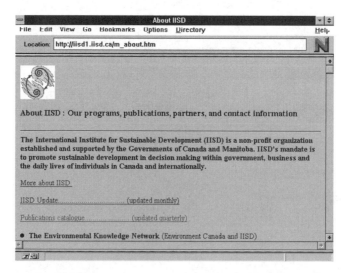

In each of these cases, not-for-profit organizations use the Internet to help the public understand their goals and objectives, an important activity for any non-profit organization or association.

Base of Support

Once a not-for-profit organization has made the public aware of its goals and objectives, the next step is to increase its public support. Not surprisingly, many such organizations do this through the Internet by educating the public about the issues in which the organization is involved.

For example, on its World Wide Web site established in Toronto, Amnesty International (**http://www.io.org/amnesty/overview.html**) provides press releases and other documents that describe human rights abuses around the world, such as this research report from an Amnesty International mission to Sudan:

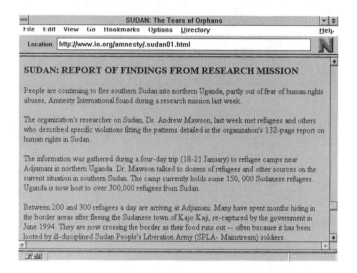

By publishing its findings on the Internet, Amnesty International hopes that more people will become aware of the situation in Sudan and lend their support to the organization's human rights campaign.

Many other Amnesty International reports are on-line as well. To build public support for its international campaign to stop human rights abuses against women, Amnesty International has made a full electronic report available on the Internet called *Human Rights are Women's Right.* While Amnesty International charges for many of its printed reports, the low cost of distributing information on the Internet means that Amnesty International can make this 135-page report available for free to Internet users. The report documents human rights abuses against women and calls on foreign governments to take action to ensure that women's civil and political rights are protected. By placing this report on its Internet site, Amnesty International hopes it can generate more public support for its lobbying efforts.

In addition to the many big-name not-for-profit organizations on the Internet such as Amnesty International and Greenpeace, the Internet contains many sites that are not run by a formal organization, but are strictly initiatives of groups of people who have united on the Internet for a common cause. An example of this is a public education initiative called HungerWeb, a U.S.-based Internet site that is dedicated to helping end world hunger. HungerWeb, based at Brown University in Providence, Rhode Island, is designed to raise awareness of world hunger and poverty (**http://www.hunger.brown.edu/hungerweb**).

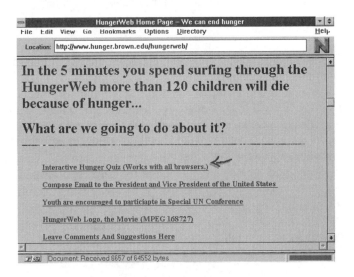

To help Internet users appreciate the urgency of the situation, HungerWeb provides an on-line, interactive quiz that tests one's knowledge about hunger and poverty in the world.

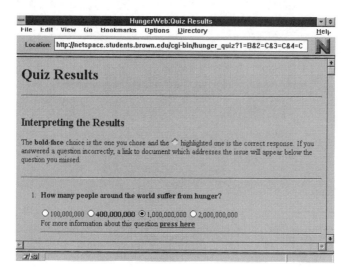

Once an individual has completed the quiz, the answers are electronically graded, and a summary of the correct responses is printed on the screen. For every mistake made in the quiz, a pointer is provided to a page of information with background facts about that particular issue. By engaging Internet users in a self-tutorial, HungerWeb is helping the public understand the issues involved in world hunger.

Free Burma is another initiative that uses the Internet to build grassroots support for its activities. Supported by volunteers who want to democratize Burma, this site (**http://www.interactivist.virtualvegas.com/freebrma/freebrma.htm**) is used to disseminate information about human rights abuses in Burma and is updated regularly with news reports from contributors around the world.

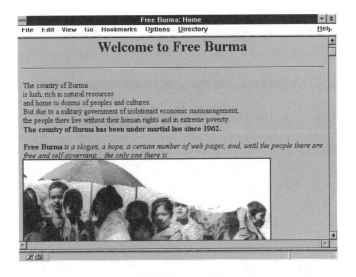

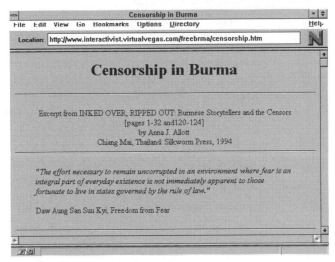

The World Wide Web's multimedia capabilities make it possible for Free Burma's organizers to add a human element to their pleas. The site displays pictures of people in Burma, such as the one above, and distributes songs recited by Burmese children. Internet users who have sound-playing capabilities on their computer can obtain the songs from the Free Burma site and listen to them on their computer.

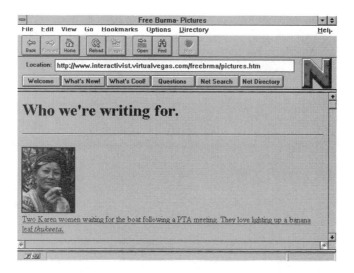

With a global audience numbering in the millions, the Internet offers not-for-profit organizations an unprecedented opportunity to increase support for their activities.

Product and Service Promotion

In the same way that businesses can market goods and services through the Internet, many not-for-profit organizations use the Internet to market and promote their products or services. For example, the Calgary Centre for the Performing Arts has established a site which includes information on upcoming concerts and special events (**http://www.ffa.ucalgary.ca/ccpa/index.html**).

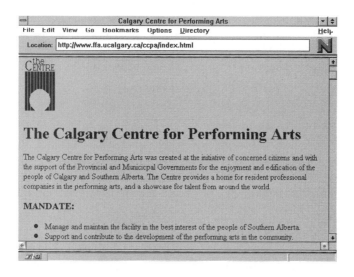

The Nova Scotia Symphony also promotes its concerts on the Internet (**http://www.nstn.ca/kiosks/sns/sns.html**). In addition to the concert descriptions, there is a section that explains the benefits of purchasing a subscription to the Symphony.

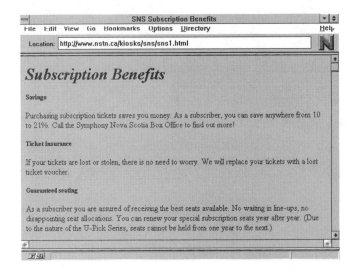

As more and more people and organizations sign onto the Internet, users will begin to rely on the Internet for up-to-date schedules from their favorite arts organizations and may perhaps even purchase a ticket on-line.

Of course, it is not just the performing arts community that actively promotes its services on the Internet. Other non-profit organizations, such as the Easter Seal Society, use the Internet to inform the public of their services. For example, one of the functions of the Ontario Easter Seal Society's World Wide Web site (**http://www.easterseals.org/CyberPlex/EasterSeals.html**) is to describe the full range of services that the organization makes available to the community.

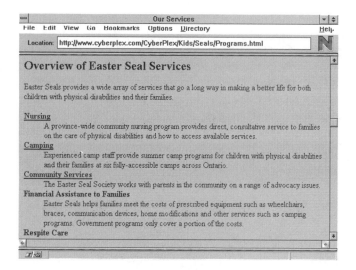

Overview of Easter Seal Services

Easter Seals provides a wide array of services that go a long way in making a better life for both children with physical disabilities and their families.

Nursing
  A province-wide community nursing program provides direct, consultative service to families on the care of physical disabilities and how to access available services.
Camping
  Experienced camp staff provide summer camp programs for children with physical disabilities and their families at six fully-accessible camps across Ontario.
Community Services
  The Easter Seal Society works with parents in the community on a range of advocacy issues.
Financial Assistance to Families
  Easter Seals helps families meet the costs of prescribed equipment such as wheelchairs, braces, communication devices, home modifications and other services such as camping programs. Government programs only cover a portion of the costs.
Respite Care

Activity Promotion

For some non-profit organizations and associations, the "product" being promoted is not a physical good or service, but an activity or discipline. This is most often the case with sport organizations and clubs/associations that are interested in furthering the growth and interest in a particular subject. For example, the Vancouver Croquet Club is interested in promoting croquet as both a professional sport and a hobby. The Club uses the Internet to stimulate interest in the sport. They have set up a World Wide Web page that provides general information about the Club and pictures from its tournaments (**http://www.wimsey.com/~dims/croquet/VCC.html**).

Another example is the Bay Area Footbag Foundation, a non-profit organization based in Santa Clara, California, that is dedicated to promoting the sport of footbag. The Foundation, which was host to the 1994 World Footbag Championships, uses the Internet to raise the profile of footbag. It has established a site on the Internet called *Footbag WorldWide*, which disseminates information about the sport, including lists of upcoming tournaments and information about footbag clubs around the world (**http://www.footbag.org**).

Another sport example is the Canadian Football League, which is interested in promoting Canadian football. Its World Wide Web site provides a detailed history of the League, profiles of each of the League's teams, and other information about the CFL (**http://www.cfl.ca**). It is hoped that this site will generate more interest in the CFL and Canadian football in general.

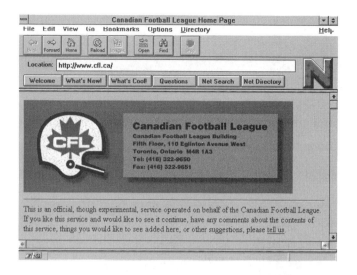

A non-sport example is the American Booksellers Association, which is interested in promoting literacy and reading. To help fulfill that mandate, the ABA has established a World Wide Web site called BookWeb, which provides a wide variety of information about books, bookstores, and authors, including bestseller lists, the latest book news, and information about authors on tour (**http://www. ambook.org/bookweb**).

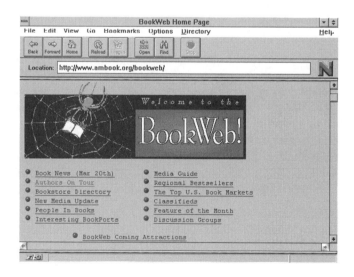

Advocacy Tool

Another goal of many not-for-profit organizations is to get people to take action on certain issues. Environmental, political, and human rights activists have long been using the Internet to mobilize people in support of a cause. For example, Amnesty International uses the Internet to expose cases of human rights abuses around the world. The organization publishes descriptions of the cases on the Internet, where they can be read by thousands, and then urges Internet users to write letters of protest to foreign governments (**http://www.io.org/amnesty/overview.html**).

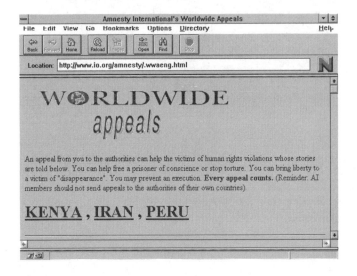

Another example of how the Internet can be used as an advocacy tool is the American Arts Alliance, which has developed an Internet site devoted almost exclusively to advocacy of the arts (**http://www.tmn.com/0h/Artswire/www/aaa/aaahome.html**). The site was created in response to U.S. government plans to reduce federal funding for the arts industry and was built with the specific objective of getting the public involved in protesting planned cutbacks. The site makes it easy for people to do so.

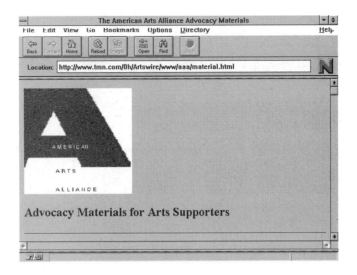

Advocacy Materials for Arts Supporters

This site is an excellent model for Canadian not-for-profit organizations that want to use the Internet for advocacy purposes. The site not only tells people *why* they should become arts advocates, but it provides them with *all the materials* they need in order to be effective advocates:

➤ a letter from the Executive Director of the American Arts Alliance, asking Internet users for their support;

➤ background information and a description of the funding crisis facing the American arts industry;

➤ guidance on how to be an effective advocate for the arts, including helpful tips on how to effectively use the media in order to build support for the arts;

➤ a list of reasons why federal funding for the arts is important; advocates are encouraged to refer to the list when writing letters to editors and when making public appearances in support of the arts industry;

➤ a list of myths and facts about national support of arts and culture;

➤ an assessment of the economic impact of arts and cultural institutions in American communities.

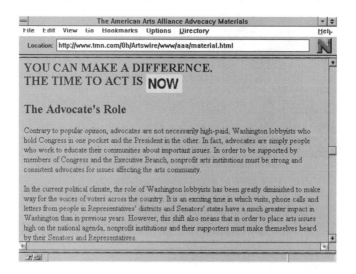

Sample letters of protest that encourage advocacy on a particular issue have become popular on Internet sites. Since they can be freely copied and distributed, it is easy for an individual to register a complaint on an issue with minimal time and effort. The American Arts Alliance, for example, has included a draft letter of protest on its Internet site. The letter can be freely copied, and the AAA encourages Internet users to use the text of the letter when sending letters of protest to their Senators and/or Members of Congress.

Another organization employing this strategy is the Manitoba Animal Rights Coalition (**http://www.umanitoba.ca/arrs/marc/marc.html**). MARC has placed numerous sample protest letters on its Internet site and invites Internet users to copy them for distribution to others. An example is the following letter to Canada's Minister of Fisheries and Oceans, condemning the government's support of seal slaughtering:

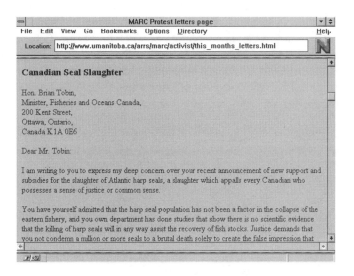

All the advocacy examples thus far have focused on the World Wide Web. Electronic mail is also a powerful advocacy tool, since it allows advocacy organizations to quickly broadcast information to supporters across the globe. For example, the Sierra Club, an environmental rights organization, sponsors an electronic mailing list that distributes environmental action alerts to its members; the following alert was broadcast to Sierra Club members on the Internet asking them to protest a bill pending in the U.S. House of Representatives:

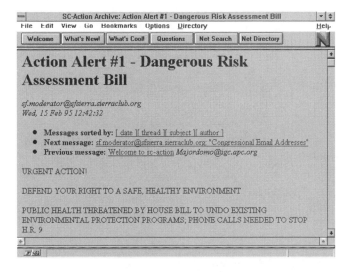

With more and more organizations, government officials, and Members of Parliament obtaining e-mail addresses, "electronic lobbying" is a tactic being used by many non-profit organizations in addition to fax and regular mail. In the United States in particular, electronic lobbying has become popular, since many Senators, Members of Congress, and government committees are on the Internet. Consequently, many not-for-profit organizations provide supporters with resources to allow them to engage in electronic lobbying. For example, the American Arts Alliance provides a link to a directory of congressional e-mail addresses from their Internet site.

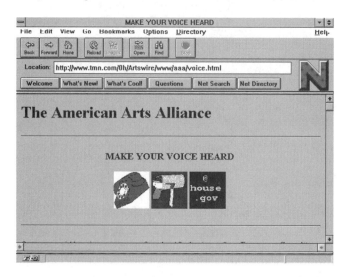

In addition to the sites that encourage advocacy on specific issues, the Internet is full of sites that offer general information to activists to help them use the Internet more effectively. For example, the Manitoba Animal Rights Coalition has created a repository of information for activists and encourages Internet users to contribute materials to the collection (**http://www.umanitoba.ca/arrs/marc/activist.html**).

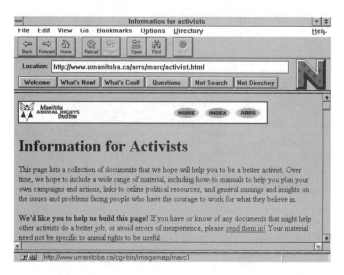

Another example is *An Activist's Strategic Guide to the Internet* (**http://www.matisse.net/politics/activist/actguide.html**). This document, which is freely available on the Internet, offers advice on how to be an effective Internet activist. If you're an activist, you'll certainly be in good company on the Internet.

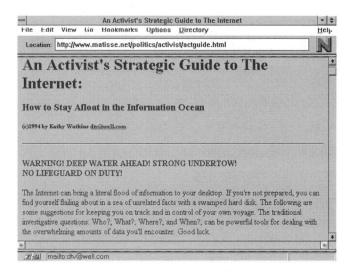

A good example of on-line advocacy at work is the controversy over the logging of the Clayquot Sound area on Vancouver Island. The issue of Clayquot Sound turned into a public relations disaster for MacMillan Bloedel and other forestry companies in British Columbia, primarily because they had a difficult time getting the public to understand and support their side of the issue. In particular, they found themselves under pressure in Germany and other European countries, where various groups threatened a boycott of B.C. forest products. What went wrong?

MacMillan Bloedel and the B.C. forest industry failed to understand that their opposition (the environmental movement) knew how to use global communication networks such as the Internet to effectively distribute information and to gain support for their cause. They failed to appreciate that even though their primary opposition was a local environmental concern, their real opposition was the entire global environmental movement, including such well-known organizations as Greenpeace and Friends of the Earth, groups which mobilized through the Internet.

The environmental movement used the Internet to build worldwide support for its cause, while MacMillan Bloedel and the forest industry pursued more traditional means of getting the word out: speaking to the press, sending the premier of British Columbia to Europe on a high-profile visit to get some press coverage, and employing other methods that have a more limited "reach." By using the Internet, environmental groups were able to instantly build *worldwide* support for their position. Is it any wonder that the Clayquot Sound situation turned into a public relations disaster for the forestry industry in British Columbia?

Clearly, the Internet is a powerful communications tool. Not-for-profit organizations and associations have long realized its potential for mobilizing international support for their causes.

Outreach Activities

Given the growing population of the Internet community, the Internet can help not-for-profit organizations with a number of outreach activities:

- fund-raising;

- volunteer recruitment;

- membership recruitment;

- disaster coordination.

We will discuss each of these activities below.

Fund-Raising

Most not-for-profit organizations are dependent upon outside support to sustain their services and activities. Sources of funding can include contributions from members, donations from individuals and corporations, and government support. Fund-raising activities are a high priority for many not-for-profit organizations and associations.

With a user base that is growing exponentially, the Internet is viewed by many not-for-profit organizations as the next frontier in fund-raising. Yet, not-for-profit organizations are learning that the guidelines that deal with advertising on the Internet are equally applicable to fund-raising activities. It is clearly not acceptable for an organization to blanket the Internet with fund-raising appeals, no matter how important the cause. The same rules that apply to business use of the Internet apply to fund-raising.

The accepted way to solicit funds on the Internet is through an organization's own World Wide Web site. For example, Canine Companions for Independence, a non-profit agency that provides highly skilled dogs to people with disabilities, solicits donations on its World Wide Web site (**http://grunt.berkeley.edu/help.html**). CCI receives no funding from the government and relies completely on private donations to support its activities. To encourage donations, CCI's World Wide Web site includes information on how Internet users can make a financial contribution to the organization.

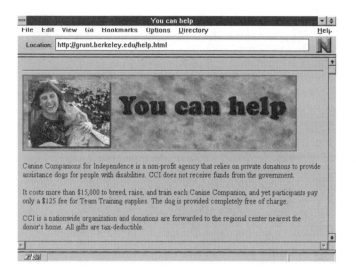

WPKN Radio (**http://www.wpkn.org/wpkn**), a public radio station in the United States, has included an area on its World Wide Web site called WPKN Needs Your Support, where they accept monetary pledges by electronic mail (**wpkn@wpkn.org**). An e-mail address has also been established so that Internet users can submit fund-raising ideas to the station (**$$$@wpkn.org**).

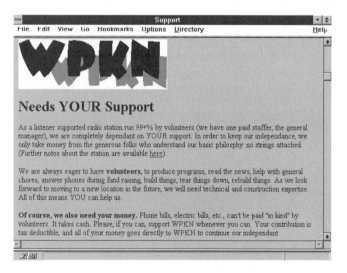

While WPKN accepts pledges by e-mail, other non-profit organizations, such as the International Rett Syndrome Association, have chosen to place a pledge form directly on their World Wide Web site (**http://www.paltech.com/irsa/irsa.htm**). (Rett syndrome is a severe neurological disorder that affects women, and has no known cure.)

The pledge form allows Internet users to make contributions of $10.00, $25.00, $100.00, $500.00, or more. Once a pledge has been made, it is transmitted over the Internet to the International Rett Syndrome Association, where it is processed by staff or volunteers. The advantage of allowing users to make pledges on-line is that users are more likely to make a pledge on impulse as they read about the organization.

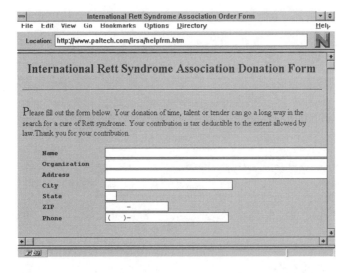

Another example of fund-raising on the Internet is the American Red Cross, which has established a page on its World Wide Web site with information on how to make a donation to the organization (**http://www.crossnet.org**).

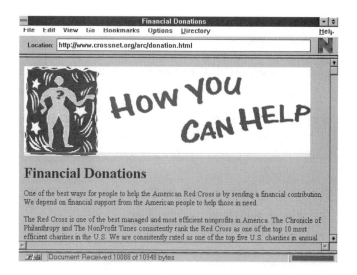

Some not-for-profit organizations have established sites on the Internet to raise money for specific one-time fund-raising activities. For example, the South Carolina-based chapter of the Independent Telephone Pioneer Association is trying to raise money for local community charities by selling a cookbook on the Internet (**http://www.sunbelt.net/palmetto_choice.html**). The cookbook is a collection of recipes contributed by chapter members.

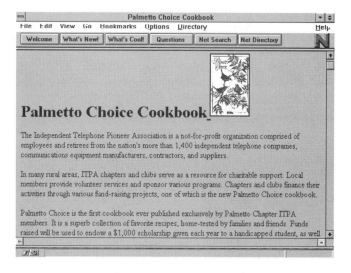

Internet users can order a copy of the cookbook directly on the Internet by filling out an on-line form and providing their credit card number. Alternatively, payment can be sent by regular mail. With the advent of the Internet, the scope of a community-initiated fund-raising effort is no longer limited to the community. The Internet gives organizations the ability to conduct their fund-raising activities *worldwide.*

Fund-raising has become an increasingly competitive activity as more and more non-profit organizations compete for the consumer's attention. To gain a competitive edge, many not-for-profit organizations are stepping up their efforts to convince consumers that their organization is the most worthy cause for their donation. This is done by designing World Wide Web sites that do more than just appeal for donations: the sites should educate the public on how their donations will be spent and illustrate how the organization is fiscally responsible. For example, the Ontario Easter Seal Society's World Wide Web site (**http://www.easterseals.org/CyberPlex/EasterSeals.html**) includes the following screen, which explains how donations are spent:

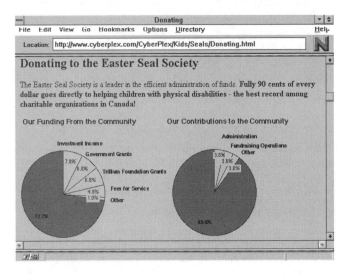

The Red Cross uses a similar approach on its World Wide Web site and provides the following details about its auditing practices to convince consumers that the organization is fiscally responsible:

> The Red Cross is one of the best managed and most efficient non-profits in America. *The Chronicle of Philanthropy* and *The NonProfit Times* consistently rank the Red Cross as one of the top 10 most efficient charities in the U.S. We are consistently rated as one of the top five U.S. charities in annual reviews in magazines like *Money* and *Forbes*.
>
> Nationwide, the Red Cross spends approximately 93 cents of every dollar on services and programs. That means that only 8 cents of each dollar is spent on administration and overhead. Only three percent of the budget is spent on generating donations from the public.

The Red Cross shares its financial information readily. Like all non-profits, it must file financial statements annually with the U.S. government, and these statements are open for public scrutiny. We print complete financial information in our annual report and distribute it widely. In addition, the U.S. Congress requires the Red Cross to undergo an annual audit by the U.S. Army Audit Agency; results are shared with the Congress and publicized in the annual report. The Red Cross also contracts with an independent accounting firm, Deloitte and Touche, to audit its performance in major disaster relief operations.

Source: How You Can Help
The American Red Cross World Wide Web
http://www.crossnet.org

In Chapter 4 we mentioned a survey conducted by the International Mass Retail Association. The survey revealed that consumers are reluctant to purchase goods or services from an on-line vendor when they are not familiar with the organization. It is reasonable to assume that consumers will take the same attitude with not-for-profit organizations that are fund-raising on the Internet. Consumers will not make a donation to an organization they know nothing about. Internet-based fund-raising efforts such as those of the Ontario Easter Seal Society and the American Red Cross will have a better chance of success because they give the consumer background information that can be used to judge the organization.

Volunteer Recruitment

Volunteers are the lifeblood of many associations and not-for-profit organizations; hence a key activity of many of these organizations is the ongoing recruitment of new volunteers. Just as businesses use the Internet to advertise job opportunities, many not-for-profit organizations use the Internet to find and attract new volunteers. For example, Wolf Haven International, a non-profit organization dedicated to wolf preservation, has set up an area on its World Wide Web site to inform the public about volunteer opportunities with that organization (**http://www.teleport. com:80/~wnorton/wolf.html**). Funded entirely by private contributions, Wolf Haven operates a wolf sanctuary for captive wolves and educates the public about wolves and their habitat. Volunteers are needed to run tours of the sanctuary, help out in the office, and assist with special events.

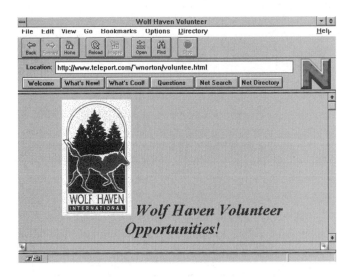

Volunteer recruitment, like fund-raising, requires some "marketing" effort. While volunteers don't get paid for the work they do, they still expect something back in return for their time. Some people volunteer to gain experience or improve their skills at a particular activity. Others volunteer to "network," and volunteer simply for the self-gratification received by helping others. Some of the most effective volunteer recruitment campaigns on the Internet are the ones that explain the benefits of volunteering. For example, the Ontario Easter Seal Society (**http://www.easterseals.org/ CyberPlex/EasterSeals.html**) has a page on its World Wide Web site called *Why Should I Volunteer?* which describes the benefits of volunteering with that organization. Wolf Haven's World Wide Web site also discusses what volunteers will gain from their volunteer work.

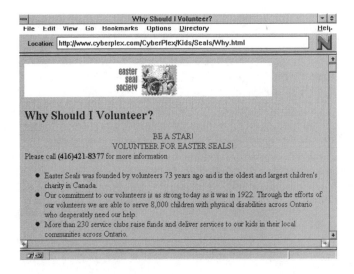

Organizations do not have to be on the Internet to seek volunteers through it. There are several formal initiatives on the Internet that act as on-line volunteer co-ordination centres and try to match volunteers with organizations. One such effort is the Volunteer Center, a California-based organization that represents 140 regional agencies and service groups (**http://www.netrep.com/local/org/vvc/vvc.html**).

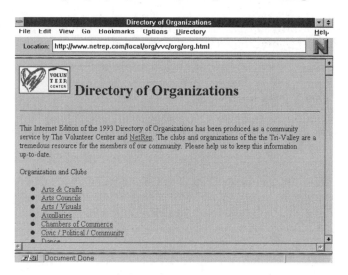

The Volunteer Center has established a World Wide Web site that provides details on the many volunteer opportunities throughout the area that it represents. A useful feature of this site is that Internet users can perform a search of the organization's "Wish List," a database of equipment, furnishings, supplies, and volunteer needs. For example, a search on the word "painting" provides a list of not-for-profit organizations in the San Francisco Bay area that are looking for volunteer painters.

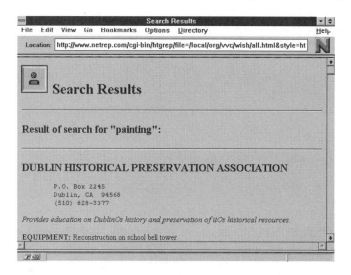

A similar initiative is the Bay Area Volunteer Information Center, an organization that provides information about volunteer opportunities in the San Francisco Bay area (**http://www.meer.net/users/taylor/index.htm**). Participating organizations include the Red Cross, Catholic Charities of San Jose, The City of Mountain View, the Humane Society of Santa Clara County, Junior Achievement, Parents Helping Parents, the Salvation Army, and The Wildlands Restoration Team. The Junior Achievement page, for example, provides background information on Junior Achievement and describes volunteer opportunities with the organization:

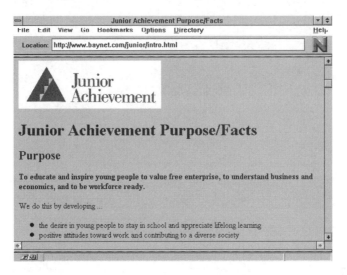

A different approach to volunteer recruitment is found with a Winnipeg-based organization called Creative Retirement Manitoba, which uses the Internet to help seniors get more involved in their communities (**http://www.mbnet.mb.ca/crm/crm/ crm.html**). Its activities are built on the premise that seniors are a great source of "wisdom, experience and knowledge."

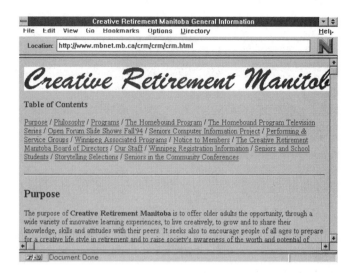

Creative Retirement Manitob

Table of Contents

Purpose / Philosophy / Programs / The Homebound Program / The Homebound Program Television Series / Open Forum Slide Shows Fall'94 / Seniors Computer Information Project / Performing & Service Groups / Winnipeg Associated Programs / Notice to Members / The Creative Retirement Manitoba Board of Directors / Our Staff / Winnipeg Registration Information / Seniors and School Students / Storytelling Selections / Seniors in the Community Conferences

Purpose

The purpose of **Creative Retirement Manitoba** is to offer older adults the opportunity, through a wide variety of innovative learning experiences, to live creatively, to grow and to share their knowledge, skills and attitudes with their peers. It seeks also to encourage people of all ages to prepare for a creative life style in retirement and to raise society's awareness of the worth and potential of

CRM's World Wide Web site describes numerous recreational programs for seniors including a volunteer program called Students and Seniors Together, which places seniors in Winnipeg-area schools where they volunteer their time to work with children on a one-on-one basis or in group situations.

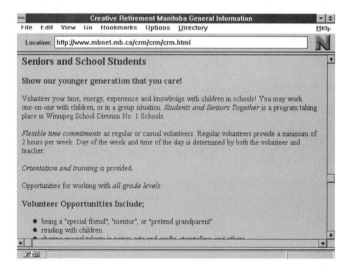

Seniors and School Students

Show our younger generation that you care!

Volunteer your time, energy, experience and knowledge with children in schools! You may work one-on-one with children, or in a group situation. *Students and Seniors Together* is a program taking place in Winnipeg School Division No. 1 Schools.

Flexible time commitments as regular or casual volunteers. Regular volunteers provide a minimum of 2 hours per week. Day of the week and time of the day is determined by both the volunteer and teacher.

Orientation and training is provided.

Opportunities for working with *all grade levels*.

Volunteer Opportunities Include;

- being a "special friend", "mentor", or "pretend grandparent".
- reading with children.

The site also encourages seniors to volunteer their time in storytelling circles, where they can share stories about their lives and their families.

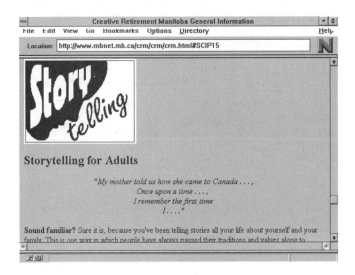

Membership Recruitment

For membership organizations, the Internet provides a new medium for membership drives. For example, the British Columbia Biotechnology Alliance, a not-for-profit trade association, has established a World Wide Web site (**http://www.biotech.bc.ca/bcba**) that provides a comprehensive overview of membership opportunities with the organization, including information on

➤ who should join the organization;

➤ networking opportunities with the organization;

➤ what you will receive in return for your membership;

➤ what the organization can do for you;

➤ how to join the organization.

This site does an excellent job of answering all the questions that a potential member might have.

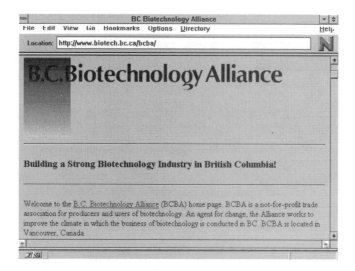

To attract new members, the site includes a few pages of quotes from current members of the Alliance, as seen in the screen below:

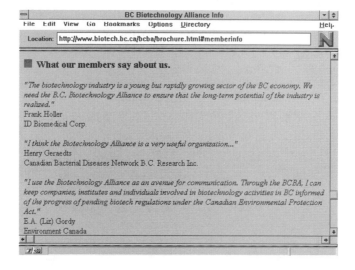

While the British Columbia Biotechnology Alliance site is a good example of membership recruitment on the Internet, it is not interactive. Many organizations recruit members on the Internet using the World Wide Web's interactive forms capabilities to handle requests for information. For example, the Sierra Club, one of the world's leading environmental movements, uses the Internet to accept electronic requests for membership kits. The organization provides a membership request form on its World Wide Web site (**http://www.sierraclub.org**). Internet users who wish to receive a membership kit can fill out the form on-line. Once completed, the form is automatically sent by e-mail to the Sierra Club for processing.

If you do not wish to wait for the membership kit and prefer to join immediately, the Sierra Club makes it easy. They provide a complete copy of the membership form on the Internet. Internet users can print out the form and mail it in.

The Sierra Club uses the Internet in another important way. To help prospective members locate their nearest chapter, the World Wide Web site includes a map that identifies the locations of all the Sierra Club chapters in the United States and Canada. The map is "clickable," meaning that Internet users can click on a location on the map to get the address of the chapter in that area. (Clickable maps like this one are popular on World Wide Web sites, since they allow users to quickly retrieve information from specific areas on the map.)

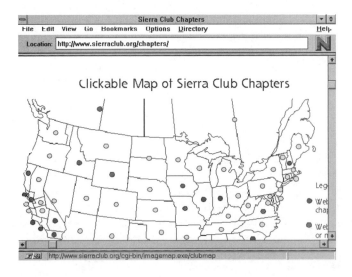

For example, if we click on the dot in British Columbia, we would receive information on the Western Canada chapter of the Sierra Club:

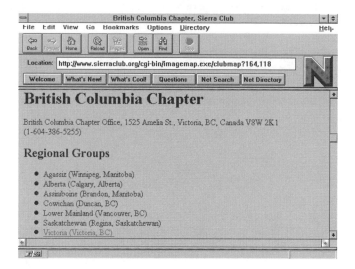

Another organization engaged in member recruitment activities on the Internet is the Alpine Club of Canada, which has prepared a comprehensive membership site on the World Wide Web (**http://www.cimtegration.com/sport/climbing/acc/acc. htm**). This site includes a description of the club's programs, publications, and other benefits of membership as well as a list of regional ACC groups.

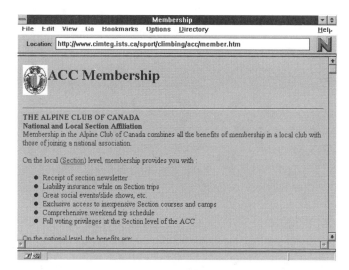

To make it easy for Internet users to locate the club chapter nearest them, the Club uses the same "clickable map" technology that was used by the Sierra Club. By clicking on a dot on the map, Internet users can retrieve information about the ACC group in that area.

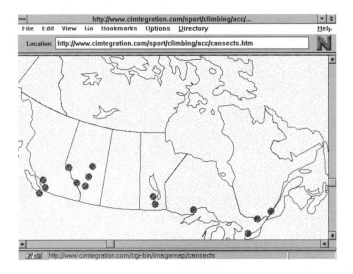

Also recruiting new members on the Internet is the Canadian Sport Parachute Association, a non-profit organization dedicated to the advancement of sport parachuting in Canada (**http://www.islandnet.com/~murrays/cspa.html**). The CSPA's World Wide Web includes a list of membership benefits and a copy of the membership application form:

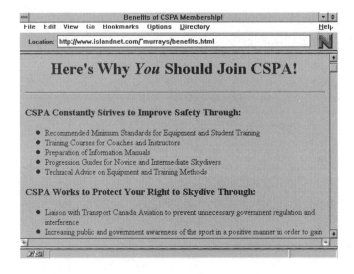

Disaster Coordination Activities

Another area where the Internet has shown significant promise is as a communications tool to assist with the coordination of disaster relief. One of the most active disaster relief organizations on the Internet is the International Federation of Red Cross and Red Crescent Societies. The IFRC maintains a site on the World Wide Web that is updated around the clock. This site contains information bulletins and requests for assistance with recent disasters, including floods, volcanoes, earthquakes, tidal waves, droughts, tropical storms, and typhoons. It also includes links to disaster preparedness and disaster management information sources on the Internet (**http://www.ifrc.org**).

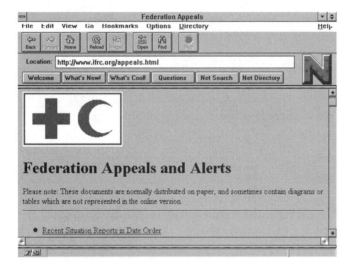

An excellent example of how the Internet can be used in a disaster situation is the 1995 earthquake in Kobe, Japan. During the crisis, the Internet was used to distribute the following types of information to the media and general public:

➤ disaster reports and updates;

➤ requests for medical aid;

➤ lists of addresses to which donations could be sent;

➤ names of the deceased;

➤ images and pictures of the damage;

➤ lists of out-of-service telephone numbers;

➤ lists of useful telephone numbers and official contacts;

➤ information on the status of railway and postal services.

With local telephone service overloaded, the Internet provided local authorities with an alternative means of dispersing information to the world. Organizations such as Sony provided their Internet facilities to help disseminate information about the earthquake to people around the world who were wondering about the fate of their families and friends. The International Red Cross and dozens of organizations quickly created "information" sites on the Internet to disseminate the latest news and updates to Internet users.

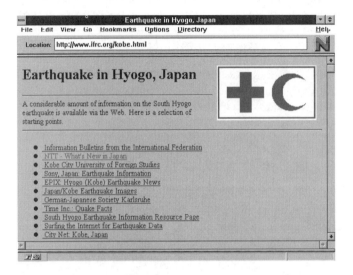

Internet e-mail is used extensively by disaster coordination centres to distribute disaster reports and bulletins to the Internet community. For example, Volunteers in Technical Assistance, an international development organization, operates a program on the Internet called the Disaster Information Resource Program (**http://www.vita.org**). This program operates a mailing list on the Internet that distributes disaster situation reports to Internet users. The reports are issued by the United Nations Department of Humanitarian Affairs in Geneva and the Office of U.S. Foreign Disaster Assistance, and are redistributed to Internet users by VITA (contact **incident@vita.org** to be added to the list).

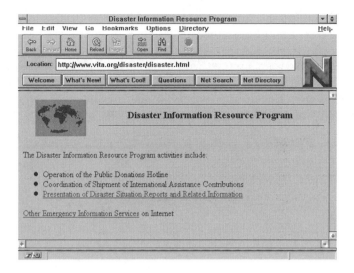

Service Delivery

The Internet is a tool that can help many not-for-profit organizations and associations in the delivery of information and services to the community and to their members. Specifically, the Internet can be used for

➤ external information dissemination;

➤ internal information dissemination.

External Information Dissemination

An integral part of the mission of many non-profit organizations is public education and information dissemination. The Internet supports these goals by making it possible for not-for-profit organizations to publish information that can be accessed by potentially millions of people. Consider the mission of the Canadian Cancer Society:

> The Canadian Cancer Society is a national community-based organization of volunteers, whose mission is the eradication of cancer and the enhancement of the quality of life of people living with cancer.

To fulfill its mission, the Canadian Cancer Society engages in public education to promote cancer prevention and inform the public of its services.

To understand how the Internet can assist with this process, consider what the Canadian Cancer Society is doing in Manitoba. As part of its public education campaign, the Manitoba Division of the Canadian Cancer Society participates in a Manitoba-based initiative called the Seniors Computer Information Project (**http://www.mbnet.mb.ca/crm**). One of the projects that SCIP is involved in is the creation of an Internet site that would act as a clearinghouse for information relevant to Manitoba seniors. To get content for the Internet site, SCIP asks local organizations to provide information. The Canadian Cancer Society is one of the local information providers participating in the SCIP Internet project.

The Society places lots of helpful information on SCIP's Internet site, including descriptions of the Society's patient services programs, information about general services available through the Society, a list of affiliated support programs, addresses of Manitoba Canadian Cancer Society offices, and descriptions of volunteer opportunities with the organization (**http://www.mbnet.mb.ca/crm/health/cancer.html**). Since this information is available on the Internet, it can be accessed by anyone in Manitoba and around the world.

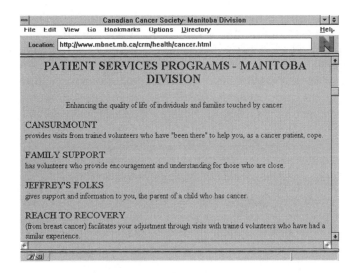

While much of this information is of local interest, there are some documents of general interest. For example, there is a document called Seven Steps to Health, which contains helpful advice for anyone interested in cancer prevention.

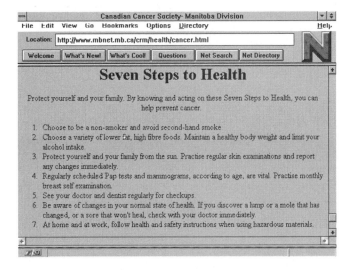

Clearly, the Internet is a medium that not-for-profit organizations should not ignore when they are engaged in public education campaigns, as it is another important distribution channel, like radio, television, and the print media.

The Center for World Indigenous Studies provides another example of how non-profit organizations can use the Internet for information dissemination purposes. Based in Olympia, Washington, the Center was founded to help people understand and appreciate the cultures of indigenous peoples. The Center uses the Internet to disseminate the works of indigenous authors, researchers, and governments to illuminate the social, political, and economic struggles being faced by indigenous populations worldwide. The Center's Internet site, called the Fourth World Documentation Project (**http://www.halcyon.com/FWDP/fwdp.html**),contains over 400 documents on indigenous populations, including essays, position papers, resolutions, organizational information, treaties, UN documents, and speeches and declarations.

Child Quest International is another not-for-profit organization using the Internet for information dissemination purposes, but for a very different reason. One of Child Quest's primary activities is finding missing children. Given the vast reach of the Internet, Child Quest uses the network to distribute information about child abductions, including pictures of missing children (**http://www.omega.com/adima/bands/child_quest/cqmain.html**).

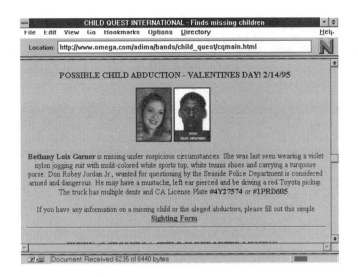

Internal Information Dissemination

Internet e-mail allows members of clubs and associations to keep in touch with each other electronically. Electronic mail can provide efficiencies in internal communications and can dramatically alter the way that organizations work. It can be especially useful for clubs and associations with a membership base that is spread out across the country. Since the cost of sending e-mail on the Internet is generally not sensitive to the number of recipients, an association will pay the same price to send a message to 2,000 members as it will to send the same message to 200 members. Hence Internet e-mail offers significant opportunities for cost savings in communications.

At the organizational level e-mail can be used to coordinate events and activities, hold votes, debate issues, and discuss policy matters. At the member level it can be used by members who want to exchange information with other members, share experiences and opinions, or seek advice.

The Canadian Sport Parachute Organization is one of a growing number of Canadian organizations using the Internet to improve communication between its members. The CSPA provides an Internet mailing list "to help the far-flung Canadian skydiving community stay in touch, make announcements, provide a forum for discussion and improve the services CSPA offers its members." Murray Stephens, the Treasurer of the CSPA, says that the organization "has made a commitment to utilize the Internet to effectively communicate with its members from coast to coast." Canadians interested in skydiving can automatically add themselves to the mailing list by using an automatic subscription form on the CSPA's World Wide Web site (**http://www.islandnet.com/~murrays/cspa.html**).

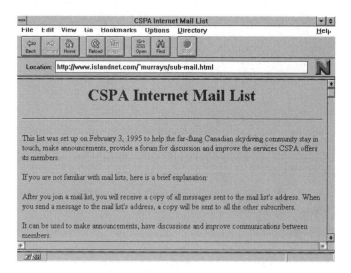

In addition to organization-wide communications, e-mail can be used to help committees and working groups within organizations carry out their work. For example, one of the CSPA's major working groups, the Coaching and Working Committee, uses an Internet mailing list to coordinate its activities. The CSPA's Board of Directors will also be using the Internet for communication purposes.

Board members of not-for-profit organizations are usually non-paid volunteers who are not involved in the day-to-day activities of the organization. Electronic mail can be an efficient means of communication for a Board of Directors, especially if the Board members live in different areas of the country. For example, it can be used to distribute agendas, proposals, minutes, and announcements of meetings. Electronic mail can effectively shorten the length of physical meetings by allowing Board members to discuss policy issues on-line thus familiarizing themselves with the relevant issues prior to a Board meeting.

Other activities

So far in this chapter we have discussed how not-for-profit organizations and associations can use the Internet for public relations and marketing, outreach activities, and service delivery. The Internet can assist not-for-profits with several other activities, including

➤ recruitment;

➤ research;

➤ topic tracking.

Each of these activities is discussed below.

Recruitment

Since the Internet is segmented into thousands of different discussion groups on a multitude of subjects, it is possible to target job postings at very specific audiences. For this reason, the Internet is evolving as a popular tool for organizational recruitment. For example, the following job opening was placed on an Internet discussion group called **soc.org.nonprofit**, which is read by people who work in the not-for-profit sector:

> From: ckunin@merle.acns.nwu.edu
> Newsgroups: soc.org.nonprofit
> Subject: Director of Development position available
> Organization: Northwestern University, Evanston, IL, US
>
> The Chicago Children's Theatre has an immediate part-time position available for a Development Director (10 hours a week) to create, coordinate and implement our annual fund-raising campaign. Responsibilities include individual solicitation, corporate, foundation and government grants, and special event planning. Please send resume, writing samples and cover letter including availability date and salary history to:
>
> Chicago Children's Theatre
> PO Box 5331
> Evanston, IL 60204
>
> or send via e-mail to us at ckunin@merle.acns.nwu.edu

Since many people who read the **soc.org.nonprofit** group will have the skills that the Chicago Children's Theatre is looking for, it is a good place for the theatre to announce its job vacancy. However, it is important to point out that the Internet should not replace conventional methods of advertising job openings. Job advertisements in magazines, journals, and newspapers may reach more qualified people than an equivalent announcement in an Internet discussion group. Remember that the majority of Canadians are not on the Internet. For this reason, the Internet should *supplement* conventional methods of recruitment, not *replace* them.

Research

The Internet is used as a research tool by many not-for-profit organizations and associations. The World Wide Web service, for example, provides access to thousands of information sites established by businesses, educational institutions, government agencies, and other not-for-profit organizations. As we have described throughout this book, organizations use these sites to make available press releases, databases, statistics, research reports, position papers, and other organizational documents. For instance, the Canada Council, which promotes music, dance, theatre, media, and literacy arts in Canada, has made its strategic plan available on the Internet (**http://www.ffa.ucalgary.ca:80/cc/index.html**).

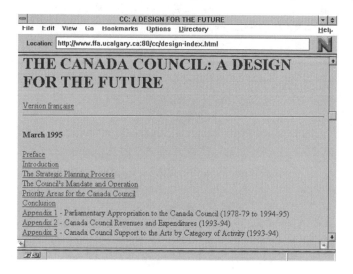

This document will be of interest to all arts organizations in Canada as well as anyone doing research on the future of the arts industry in Canada.

Electronic mailing lists and USENET discussion groups provide another way for not-for-profit organizations to do research on the Internet. Discussion groups and mailing lists allow people that work in similar jobs to compare experiences and seek advice from each other. For example, the Royal Life Saving Society of Canada sent out the following message to an Internet discussion group dedicated to the discussion of not-for-profit organizations:

From: Leslie Fast <lfast@sfu.ca>
Newsgroups: soc.org.nonprofit
Subject: Recognizing Volunteers for Their Contributions
Organization: Simon Fraser University

The Royal Life Saving Society of Canada is presently revising its volunteer recognition program. Does any nonprofit have a volunteer recognition program that they would recommend. We would like to recognize our volunteers' accomplishments based on quantity and quality. Any information on the following would be appreciated:

1. Methods of recognition.

2. Methods of measuring contribution in terms of quality.
3. And, environments in which the volunteer is recognized. (formally and informally)

Thanks for your time. We look forward to your input.

In this case, Leslie Fast is using the Internet to canvass her peers around the world for advice on volunteer recognition programs.

In another example an individual from a hospital foundation has used an electronic discussion group called "Non-profit Gift Planners" to seek advice on a new donor program:

Reply-To: Non-profit Gift Planners
<GIFT-PL@UMINN1.BITNET>
Sender: Non-profit Gift Planners
<GIFT-PL@UMINN1.BITNET>
From: Tom Akins <Fundseeker@AOL.COM>
Subject: Donor Recognition Wall

Happy Monday everybody!

We are in the process of finalizing design plans for a donor recognition wall at our hospital. The wall will recognize three distinct groups — those who have made cumulative contributions to the hospital of $5,000 or more, those who are current members of our President's Council ($1,000 or more during the calendar year), and members of our Franciscan Club (planned giving donors).

How have you announced/previewed/unveiled donor walls at your hospital/institution? What kinds of letters/promotional pieces have you sent out ahead of time encouraging others who are not currently members of one of these three groups to join so that they can be featured on the wall? What has your dedication event been like?

Any feedback would be much appreciated!

Tom Akins Fundseeker@aol.com
St. Francis Hospital Foundation
1700 SW 7th
Topeka, KS 66606
913/295-8082

In the following case an individual is seeking guidance on the issue of board compensation. This message was posted to the **soc.org.nonprofit** discussion group mentioned earlier:

From: brand@panix.com (Gerard Brandenstein)
Newsgroups: soc.org.nonprofit
Subject: Board fees
Organization: PANIX Public Access Internet and Unix, NYC
Lines: 5

Does anyone know of a summary publication that examines the topic of board compensation? We are a private foundation supporting education in the sciences that will be visiting this topic in the next week or so and would like to have some background information. Thank you in advance.

Finally, here is a message from a not-for-profit organization in Newfoundland asking for fund-raising ideas:

From: lorim@public.compusult.nf.ca (Lori from Newfoundland)
Newsgroups: soc.org.nonprofit
Subject: Fundraising ideas??
Organization: Compusult Limited - Public Access Unix BBS
Lines: 15
Keywords: fund-raising

Hi,

I'm currently involved in a major fund-raising project for a non-profit organization and I was wondering if anyone out there might have some really *INNOVATIVE* fund-raising ideas to share. Our project is long-term; we've already tried a lot of the traditional things like dances, variety shows, selling chocolates, etc., and we need something new and different to get people "excited" again.

Thanks in advance for your help!

Lori
e-mail: lorim@public.compusult.nf.ca

In all four of these examples, people working in the non-profit sector have used the Internet to seek guidance and information from their peers. The unique spirit of the Internet, and the global cooperation that is found on the network, means that requests for information occur daily, and Internet users volunteer their time to provide answers and advice.

Topic Tracking

Using the Internet for research entails looking for answers to specific questions or problems. Another important but distinct use of the Internet is monitoring relevant Internet discussion groups and mailing lists to keep up with news and developments in your field, just as we subscribe to newsletters and magazines to keep up with news in our professions, such as dentists subscribing to various industry periodicals to keep abreast of the latest research and news in the field of dentistry. On the Internet, people subscribe to electronic newsletters and discussion groups for the same reason.

If your organization is an arts theatre, you might want to track the USENET discussion group called **rec.arts.theatre.misc**, a place on the Internet where people talk about theatre issues. Here is a sample message from the discussion group where someone has contributed a recipe for stage blood:

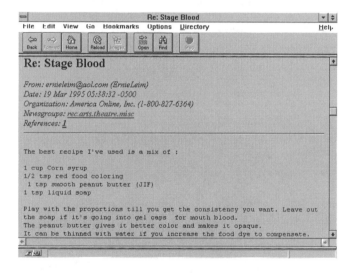

If you belong to an environmental organization, you might want to follow the **sci.environment** USENET discussion group, where people from around the world discuss environmental issues.

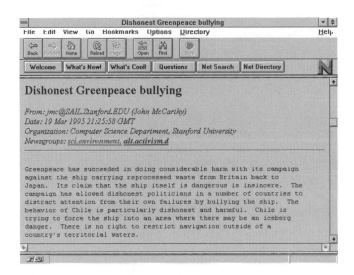

Other sources for topic tracking, in addition to USENET discussion groups, are electronic journals and newsletters. The Internet carries electronic publications on a wide range of subjects. An example is ECO, a newsletter that is prepared on-site at major international climate conferences by non-governmental environmental groups, and then distributed worldwide through the Internet (**http://www.igc.apc.org/ climate/Eco.html**). For people around the world the newsletter is a valuable source of feedback and commentary about the conference proceedings.

It is possible to automate topic tracking to some degree by using one of the filtering programs found on the Internet. For example, Infoseek (**http://www.in-foseek.com**) keeps a database of 4 weeks worth of USENET newsgroups that is searchable by keyword. Over 10,000 newsgroups are archived in the database. InfoSeek costs $9.95 (U.S.) per month for 100 free transactions (a query of the database or the retrieval of a message or document from the database counts as a transaction). Additional transactions are $0.10 (U.S.) each. The database can be used to find out what people on the Internet are saying on a particular topic or issue, to find messages that have been posted by a particular organization or person, or to find messages about a particular subject, product, person, or organization. It is this type of topic tracking that will provide associations and not-for-profit organizations with yet another powerful incentive to use the Internet on a regular, day-to-day basis.

The Web

Finally, we close this chapter with an overview of a major Canadian Internet success story — Web. Web is a Canadian computer network that specializes in the not-for-profit community. The Web network links Canadians across the country and around the world who are working in the fields of social justice, international development, environment, peace, health, human rights, economic development, and education. Web users have full access to the Internet, but Web also carries a number of news services and databases not available on the Internet, including over 1,000 specialized conferences of interest to non-profit organizations.

Web, in existence since 1987, plays a vital role in supporting collaboration, communication, and advocacy among Canadian not-for-profit organizations. Contact information for Web is listed in Appendix A. The Web's Internet site, illustrated below, can be reached at **http://www.web.apc.org**:

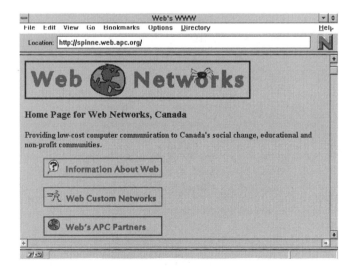

In this chapter we have alluded to the powerful capabilities that the Internet provides to all kinds of associations and not-for-profit organizations. The Web has been using computer-based communications technology for close to a decade, even before the Internet became a mainstream business application. As a result, it is a powerful international success story and is now at the forefront of international activist efforts, as reported widely in a story in the *Globe & Mail*:

> Canadian social activists blasted Prime Minister Jean Chretien yesterday for staying away from the United Nations social-development summit — and they'll be using a rapidly growing alternative computer network to drive the message home....It will be posted on a non-profit activists' network called the Web, perhaps with a call to sympathizers at home to put pressure on the Prime Minister to change his mind. From there, it should be accessible to the Canadians' counterparts in 50 countries through a global link that is having a significant impact on policy-making and the conduct of international relations.
>
> Nevertheless, the summit, which opened yesterday with appeals for renewed vigour in attacking global poverty, is the latest example of the new power that instant communication has given pressure groups. By linking activists in rich and poor countries and by providing widespread access to documents under discussion, the computer link allows opinion to be galvanized and pressure to be mounted much more rapidly.
>
> "It does keep us on our toes," said George Green, director-general of policy development for the Canadian International Development Agency. "They can co-ordinate positions between North and South better than governments can."
>
> Mr. Green and Web manager Rory O'Brien said the cancellation of the Great Whale power project in northern Quebec happened in part because the network allowed Cree activists and U.S. environmentalists to trade information rapidly and launch appeals for support from New York State power consumers.[1]

---

[1] Chretien blasted for summit absence — Canadian social activists at UN meeting use alternative computer network to spread criticism of PM, *Globe & Mail*, March 7, 1995.

Finally, perhaps the real power of the Internet to associations and the not-for-profit community will be the dramatic impact that it will have on global power structures, as the following quotation suggests:

> The closer links among the world's non-governmental organizations have led to suggestions that a "global civil society" is emerging to match the reach of institutions such as the UN, global markets and multinational corporations.[2]

---

[2] Chretien blasted for summit absence — Canadian social activists at UN meeting use alternative computer network to spread criticism of PM, *Globe & Mail*, March 7, 1995.

CHAPTER 8

Health and Medicine on the Internet

....the use of cyber-health systems is not limited to healthcare professionals or to hackers wielding sophisticated hardware. A new generation of medical computing systems is serving the lay population as well as doctors. In fact, a panel of consumer health informatics experts recently predicted that these new systems will become an important part of our effort to reinvent healthcare, turning patients into providers and offering customized health information at the touch of a button.

Consumer health informatics,
Healthcare Forum, January/February 1995

It's the most fundamental shift since Gutenberg.... The Internet is basically a space and time destroyer. It shrinks distance and time to zero. It's as if all the world's scientists were in one room, available at one computer.... In the 1980s, the so-called GenBank at Los Alamos collected research from scientists around the world on the DNA sequences at the heart of all genetic codes and distributed the data as printed books. The turnaround time was up to 13 months. Now the dissemination is all electronic, with data coming in over the networks and going out over them. Turnaround is less than 48 hours.

How the Net caught science,
Globe & Mail, June 16, 1993

*W*hen asked about the role of the "information highway" in health care services in Canada, most Canadians probably have a quaint and romantic image of a young, brave doctor at a medical clinic in the remote Yukon, using the latest in satellite technology to transmit live videos of a gravely injured snowmobiler to Toronto. There, a heroic, dashing team of medical specialists use the "high-tech highway" to maneuver a miniature camera over a damaged leg, quickly narrowing in on the critical hairline fracture missed by the doctor in the North. Using a remote manipulator arm, the Toronto specialists carefully patch up the leg, and the patient is saved! A diagnosis is made, and a solution is put into place. *Voilà* — the "information highway" comes to the rescue.

STRATEGIC USES OF THE INTERNET FOR HEALTH AND MEDICINE

(1) Health and Safety Organizations
- public education
- prevention
- institutional promotion

(2) Patients
- communication tool
- research tool

(3) Medical Profession
- medical education
- information sharing
- dissemination of medical research

(4) Veterinary Medicine
- electronic networking
- institutional promotion
- dissemination of medical research

(5) Alternative Medicine
- promotion of alternative medicine

It is sort of like the *Fantasic Voyage* movie of the 1960s, where a group of heroic, dashing medical specialists traveled within the body to solve a particularly nasty medical situation. While such Buck Rogers flights of fancy are wonderful in helping to convey the potential of computer technology within the health profession, the reality is that these capabilities are still many years from widespread implementation and use.

Use of the Internet in Health Care

In contrast, the Internet is already here and in widespread use throughout the health care industry in Canada and around the world. Given the perilous state of our current health care system, due to ongoing government funding cutbacks, there is a need to "re-engineer" the manner in which health care is delivered and provided. One of the major means by which this can occur is through "telemedicine," the application of modern telecommunications technology to medicine, both human and animal.

Telemedicine does not necessarily mean the actual delivery of health care services through the Internet (i.e., from doctor to patient, or as found in the sophisticated scenario above). Instead, it can refer to the simple, effective use of telecommunications within various areas of health care delivery. It can involve medical research, patient education, or electronic communications between medical specialists.

Telemedicine is simply the use of computer and telecommunications technology to support communications between doctors, health care professionals, patients, and virtually anyone working in the medical field — and the Internet is emerging as one of the most important applications of telemedicine. "Almost half of U.S. hospitals now use Internet, according to a 1994 survey by the Healthcare Information and Management Systems Society, Chicago, and Hewlett-Packard Co., Andover, MA." [1]

Led by the early involvement in the Internet by the medical education and medical research communities, the Internet is now extending into hospitals, medical practitioner offices, and into the patient community as well.

This chapter will discuss how the Internet is being used by health and safety organizations, doctors, and medical researchers. In addition, we review how the Internet is used by patients, since, as we shall see, patient education is becoming an increasingly important part of health care delivery. We will also look at use of the Internet within the veterinary and alternative medicine fields.

---

[1] The world at their fingertips — Rural providers turn to the Internet, *Hospitals and Health Networks*, July 20, 1994.

Health and Safety Organizations

At the organizational level the Internet is being used for three distinct purposes:

➤ public education;

➤ prevention;

➤ institutional promotion.

Each of these strategies will be discussed below.

Public Education

There is a growing belief in the medical profession that our nation's health costs can be minimized by ensuring that patients have access to appropriate medical information when they need it, a concept referred to as "consumer health informatics." The belief is that educated patients are less likely to run for medical care at the first sign of a potential health problem. As stated in the January/February 1995 issue of HealthCare Forum, "consumer health informatics provides citizens with the tools, skills, information, and support they need to play the role of primary practitioner in the emerging new healthcare system. The biggest change in thinking this will require for health professionals is that consumers will now increasingly be seen not only as problems but also as resources."

To help educate patients, for many years the health industry has published brochures, booklets, and other information on particular ailments. Now, several health-related organizations, including hospitals, health associations, and medical research institutions, are starting to publish such information on the Internet for direct access by the public. This is characteristic of a general trend in the medical profession toward self-education by patients. *HealthCare Forum* noted the following in its January/February 1995 issue:

> With the support of effective consumer health informatics systems, the old configuration will be replaced with a new Information Age map. In the Information Age healthcare system, people with a health concern or problem will begin by managing it themselves; they will move on to other resources only as needed…the emerging information highway is making it much easier for people with health problems or concerns to reach out for information, advice, and support.

If you work for a health organization that is engaged in public education, the Internet can support your public education activities; a quick tour of the Internet will reveal a wealth of health education activities from a variety of different organizations.

Non-Commercial Initiatives

One example is the Diabetes Knowledgebase, a project of Dr. Donald A. Lehn at the University of Wisconsin Medical School. The Diabetes Knowledgebase disseminates information on diabetes to Internet users worldwide (**http://www.biostat. wisc.edu/diaknow/index.htm**). The site provides a lot of detailed information about diabetes, including diabetic recipes, statistics, a list of frequently asked questions and answers about diabetes, a "diabetes dictionary," and an on-line newsletter about diabetes. Families of diabetics will find this site useful as well. For example, there is a document called "Dealing with a Child Having an Insulin Reaction." There is also information from national diabetes associations, including the Canadian Diabetes Association:

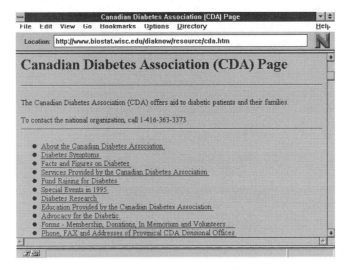

Another example of a comprehensive patient information site on the Internet is OncoLink (**http://cancer.med.upenn.edu**). OncoLink provides Internet users with information about the field of oncology, the study of cancer. OncoLink's administrators use the Internet to rapidly collect and disseminate cancer information to educate health care personnel, patients, families, and other interested parties about the disease. The service is provided free of charge to Internet users around the world and includes reviews of books related to cancer, frequently asked questions about cancer, and cancer news bulletins. A powerful feature of OncoLink is its search capabilities. Internet users can search OncoLink's database for information on specific subjects.

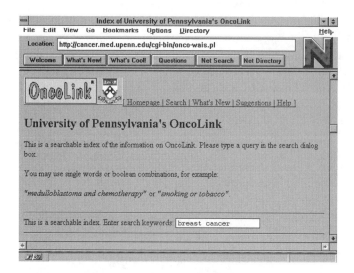

For example, in the screen above we asked OncoLink to search its database for any information pertaining to breast cancer. The search quickly returned a number of matching documents, as seen in the screen below:

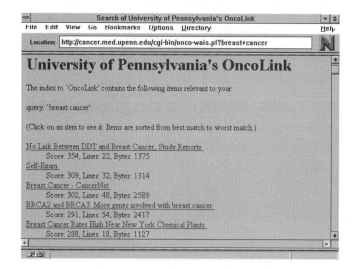

OncoLink also provides information on the various forms of cancer, as seen in the next screen:

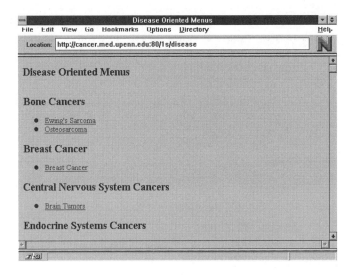

There is also extensive information related to cancer support. For example, there is information on pain management, caring for cancer patients, books and videos for coping with cancer, and a list of cancer support groups.

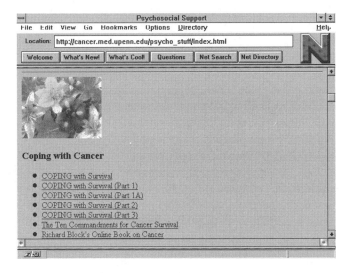

An outstanding example of an academic public health education initiative on the Internet is Ask Alice, an anonymous question and answer service run by the Health Education and Wellness Program of Columbia University (**http://www.columbia. edu/cu/healthwise**). Students at Columbia University can submit questions to the service on any health topic, including emotional well-being, relationships, nutrition and diet, drugs, sex, alcohol, stress, or general health. The answers to the questions are made public so that Internet users all over the world can benefit from the advice. Every answer that Alice has ever given is archived on the Dear Alice site, providing a wealth of health information to Internet users worldwide. There are hundreds of answers to hundreds of different health questions. Here is a sample:

Q. Dear Alice

I hardly drink any fluid during the day; maybe a glass of water with my evening meal. I've been like this my whole life — I just don't get thirsty. Someone told me that this is dangerous. What do you think? I don't handle warm temperatures very well. Could it be related? — The Lizard

A. Dear The Lizard,

Your body absorbs water not only through liquids that you ingest daily, but also extracts it from foods that you eat, as many fruits and vegetables are more than 80% water. Additional water is also produced as a by-product of the metabolic process. If you do not drink enough water, and your total body water falls by 1%–2%, your thirst mechanism is automatically activated. Only in certain situations is your thirst signal unreliable, such as when you are ill or exercising vigorously. In these situations, you need to be more aware of replenishing your body with fluids. This is also very true in warm climates where water loss through perspiration can be significant, so rehydration should be undertaken regularly.

Limited fluid intake results in fluid conservation. This forces the kidneys to conserve water, the results of which manifest in reduced urine flow, or more concentrated urine. If a person actually loses up to a 4% loss of body weight in fluids, then their muscles can lose their strength and endurance. This may be the danger that some of your friends have been talking about.

Some individuals actually do not have an active thirst mechanism. This is a result of not having responded to the thirst mechanism when they were young, and therefore their body has stopped sending this signal. Sounds like it couldn't hurt to be conscious about drinking more than one glass of water or other non-caffeinated beverage each day.

If you work within a university or college environment, consider implementing a similar service on your campus.

Many health education sites on the Internet are funded through government-supported initiatives. For example, the New York State Science and Technology Foundation has funded a site on the Internet for the dissemination of information about bone marrow transplants (**http://nysernet.org./bcic/bmt/bmt.news.html**). The site includes the full text of a publication called *Bone Marrow Transplants — A Book of Basics for Patients*, a guide that explains the issues related to bone marrow transplants.

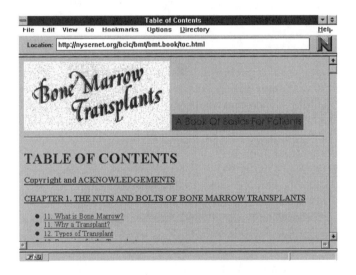

The site also contains a monthly newsletter about bone marrow transplants, written by a former bone marrow transplant patient. Called *The Bone Marrow Transplant Newsletter*, it provides information ranging from detailed medical information to contributions and questions from BMT patients.

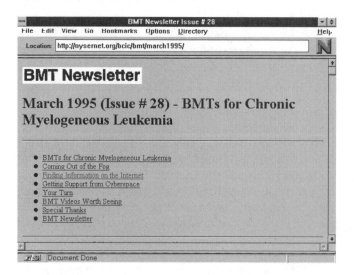

Commercial Initiatives

A number of commercial organizations also provide free public education material on the Internet. The On-line Allergy Center (**http://www.sig.net/~allergy/welcome.html**) is an example of a commercial patient-education initiative. Established by Dr. Russell Roby and his clinic, The Allergy Centre, the site provides a wealth of information for allergy sufferers, including allergy facts and symptoms, allergy news, information about food allergies, and an overview of allergy treatment. The site notes that "allergy is not easily treated or understood, and the patient needs a great deal of information so that they can treat themselves."

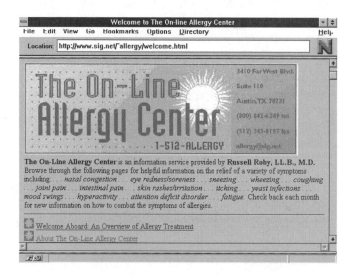

Although Dr. Roby uses this site to market the services that his clinic offers, he is also providing helpful allergy information to Internet users worldwide. In this way, he is creating goodwill toward his clinic and giving something back to the Internet community.

A similar initiative is DentalNet, operated by two Austin, Texas, dentists (**http://www.dentalnet.com/dentalnet**):

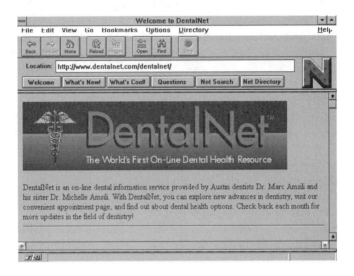

On DentalNet you can learn how to book an appointment with either of the dentists. To make it easy, they even provide you with a map:

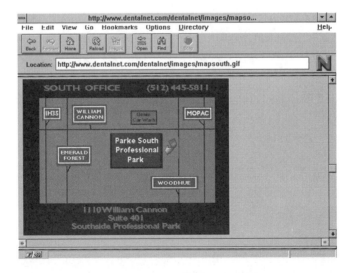

The commercial aspects of DentalNet are offset by the free information that the dentists provide to the Internet community. The dentists frequently publish articles on their site that provide dental tips to the general public. These articles help educate Internet users about proper dental care.

These examples demonstrate that if you are part of a commercial health care organization that is planning on marketing its services through the Internet, you may want to consider providing some free health care information on your Internet site. This will serve two objectives: it will help draw people to your site, and it will create goodwill toward your organization. We discuss this concept in greater depth in Chapter 10, where we outline steps to make your Internet strategy a success.

Prevention

The key objective of many Internet-based health initiatives is prevention. For example, consider the Internet site established by the U.S.-based International Food Information Council (**http://ificinfo.health.org**). The Council helps consumers make informed food choices by "developing and supporting information and educational programs on food safety, nutrition and health." The Internet supports this mandate by allowing the Council to publish its educational materials on-line, where they can be accessed by consumers around the world.

The Council's Internet site includes lots of useful food information for educators, parents, consumers, reporters, and health professionals. For example, the consumer section includes publications on the effects of caffeine, sugar, MSG, food additives, food coloring, as well as a guide called "10 Tips to Healthy Eating for Kids":

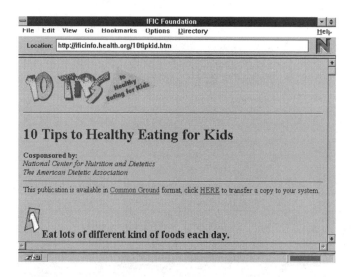

The section for parents includes publications on teen nutrition, hyperactivity, breakfasts, and healthy eating during pregnancy.

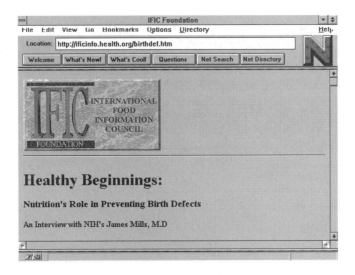

The Center for Injury Research and Control at the University of Pittsburgh sponsors The Injury Control Resource Information Network, an on-line directory of injury-related information sites on the Internet (**http://info.pitt.edu/~hweiss/ injury.htm**).

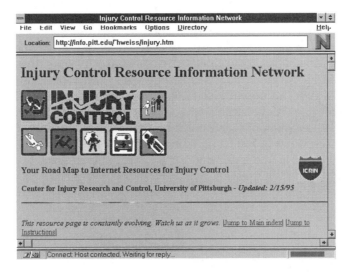

There are a variety of safety subjects indexed on this site, ranging from poisons to firearms to farm safety.

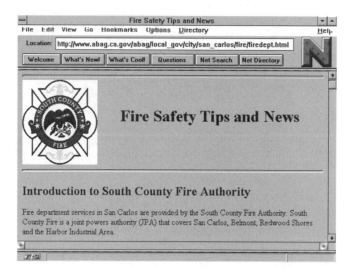

For example, if we select the Fire Safety and Burns section (not shown), we can view fire prevention information that is published by a city fire department in California (**http://www.abag.ca.gov/san_carlos/fire/firedept.html**). The site includes the addresses of local fire halls as well as handouts that describe how to protect your home from a fire. The City of San Carlos Fire Department holds the distinction of being one of the first North American fire departments to distribute fire safety information via the Internet. Canadian fire departments should consider implementing similar Internet programs in order to educate the public about fire safety.

A number of safety organizations are also on the Internet. For example, the Bicycle Helmet Safety Institute in Arlington, Virginia, provides information about bicycle helmet safety to the Internet community. BHSI's World Wide Web site includes a helmet safety newsletter, a bibliography of over 500 helmet safety studies, articles, papers, and pamphlets, program information for organizers of bicycle helmet campaigns, reviews of helmet promotion videos, helmet statistics, a list of manufacturers of bicycle helmets, and much much more (**http://www.bhsi.org**).

Institutional Promotion

The Internet can be used as a promotional tool by health organizations. For example, the Canadian Centre for Occupational Health and Safety has established a World Wide Web site to increase awareness of the products, services, and courses offered by the organization (**http://www.ccohs.ca**).

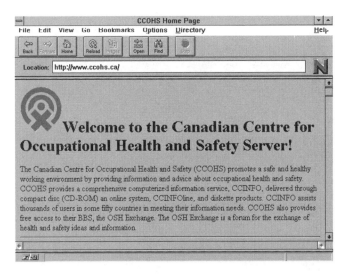

A useful feature of the CCOHS site is that Internet users can obtain demonstration versions of the organization's software products directly off its Web site.

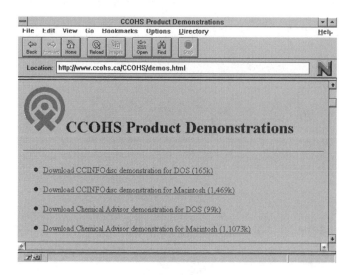

An increasing number of hospitals are also joining the Internet and establishing a presence on the World Wide Web. Hospitals can use the Internet to promote their accomplishments and research activities, thus enhancing their reputation and image in the community and throughout the world — an important step in drawing funding, participating in reseach projects, and in recruiting specialists. The Arkansas Children's Hospital, for example, has the following page on its World Wide Web site, which lists the accomplishments for which the hospital is renowned (**http://www.ach.uams.edu**):

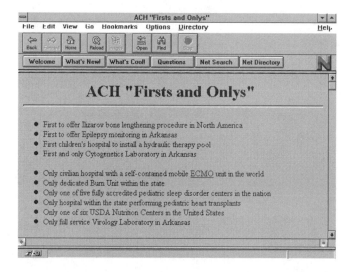

The Dermatology Department at the New York University Medical Center has established a World Wide Web site that describes how it is "the largest single provider of skin care in the United States and an international referral center for rare skin diseases" (**http://www.med.nyu.edu/Derm/HomePage.html**):

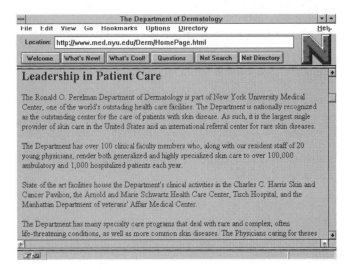

To illustrate the importance of the hospital's work, the hospital has placed two patient "success stories" on its Web site. The profiles describe how two women, one with a facial discoloration and one with melanoma, were able to overcome their medical problems with the help of doctors at the hospital.

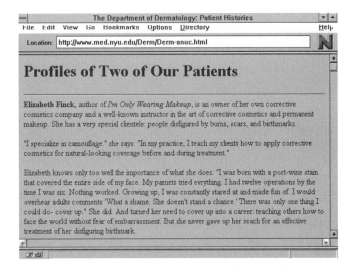

Hospitals can also use the Internet to provide general information about their services, departments, and medical staff to the general public. For example, the Arkansas

Children's Hospital has established a World Wide Web site for its eye clinic. The Web site describes the clinic, the types of patients it services, the services it provides, and its research activities (**http://www.ach.uams.edu/services/ophth/ophth.html**):

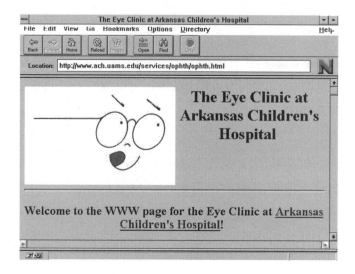

Patients

An important concept of telemedicine is in seeing that patients have access to up-to-date medical literature, support groups, and support information. Through the Internet patients have access to both a communication and research tool.

Communication Tool

The Internet is used on a regular basis by patients who wish to communicate with others who have the same medical condition or have undergone similar medical treatments. Medical professionals often place patients in support groups as an important part of the therapeutic process. Now there is an opportunity for doctors to encourage their patients to participate in such groups through the Internet. Medical professionals can become familiar with how the Internet is used in this way by spending time on-line; this is the best way to understand that the concept of on-line therapy is a valuable addition to the medical "tool kit." To help the medical profession understand how these groups work, we will take a look at the concept in a bit more depth.

By allowing people who have experienced similar medical problems to communicate with each other, the Internet becomes an extremely powerful emotional support tool. The Internet has dozens of mailing lists for people afflicted with specific diseases or medical ailments. Here are just a few examples:

➤ **alt.support.arthritis** (discussion for arthritis sufferers)

➤ **alt.support.asthma** (discussion for asthma sufferers)

➤ **alt.support.sleep-disorder** (discussion for people with sleep disorders)

➤ **DOWN-SYN** (Down's syndrome discussion)

➤ **MSLIST-L** (discussion of multiple sclerosis)

➤ **PARKINSN** (Parkinson's disease network)

➤ **STROKE-L** (stroke discussion list)

➤ **TRNSPLNT** (discussion of organ transplant issues)

These Internet discussion groups are used by people seeking advice or opinions on specific medical issues. On the Internet it is not difficult to locate discussion groups where people with similar medical conditions are gathered. For example, if you are having trouble sleeping, you might want to try seeking advice from the **alt.support.sleep-disorder** discussion group. Gathered there are people from around the world who are interested in this topic. They include researchers, doctors, people with sleep disorders, and former sleep disorder patients.

A snapshot of the discussions that were taking place in early 1995 provides an example of how this self-help group works. Each of the bullets down the left side of the next screen represents a different discussion topic. As you can see, people are seeking advice on topics such as "How Do I Cut Down on My Sleep" to "How Can I Cure My Insomnia."

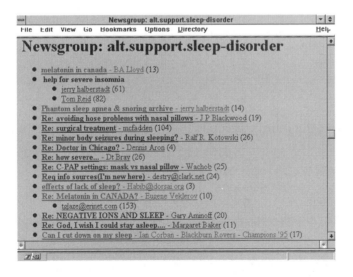

While there are many people asking questions in health discussion groups, there are just as many responding with tips and advice. For example, the following message from Prince Edward Island appeared on the **alt.support.arthritis** discussion group, where people exchange information about arthritis.

From: bjudson@bud.peinet.pe.ca (Barry Judson)
Date: Sat, 8 Apr 1995 07:07:58
Subject: Emu oil: What is it
Organization: PEINet
Newsgroups: alt.support.arthritis, misc.health.arthritis

Hello

Emu oil has been helping a lot of people here on P.E.I. Emu oil is FDA approved. I know a man who has arthritis in his hands. One finger was crooked, knuckles swelled, and he could only close his hand partially with pain. After using the emu oil for a few days the pain and swelling had disappeared and his hand appeared to be normal as long as he kept using the oil. Another woman was going to have to quit her job because of the arthritis but after using the oil she can now keep working. Emu oil is not a cure, but it can relieve the pain as long as you keep using it. Emu oil has a unique composition that cannot be duplicated. It is the only product that can penetrate all layers of the skin. Our skin is phospo-lipid deficient. Any time you put anything on our skin that lacks phosphorus it goes right through. Emu oil is deficient in phosphorus. If you would like more specific info let me know.

People also use health discussion groups to keep each other informed of relevant scientific discoveries or important medical news. For example, the following message appeared on the Parkinson's Disease Information Exchange Network, an Internet discussion group for the discussion of Parkinson's disease:

Date: Mon, 3 Apr 1995 09:57:12 -0400
Reply-To: Parkinson's Disease - Information Exchange Network
<PARKINSN@UTORONTO.BITNET>
Sender: Parkinson's Disease - Information Exchange Network
<PARKINSN@UTORONTO.BITNET>
From: Melony Winkelmann
<WINKELMANNMH@CONRAD.APPSTATE.EDU>
Subject: PD RESEARCH FOR A GENE

Greetings from Boone, NC

The *Charlotte Observer* this morning, April 3, 1995, reports that Duke University neurologist, Allen Roses, whose theory about a gene for Alzheimer's disease is gaining support, is now launching a search for a gene that causes PD. Charlotte neurologist Fred Allen, director of the Metrolina Memory Center at Carolina Neurological Clinic, is among the researchers at seven sites across the country who will be helping Roses find families affected with PD [...].

Research Tool

The other resource to which medical professionals can steer their patients is the on-line research sites. In many ways, pointing a patient towards on-line information is similar to providing them with a brochure or books to read for further information. Earlier in the chapter we discussed how health and safety organizations use the Internet to disseminate information about health topics. The end users of this information are often members of the general public who use the Internet to research information about specific health and safety issues, sometimes at the encouragement of their doctors

Internet resources exist for hundreds of different medical topics. For example, if you are interested in issues related to organ transplants, you will probably be interested in Transweb, an Internet resource that provides general information on topics related to organ transplants and organ donations (**http://www. med.umich.edu:80/trans/transweb**). The site includes a list of recommended readings, information on legislation relevant to organ donations, research reports, and links to transplant centres on the Internet. (Keep in mind that any information you obtain on the Internet is not a substitute for professional medical advice. Seek the advice of your family physician before acting on any medical information you obtain through the Internet.)

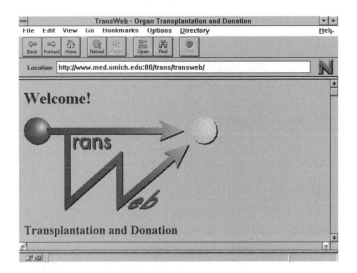

Medical Profession

Medical practitioners use the Internet in three significant ways:

> medical education;

> information sharing;

> dissemination of medical research.

We will discuss each of these applications separately.

Medical Education

The Internet is changing the way that students acquire medical knowledge by providing them with quick access to health information from medical specialists, researchers, and students around the world. The entire process of medical research is being transformed by the instantaneous exchange of knowledge that occurs through the Internet.

Many medical schools have established on-line resources for use by their students. Yet, because of the wide reach of the Internet, these resources are available to medical students around the world, resulting in a variety of learning sources for students. For example, The University of Tennessee at Memphis provides a quiz on the Internet that tests students' knowledge of gross anatomy. After reading each question, students can click on an area of the screen to reveal the correct answer (**http://planetree1.utmem.edu/StudentPages/classes/gross/grossquiz.html**):

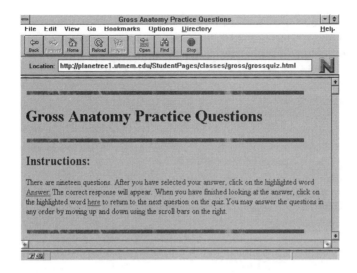

Medical education through the Internet is becoming more promising with advances in the Internet's multimedia capabilities. For example, if you have the right hardware and software on your computer, you can view pictures, listen to sounds, and watch videos. Consider some of the following examples of multimedia applications of the Internet for medical education.

Sounds

Synapse Publishing, a medical publisher based at the University of Alberta, provides audio files of "heart sounds" on its World Wide Web site (**http://synapse.uah.ualberta.ca/synapse/00b10000.htm**). This helps students specializing in this area, as well as general practitioners, learn how to relate particular heart murmurs and other problems to the sounds the heart makes.

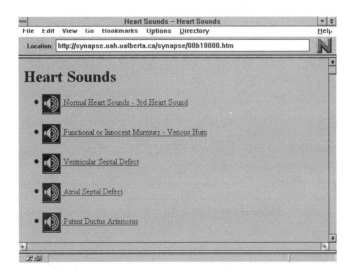

Video

General Electric's research division is making available video clips of various medical simulations on its World Wide Web site (**http://www.ge.com/crd**), including a simulation of a baby delivery, as seen in the next screen. To view the videos, you need a piece of software known as an MPEG viewer, which is available at various locations on the Internet.

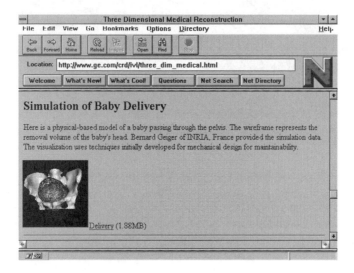

Pictures

The Department of Radiology at the University of Washington uses the Internet to help radiology students learn how to read x-rays. The Department has established a World Wide Web site (**http://www.rad.washington.edu**) that provides pictures of x-rays from real medical cases. Students can view the x-rays on the Internet and make a diagnosis based on what they see. They can then test the accuracy of their diagnostic skills by comparing their diagnosis to the correct answer which is provided on the Web site.

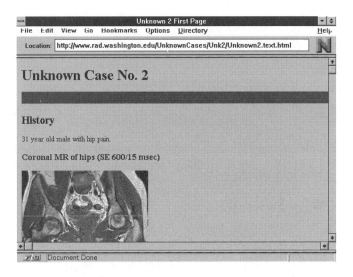

The department regularly runs an "x-ray diagnosis contest" on its Internet site. An x-ray is posted and students and other radiology professionals from around the world are invited to submit their diagnoses. Those with the correct diagnosis have their names publicly posted on the department's Web site.

Cornell University Medical College (**http://edcenter.med.cornell.edu/**) uses the Internet for a similar purpose. It publishes cases (with pictures) on the Internet to allow students to test their diagnostic skills:

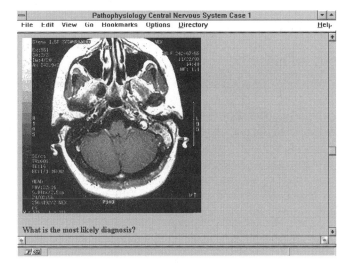

Medical Indices

New medical education resources are emerging every week on the Internet. To make it easier for medical students to locate educational materials on the Internet, a first-year medical student at Loma Lindu University in California has created a site called "The Medical Education Page," which provides pointers to medical educational resources throughout the Internet. The resources include Internet discussion groups, medical teaching materials, medical schools, and medical centres (**http://www.primenet.com:80/ ~gwa/med.ed**).

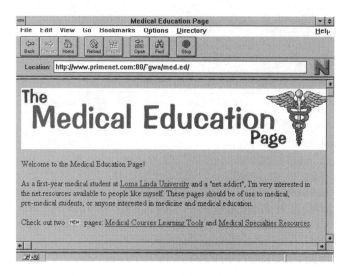

Information Sharing

Around the world medical students, physicians, researchers, and other medical professionals are using the collaborative powers of the Internet to share information with other physicians and seek advice from medicial specialists. The wide reach of the Internet means that information can quickly be broadcast to doctors worldwide. For example, the Arkansas Children's Hospital Eye Clinic maintains a Patient Picture Gallery on its World Wide Web site that shows pictures of patients with "interesting ocular findings." Other physicians who have encountered similar findings with their own patients or who have any comments are encouraged to contact the Eye Clinic (**http://www.ach.uams.edu:80/services/ophth**) so that notes can be compared. The Internet improves the likelihood that doctors with similar findings and/or interests will discover each other, thus improving opportunities for collaborative research.

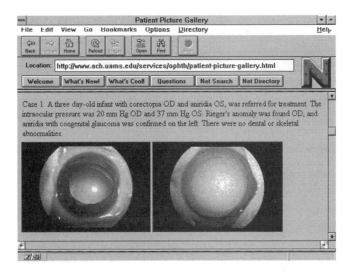

There are hundreds of discussion groups from which medical professionals can choose to link up with their colleagues around the world. There are specialized discussion groups for virtually every medical profession. Topics include anesthesiology, bariatrics, cardiology, dermatology, emergency medicine, family medicine, gastroenterology, geriatrics, gynecology, immunology, infectious diseases, neurology, oncology, ophthalmology, orthopedics, pathology, pediatrics, public health, psychiatry, radiology, rheumatology, sports medicine, surgery, and many other medical disciplines.

To understand how these discussion groups are being used, consider the following messages, which were posted to a discussion group on pediatric emergency medicine with over 250 subscribers from around the world. The first message, posted by a doctor in Boston, asks for information about the use of radio base stations in pediatric hospitals.

Date: Mon, 6 Mar 1995 16:46:00 EST
Reply-To: Pediatric Emergency Medicine Discussion List
<PED-EM-L@BROWNVM.BITNET>
Sender: Pediatric Emergency Medicine Discussion List
<PED-EM-L@BROWNVM.BITNET>
From: "Baruch Krauss, M.D." <KRAUSS@A1.TCH.
HARVARD.EDU>
Subject: Radio Control Base Stations

I would be interested in knowing if anyone on this list is
working at a children's/pediatric hospital that serves as
a radio control base station (gives radio control to the

---

paramedics) for the local EMS system and what your experience has been with it.

Thanks,

Baruch Krauss, MD
Emergency Department
Children's Hospital, Boston
Internet address: Krauss@A1.TCH.harvard.edu

This doctor was able to receive a number of responses from other pediatric departments that described their experiences with radio base stations. For example, the following message was posted to the list from a pediatric hospital in New York:

Date: Tue, 7 Mar 1995 20:11:51 -0500
Reply-To: Pediatric Emergency Medicine Discussion List
<PED-EM-L@BROWNVM.BITNET>
Sender: Pediatric Emergency Medicine Discussion List
<PED-EM-L@BROWNVM.BITNET>
From: Thomas Terndrup
<TERNDRUT@SNYSYRV1.BITNET>
Subject: Re: radio control

Our experience with on-line medical control has been very good. We are blessed with many highly trained paramedics and other out-of-hospital providers. Generally, we find they are somewhat less comfortable with assessing and treating younger children. It seems (anecdotally) that we are able to increase their comfort level on-line or after arrival at the hospital (the latter through verbal feedback on their proficiency).

Tom Terndrup, MD
Director, Pediatric ED
SUNY Health Science Center at Syracuse

In another example from the pediatric medicine discussion group, one of the physicians on the list posted the following message:

Date: Fri, 24 Mar 1995 12:58:57 -0500
Reply-To: Pediatric Emergency Medicine Discussion List
<PED-EM-L@BROWNVM.BITNET>
Sender: Pediatric Emergency Medicine Discussion List
<PED-EM-L@BROWNVM.BITNET>
From: "Jeff Hoffman, M.D." <KiddyDoc@AOL.COM>
Subject: Re: Security

We just had one of our luckily rare incidents in Kansas City the other night. A disgruntled father became physically violent during an IV attempt on his child. He pushed two of our nurses into the cabinets and picked up a chair to threaten everyone else. Despite the direct effect of this violence, he also scared the !#*$*! out of the rest of the parents in the department (not to mention the effect on the children).

We have a panic button system to alert security to immediate threats and the ability to lock-down the ER with magnetic door locks. However, our security guards don't carry weapons…so in an armed crisis they are no better than human bullet shields (and perhaps more likely targets). We called the police (since the nurses wanted protection and to have the father charged with battery), but it took several minutes for them to arrive.

Unlike our adult counterparts, I'm not aware of any pediatric ERs that have had episodes of armed violence. But I don't believe we have to wait for such episodes to occur before taking necessary precautions.

This message generated responses from other pediatric physicians in the discussion group who described how their hospitals handled security.

Another popular use of medical discussion lists is exchanging case notes and asking for advice from other physicians. For example, if a doctor is unsure how to diagnose or treat a patient, the Internet is often used to seek feedback from other physicians.

In all these examples the Internet made it possible for the doctors to quickly obtain advice and feedback from their colleagues. For hundreds of years, consultation between medical professionals has been an important part of medince, and the Internet permits any doctor or medical professional to consult with peers worldwide. In this way, it promises to dramatically extend the capabilities of medical professionals and help them solve difficult and unusual problems.

Dissemination of Medical Research

The Internet has had a big impact on how medical research is disseminated around the world. One of the articles used to open this chapter (How the Net caught science, *Globe & Mail*, June 16, 1993) commented on the manner in which information in the scientific community is distributed:

> ...the speed with which ideas are communicated has often been a basic regulator on the pace of scientific progress. In the 17th century, books were the main way of disseminating new ideas. The process was costly, haphazard and slow. This spawned the scientific journal, which made its debut in 1665. The *Philosophical Transactions of the Royal Society of London* was published monthly, and its success prompted a deluge of such periodicals.
>
> ...Publication can still entail delays of many months, and sometimes years...Ann Okerson, head of scientific publishing at the Association of Research Libraries, a trade group in Washington, said...these libraries dramatically increased their use of the computer networks. "They really do transform the way work is done," she said from a conference in Hawaii, where she periodically tapped the Internet from a portable computer hooked up to a hotel telephone...

In addition to being a source of advice and a place for information sharing, the Internet is used to disseminate research findings to medical researchers and practioners around the globe. For example, the United States National Library of Medicine uses the Internet to distribute "clinical alerts" that announce clinical findings from research studies sponsored by the National Institutes of Health. Normally, these findings would first be announced in medical journals, but because of the lengthly process involved in publishing findings in print, the announcements are circulated on the Internet so that more lives can be saved. Here is an extract from a typical announcement:

> Clinical Alert: Drug Treatment for Sickle Cell Anemia
> National Heart, Lung, and Blood Institute (NHLBI)
> January 30, 1995
>
> Abstract:
> The National Heart, Lung, and Blood Institute (NHLBI) today announced a drug treatment for sickle cell anemia.

Findings from a multicenter clinical trial show that daily administration of the drug hydroxyurea reduced by about 50% the frequency of painful episodes and hospital visits for those episodes. The treatment also reduced the frequency of acute chest syndrome and the number of blood transfusions for patients in the study.

Source: National Institutes of Health Clinical Alerts
gopher://gopher.nlm.nih.gov

Harvard Medical School publishes its bi-weekly newsletter on the Internet. Called "Focus," it features news about clinical and basic research undertaken by faculty and students in Harvard's Medical School, School of Dental Medicine, and School of Public Health. The newsletter is free to Internet users.

Cancer:

PROTEIN PATHWAY: HOW A TAME VIRUS TURNS WILD

In the menagerie of pathogens, the Epstein-Barr virus is usually one of the tamest. Ninety percent of all Americans are infected with the virus, but in the vast majority of people, it causes no problems once the initial illness — a sore throat or infectious mononucleosis — has passed. However, in people whose immune systems have been compromised by organ transplantation or the AIDS virus, the Epstein-Barr virus can cause fatal cancers of the immune system. Researchers have long puzzled over how the virus stirs cancer, and now a team of Harvard Medical School scientists appear to have found an answer. In a paper published in the Feb. 10 issue of *Cell*, HMS researchers report that they have identified an interaction between a viral protein and a cellular protein that produces unfettered cell growth.

Focus
March 17, 1995
**http://count51.med.harvard.edu/publications/Focus/
.index.html**

A great number of medical journals are migrating towards electronic versions on the Internet to ensure that information gets out to the medical research community as quickly as possible. While some journals charge for electronic versions, other journals are available without charge on the Internet. *The Journal of Medical Imaging*, for example (**http://jmi.gdb.org/JMI/ejourn.html**), is an experimental effort to get around the problems of delays in information distribution. As it notes on-line, "the purpose of *The Journal of Medical Imaging* is to improve the communication of scientific and engineering developments in the field of medical imaging. This journal can offer a solution to the problems of long delays between acceptance of a paper and its publication, the inferior quality of image reproduction, and the lack of color and dynamic cine displays."

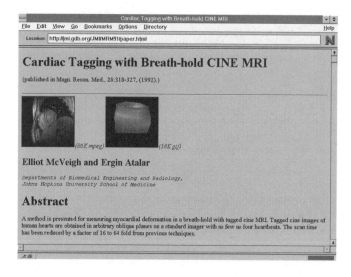

The Atlanta-based Centres for Disease Control and Prevention publish the journal *Emerging Infectious Diseases* through the Internet. The entire contents of each issue are available for free on the Internet through CDC's Web site (**http://www.cdc.gov**). The CDC makes each issue available in a special format (called Adobe Acrobat) so that complex charts, graphs, and images can be viewed in their entirety, *exactly* as they appear in the printed version of the publication. The software required to view a journal in Adobe Acrobat format is available free of charge on the CDC's Web site.

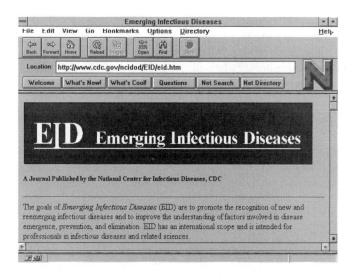

The Global Emergency Medical Archives (**http://solaris.ckm.ucsf.edu: 8081/**) is another Internet-based electronic journal and a "pilot project demonstrating the use of the Internet to share Emergency Medicine information." Emergency medicine specialists from around the world contribute articles to the journal. There is no print version. Articles that are accepted for publication are immediately placed on the journal's World Wide Web site where they can be read by Internet users all over the globe.

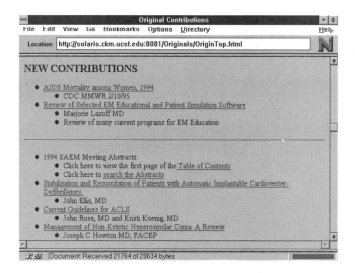

Electronic journals have many advantages over paper journals since letters to the editor and comments about articles can appear immediately. The Global Emergency Medical Archives allows anyone on the Internet to submit a letter to the editor or contribute a comment about an article through the journal's "interactive forum page," which serves as a place for on-line discussion and debate among readers.

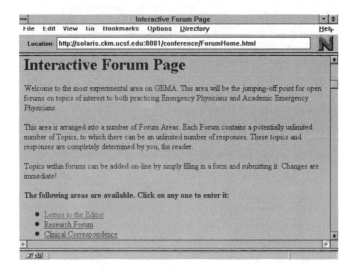

Many medical journals do not publish the full text of their articles on the Internet, but instead use the Internet to distribute the table of contents of their publication to increase readership and encourage sales and subscriptions. For example, the following screen shows a detailed summary of the April 1995 contents of *Radiation Research* published on the USENET group **bionet.journals.contents**:

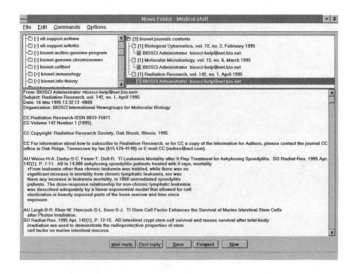

Specialized World Wide Web sites are emerging on the Internet that act as clearinghouses for research on specific areas of medicine. These sites are useful to doctors and medical researchers because they provide a common meeting place for specialists in particular areas of medicine. Here are a few examples of specialized medical Web sites.

A site called the Alzheimer Web has been established to disseminate information on Alzheimer's disease (**http://werple.mira.net.au/~dhs/ad.html**). The site contains articles on Alzheimer's, conference information, hypotheses on the cause of Alzheimer's disease, and general information on the treatment and diagnosis of Alzheimer's. The site also maintains links to research laboratories and organizations on the Internet that have some connection with Alzheimer's.

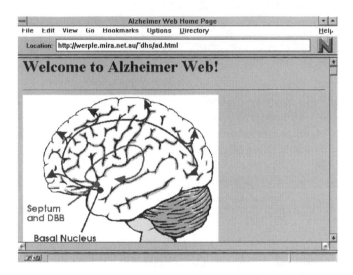

The Johns Hopkins University School of Medicine has established a site on the Internet for the dissemination of information and research pertaining to hearing and balance (**http://www.bme.jhu.edu/labs/chb**). The site includes a glossary of balance terms and balance disorders, case studies, research results, and frequently asked questions about dizziness. There are links to other auditory and balance sites on the Internet.

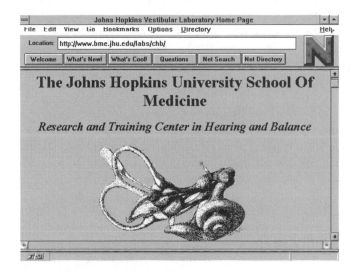

The Marshall University School of Medicine has created a site on the Internet called RuralNet, which acts as a clearinghouse for information and research pertaining to rural health care (**http://ruralnet.mu.wvnet.edu**). The site provides links to documents, research reports, and Internet sites related to rural health care.

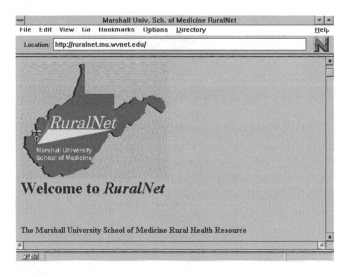

In all these examples the Internet is being used as a communication tool that permits medical professionals worldwide to share information, which greatly helps to advance the cause of global medical research.

Veterinary Medicine

The Internet's health care resources are not limited to information about human health. As we noted in the chapter opening, telemedicine is defined as the "application of modern telecommunications technology to medicine, both human and animal." As might be expected, there is a lot of health-related activity in the veterinary field as well.

Electronic Networking

There are dozens of veterinary mailing lists where veterinarians from around the world discuss topics of mutual interest and share information with each other. Veterinary mailing lists not only provide a place to seek advice from other veterinarians, but they also provide an opportunity to keep up with news and research in the veterinary field. A sample of some of the veterinary discussion groups available on the Internet provides an indication of the diversity of topics:

- **VETADM-L** (discussion of veterinary hospital administration);

- **VETIMM-L** (discussion of veterinary immunology);

- **VETLIB-L** (discussion of veterinary libraries);

- **VETMICRO** (discussion of veterinary microbiology).

To illustrate how these veterinary discussion lists are being used, consider the following sample messages from **VETMED-L**, a discussion group for students, professionals, and others employed in or interested in the veterinary profession. The first two messages are from veterinarians, while the latter two are from members of the general public.

Date: Thu, 2 Mar 1995 13:45:22 -0500
Reply-To: Veterinary Medicine <VETMED-L@UGA.BITNET>
Sender: Veterinary Medicine <VETMED-L@UGA.BITNET>
From: Chip Ridky <afcridk@gatekeeper.ddp.state.me.us>
Subject: Hedgehogs and other "pocket pets"

Hedgehogs are not currently permitted to be sold in pet-shops in Maine. A request has been made to the State's wildlife department to allow their sale. As a state veterinarian I have been asked for my opinion from a health (including public health) standpoint. To say the least I am no expert on these critters and could use some advice [...]

Chip Ridky, D.V.M.
Maine Dept. of Agriculture
Veterinary Services
Augusta, Me. 04333
afcridk@state.me.us

Date: Wed, 25 Jan 1995 11:36:01 -0500
Reply-To: Veterinary Medicine <VETMED-L@UGA.BITNET>
Sender: Veterinary Medicine <VETMED-L@UGA.BITNET>
From: Evan Blonder <blondee@IIA.ORG>
Subject: Psychomotor Disease in German Sheperd Dog

My colleague has a case that presents an interesting diagnosis, and we need some help and direction from members with experience in this field.

We have a 16-month female spayed German sheperd mix that experiences episodic bouts of disorientation, space staring, and lethargy coupled with hypothermia (cold ears, paws, and tail). It has happened 4 times so far every 2–4 weeks, and the episodes lasts about 12 hours, before she becomes normal again [...]

Any comments?

Evan Blonder, D.V.M.
Lisa Bongiovanni, D.V.M.
Bayonne Animal Hospital

Date: Wed, 8 Mar 1995 15:00:54 -0500
Reply-To: Veterinary Medicine <VETMED-L@UGA.BITNET>
Sender: Veterinary Medicine <VETMED-L@UGA.BITNET>
From: LBaer2@aol.com
Subject: Equine Chiropractic

I am interested in hearing comments from veterinarians and others in the horse industry regarding the use of chiropractic techniques for pleasure/show horses [...]

Date: Fri, 13 Jan 1995 13:00:06 -0800
Reply-To: Veterinary Medicine <VETMED-L@UGA.BITNET>
Sender: Veterinary Medicine <VETMED-L@UGA.BITNET>
From: "Betty J. Goetz"
<Betty_Goetz@RACESMTP.AFSC.NOAA.GOV>
Subject: Siberian husky temperament

This discussion group provides me with a forum for asking
a question to all vet medicine practitioners. How would
you characterize the temperament of the purebred Siberian
husky patients you deal with? I ask this question to help
me approach a temperament issue with our regional and
national breed clubs [...]

Institutional Promotion

Dozens of veterinary colleges and university departments of veterinary medicine
have a presence on the World Wide Web and use it to disseminate information on their
academic programs and research activities. The Ontario Veterinary College, for example, maintains a site (**http://www.ovcnet.uoguelph.ca/HomePage.html**) that
provides general information on the college and its programs and departments.

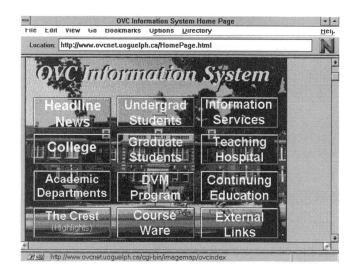

Dissemination of Medical Research

The veterinary profession also uses the Internet for the dissemination of medical research. An excellent example is NetVet, an initiative of Dr. Ken Boschert, a U.S. veterinarian. NetVet provides links to veterinary resources on the Internet, including discussion groups, professional associations, veterinary colleges, research laboratories, veterinary legislation, and information sites for various animal species, ranging from birds and cats to reptiles and rodents (**http://netvet.wustl.edu**).

Thus the veterinary medical field has discovered that the Internet can be used for the same objectives as the human medical field.

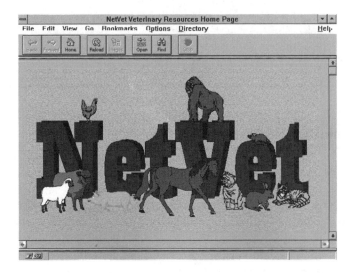

Alternative Medicine

Finally, since anyone can be a publisher on the Internet, it should come as no surprise that there are a number of sites on the Internet that are dedicated to alternative medical methods and practices.

Promotion of Alternative Medicine

There are numerous Internet sites that provide access to a variety of information sources on alternative medicine. An Internet site called Healing Methods, for example, offers information on ancient healing techniques (**http://zeta.cs.adfa.oz.au/Spirit/healing.html**).

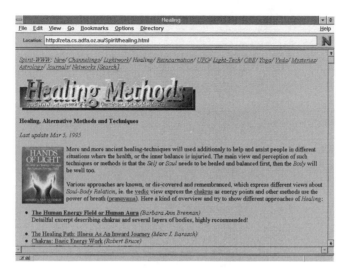

Some of the alternative medicine sites are commercial ventures, such as the site illustrated below, which sells videos and books on alternative medicine as well as nutritional supplements (**http://www.maui.net:80/drbill**):

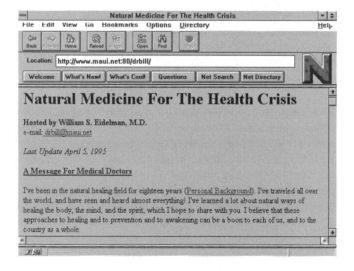

There are also numerous discussion groups dedicated to alternative medicine, such as the USENET newsgroup **misc.health.alternative**, depicted in the next screen, where people from around the world are exchanging information on non-conventional forms of medical treatment.

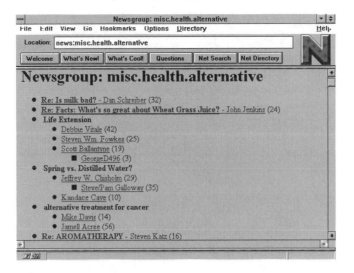

Many may wonder whether people who use the Internet in this way are obtaining improper medical advice. The answer is yes, but the same risk exists for all the medical sites presented in this chapter. Medical professionals must be aware that patients now have, through the Internet, access to a wide variety of medical information, and they must thus become more involved in counselling their patients on the adequacy of particular medical solutions.

Telemedicine Skepticism

Some people are skeptical about the whole concept of health care via telecommunication networks. A recent initiative in Ontario concerning health information being made available via a 900 telephone number drew this response: "At least one healthcare advocacy group wonders whether the information highway has stretched too far into health care. 'Once upon a time we had the family doctor coming to us, then we had to go to the family doctor and now you don't have to go at all,' said Stephen Learey, spokesman for the Canadian Health Coalition in Ottawa. 'I'd hate to think people would replace seeing a doctor with pressing buttons.'"[2]

Telemedicine is not about replacing visits to the doctor, and by no means is it about changing the medical profession as we know it today. Telemedicine is about trying to improve the delivery of health care services in Canada and reducing demand on a resource that will become increasingly scarce as public budgets continue to come under increasing strain in Canada. It is about allowing medical research to continue unabated, so that medical knowledge is shared worldwide, permitting more rapid

---

[2] Dial-a-doctor 900 service starts: $6 house call, *Business Information Wire*, July 13, 1994.

advances in finding new solutions to difficult medical problems. It is about empowering medical professionals with the ability to network with their colleagues worldwide, wherever they might be. Finally, it is about encouraging people to get more involved in health care by giving them tools so that they can learn more about particular problems and ailments before requiring services from the health care system.

CHAPTER 9

The Importance of an Internet Strategy

> The place to start creating an organization strategy for telecommunications is with the business opportunity, not the technology...the firm's leaders have to take a fresh look at the opportunities of the future.
>
> *Competing in Time*, Peter G.W. Keen

*T*he Chief Executive Officer of a publicly traded company recently used the Internet to publicize his position with respect to a proposed corporate takeover. Accounting firms, mutual fund companies, and major banks in Canada are establishing information sites on the Internet. Major media companies are investing heavily in the network. Business in Canada is clearly gaining an interest in the potential of the Internet.

Bay Street, *Fortune* 500 organizations, and other large business organizations seem to be waking up to the fact that the Internet has become a serious business network, full of normal, everyday people who use the network to retrieve information, perform research, or communicate with others. There is also the growing recognition that "*our customers are using this thing!*"

Yet, a preliminary look around the Internet would indicate that the Internet activities of many of these organizations are nothing more than an exercise in public relations. For many organizations the Internet is still treated as an experiment and hence is low on the corporate priority list. In many cases, corporate Internet initiatives are backroom activities supported on shoestring budgets by information technology staff. In these situations the Internet is not part of an organization's corporate strategy, and senior management provides little support for the organization's Internet activities.

THE IMPORTANCE OF AN INTERNET STRATEGY

15 Steps to an Internet Strategy

(1) Get on-line!

(2) Determine the state of Internet planning in your organization.

(3) Determine the scope of your Internet strategy.

(4) Understand how your industry and market are responding to the Internet:
- Assess Internet activity in your industry or market;
- Assess the Internet activities of individual firms in your industry or market;
- Think about your customers and target audience;
- Think about Internet initiatives and programs that might support your Internet strategy.

(5) Determine the extent of Internet knowledge in your organization and educate accordingly

(6) Determine your organization's Internet objectives.

(7) Be a good Internet citizen.

(8) Define the benefits of the Internet.

(9) Develop a vision for the Internet.

(10) Determine the Internet tools that you will use:
- Electronic mail;
- Mail robots;
- Announcement-only mailing lists;
- Discussion mailing lists;
- USENET newsgroups;
- The World Wide Web.

(11) Determine how you will use these Internet tools.

(12) Determine whether you should hire a subcontractor to design and implement your system:
- In-house Internet connections;
- Third-party services.

(13) Define the costs of establishing Internet services:
- Equipment and telecommunications;
- Training.

(14) Add the finishing touches.

(15) Create your plan and establish a time line.

Management Understanding is Critical

Senior management within corporate Canada must understand what is happening on the Internet — not technically, but *strategically*. In his book *Competing in Time: Using Telecommunications for Strategic Advantage*, Peter G.W. Keen observed that "creating an organizational strategy for telecommunications requires a new style of business thinking among senior managers, who must also have some insights into the key aspects of the technology itself."

Sadly, he later quotes someone who observes that "most of our top management team really don't have a clue what to do about IT (information technology). They are at the mercy of the techies. They just nod their head and hope they don't show their ignorance." This is a typical problem in many companies across Canada when it comes to the Internet. Unfortunately, management fails to realize what is happening here. They fail to grasp the opportunities that the Internet can provide, and they do not take the time to learn how the Internet can be used to reach key business objectives.

Perhaps this is so because much of the talk about the Internet in Canada has focused on Internet technology, with very little focus on the Internet's role in business strategy. Whatever the reason, the result is that the Internet does not get a sufficient degree of management attention in Canada.

Be Serious about the Internet at a Senior Level

Organizations can no longer plead ignorance when it comes to the Internet. With the massive amount of corporate, government, and not-for-profit activity under way on the network, management *must* take the time to understand the strategic opportunities to be found on the Internet.

Unfortunately, in many organizations Internet activities are still the private domain of the techies — computer support personnel in information systems departments. These people recognize that the world's first universal information utility has arrived on their desks in the form of the World Wide Web. These technical staff try, often with great difficulty, to get senior management to recognize that the information highway is being built right under their noses. They build company World Wide Web sites on their own time to try to get their organizations to understand what is happening. These people recognize that a global information revolution is occurring through the Internet and passionately believe that they must get their organizations involved.

In the meantime, management waits, cheque in hand, ready to invest in the information superhighway promised by entertainment, cable, and telephone companies, a system that everyone knows is many, many years away. Consequently, Internet initiatives are often built by staff who are underfunded, do not have a sufficient degree of corporate guidance and support, and who do not have a mandate to pursue the Internet as a project.

In some situations management only gets involved with the Internet when it becomes opportune to do so. The authors of this book have witnessed many situations like this. In one case, a national TV show approached a particularly high-profile organization that had a presence on the Canadian Internet. The World Wide Web site, well known throughout the Internet, had been built as a part-time effort by a member of the organization's technical staff. As a result of the media attention, the public relations department of this organization immediately demanded the right to participate in the interview to express the company's "strategic vision" concerning the use of the Internet as a customer service tool. Yet, the first question they asked of the staff member who built the Internet site was "what's the Internet?" The public relations staff were clueless about the Internet and its strategic potential, as were the rest of management. If it wasn't such a sad situation, it would be laughable.

Business Strategies and the Internet

In previous chapters we reviewed the strategic opportunities that exist on the Internet for business, government, not-for-profit organizations and associations, and organizations in the educational and health care sectors. Identifying the opportunities is a natural starting point for dealing with the Internet, but in order for an organization to successfully use the Internet, an Internet strategy must be developed. An organizationwide Internet strategy will make use of the strategies that we discussed in previous chapters.

Any organization can dabble with the Internet and play with its technologies. Without question, the Internet can be a lot of fun. Any organization can send its staff to explore the Internet and have them come back with a summary of their discoveries. But for an organization to be truly successful with the Internet, it must approach it seriously. The organization must develop a strategic plan.

Strategic planning, in general, is an important step to success for any organization. Use of the Internet should be part of an organization's strategic plan. We are not suggesting that you form committees and hold meetings and discuss and debate the Internet *ad nauseam* within your organization. We are suggesting that you spend time planning, thinking, preparing, and plotting. We are suggesting that you not only identify the opportunities that you see on the Internet, but that you prepare a plan that identifies how you hope to exploit those opportunities.

In this chapter we will outline a few of our thoughts on how you can prepare an Internet strategic plan for your organization. This chapter is applicable to business, government, not-for-profit organizations and educational and health care organizations. While it might seem less applicable to educational bodies and institutions, strategic planning within these organizations is just as critical as for those in the business sector, and much of the guidance herein will be equally applicable to those organizations.

A 15-Step Approach to an Internet Strategy

To maximize the use of the Internet in your corporate strategy, you first need to know what your organization's corporate strategy is. A corporate strategy defines an organization's goals and objectives and outlines the courses of action required to achieve those goals and objectives. A corporate strategy may not exist or be known to all levels of management within your organization. If this is the case, you will need to spend some time identifying what senior management views as the goals and objectives of your business. These goals and objectives can often be found in your organization's mission statement, vision statement, or annual report.

For example, Fisher-Price, a world-renowned manufacturer of children's toys, has established the following strategic objectives for its organization, which form part of the organization's vision:

FISHER-PRICE
STRATEGIC OBJECTIVES[1]

➤ To ensure that Fisher-Price continues to be the most trusted name in children's products

➤ To increase our worldwide recognition as the leader in children's products

➤ To provide children with innovative toys that will allow them to have fun and enjoy long-term imaginative play

➤ To achieve excellent performance through people, Fisher-Price will create an environment of team-work, empowerment, recognition, and personal growth

➤ To provide our retail customers outstanding service and the opportunity for sales at competitive margins throughout the year

➤ To enrich the lives of others in our communities, particularly children, by contributing generously of our human and financial resources

---

Once you know your organization's goals, you can more confidently "surf" the Internet to discover how the Internet might be used in your organization, by relating those goals to use of the Internet.

---

[1] Fisher-Price Vision Statement, May 3, 1994.

An Internet strategy is more than just a list of what you want to accomplish on the Internet. Below is a suggested series of steps that may help you in defining your Internet strategy.

- Get on-line!
- Determine the state of Internet planning in your organization.
- Determine the scope of your Internet strategy.
- Understand how your industry and market are responding to the Internet.
- Determine the extent of Internet knowledge in your organization and educate accordingly.
- Determine the objectives.
- Be a good Internet citizen.
- Define the benefits.
- Develop the vision.
- Determine the Internet tools that you will use.
- Determine how you will use these tools.
- Determine whether you should hire a subcontractor to design and implement your system.
- Define the costs.
- Add the finishing touches.
- Create your plan and establish a timeline.

Much of the material in this chapter assumes that you need to justify an Internet presence to your management. In many ways, the chapter is a tutorial on business planning fundamentals as they relate to the Internet. However, this may not be the case for many of you. Your role as decision makers will mean that you will not need guidance on basic Internet business strategies. In that case, you can skip the fundamentals and take a look at Step 10, where we describe some of the key Internet tools.

Step 1: Get On-Line!

The first step in developing an Internet strategy is to actually use the network. You cannot figure out what the Internet is all about without getting on the network and looking around. The Internet, like good food and fine wine, is best appreciated through actual experience: reading about a good restaurant is never as satisfying as actually going there.

For many people the first "live" exposure to the World Wide Web is a magical experience which transforms their view of the world. Observing marketing and communication strategies in action on the Internet is eye-opening. Visiting government sites provides insight into how government services can be delivered through the Internet. Similarly, visiting educational sites shows how the Internet is affecting education. Visiting business sites provides an appreciation for how the Internet is redefining corporate communications and marketing, and gives new meaning to the words "customer service." Just observing some of the 100 to 400 new sites that appear *each week* is stunning.

Observing what is happening in USENET discussion groups and electronic mailing lists will change your view of human knowledge exchange. For businesspeople, witnessing the new consumer dynamics that occur in Internet discussion groups changes their view of consumer power. A teacher can observe how students use the Internet to communicate worldwide and how teachers can talk to other teachers about any aspect of education. A politician can use the Internet to observe the grassroots discussions happening in a local area or on a national level. An advocacy or not-for-profit group can observe what people have to say about a particular emerging issue.

There is no other way to get a feel for what is happening on the Internet than getting on-line. There is no better way of judging what might be possible with the Internet than observing what is already happening on the Internet. If you wish to develop an Internet strategy for your organization, you need to get on the Internet.

Step 2: Determine The Current State of Internet Planning Within Your Organization

Before you proceed with an Internet strategy, determine the current state of Internet planning within your organization so that you do not duplicate what someone else has already done. Do research to determine whether anyone else within your organization is currently working on an Internet strategy or has prepared a strategy paper that was rejected by management. If this is the case, you may want to coordinate your efforts with that person. (If the previous strategy was rejected, find out why, so that you can address management's concerns in your own proposal. The Internet is changing so quickly that the circumstances under which the strategy was originally rejected may no longer be valid. Moreover, there may be new reasons for the organization to get connected, such as recent competitor activities, new technologies, or other developments.)

Step 3: Determine the Scope of Your Internet Strategy

This step is an important one. You will have to decide at what level you want to tackle the Internet. For example, do you want to prepare a strategy for the overall company or just for your particular department? If you are part of a small company (e.g., 2 – 50 employees), this is not really an issue. You will probably prepare an Internet strategy for the entire organization. However, if you are part of a large company with hundreds of employees and multiple divisions, offices, departments, and subsidiaries, you will need to determine the scope of your Internet strategy and how it interrelates with other Internet strategies within the organization.

For example, if you work in one division of a large company, are you working on an Internet strategy for your division only, or is your strategy an organization-wide strategy? If you restrict your strategy to your division, you will need to ensure that your activities do not conflict with or duplicate other corporatewide Internet plans being made by your organization.

Rather than having a single comprehensive Internet strategy, many organizations will have a set of interrelated Internet strategies, with each strategy being formulated by a different division of the firm. This is because the Internet strategies required by one division or department of the firm may be very different from the Internet strategies required by another division or department.

For example, the Lubricants Division of Dupont will have different Internet needs than DuPont's Plastics Division. Therefore, different Internet strategies are required. Yet, despite this decentralized approach, a corporate-level Internet strategy should still exist that sets the direction of the strategy within the entire organization, sets standards for corporate image, and ensures consistency and cohesion across all the departmental or division Internet strategies. For example, DuPont could have a corporate Internet strategy that would establish Internet policy for the organization as a whole.

Anyone involved in Internet strategic planning should carefully determine the boundaries of the strategic plan and coordinate that plan with other Internet activities within the organization.

Step 4: Understand How Your Industry and Market are Responding to the Internet

Once you're on the Internet, take some time to examine what is happening in your industry. You do not need to be precise at this stage. Later we will talk about how you will reconcile the Internet opportunities you identify to the business strategies of your organization. At this time, you simply want to identify some of the key Internet opportunities that might be of value to your organization. It is important to gauge the extent of Internet activity in your industry or market, and then summarize what you have learned. This includes the following steps.

Make a General Assessment of the Level of Internet Activity in Your Industry or Market

➤ Are there any Internet initiatives already?

➤ Are there Internet discussion groups related to your industry or market?

➤ Are there any Internet addresses in industry and trade publications to which you subscribe?

➤ Is the Internet being discussed at industry conferences?

➤ Is the Internet receiving coverage in industry publications?

➤ Are industry associations working on any Internet activities?

➤ Are there any Internet success stories? Are there obvious failures?

Assess the Internet Activities of Individual Firms Within Your Industry or Market

This means determining who in your industry or market is on the Internet. For Fisher-Price, for example, this would mean identifying which toy manufacturers, toy retailers, industry associations, and suppliers are using the Internet.

➤ Are they marketing through the Internet? If so, what is the nature of the marketing activities?

➤ Are they providing for on-line ordering or customer support? What electronic commerce tools are being used?

➤ Are they providing interactive feedback?

➤ Are they engaged in electronic publishing?

➤ If they have a site on the Internet, is it being maintained in-house, or did they hire a third party to set up and maintain the site for them?

➤ Do they appear to have the support of senior management, or do they seem to be just dabbling in the Internet?

➤ Are they promoting their Internet presence through print and broadcast media?

➤ Are they participating in Internet discussion groups?

➤ Are their employees using Internet e-mail?

Think About Your Customers and Target Audience

A critical step in developing an Internet strategy is to examine the audience you are trying to reach and determine if they are likely on the Internet, or might be joining the Internet soon. This step is as applicable for a business as it is for a government department or not-for-profit organization. Try to obtain answers to the following questions:

➤ Is your customer or user base a relatively technically advanced audience?

➤ Are end users of your products/services using the Internet?

➤ Are the people who purchase/use your products or services using the Internet?

Determining the extent of Internet usage within your target audience provides valuable background information that will influence your strategy. In many cases, the target audiences are the purchasers of a product, not the end users. For example, a company such as Fisher-Price markets to parents, not children, since parents are most often responsible for the purchase of Fisher-Price toys. Fisher-Price would therefore want to find out the extent of Internet usage among parents.

Similarly, a non-profit organization like the Canadian Cancer Society would need to determine whether the people the organization is trying to serve are on the Internet. In an organization that has many functions and roles, such as the Canadian Cancer Society, the Internet may be more suited to specific activities than others. For example, where cancer prevention is concerned, the entire Internet population in Canada is a potential target audience.

Think About Current Internet Initiatives and Programs that You Might Want to Get Involved in to Support Your Internet Strategy.

There may be existing Internet projects or activities that your organization may want to consider as part of its Internet strategy.

➤ Determine which Internet initiatives might already be in existence in your industry that could influence your own plans and activities.

➤ Is your industry or trade association involved in any Internet projects?

➤ Are there industry or business initiatives appearing on the network that could influence your own activities?

For example, if you are in the hotel industry, you might be interested in participating in TravelWeb, an Internet initiative that acts as a central location for hotel, motel, and lodging information on the Internet (**http://www.travelweb.com**). Among the participating hotel chains are Best Western and Hyatt Hotels.

If you work in the automobile industry, as a dealer or manufacturer, you might want to get involved in DealerNet, an Internet initiative that helps users shop for cars and other automotive products (**http://www.dealernet.com**).

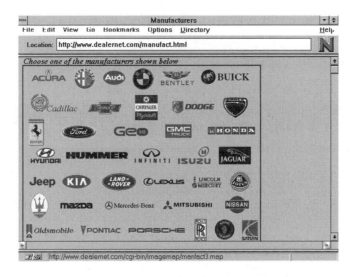

If you work in the finance sector of the government, you will want to find out more about FinanceNet, an Internet initiative that we discussed in Chapter 5. FinanceNet acts as a clearinghouse for government financial information world-wide. If you work in the educational sector, you will want to become more familiar with the national SchoolNet project, which we discussed in Chapter 6, and other Internet projects and programs that are helping schools get onto the Internet.

TravelWeb, DealerNet, FinanceNet, and SchoolNet are just some of the many industry-specific initiatives available throughout the Internet. Some initiatives will provide funding to help your organization establish a presence on the Internet, while others will simply provide a location on the Internet for you to market your organization's products and services.

In searching for relevant Internet programs, do not restrict yourself to the on-line world. Keep in mind that there are many government initiatives designed to help organizations develop and support telecommunications projects. Check with the federal government and your provincial government to determine what grants and funding opportunities are available. For example, as a municipal government, you should be aware of a federal government program that provides matching grants to municipalities seeking to extend communication networks based on the Internet to their region. Provincial programs were also available at time of writing. For example, the Ontario Network Infrastructure Program provides matching grants to various Internet-related networking initiatives.

As we mentioned at the start of this section, you do not need to be precise at this stage. You just want to summarize what you think might be possible for your organization on the Internet and identify what some of the key opportunities and strategies might be.

Step 5: Determine the Extent of Internet Knowledge and Educate

The next critical step in developing an Internet strategy is to determine the extent to which senior management understands the Internet. Senior management, as well as staff with strategic and information technology (IT) responsibilities, need to understand the strategic opportunities and benefits of the Internet. At this point, you do not have all the solutions, but you can at least help them understand that the Internet is more than just a technology.

There is a lot of hype about the network, and, as we indicated in Chapter 1, there is a fair amount of misreporting about the Internet in the media. It is critical that senior management and the IT department understand that the Internet represents a *strategic* opportunity for the organization. They need to understand that although the Internet of today is still at a very early stage of development, it is already profoundly changing how organizations do business. They need to understand that, even at this early stage, the organization can realize many strategic benefits by getting involved with the Internet. Only if senior managers understand the management benefits of the Internet will they give their support (and funding).

Education must start with the most senior managers and then continue with other management groups that will be affected by the decision to use the Internet. People need to understand the Internet, not as some exciting new technology, but as a fundamental change in the way the world will operate, and as a development that will present a number of strategic opportunities for the organization. To help senior managers understand this, you must be prepared to speak their language. They will not be interested in hearing technical jargon. Rather, they will want to hear, in business terms, what the Internet is, what it is all about, what is going on, why it is important, and, most importantly, the benefits and opportunities that it will present.

How do you best do this? Put together a presentation for management that outlines some potential Internet opportunities for your organization. Accompany your presentation with a "live" demonstration of the Internet to help them see the opportunities firsthand. Show them some of the industry activities already happening on the Internet. Show senior managers what their competitors are doing on the Internet: that will get their attention. If you cannot pull it together on your own, you should be aware that there are a number of Internet companies and consultants who can help put the Internet into perspective for your organization.

If you are part of a business, not-for-profit organization, government body or association, there are a number of places on the Internet that you might look for guidance in the process of educating senior management. The Internet Marketing list, for example, is an Internet forum where Internet users discuss the use of the Internet for marketing. The archives of the discussions are fully searchable. In this group you might discover some powerful ideas that apply to your own organization. You may also want to follow the Internet training discussion group (NETTRAIN), where Internet trainers worldwide discuss strategies for educating people about the Internet. Addresses for both of these discussion groups are listed in Appendix A.

If you work for the government, browse some of the government discussion forums on the Internet and feel free to ask people for advice on making senior management aware of Internet opportunities. If you work with a not-for-profit group, spend time in some of the many not-for-profit discussion groups and USENET newsgroups and ask other non-profit organizations about their experiences in educating senior management about the Internet. If you work in the educational sector, consider joining one of the many educational discussion forums, where you can find out how educators have been able to obtain funding and support for their school's connection to the Internet. There are many people already on the Internet who have been in your shoes before and are willing to offer advice and suggestions.

Step 6: Determine the Organization's Internet Objectives

The next step is to relate the Internet to the business goals and objectives of the organization and define the objectives that you would want to meet through the use of the Internet. This is a critical step, for it is the only way to relate the Internet to the decision makers — senior management.

Management strategy is never dictated by the presence of a neat, hot, exciting technology. Management will not support the Internet because it is "significant," "profound," or "revolutionary." Management is not sold by adjectives. Management is concerned about the bottom line. Management will understand the role of the Internet if its use can be described in terms of the strategic advantage it might present to the organization, in terms of the business opportunities it will present and in terms of the benefits that will accrue from it. Management will pay more attention to the Internet if you can relate its benefits to the mission and strategic objectives of the organization.

How do you do this? It's simple, once you get the hang of it. On the left side of a page of paper, identify the strategies of your organization. On the right side, write down how the Internet could help to achieve those strategies. Here are a few examples:

> If your business has stated that one of its key strategic goals is to "improve levels of service to the customer," and your review indicates that quite a few customers might be on the Internet already, then you can categorically state in your Internet strategic plan that "the Internet will help us to improve service to customers, by permitting them to query us directly for information, by permitting them to access our support library seven days a week, 24 hours a day, and by permitting them to engage in active, e-mail-based dialogue with their account representatives." *This is language that management will understand.*

> If one of your key business objectives is to "become the leader in the intelligent deployment of communications technology to solidify business relationships with existing customers," you can state that "using Internet

e-mail will open a new line of communication between ourselves and our customer base and will provide for more direct communications between our sales representatives and our customers."

➤ If a key educational objective is "to introduce students to the use of computers in the classroom, through access to new and innovative technologies at minimum cost," your objective would be "to use the Internet to take advantage of some of the leading scientific and educational sites designed for children."

➤ If, in a not-for-profit association, a key management objective is to "strengthen the membership relationship by providing members with up-to-date, current information," then your Internet strategy could state that "use of the Internet as a publishing medium will permit us to make information available to members on an immediate basis. In addition, we can use Internet electronic mailing lists to quickly notify members on the Internet of the importance of new, emerging issues."

Consider Fisher-Price's strategic objectives, which we mentioned earlier in the chapter. One of their objectives is "To increase our worldwide recognition as the leader in children's products." Fisher-Price's Internet strategy could state that "the Internet can help us strengthen our image by giving us the ability to disseminate information worldwide about the quality, safety, and durability of our products."

It is important to relate each objective or strategic item to the Internet. To do so requires that you understand the key possibilities behind each particular Internet technology. We explain these possibilities in Step 10, the Internet tools.

Test your Internet strategic ideas with a number of people. Bounce them off people to see if they will work, to see if people understand, to determine if there are obvious points that you are missing. Get others, particularly those who are involved in strategic planning for the organization, involved in the process of relating organizational strategies to Internet opportunities.

Step 7: Be a Good Internet Citizen

Another part of your Internet strategy is to learn how to be a good Internet citizen; this is often a key to the success of your strategy. As we indicated in Chapter 4, the Internet is as much a culture as any nation. You will not succeed in doing business in France without understanding French culture. In the same way, you will not succeed in doing business on the Internet without an understanding of Internet culture.

One of the key cultural aspects of the Internet is that it has grown from the grassroots as a unique global cooperative network. Some have said that the Internet is a place where people are "still nice to each other." Others have said that the idealism of the 1960s is reemerging in the network. Whatever it is, the Internet is a unique and fascinating culture and hence organizations need to learn about this culture and respect it in their Internet activities.

What is the culture of the Internet? Beyond a hatred for junk mail, it is many other things. On the Internet, people cooperate. They share information. They go out of their way to be helpful to other people. They volunteer time to assist others. They write software and contribute it to the world as shareware so that people can try it out before purchasing it. Or they write it and make it available for free. They write book, movie, and product reviews, and make them available to the world. They answer questions posted in a USENET forum, or volunteer to take questions from students at a school. Why do they do this? Because many people believe that cooperation, generosity, and sharing make the Internet a useful and enjoyable place to be. And many people simply enjoy this aspect of on-line communication.

The Internet functions so well because of this unique culture. Many passionately believe that it is a culture that needs to be preserved. Organizations can build goodwill on the Internet by respecting the Internet culture in *all their activities*. Organizations that want a successful Internet strategy will want to be seen as good citizens and neighbors on the Internet in the same way that they want to be recognized as good corporate citizens outside the Internet.

It should not be difficult to get management to appreciate this aspect of Internet strategy, since many organizations explicitly recognize the importance of good corporate citizenship in their mission or vision statements. For example, recall the list of Fisher-Price's strategic objectives at the beginning of this chapter. The last objective is "to enrich the lives of others in our communities, particularly children, by contributing generously of our human and financial resources." Many other organizations have similar statements in their corporate mission statements, where the community is recognized as important. Being a good Internet citizen is simply an extension of being a good corporate citizen.

One of the key ways of building goodwill with the Internet community is by giving something back to the network. Organizations that contribute something to the Internet, for example, information, computer resources, or sponsorship, gain goodwill from the Internet community. For example, DuPont Lubricants has gained goodwill on the Internet by providing Internet users with reports from the 1995 Tour DuPont bicycle race. During the race, statistics and daily updates were available on the firm's World Wide Web server along with course maps and team and schedule information (**http://www.lubricants.dupont.com**).

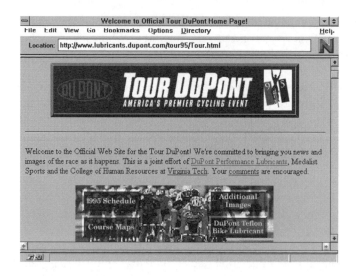

There is a lot of free material on the Internet as a result of this Internet culture. In fact, the Internet culture is best exemplified by people's attitude toward information on the network. Many believe that certain types of information (e.g., government information) should be freely available on the Internet.

Organizations generally have all kinds of information that could be useful to people on the Internet. If this is the case in your organization, contribute it to the Internet (if possible), and make it available for free. The astute businessperson will ask why an organization should "give" to the Internet. Not only is it a good way to draw people to your Internet site, but it is a method of building goodwill on the Internet and being seen as a good corporate citizen.

As many organizations are discovering, it can be difficult to make money *selling information* on the Internet. It is easier to leverage your core business objectives (e.g., sell more of your core product) by using free information as a draw.

SchoolNet

When it comes to being a good Internet citizen, you should also think about getting involved with, and sponsoring, SchoolNet. Business in Canada complains about many aspects of our educational system: the lack of adequate schooling, students graduating without basic literacy skills, and a drop in science education.

Now, business in Canada has an opportunity to do something about it: business can support the use of the Internet within the educational community. In doing so, a business can build goodwill on the network and be seen as a good Internet citizen while helping the education system.

SchoolNet, as we mentioned in Chapter 6, is an initiative that provides students in elementary and high schools across Canada with access to the Internet. Business can help SchoolNet and the community in several ways:

➤ Participate in the "Ask an Expert" program. Business can make experts available to students across Canada to help with particular class projects and can provide on-line career counseling, by taking questions from students about their company. It is not necessary to take a lot of time; indeed, business can determine the extent that it wants to communicate. But participation in such a program is a powerful way to help our young people in Canada.

➤ Donate server space to schools seeking to establish their own World Wide Web sites. As we discussed in Chapter 6, many schools have introduced students to the concept of global publishing via the Internet, yet lack the resources to do so. Businesses with their own World Wide Web sites can donate some space on their Internet servers. After all, what's a few megabytes of space to a large business? Nothing, really, so there is no real cost for the donation. A business that donates space to a school is helping to foster a creative, high-tech environment in Canada's school system, for a minimal cost. This is perhaps one of the best investments a business can make.

➤ Help schools to access the Internet. In many places in Canada, access to the Internet through SchoolNet is through a long distance call, a cost that is beyond the budget of many schools. Yet, in the same town a business might have a high-speed, dedicated link to the Internet. Donation of a little bit of access time to the school will cost the business little and provide students with access to a much-needed resource.

➤ Donate equipment, money and services. Computers, modems, software, computer experts, cash. There is a lot that business can do. Schools often lack the infrastructure necessary to get on the Internet. There is a natural opportunity for business to help solve the problem. Given the returns that we already see from the use of the Internet within the educational community in Canada, the investment is well worth it.

➤ In the same way that business should get involved with SchoolNet, it should also get involved in helping charities and not-for-profit organizations to participate in the Internet. Many associations and not-for-profit organizations would like to be able to publish on the World Wide Web. Businesses can help them by donating space on their World Wide Web servers. Business can also provide them with equipment and other resources to get on-line.

Step 8: Define the Benefits

The next step is to define the benefits that the organization might achieve from the Internet strategies you have identified. Categorize the benefits. What will the organization gain through the objectives that you set? Will there be any cost savings?

Increased awareness of the organization's activities? Improved corporate image? More satisfied customers? More efficient communications? Do you anticipate new markets? Do you plan on providing access to some new research information that was previously unavailable, thus reducing the amount of time that it takes to research particular topics?

It is critical that senior management recognize that many of the benefits that will arise from the Internet will be *intangible*, and it might not be possible to identify a direct monetary benefit. For example, if you use the Internet to provide better customer service, there is no direct monetary gain for the organization. However, improved customer service can indirectly lead to repeat customer sales and higher income for the organization. Similarly, if you are using the Internet for market intelligence activities, there is no direct monetary benefit to the organization. Yet, the information gleaned from market intelligence activities can provide new product ideas and new insights into levels of customer satisfaction. This type of information will indirectly affect the bottom line in the long term.

Define, in advance, how your organization will measure the success of the project. Make sure that everyone understands that success is unlikely to be immediate. Be realistic and conservative in your plans; do not overstate the benefits in order to get management on side. If the benefits that you identify fail to materialize immediately, you will be left with egg on your face, and the overall Internet initiative will be damaged. It is better to be conservative in your projections than to be too aggressive. As we stated in Chapter 1, the Internet is for the long term.

Step 9: Develop the Vision

Once you have outlined the Internet opportunities within your organization and you have determined the benefits associated with those opportunities, you can create or prepare the "Internet vision" for your organization. Exactly how you do this depends on what you need to do to convince management to move forward with your Internet strategy. In some organizations all that is required is a discussion around a table in a meeting. In other cases, management will require a document, presentation, "white paper," project plan, or some other type of prepared material. The particular requirements depend on the working style and culture of your organization when it comes to new activities and plans.

Develop whatever is appropriate for your organization. Do not get bogged down in the development of lengthy discussion papers or unending committee meetings. Move quickly since the Internet is evolving quickly. If you spend too long formulating plans and reports, the reports will be outdated by the time you get them to senior management.

Whatever you prepare, your "vision" should state, clearly and emphatically, the role of the Internet within your organization. Specify what it will be used for, how the proposed uses relate to the strategies of the organization, and outline the benefits that the Internet will bring to the organization. Your report should draw on real examples where possible: include examples of what is already happening on the Internet in your industry or market.

When it comes to development of an Internet strategy, the key is to move comprehensively, but quickly.

Why is a vision important? For several reasons. A vision will help to

➤ *Get people talking about the Internet.* You want the Internet to become an item on the agenda of a weekly management meeting. You want management and other staff to be thinking about it. You want to create discussion and debate about your plans and recommendations. You want people to start talking, thinking, and asking about the Internet.

➤ *Get everyone to understand the Internet.* A vision is often a critical part of the educational process, for it helps to summarize the issues at hand. It is, in many ways, an educational tool.

➤ *Get people on side,* by building concurrence and agreement with the direction you are suggesting, and by helping to build enthusiasm for the project. Clearly, there will be many who will have heard of the Internet, but will remain skeptical of its benefits. They can be won over, in some cases, by a clearly stated vision, which categorically outlines, in business terms, the role of the Internet within the organization.

➤ *Build commitment from management.* Developing a vision and getting people to take the time to understand the vision starts you on the road towards getting management commitment to the project. A necessary step by all means.

➤ *Attract the necessary funding.* Obviously, the organization will have to spend money on implementation of Internet capabilities. The vision, by getting management attention, also puts them on notice that there must be some funds made available in order to move forward. You need to avoid being saddled with an effort built on a shoestring budget. This is most likely to happen if you do not get the proper degree and level of management attention and respect.

➤ *Identify the benefits.* After all, everyone is going to want to know the answer to the question, "What's the impact on our bottom line?"

➤ *Put issues on the table that will need to be resolved.* Getting involved with the Internet might introduce a number of tricky questions for the organization. These include intellectual property and security issues, which are discussed in Chapter 11. As early as possible, identify the issues that management will need to address. This will get people thinking about the possible alternatives.

You need to make everyone understand that things move at light speed on the Internet. Preparing your vision, while important, is not a stage to which a lot of time can be devoted.

Step 10: Determine the Internet Tools that You Will Use

Now that you have prepared a vision clearly outlining the opportunities for your organization, you must determine what must be accomplished to achieve those opportunities. Even if you do not want to become a technical expert about the Internet, you must have a basic understanding of the various Internet tools, what they can be used for, and most importantly, how they relate to particular Internet opportunities. Thus the next step in developing an Internet strategy is to clearly outline the Internet tools or technologies that you expect to use, and what they will be used for. The six most important Internet tools are

- electronic mail;
- mail robots;
- announcement-only mailing lists;
- discussion mailing lists;
- USENET newsgroups;
- the World Wide Web.

We will discuss each of these six tools separately.

Electronic Mail

Electronic mail was covered in Chapter 3, but because it is one of the most important tools, it bears repeating and expanding.

Electronic mail is a tool that allows people on the Internet to send and receive electronic messages. Every Internet user has an Internet address that is used for electronic mail correspondence. Electronic mail addresses, like telephone numbers, are unique. For example, the e-mail address for Rick Broadhead is **rickb@hookup.net**, and the e-mail address for Jim Carroll is **jcarroll@jacc.com.**

Internet e-mail has the farthest reach of any Internet tool. Because of the vast number of interlinked e-mail systems around the globe, it is believed that you can reach some 60 to 80 million people via Internet e-mail. An important trend to note is that corporations and other organizations are linking internal e-mail systems to the Internet to support their interorganization communications.

Internet e-mail

- Provides one-to-one communications, that is, communications between one individual and another.

- Provides one-to-many communications, that is, communications between several individuals; you can send a single message to several of your customers or co-workers at one time.

- Provides significant cost savings. The cost of an Internet e-mail message is significantly less than the cost of a fax or telephone call, and is insensitive to distance or geographical location. In most cases, it costs as much to send an e-mail message to your neighbor as it does to send a message to someone in Australia.

➤ Provides efficiency in communications. Many organizations have already discovered the advantages of e-mail for internal communications. Linking an internal e-mail system to the Internet provides efficiencies in communications with clients, customers, business associates, trading partners, and others.

➤ Reduces dependency on ordinary mail, which is comparatively slow and expensive. There are other factors: e-mail requires no envelopes, postage meters, office mail carts, mailboxes, or mail room clerks. It is also more efficient: e-mail posted anywhere in the world can often be delivered to its destination in mere seconds.

➤ Can be used to communicate certain items better than the telephone; these include items that are for the record, require thought before responding, relate to complicated matters, are not urgent enough to disrupt the recipient's day, or need to be communicated to many individuals in many different geographical locations.

➤ Eliminates telephone tag and the undesirable effects of time zone and geographical differences. In most cases, e-mail is less expensive than a long distance telephone call.

➤ Competes effectively with a fax in a number of ways: transmission costs are often lower; e-mail will transmit documents (spreadsheets, documents, pictures, and other computer-based information) in electronic form, so that they can be reused, without rekeying; there is no need to transport the documents to and from the fax machine; there are fewer fax machine line-ups; e-mail can provide better quality output; and it is more direct, since transmissions go right into the recipient's computer instead of arriving on a fax machine somewhere in the office.

In many ways, Internet e-mail addresses are becoming the "fax machine numbers" of the 1990s: they are quickly becoming ubiquitous and almost a necessity on business cards.

Examples of the use of Internet e-mail throughout corporate Canada are many. Organizations ranging from the Ontario Milk Marketing Board to the Canadian Broadcasting Corporation to small one- and two-person consulting firms have the ability to send and receive Internet e-mail worldwide. It has been estimated that there are over one million Canadians with the ability to send and receive e-mail through the Internet.

Hewlett Packard makes extensive use of Internet e-mail worldwide: all 98,000 users are provided with an Internet e-mail address the minute they get on the internal HP mail system, known as HP Desk, which permits them to communicate with customers, partners, and suppliers. A total of 21 million e-mail messages are sent through the system each month, 500,000 of which are to external contacts via the Internet.

Mail Robots

An Internet mail robot, also called an auto-responder or mail reflector, is an automated tool that permits Internet users to request documents or information from an organization by electronic mail.

Given the extremely wide reach of Internet e-mail, a mail robot is an effective way of allowing people to easily obtain information from an organization. By sending a message to a certain e-mail address, Internet users can request documents and files from an organization. A computer responds with the requested information, so there is no need for human intervention. Mail robots provide a very low-cost method of distributing information, given the low cost of Internet e-mail.

The authors of this book have a mail robot related to this book and the *Canadian Internet Handbook*. Our mail robot allows people to retrieve information about these books, including order instructions, press releases, and other information. This is how it works: Send a message to **info@handbook.com** by e-mail. You will soon receive an e-mail message back that details how you can obtain press releases, order instructions, and other information. You do this by sending a message back to the mail robot, and by inputting a phrase in the text of the message. For example, sending a message to **info@handbook.com**, and inputting "send order" on the first line of the body of the message will get you information on how you can order the *Canadian Internet Handbook*.

Mail robots are becoming a common means by which organizations and people can make information available through the Internet. We have included some examples below. A message sent to

➤ **ran-info@igc.apc.org** provides information about an initiative called the Forest Action Network, which protects rainforests around the world.

➤ **windpubs-info@igc.apc.org** provides the publications catalogue of the American Wind Energy Association.

➤ **info@ablelink.org** provides information about Ability On-Line, an organization that provides disabled children and others with access to electronic tools such as the Internet.

➤ **info@wired.com** provides information about WIRED Magazine.

➤ **info@cathay-usa.com** provides information from Cathay Pacific Airways.

An Internet mail robot provides a quick, efficient, and effective means of permitting people throughout the Internet world to conveniently retrieve information from your organization. Organizations can make virtually any type of document available through a mail robot, including price lists, order forms, product and service information, brochures, newsletters, and press releases.

A mail robot also extends the reach of your information. Many people who do not have full access to the Internet cannot use tools such as the World Wide Web but can send and receive Internet e-mail through a corporate e-mail system that is linked to the Internet. Given that many people know how to send and receive Internet e-mail messages, a mail robot is often an excellent method of making your information available to the Internet community.

Announcement-Only Mailing Lists

Announcement-only mailing lists are used by organizations to reach multiple people simultaneously through Internet e-mail. Any message sent to the mailing list is automatically sent to every member of the list. Some announcement-only mailing lists have thousands of subscribers. Such a list is typically used by an organization to send out product announcements, sales information, and other pieces of information to interested customers and members of the general public. The organization sponsoring the mailing list controls who may belong to the list, and only the sponsoring organization can send messages to the subscribers. Generally, anyone can request to join the list, either by sending a specially formatted e-mail message to a certain Internet address or by filling out a form on a World Wide Web server.

In order to avoid any infringement of Internet culture, the mailing list must be voluntary, that is, consumers have the choice of whether or not they wish to join the list. Adding an Internet user to a mailing list without seeking permission first is considered bad etiquette.

Announcement-only mailing lists provide organizations with a very simple and inexpensive way of reaching existing and prospective customers with new product and service information. Roswell Computer Books, for example, mentioned in Chapter 4, has established an announcement-only mailing list. Roswell uses the mailing list to inform its customers of new book arrivals and other product information. In Chapter 7, we discussed how the Sierra Club provides a mailing list that members and others can join. The Sierra Club uses the list to send out notices advising members of important environmental issues.

Discussion Mailing Lists

Discussion mailing lists are used for discussion, and any member of the list can send a message to all the other members of the list. This is in contrast to announcement-only mailing lists, where only the sponsoring organization can distribute information to members of the list. Discussion mailing lists provide a forum for ongoing, open discussion. They can have a local, national, or international base of subscribers, depending on their mandate.

Discussion mailing lists are either "unmoderated" or "moderated." If a list is *unmoderated*, a message posted to the list is immediately distributed to all the members of the list. If the list is *moderated*, a message posted to the list is screened by a moderator before it is distributed to the list. The moderator's job is to keep the discussion focused and intercept any messages that are off-topic. Discussion lists can also be "public" or "private." Anyone can join a public mailing list: it is open to members of the public. A private mailing list restricts who can join. Many organizations set up private mailing lists on the Internet for internal communications between employees or members.

Discussion mailing lists provide an opportunity for people with similar interests to share ideas, experiences, and opinions. Some discussion lists are used for debate, others are used for collaboration purposes, and still others are used for information exchange. Not-for-profit organizations can use discussion lists to improve internal communication among Board and staff members and committees and working groups. For example, the Canadian Sport Parachute Association, mentioned in Chapter 7, has a private Internet discussion list to improve communication among Board members. Governments can use discussion lists (either moderated or unmoderated) to start a dialogue with citizens on particular topics. Businesses can create discussion lists to obtain customer feedback about specific products and services. Internet users can set up a discussion list to discuss their favorite hobby or pastime.

There are several thousand public discussion lists on the Internet covering thousands of different topics. The diversity of the topics under discussion is staggering. Examples include Kodak, which has set up a public mailing list to discuss its photo CD products (**http://www.kodak.com**), and the United States Government, under the auspices of the FinanceNet project, which sponsors the use of several Internet discussion groups to promote the sharing of information among U.S. government financial officers.

Nova South Eastern University maintains an extensive list of several thousand electronic mailing lists on its World Wide Web site (**http://alpha.acast.nova.edu/listserv.html**). A few examples of some of these mailing lists will demonstrate the wide array of subjects being discussed on the Internet:

➤ MAR-FACIL is a mailing list for managers and technical staff at marine research facilities, aquaculture operations, public aquaria and other facilities supplying seawater for the support of marine life. The list is intended as a forum for the discussion of technical and business topics; however, discussion of other matters is welcome and encouraged. The list is managed by the staff of the Aquatron Laboratory, which is situated at Dalhousie University in Halifax, Nova Scotia.

➤ EAP is a discussion list and powerful networking tool for anyone with an interest in any aspect of employee assistance counselling or psychological interventions in the workplace. Professional associations, managed care companies, university faculty, and students as well as corporations are subscribers. Practitioners, researchers, and educators may use this list for any purpose.

➤ FISH-JUNIOR is a forum for interaction between marine scientists and children and high school students. The list was initially set up by the Swedish University Network (SUNET) on behalf of a pilot project to be conducted by the British Columbia Ministry of Education. The aim of this forum is to teach children to interact with scientists and discuss scientific issues mainly related to fisheries ecology and related topics.

Because anyone with the appropriate software can set up a public mailing list, new mailing lists are being created every day on the Internet.

USENET Newsgroups

USENET is an area within the Internet where there are several thousand topical discussions taking place. USENET is similar in concept to public mailing lists except for a few fundamental differences:

- USENET messages do not come to your mailbox. You have to have special software (called a USENET newsreader) to read USENET messages.

- USENET messages are organized into categories (e.g., science topics, recreational topics, computer topics, social topics).

- Creating a USENET group is more complicated than creating a mailing list. While anyone can set up a mailing list at will, the creation of most USENET newsgroups is subject to a 2–3 month discussion and voting process.

- With a few exceptions, USENET is non-commercial in nature. Advertisements about commercial products or businesses are explicitly forbidden in most areas of USENET.

USENET provides an opportunity for organizations to seek advice and information from Internet users and other organizations on the Internet. Organizations can also use USENET to monitor what people are saying about certain topics or issues.

USENET is perhaps the most controversial part of the Internet. It is the area of the Internet where much of the pornography and other information of a controversial nature is distributed. USENET has a very distinct and sometimes unforgiving culture. It is a part of the Internet that is often in complete anarchy. People say anything they want in USENET, so a visit is sometimes a cultural shock. Be prepared if you decide to visit.

There are thousands of topics within USENET, ranging from **rec.aviation.homebuilt**, about selecting, designing, building, and restoring aircraft, to **sci.engr.biomed**, for the discussion of biomedical engineering, to **alt.fan.stephen-king**, for the discussion of Stephen King and his novels, to **alt.wedding,** for talk about weddings. In Chapter 4, we discussed how Snapple Beverage Corporation monitors the Snapple USENET group (**alt.drinks.snapple**) to obtain customer feedback.

The World Wide Web

The World Wide Web is the part of the Internet where people can access information sites established by thousands of organizations and individuals worldwide. The World Wide Web is a "multimedia" service, meaning that these sites can contain text, graphics, pictures, sound, and even full motion video. In addition to accessing World Wide Web sites established by other organizations, organizations can establish *their own* sites to promote their products and services. To access the World Wide Web, you need to have a World Wide Web navigator program, such as Netscape or Mosaic.

The World Wide Web is the most popular area of the Internet, and the area that is receiving the most media attention. It has been at the heart of much of the discussion about the Internet in this book. The World Wide Web provides access to a vast number of information sites around the world that contain information from companies, government departments, schools, individuals, not-for-profit organizations, associations, research bodies, and countless other organizations.

How many sites are there? No one knows, since anyone with the proper computer equipment can establish a site and make it available to the rest of the world. Yet, it is the fastest-growing application on the Internet; it is the application that has gained the attention and notice of the business community and business press. The World Wide Web is where many of the more innovative and leading-edge developments are occurring on the Internet. For example, the World Wide Web can support fill-out forms that allow organizations to place surveys, quizzes, and customer feedback forms on the Internet.

We have used many examples from the World Wide Web: most of the screens reproduced in chapters 4, 5, 6, and 7 are from the World Wide Web.

The best way to get an appreciation for the vastness of the World Wide Web is to examine some statistics provided by an Internet service called Yahoo, which is attempting to index many of the sites on the World Wide Web. As of early 1995 Yahoo indexed the following numbers of World Wide Web sites:

> 7,171 corporate sites, including 42 in the aerospace category, 4 in cosmetics, 63 health and fitness corporations, and 99 in sports;

> 1,214 government sites, including 34 in Canada;

> 1,122 sites about specific countries, ranging from Afghanistan to Vietnam;

> 3,232 sites related to science information, including 20 anthropology, 330 biology, and 15 environmental health sites.

Another well-known index is City.Net, which provides access to information from cities around the world. As of early 1995 it pointed to 580 cities and towns around the world that had some type of information accessible through the Internet.

How quickly is the Web growing? A number of people have attempted to quantify this. For example, a study by Matthew Grey (**mkgray@netgen.com**) produced the following graph, which gives you an idea of how quickly the World Wide Web is growing (**http://www.netgen.com/info/growth.html**):

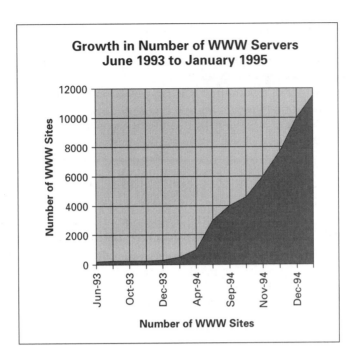

**Growth in Number of WWW Servers
June 1993 to January 1995**

Number of WWW Sites

Number of WWW Sites

Step 11: Determine How You Will Use the Tools

Having reviewed the various tools that you might use within your Internet strategy, it is time to relate your Internet opportunities and strategies to various Internet tools. How do you do this? At this stage you need to link the opportunities and strategies previously identified to the Internet tools. Recall that earlier we started a list on a piece of paper. Column 1 lists the business strategies; column 2 lists the Internet opportunities to meet those strategies. Now add column 3 — the Internet tools you will use to fulfill these strategies.

This step involves answering some questions. Should you establish a mail robot to permit people to retrieve product and sales information by e-mail? Can you establish a World Wide Web site? Are there business opportunities for the organization in establishing a mailing list that customers can join?

Each tool has advantages and disadvantages over each of the other tools. In some cases, you will want to use multiple tools to accomplish the same objectives. For example, since not everyone has access to the World Wide Web, you might want to distribute corporate information using both a mail robot and the World Wide Web. The mail robot can be used by people who only have e-mail access to the Internet, while the World Wide Web site will allow you to present your information graphically and in full color for those people who have access to the Web.

There will also be trade-offs. A World Wide Web site is more expensive to create and maintain than a mail robot. However, it has much more functionality and power. If your competitors are using the World Wide Web, you do not want to be perceived as being slow to adapt.

Your on-line tour of the Internet will help you relate the tools to the strategies. Take a look at what others are doing, and review the strategy behind their efforts. Summarize everything at this point, by identifying the actions that you plan on taking and the Internet tools that will support those actions.

Step 12: Determine Whether You Should Hire a Subcontractor to Implement Your System

The next step is to determine how to proceed and involves a simple answer to a complicated question: Do you have the capability, resources, and technical staff to support a direct link from your corporate network to the Internet? This would involve purchasing an Internet connection from an Internet access provider, and your organization would be responsible for setting up and running its own Internet services (e.g., mailing list, World Wide Web site). Or should you use a third-party organization, an Internet presence provider, that helps companies implement the Internet tools discussed above?

Establishing Your Own Link to the Internet

If you want to provide your employees with *full* access to the Internet so that they can use Internet tools in their jobs, there are two alternatives. The first option is to register your employees with dialup Internet access providers — companies that sell access to the Internet (see Appendix C for a list of Internet access providers). A dialup Internet access provider will allow your employees to access the Internet using a dialup modem. Dialup Internet accounts generally cost $25 to $30 per account per month, and provide about 35 to 50 hours of usage per month. This can become expensive if you belong to a large organization with many employees: for example, paying approximately $300 per year for each employee that requires Internet access will cost close to $6,000 per year to permit 20 employees to access the network.

For large organizations a better option may be to implement a dedicated (or high-speed) connection to the Internet. Putting in place such a link means that all employees have direct access to the Internet from their desktops without having to use a modem. If you have a large number of employees to hook up to the Internet, dedicated connections can be less expensive than multiple dialup Internet accounts. The disadvantage of dedicated connections is that they require a lot of time and expertise to administer (see the section "Third-Party Services" below).

If you decide to establish a dedicated connection from your organization to the Internet, the first step is to link your internal e-mail service, if you have one, to the Internet so that employees can use Internet e-mail and Internet mailing lists. The second step with a dedicated link is to provide your employees with access to the full suite of Internet services from their desktops, including the World Wide Web and other interactive Internet services. With a dedicated link to the Internet, your organization can also set up its own World Wide Web sites for the Internet community to use.

A high-speed dedicated link will probably cost at least $700 per month to maintain (if not more, depending on the speed of the link and your location in Canada). The computer equipment required to support a dedicated Internet connection can be tens of thousands of dollars. Then there may be the additional expenses of hiring at least one person to maintain your network ($40,000 to $80,000 per year) and someone, if you wish to provide services on the World Wide Web, with HTML programming experience ($50 to $150 per hour). (HTML is the language of the World Wide Web.)

An additional issue, should you establish a direct link to the Internet, is security. There are security risks associated with linking your computer network to the Internet. These risks can be minimized by taking appropriate security measures (see Chapter 11 for elaboration on this topic). Hence security planning should be an important part of your strategy in this case.

Third-Party Services

Even if your organization does not have its own dedicated connection, you can still publish on the Internet by renting space on another organization's Internet server. In other words, you buy space on another organization's dedicated Internet connection. Why would you want to do this? Many organizations that want to "publish" information on the Internet do not have the necessary physical or human resources to run their own dedicated Internet connection. Therefore, some organizations have chosen to enlist the services of an Internet presence provider rather than purchase their own dedicated Internet connection.

Internet presence providers are organizations that maintain dedicated Internet servers and sell space to other organizations that want to publish information on the Internet. Most Internet presence providers offer a full suite of Internet presence services, including

- *marketing services*, to help organizations promote their Internet presence through traditional media such as radio, television, and print advertisements;

- *electronic conversion services*, to help organizations turn paper documents into electronic formats;

- *HTML coding services*, to help organizations convert documents into formats suitable for the World Wide Web;

- *creative services*, to help organizations design visually appealing World Wide Web sites.

Internet presence providers are useful to those organizations that want to take full advantage of the World Wide Web's interactive and multimedia capabilities (e.g., sound, graphics, fill-in-forms), but do not have the in-house expertise necessary to do so. While they are not the perfect solution for all organizations, Internet presence providers represent an increasingly popular alternative to setting up your own dedicated Internet connection.

Step 13: Define the Costs

The next step in your Internet strategy is to define the costs.

Equipment and Telecommunications Costs

Roughly, what will it take to accomplish what you want to do? If you determine that it is necessary to link your organization's internal e-mail system into the Internet, what is the cost for doing so? If you plan to build a World Wide Web server, what will it cost to have an outside organization create it on your behalf? What will it cost to provide a dedicated corporate link to the Internet? If you plan to make customer service manuals available via the Internet, what will it cost to get each of them in an electronic form suitable for loading into a World Wide Web site?

Many of the Internet access providers in Appendix C can give you an estimate of the cost of a dedicated Internet connection or the setup of a single World Wide Web site or Internet mailing list, but determining the other costs will require your involvement. This area will require extensive effort and hence will require even more familiarity with certain aspects of the Internet. If you decide to utilize a third party to establish mailing lists or a World Wide Web site, you will need to research how much the third party will charge you to implement and maintain the site on your organization's behalf.

Keep in mind that the Internet market is very competitive; therefore, prices vary widely. When shopping around for a dedicated Internet connection or third-party Internet services, check prices with at least three of four different vendors before making a final selection. However, price should not be the only criterion; in fact, it should not be the deciding factor at all. Service, support, reliability, and the professionalism of the Internet service provider should be the deciding factors. Be sure to include the following steps in your research:

➤ If you are purchasing a dedicated Internet connection, ask about service level guarantees and the availability of technical support.

➤ If you are purchasing World Wide Web services from a third party, find out how fast their Internet connection is and ask to see examples of work done for other clients. The quality of the layout and design is extremely important, as we will discuss in the next chapter.

Training Costs

When assessing the costs of implementing the Internet within their organizations, people frequently forget about training costs. We have stressed in this chapter that it is important that all employees, not just senior managers, have a full understanding of the Internet and its role in the organization. Not only that, they have to know how to use the Internet so they can explain it to other people.

For example, customer service representatives who answer the telephone have to be Internet-literate so they can tell callers how to interact with the company through the Internet. Recall the Federal Express parcel-tracking system we noted earlier in the book. If you call Federal Express and ask how to track your parcel over the Internet, you will expect the Federal Express representative to be able to explain it to you in clear, non-technical terms. If Federal Express employees cannot explain this to customers, not only does it look bad, but it defeats the purpose of having the Internet service in the first place. Training is a vital component of an Internet strategy. Hence training costs should be estimated and included as part of the Internet budget.

Step 14: Add the Finishing Touches

If a World Wide Web site is part of the strategic plan, a number of related issues need to be addressed in the plan. The people in the organization who are responsible for marketing, advertising, and corporate identity will need to be consulted to ensure that the organization's public services on the Internet project the desired public image. Representatives from the legal department will need to be consulted on legal issues. Other divisions and subsidiaries of the company will need to be informed about the organization's Internet activities so that Internet projects can be coordinated.

Your plan should address how other departments and company divisions will be involved in the implementation of your organization's Internet services. Coordinating all the various departments will be a challenging task, but it is important that the Internet be a team effort. (We discuss the issue of corporate image in the next chapter, while some legal issues are reviewed in Chapter 11.)

Step 15: Create the Plan and Establish a Timeline

You are now at the stage where you have enough material to implement your Internet strategy. You will have pulled together information on

➢ how the Internet can be used in your organization;

➢ Internet objectives and how these relate to the strategic goals of your organization;

➢ a vision of how the Internet can be used in your organization;

➤ the benefits that will come from use of the Internet;

➤ Internet tools and potential costs of implementing those tools;

➤ logistics, including who will be involved from each of your organization's departments.

The next step is to create your strategy, establish a timeline for its implementation, and present it to management for approval. With luck, you will be given the green light to proceed.

CHAPTER 10

Corporate Image on the World Wide Web

Something's missing from the Web, and I bet you don't know what it is. It's not a search mechanism, it's not a general index, and it's not higher bandwidth.

What's missing is the corporate image.

When a corporation hires an agency to create a million dollar ad campaign, the CEO gets involved, Vice Presidents get consulted, marketing joins ranks with sales and provides focus groups, test beds, etc.

When a company is about to bring a new piece of software into their product line, there are alpha sites, beta sites, test groups, and developers meet and meet and meet.

When a brochure is being developed for an organization, artists are hired, graphic designers are contracted, art directors are given direction and printers are told what quality of paper, type of ink and printing style to use.

This is not happening on the Web.

Christine A. Quinn,
Director, Electrical Engineering Computer &
Network Services, Stanford University
quinn@eecns.stanford.edu

*W*e noted in Chapter 9 that "use of the Internet for competitive business advantage does not get the proper degree of management attention that it should" and outlined some of the steps needed to put together an Internet strategy.

Much of what you will do with your Internet strategy will focus around the use of the World Wide Web. In many ways your World Wide Web site will become associated with your corporate image, and in the same way that you protect your corporate image outside the Internet, you need to protect it on the Internet.

Many organizations have ignored this reality in their early efforts with the Internet, and the quote that opens this chapter sums the situation perfectly. While senior management normally gets involved in many aspects of corporate communications and public relations, corporate

CORPORATE IMAGE ON THE WORLD WIDE WEB

(1) Do it Right the First Time
  - Don't announce your World Wide Web site before it is ready

(2) Draw People to Your World Wide Web Site
  - Give people a reason to visit you
  - Provide up-to-date information
  - Link internal databases to your World Wide Web site
  - Appeal to the sense of "cool"

(3) Pay Attention to Content and Layout
  - Get management involved
  - Seek feedback and suggestions
  - Highlight new additions to your site
  - Do not overuse graphics

(4) Maintain a Consistent Corporate Image
  - Be aware of how many World Wide Web sites your organization has
  - Ensure that your organization has a consistent image on the World Wide Web
  - Work out the logisitics
  - Watch out for unsanctioned World Wide Web sites

(5) Market Your Internet Presence
  - Let the Internet know your World Wide Web site exists
    - Announcement-only mailing lists and USENET newsgroups
    - Discussion mailing lists and USENET newsgroups
    - Major directories of World Wide Web sites
    - Smaller directories of World Wide Web sites
    - World Wide Web search engines
    - Ask other sites to link to your site
  - Let the "outside world" know your site exists
    - Include your Internet addresses in external communications
    - Issue a press release

(6) The Evolution of World Wide Web Sites
  - First-generation World Wide Web sites
  - Second-generation World Wide Web sites
  - Third-generation World Wide Web sites
  - Fourth-generation World Wide Web sites

communications through the World Wide Web are not afforded the same degree of attention. When it comes to the World Wide Web, many sites are built by technical staff on their own time and initiative, often with brilliant results. Yet, when a World Wide Web site is created by the information technology department without guidance from senior management, it is easy for incorrect or unofficial information to be "published" on the network, where it is instantly accessible to millions of people around the world. Or, in other cases, technical staff might build a World Wide Web site that is technically fabulous, but has little strategic impact or potential.

Given the wide reach of a World Wide Web site on the Internet, the same degree of *management attention, respect, and funding* must be given to any Internet initiative. If a World Wide Web site is not done right, the potential for public relations *damage* exists, since thousands may visit a corporate World Wide Web site as soon as it is available — and before it is ready.

In this chapter we outline some of the key issues that an organization must consider to ensure that its World Wide Web site is a success. We focus exclusively on the use of the World Wide Web, since it is becoming the primary medium for establishing a corporate identity on the Internet.

Establishing Your Corporate Image

Doing it Right the First Time

It is time that corporate Canada became serious about the Internet and the World Wide Web. If you are going to do it, *do it right*. As the Internet becomes a mainstream business application, management *must* be involved and must be prepared to support that involvement with the proper funds and commitment.[1]

Do you really want people to visit your corporate site if it is a shoddy job? Do you want people to visit your site if it is incomplete, full of errors, or has a number of empty screens? Do you want people to visit a site full of spelling mistakes and erroneous, outdated, or unofficial information? Do you want people to ridicule your site in public? It has happened — and can happen to you. When it comes to the Internet, an organization must ensure that the creation of its World Wide Web site is done properly the first time.

Do Not Announce Your Site Before it is Ready

If you establish a World Wide Web site, do not make it available and certainly do not announce it before it is ready. The Internet learns about new sites very quickly,

---

[1] On the other hand, there are lots of technologies that are examined by "lower echelons" of an organization before being adopted by senior management. These efforts should not necessarily be stopped, since experimentation is at the heart of many successful information technology strategies. Thus a more balanced, moderate approach is required, one that recognizes the benefits of the experiments but also encourages management support.

and curious Internet users are known to go searching for new company sites that have not been officially announced. It is relatively easy to do.

Someone who discovers your World Wide Web site can immediately create a link to it, with the result that hundreds or perhaps thousands may visit the site every day, even though it might not be ready for public consumption. A good strategy to avoid this situation is to put a note on the site advising users that it is being prepared and will be launched "soon," as Bell Mobility did when their World Wide Web site was being constructed (**http://www.mobility.com**):

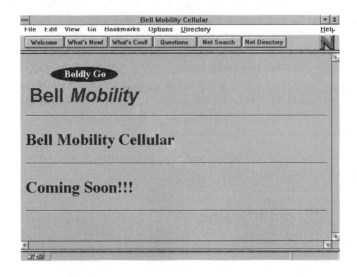

The Internet has a very efficient system of "jungle drums": many people around the world know about new sites within a day of their announcement on the Internet. This means that not only do people discover new World Wide Web sites quickly, but they begin to critique them quickly as well. These jungle drums can be very unfriendly. New sites are rated through informal discussions within the Internet community, and if a site is bad, everyone knows it is bad.

One of the most bizarre premature site situations in Canada involved press releases issued on the same day in January 1995 by the Bank of Montreal and the Royal Bank, each purporting to be the first Canadian bank on the Internet. (**http://www.bmo.com** and **http://www.royalbank.com**). As a result of the press releases, both sites were announced in the *Toronto Star's* business section the next day.

Prompted by the press coverage, people immediately visited these sites, only to discover that they were rather barren in information content. At the time, the Royal Bank site contained only a little bit of information, most of it public relations fluff. While the Bank of Montreal site went one step further, providing access to interest rates, foreign exchange information, and daily economics reports, selecting several of these items presented a page that merely stated "the information you requested is not available." Internet users were very frustrated, and negative "reviews" were quickly posted throughout various areas of the Internet. The efforts by the banks backfired. It is not a good way to start.

It was laudable that each bank made a tentative effort into the Internet, but it is also evident that these efforts were nothing more than experiments. (It is also likely that by the time that you read this, both banks will have changed their World Wide Web sites somewhat.) There is nothing wrong with experimentation, but an organization cannot afford to experiment by opening a site on the Internet before it is ready. The Internet community will be unforgiving and critical. The public is not looking for public relations; they are looking for content. If your World Wide Web site has nothing to offer, Internet users will not come back again. Think of it this way: a corporate World Wide Web site is like a good bottle of wine; opening it too soon will spoil it.

Drawing People to Your World Wide Web Site

Keeping in mind that a World Wide Web site should be more than just a public relations exercise, one of the key things that you want to do with your site is draw people to it on a regular basis. Some companies ignore this fact, and while they do invest time to build impressive World Wide Web sites, full of colorful graphics, corporate information, annual reports, and other information, there is really nothing there to keep people coming back. Consequently, many people visit the site when it is first announced. Then interest quickly drops off, and visitors do not return.

Obviously, if your site has a marketing purpose, you want to attract people to it on a regular basis. To keep people coming back to your site, it must provide current information.

Give People a Reason to Visit You

If you intend to use your World Wide Web site to promote your organization, your product, or your services, you have to give people a reason to want to visit you. You won't get a regular stream of visitors if your site contains boring press releases, dull corporate information, and other mundane material. Internet users want relevant information and content that will pique their curiosity and interest. The key is to use content that has drawing power. However, what works in your particular case will depend on many factors, and you might have to try several types of content to see what will be successful. Many organizations have solved this problem by ensuring that their site provides value to visitors.

One of the best ways to provide value to visitors is to include pointers to other related sites from your site. If you keep your pointers up-to-date, people will come and visit your site in order to discover other Internet-related information resources.

An example is the World Wide Web Tennis Server, sponsored by the Racquet Workshop, a specialty tennis store in Texas. The Racquet Workshop sells tennis merchandise on the World Wide Web, such as tennis racquets, shoes and socks, and tennis accessories. To attract visitors to their on-line store, the Racquet Workshop, in conjunction with an Internet company in Texas, has set up an Internet site devoted to tennis information. The site is free and provides links to tennis resources all over the Internet as well as tennis tips and pictures of tennis pros (**http://arganet. tenagra.com/Racquet_Workshop/Tennis.html**).

Another way of using content as drawing power is to provide, within your World Wide Web site, information that you already make available to the public — research papers, brochures, newsletters, documents, discussion papers, and other documents in the public record — and update this information regularly. In many cases, you will find that this information already exists in electronic form and can be easily converted so that it can be made available on the World Wide Web.

In Chapter 4, we looked at DuPont Lubricants and noted how they made over 300 pages of technical literature related to their products available on-line. Also in Chapter 4 we noted how Godiva Chocolates makes chocolate recipes available on its World Wide Web site to attract visitors and Ragú places pasta recipes on its Web site with the same objective.

The Energy Sector of Natural Resources Canada has made dozens of its publications available on the Internet, including energy statistics, forecasts, publications, and reports (**http://es1.es.emr.ca**). For example, the full text of a study on Canada's energy markets is freely available on its World Wide Web server, as illustrated below:

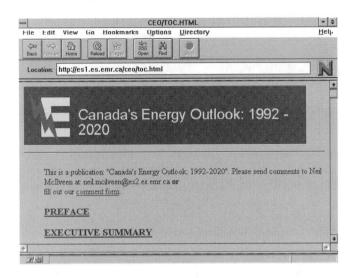

Another good example is Best Western Hotels, which has provided a list of traveler safety tips on its site on the World Wide Web. As a service to Internet users, the tips are offered in several different languages (**http://www.travelweb.com/thisco/bw/common/bw.html**).

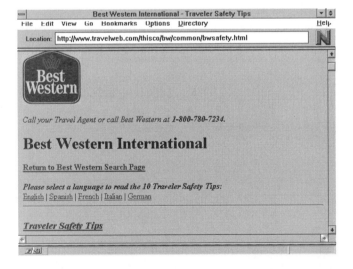

You don't have to be a large organization to make useful information available to Internet users. For example, you could create a monthly newsletter that provides helpful advice to your customers and place it on your World Wide Web site.

Finally, be creative! One strategy is to place a "tip of the day" or "tip of the week" on your World Wide Web site that will draw people on a regular basis.

General Electric's Plastics Division, for example, includes a "technical tip of the week" on its site (**http://www.ge.com**). Because this information is not time-sensitive, GE keeps an archive of the previous weeks' technical tips on its site. Thus GE can start building an electronic library of technical tips that will be of immense value to Internet users.

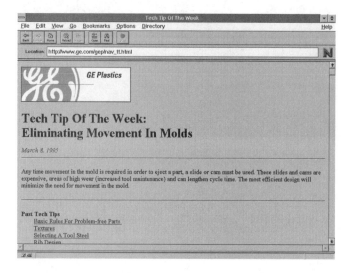

KPMG uses a similar strategy on its World Wide Web site. To attract users to its site (and to provide a public service to the community), KPMG places a new tax tip on its site every business day (**http://www.kpmg.ca**).

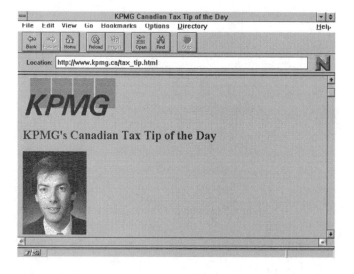

Like General Electric, KPMG keeps an archive of all the previous tax tips on its World Wide Web site. Over time, this will become an extremely valuable collection of tax tips for consumers and will help to draw people to KPMG's World Wide Web site.

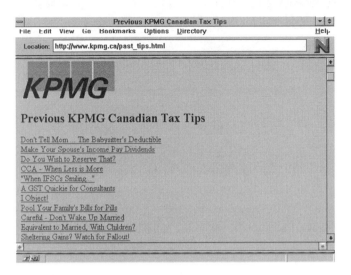

Regardless of how it is done, certainly one of the key strategies in building a World Wide Web site is to ensure that it contains information that will entice people to visit the site on a regular basis.

Provide Current Information

It is important that organizations on the World Wide Web let their customers know that their site is being updated regularly. If Internet users know that they can count on your site for reliable and up-to-date information, they are likely to make repeat visits. Altamira, an investment company, has established a World Wide Web site to make information available about its mutual funds (**http://www. altamira.com**). This is a good example of a site that is updated with recent, relevant information. Through it, a customer can, for example, obtain mutual fund prices and "net asset values" as of the previous day, read through full fund descriptions, and retrieve research reports.

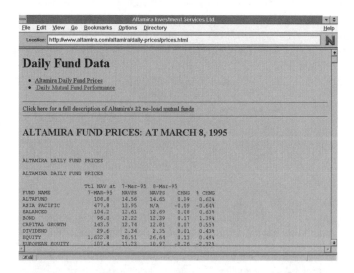

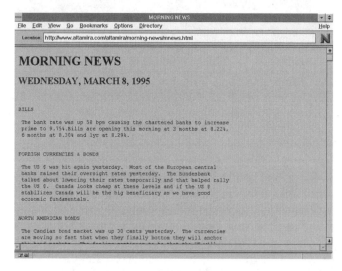

If the nature of the content you are providing is not time-sensitive, make sure you provide some indication that your World Wide Web server is being updated. You can do this by including a line at the top or bottom of your Web pages that indicates the day the pages were last revised. This way, Internet users can be confident that the information they see is reliable and current.

Link Internal Databases To Your World Wide Web Site

One way to provide information that is current and relevant is to link your World Wide Web site into an internal database or information system. When you update your database internally, it is also updated on the World Wide Web. This is how

Federal Express, mentioned in Chapter 2, is able to allow its customers to query the package-tracking system through the Internet. This type of application represents the real future of the Internet, for it indicates that the Internet is increasingly becoming the "front end" to an organization's internal information systems. Organizations that want to build strategic applications to reach their clients, customers, suppliers, or others can do so through the World Wide Web.

This trend is gaining momentum. Major database vendors such as Oracle, Sybase, and IBM are releasing tools that permit computer developers to easily and simply prepare a link from the World Wide Web into an internal corporate database. Organizations have a wealth of strategic information in their internal information systems, and this technology will open the door for the customer, and the organization.

Appeal to the Sense of Cool

In many ways the Internet is a youth culture as well as a culture of people who are fascinated by the advancements in computer technology, regardless of their age. The result of this culture is that "cool" sells on the Internet. "Cool" is a method of drawing people to your site. Do something "cool" on your site, and the Internet will learn about it — quickly.

A number of organizations have done something "cool" with their World Wide Web sites to encourage visitors. There are even sites throughout the Internet that provide an index to "cool" sites. If you want to get your site noticed, do something cool.

Time Warner and Disney were rated as "cool" sites to visit when they established their sites. In Time Warner's case, it was because of their on-line publications, while with Disney, it was because they chose to make available clips of various videos for those with high-speed links to the Internet. Encyclopedia Britannia established a calendar that lets users look up who was born on any particular day of the year, and it was rated as "cool" in the popular Yahoo index at Stanford University (**http://www.yahoo.com**).

Another good example is Reebok, the shoe company, which provides live interviews over the Internet with popular sports figures, as seen in the following screens (**http://planetreebok.com**):

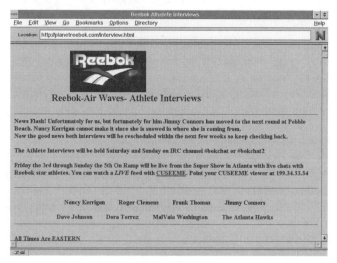

The "cool culture" on the Internet gets a lot of attention. One Internet user has gone so far as to establish a "Cool Site of the Day" listing, which recognizes a new "cool" spot on the Internet each day (**http://www.infi.net/cool.html**). The site receives thousands of visits from Internet users every day. The site has become so popular that at one point in early 1995 it had received 22,000 visits in a single day. Sites that have the honor of being listed in the "Cool Site of the Day" therefore receive a lot of attention and exposure.

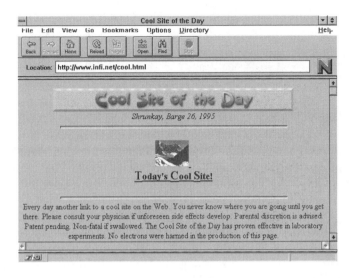

Perhaps the ultimate display of cool on the Internet is "The Amazing Fish Cam," developed by a U.S. Internet user (**http://home.mcom.com/fishcam/fishcam.html**). This person has focused a video camera on a fish tank in his office, and he displays the picture on the World Wide Web for the world to see. The picture is updated every minute. The site has become legendary throughout the Internet, guaranteeing an almost steady stream of visitors to the site of the company that he works for. He is currently running a fund-raising campaign to help him buy a better camera.

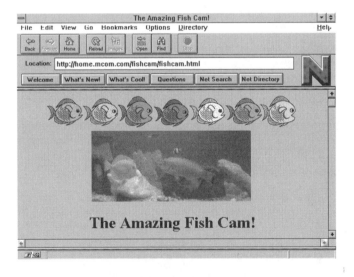

While all this might seem lighthearted and fun (and even downright weird), the key point on the Internet is to get peoples' attention. In the same way that television commercials are designed to get the attention of viewers, World Wide Web sites are designed to get the attention of Internet users. Think of something innovative and creative, and people are guaranteed to visit.

Paying Attention to Content and Layout

Get Management Involved

You must think of your corporate image when you design your World Wide Web site. Your corporate image on the Internet is as important as the corporate image you want to project in any print or TV-based media campaign. This means that when designing a World Wide Web site, you should get the same people involved from your organization that would be involved in the creation of a print, TV, or radio ad.

Designing a World Wide Web site is straightforward. It is not difficult to figure out how to do it. As a result many Web sites are often built by people who do not have a great degree of creative talent, who do not understand the organization's objectives, and who do not understand much about the importance of corporate image. This is a big mistake. People will develop impressions about your organization based on what they see on your World Wide Web site. If 22,000 people visit your organization's site because it was listed in the "Cool Site of the Day," that's 22,000 people who may get the wrong message about your organization if it has not been designed properly. It is critical that the World Wide Web site be designed in a manner that is consistent with the image that corporate management wants to project to the public.

Some of the most common design and content flaws on World Wide Web sites include:

➤ too many images;

➤ too many different fonts;

➤ a confusing layout;

➤ too much information crammed onto a page;

➤ outdated or incorrect links and pointers to other information pages;

➤ no information on when the site was last updated;

➤ no contact information.

The solution? In addition to getting management involved to ensure that the content is properly maintained, get creative people involved — people who understand design issues, such as proper layout, the use of white space for balance, the use of eye-catching graphics, color balance, and all kinds of other creative issues. These people will be found in your organization's marketing department or advertising agency. There are also many Internet consulting firms that can help you build a World Wide Web site. These are the people who truly understand what it takes to build a site that is visually and interactively pleasing — an important component of its eventual success.

Seek Feedback And Suggestions

Make sure that your World Wide Web site is designed so that Internet users can send feedback, not only about your organization and its products and services, but also about the quality of your Web services. One of the biggest mistakes that organizations can make is to design an effective World Wide Web site, but not provide any contact information. The experience is similar to getting into an organization's voice mail system and not being able to reach a human being. It can be extremely frustrating.

You can seek feedback from Internet users by providing a form on your site that users can fill out with suggestions and comments. You might be surprised at how willing people are to offer suggestions and hints on how your site could be made more pleasing or useful. It is important to give your customers the opportunity to tell you what services they want to see on your World Wide Web site. This will help your organization develop Web services that are consistent with customer needs. A survey that asks Internet users what services they would like to see on your Web site is a good strategy.

There are many examples of organizations that have feedback forms on their Web sites, such as Goodyear Tire (**http://www.goodyear.com**):

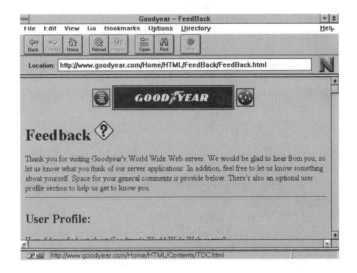

Highlight New Additions To Your Site

Make sure that your site clearly identifies an area where people can find *new* information.

Serious World Wide Web sites are updated with new information on a regular basis, which draws repeat visitors. As these repeat visitors return to your site, they will want to zero in on the most recent additions. If you make it difficult for users to locate new information, by forcing them to scour through every nook and cranny of your site, they will become quite frustrated and may not visit again.

On the Internet organizations have adopted two methods to draw peoples' attention to new information:

➤ Many establish a "What's New" section that can be accessed right from the home page for the site. A "What's New" item on the first page is one of the first things that people see when they visit. For example, Delrina includes a "What's New" item on its World Wide Web home page (**http://www.delrina.com**):

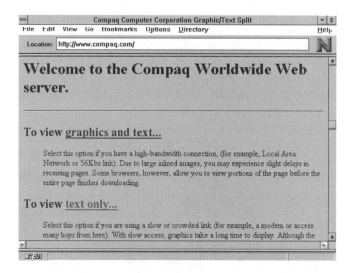

Internet users who select the "What's New" item are taken to a page that summarizes the new features on Delrina's World Wide Web site.

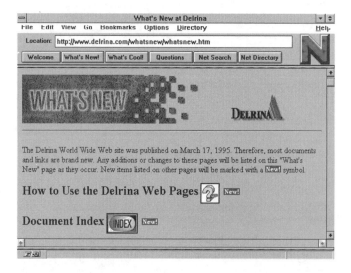

Organizations that don't have separate "What's New" pages can use special "New" graphics to indicate recent additions to their sites. For example, the Ontario Milk Marketing Board (**http://www.milk.org**) used a "New" graphic to alert Internet users to a new page of information about nutrition month:

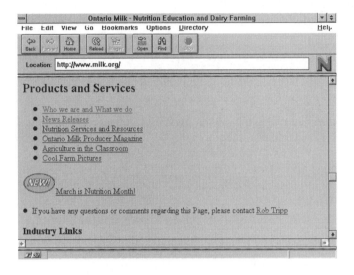

Similarly, Northern Telecom uses "New" graphics to identify new features on its World Wide Web site (**http://www.nt.com**):

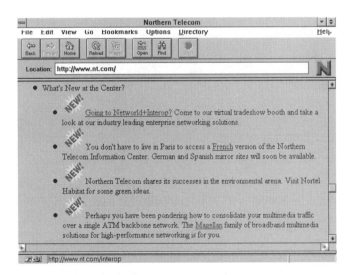

Do Not Overuse Graphics

The World Wide Web is exciting because it combines the use of text, graphics, images, and sound. Some organizations go overboard and load their sites with "awesome" graphics. The problem in doing this is that many people access the Internet with a dial-up modem, and while performance is improving, it can take a long time for a full page of graphics to appear on the screen.

A World Wide Web page should

➤ use a mixture of text and graphics that offers a compromise between those who access the Internet using a slow-speed modem and those who have a direct, high-speed link to the network;

➤ provide an option for individuals to access a "text-only" version of your site.

Compaq's World Wide Web site (**http://www.compaq.com**) is an excellent model to follow. The first page contains no graphics or company information at all. The first thing users see is a welcome message and then they are asked to select between a graphics display and a text-only display. This allows users to select the type of display that is most appropriate for the speed of Internet connection that they are using.

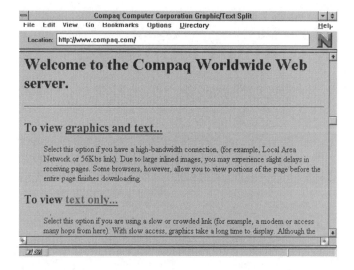

Maintaining a Consistent Corporate Image

It's 11:00 p.m. Do You Know Where Your Web Sites Are?

Do you know how many World Wide Web sites your organization is running? If you are part of a large organization, take a look around. You might be surprised. If senior managers are not aware of an organization's Internet activities, they cannot take responsibility for their company's World Wide Web activities. This is a particularly dangerous position for a company to be in, especially if a single person somewhere in the company has built a Web site that is unknown to senior management.

What often happens is that the person maintaining the site relocates to another job and leaves the site running without telling anyone. Despite being abandoned, the World Wide Web site is still alive on the Internet, receiving visits from hundreds of potential customers a week from around the world. And because the site is no longer being maintained, the information on it is stale. This leaves a poor impression on potential customers who continue to visit the site. Can you imagine what would happen if this forgotten Web site contained out-dated price information?

The case of the "missing Web site" is not uncommon (in fact, we know of one example for a large Canadian organization, but in the interest of fairness, we will not mention the name). It underscores the need for senior management to be involved in a company's Internet activities from the start.

Does Your Organization Have A Consistent Image on the World Wide Web?

It is important that senior management, especially in large organizations, keep track of all its Web sites. Clearly, World Wide Web sites created by customers of your organization, as we discussed in Chapter 4, are unofficial. But what happens if you are in an organization that has independent sales agents or branch offices worldwide? Many of these branch offices and sales agents may start building their own sites. How do you ensure that all these sites present a unified and consistent image to the public?

If your branch location in Hong Kong puts up a World Wide Web site, it is immediately accessible to Internet users worldwide. Internet users who visit your company's Hong Kong site will form impressions about your company based on what they see and do there.

Corporate image is a tricky thing, and it must be very carefully managed. The situation with the World Wide Web is analogous to the corporate image of a hotel chain. For example, if you have a bad experience at a Holiday Inn in France, it will affect your perception of the whole hotel chain. Likewise, a bad experience at any of your company's World Wide Web sites will affect an individual's perception of your organization. How can this happen? Say a user fills out a comment form on the Hong Kong Web site, requests a return telephone call, and does not receive a response. His or her impression of your organization has been adversely affected. Similarly, the design, layout, and content of the Hong Kong Web page will affect how Internet users *worldwide* perceive your organization.

There are cases where corporate image is being affected by local initiatives. Not coincidentally, within the hotel industry there are already several cases of large hotels putting up their own World Wide Web sites. For example, here is the introductory screen of the Web site created by a Holiday Inn Crowne Plaza Hotel in California (**http://www.geninc.com/geni/USA/CA/Redondo_Beach/travel/crowne_plaza/index.html**):

This site is an independent initiative and is not part of a Holiday Inn corporate site on the World Wide Web. Yet it is operating under the Crowne Plaza brand name, and it is viewable worldwide. It therefore raises some important managerial issues for Holiday Inn. Does the head office know that one of their hotel chains has a site on the World Wide Web? What happens if the site crashes or is inaccessible on a regular basis? What if there are errors? What if the operators do not return comments? What if there are outdated prices?

The challenge for senior management at Holiday Inn's head office is to ensure that the content and design of the site conform with the Crowne Plaza image. If more and more Holiday Inn hotels establish their own World Wide Web sites, it will be important for the head office to create a companywide Internet strategy that establishes guidelines on World Wide Web use. This will ensure that all Holiday Inn sites are consistent in both content and image.

Hewlett Packard has approached this issue of corporate image on the Internet. Walid Mougayar of Hewlett Packard, notes that "a central corporate resource called Web Central provides information for developers of WWWeb servers that are to be accessed by people outside of HP. This includes a standards architecture, style guide, library of gif files, on-line topic editor, and other information." This is a good example that any organization should follow.

Work Out the Logistics

Trying to implement a World Wide Web strategy within an international organization involves a number of tricky logistical questions. For example, continuing with the hotel example, what happens if seven different Holiday Inn hotels suddenly have their own independent World Wide Web sites? The following questions would then need to be addressed by the head office:

- How should the different hotel sites be linked to each other, and who should coordinate the linkages?

- Should Holiday Inn establish a single corporate World Wide Web site that would act as a one-stop location for Holiday Inn information on the Internet?

- What should the role of the corporate World Wide Web site be? For example, should it only provide corporate information such as press releases and annual reports, or should it contain detailed information on each of the hotels in the chain?

- How does the hotel chain avoid redundancy and duplication of efforts on its World Wide Web sites? For example, is each hotel paying to put the same information on the Internet?

- What policies should exist for other Holiday Inns that want to create their own World Wide Web sites? For example, does each site have to be registered and approved with the head office, and should there be a consistent style?

As the Holiday Inn example demonstrates, establishing a companywide Internet strategy is critical for large organizations, especially those with national or worldwide operations, because many logistical problems can arise. The earlier a corporate Internet strategy is laid out, the fewer logistical problems the organization will encounter.

Watch Out for Unsanctioned Web Sites

Management must also be on the lookout for sites that give the impression that they are officially sanctioned when they are not. For example, consider the case of Mary Kay Cosmetics. The following announcement was circulated on the Internet in late 1994:

ANNOUNCE: Mary Kay Cosmetics
World Wide Web:
http://cyberzine.org/html/Cosmetics/cosmetics2.html

Cosmetics for you are now online at www:
http://cyberzine.org

For all your special cosmetic needs you will find them on-line with Mary Kay Cosmetics. Check out the site and welcome Mary Kay and Cosmetics to the Internet.

E-mail feykay@CyberZine.ORG

This announcement gives the impression that Mary Kay Cosmetics has established a site on the World Wide Web. Yet, when Internet users travel to the site noted in the above message, they see a site that is operating under the May Kay name, but run by a Mary Kay consultant.

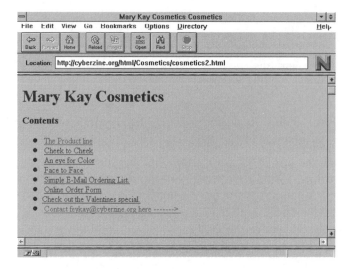

The impression is given that Mary Kay (as an organization) is active on the Internet, but it is not. What should the policy be in such a case? This is a difficult question, and one that should be addressed by management.

Marketing Your Internet Presence

Many organizations create a World Wide Web site without adequately advertising it or making people aware that it exists. They then complain that no one is accessing their site. Of course, this is like setting up an 800 number and not telling anyone what the number is. Publicizing your World Wide Web site involves marketing both off and on the Internet.

Let the Internet Know Your Web Site Exists

Once you have established your Internet site, you need to let the Internet know that your site exists. There are many places on the Internet where you can announce new World Wide Web sites.

Announcement-only Mailing Lists and USENET Newsgroups   The Internet loves to report on itself. One result is that there are several mailing lists and USENET groups that are devoted exclusively to the announcement of new Internet sites. You can send a message to these areas announcing your new site. When you send your announcements to such a mailing list or USENET group, be short, concise, and to the point. Remember that the purpose of your announcement is to "announce" your site, not to advertise your company or its products. Announcements that are too commercial in nature will be frowned upon. A good announcement will meet the following three basic criteria:

➤ it identifies the organization;

➤ it identifies the location of the World Wide Web site;

➤ it describes what the site contains.

For example, here is the announcement that Goodyear Tire circulated on the Internet when it launched its company World Wide Web site. Notice that it contains the three basic elements that we noted above.

Goodyear Introduces Home Page on the World Wide Web

Akron, OH, March 1 — Goodyear Tire & Rubber Co., North America's leading tire manufacturer, introduces the Goodyear Home Page. Goodyear's server provides valuable product information, plus a wealth of knowledge on tires and vehicle maintenance.

The Goodyear Tire & Rubber Co. server address is:

<URL:http://www.goodyear.com>

The server contains a complete catalog of Goodyear's consumer tire lines, including features, benefits, and a good look at the tire. The Goodyear "Tire Selector" recommends a tire line based on the individual user's vehicle and driving needs.

The server's "Retailer Locator" finds the Goodyear retailer closest to the user and provides important information about that location.

Goodyear's "Tire School" provides tips on tires, vehicle maintenance, and driving skills. In addition, it contains a comprehensive auto racing schedule and a calendar of Goodyear Blimp appearances.

Many of the announcement discussion groups mentioned below have specific guidelines that you must follow when making a submission. It is therefore a good idea to follow the discussion group for a few days to familiarize yourself with the format of announcements. Here are a few places to send your announcements:

➤ **comp.infosystems.www.announce**, a USENET newsgroup for the announcement of new World Wide Web sites. Look for the posting entitled

"How to Announce in comp.infosystems.www.announce" for information on how to submit announcements to this newsgroup.

➤ Net-Happenings, a mailing list for the announcement of new Internet resources including, but not limited to, World Wide Web sites. Send your announcements to Gleason Sackman, who is the moderator of Net-Happenings (**sackman@plains.nodak.edu**).

➤ EDRES-L, a moderated mailing list for the announcement and review of new educational resources. You can e-mail your announcements to **EDRES-L@unb.ca**. See Appendix A for information on how to join.

In addition to general announcement newsgroups and mailing lists like comp.infosystems.www.announce and Net-Happenings, a number of subject-specific announcement groups exist. For example, if you are a ski resort launching a World Wide Web site, you could announce it in the USENET newsgroup **rec.skiing.announce.**

Discussion Mailing Lists and USENET Newsgroups   You can also announce your World Wide Web site on some of the Internet's general discussion groups, where appropriate, if you respect the etiquette of the particular group while doing so. For example, suppose you work for Toyota and you want to announce a new World Wide Web site that your company has developed. You will probably want to announce your new site on the Toyota mailing list, where Internet users discuss Toyota cars. You will also want to announce it on some of the general automotive discussion groups. If you are a telecommunications organization, you will want to announce your World Wide Web site on some of the telecommunications discussion groups. If you are a not-for-profit organization, you will want to announce your site on some of the general not-for-profit discussion groups, as well as on any of the discussion groups that relate to your organization's primary activities.

The key is to find mailing lists and USENET newsgroups where your announcements reach the right target audience. Make sure that announcements are welcome on the discussion group before you post anything. Monitor the discussions for a few days to see what types of postings are acceptable. There are several places to look on the Internet for relevant mailing lists and discussion groups:

➤ The List of Publicly Accessible Mailing Lists (**http://www.NeoSoft. com:80/internet/paml**) contains a directory of several hundred mailing lists in dozens of different subject categories.

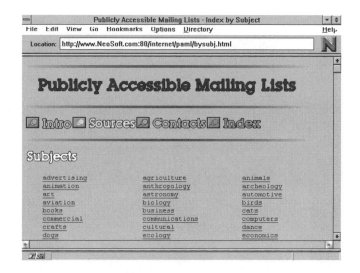

> The Clearinghouse for Subject-Oriented Internet Resource Guides contains subject-specific guides to Internet resources, prepared by people on the Internet. The guides usually contain pointers to mailing lists. You can access the guides at **http://asa.ugl.lib.umich.edu/chhome.html**.

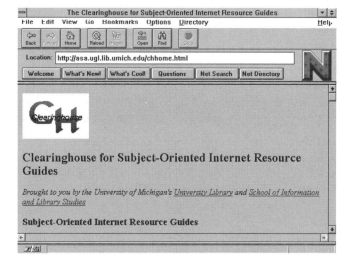

➤ The World Wide Web Virtual Library (**http://info.cern.ch/hypertext/DataSources/bySubject/Overview.html**) provides pointers to Internet resources (including mailing lists) on dozens of topics.

➤ The USENET FAQ (frequently asked questions) documents provide information on dozens of different topics, including pointers to Internet mailing lists. A directory of USENET FAQs is available at **http://www.cis.ohio-state.edu/hypertext/faq/usenet/FAQ-List.html**.

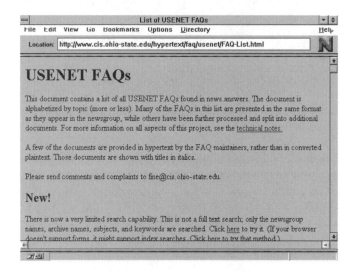

Major Directories of World Wide Web Sites   Many people will discover your site by finding it listed within one of the many directories found throughout the Internet. Thus one of your key activities should be to get your site listed in as many World Wide Web directories as possible. Here are a few suggested directories:

➤ Open Market's Commercial Sites Index is one of the best places to announce a new organizational World Wide Web site if you are a "for-profit" company. To announce your organization's World Wide Web site there, fill out the on-line form at **http://www.directory.net**.

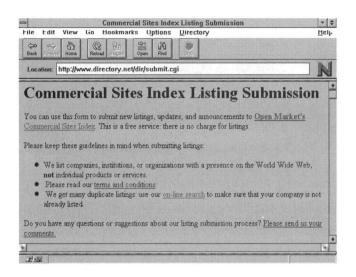

NCSA What's New is for the announcement of new World Wide Web sites in all categories. NCSA stands for "National Center for Supercomputing Applications." To submit an announcement to the What's New page, fill out the on-line form at **http://gnn.com/gnn/wn/whats-new.html**.

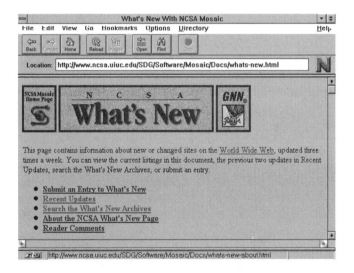

The Central Index of Canadian World Wide Web servers is for the announcement of new Canadian World Wide Web sites in all categories. To submit an announcement, fill out the on-line form at **http://www.csr. ists.ca/w3can/Welcome.html**.

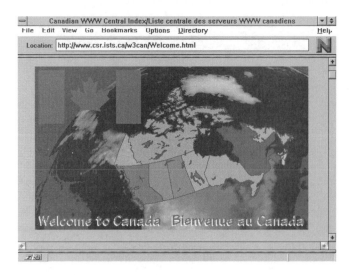

➤ The World Wide Web Virtual Library provides links to dozens of subject-specific directories of World Wide Web sites. To add your site to a subject directory, connect to the Virtual Library and locate the subject directory that most closely approximates your business or organization. There you will find instructions on how to register your site with the directory. The master list of subject directories is at **http://info.cern.ch/hypertext/DataSources/bySubject/Overview.html**.

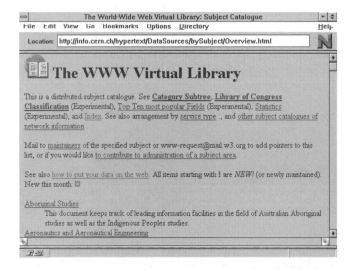

➤ City.Net is a directory of communities worldwide that have World Wide Web pages, including cities, towns, provinces, states, and countries. Municipal or provincial governments establishing World Wide Web sites should register them with City.Net. Registration is free. To register, fill out the form at **http://www.city.net**.

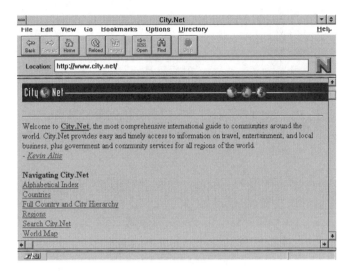

➤ Yahoo is an Internet-indexing project undertaken by two Stanford University students. It provides one of the best indices to World Wide Web sites, and contains over 40,000 entries (**http://www.yahoo.com**).

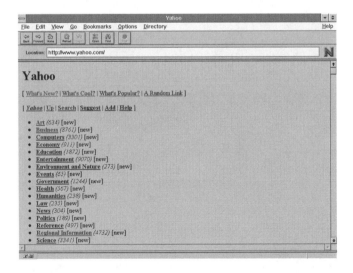

➤ Registration with the Yahoo directory is free. Anyone can register a new World Wide Web site with Yahoo by filling out an on-line form at **http://www.yahoo.com**.

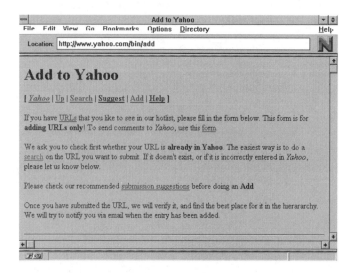

Smaller directories of World Wide Web Sites   In addition to the large Internet directory initiatives noted above, there are hundreds of smaller Internet directories in which you can list your World Wide Web site. For example, there is a site in Manitoba that is attempting to catalogue all the known World Wide Web sites in that province. If you are a Manitoba-based organization with a new World Wide Web site, you should certainly list it there (**http://www.umanitoba.ca/ALICE/manitoba.html**).

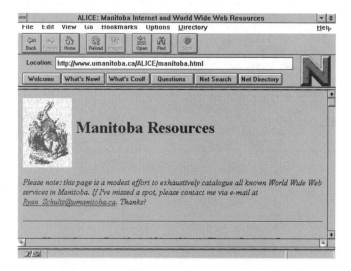

In British Columbia the Victoria Free-Net maintains a directory of World Wide Web servers in that province (**http://freenet.victoria.bc.ca/bcw3list.html**).

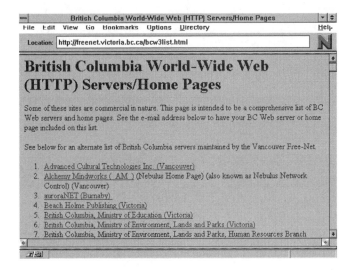

There are many other smaller Internet directories that are listed within the large Internet directories like Yahoo (**http://www.yahoo.com**) and City.Net (**http://www.city.net**). Discovering them and getting yourself listed in each of them might be an arduous task, but it is part of getting your site noticed on the Internet.

World Wide Web Search Engines   Another way of making your site known on the Internet is to register it with some of the World Wide Web search engines. Search engines are large databases that index the content found in thousands of World Wide Web sites. Typically, these systems "travel" the Web on a regular basis and update their index with new sites discovered; they are quite often very up-to-date. Each database is searchable by keyword. Search engines are used by individuals conducting research or by individuals looking for a particular company or organization on the Internet. (They differ from directories like Yahoo, City.Net, and the Commercial Sites Index, which provide categories of topics.)

Three of the most popular search engines on the World Wide Web are Infoseek (**http://www.infoseek.com**), Lycos (**http://lycos.cs.cmu.edu**), and WebCrawler (**http://webcrawler.cs.washington.edu/WebCrawler/WebQuery.html**). WebCrawler is illustrated below:

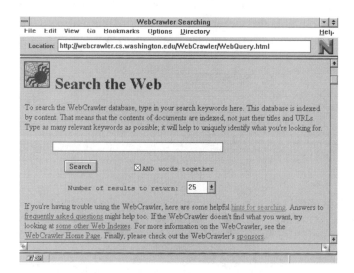

While most search engines scour the World Wide Web automatically for new sites, it is also possible to manually request that your site be added to a search engine's database. To add a new site to WebCrawler's database, for example, you simply fill out an on-line form on the WebCrawler site (**http://webcrawler.cs.washington.edu/ WebCrawler/WebQuery.html**).

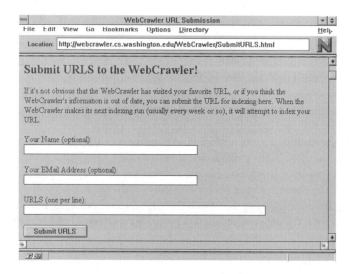

Ask Other Sites to Link to Your Site　On the World Wide Web any site, anywhere in the world, can contain a link to your site. Naturally, the more sites that contain links to your site, the more visitors you will have. One of the most important marketing tactics on the World Wide Web is to get as many sites as possible to link to your site.

Thus one of the key objectives in your Internet plan should be to determine how you can get other sites to establish a "pointer" to your site. This "hypertext" linking found in the Web is what has made it so popular, for it means that people can quickly travel the globe in search of information. People spend a great deal of time surfing the Internet — traveling from site to site, and from country to country — often for enjoyment, but also in the pursuit of knowledge and information.

By making your site more attractive to visitors (using ideas suggested earlier in this chapter), other sites will want to create a link to your site. But don't wait for this to happen. Actively seek out sites that are related to yours and ask them to create a link to you. For example, suppose you are a retail store that sells kites, and you have just launched your World Wide Web site. You should find as many kite-related World Wide Web sites as you can, and ask the people who created them to include a pointer to your site. You will find that most people will be more than happy to create a link to your site *if you ask politely and if your site has useful information to offer.*

The World Wide Web site pictured below, which we found using the Yahoo directory described earlier, contains all kinds of information about kites (**http://www. mathcs.emory.edu/~kml/kites/kites.html**). The site includes links to other kite sites on the World Wide Web, including stores that sell kite supplies. Since this site was listed in the Yahoo directory, it probably receives many visits from people around the world who are looking for information about kites. Therefore, as you are trying to publicize your kite site, it would be a good idea to approach the person who created this site to determine if he/she can create a link to you. That way, when people visit that kite site, they will be able to travel directly to your kite site.

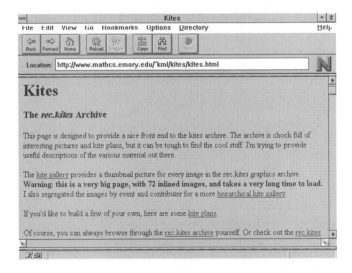

But how do you go about finding sites to link to? Spend some time surfing the Web and using the various directories and search mechanisms described over the last several pages. To discover World Wide Web sites that relate to your primary business activity, search the databases and directories using key words that describe your industry or business. Here are some directories and databases that you can try:

- the Yahoo directory (**http://www.yahoo.com**);

- the World Wide Web Virtual Library (**http://info.cern.ch/hypertext/ DataSources/bySubject/Overview.html**);

- the Commercial Sites Index (**http://www.directory.net**);

- as many of the World Wide Web search engines as possible (e.g., InfoSeek, WebCrawler, Lycos). A directory of search engines is available at **http://home.mcom.com/home/internet-search.html**.

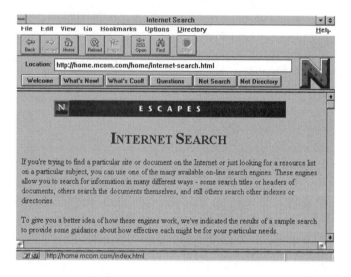

Finally, one last point about getting others to point to or link to your site: the principle of reciprocity is important. Tell others that in exchange for linking their World Wide Web site to you, you will link your site to them. In this way both organizations benefit.

Let the Outside World Know Your World Wide Web Site Exists

Publicizing your site on the Internet is only part of the challenge. You also have to advertise your site in the outside world. There are several things you should consider.

Include Internet Addresses in External Communications   It is important to publicize your Internet presence through traditional marketing channels so that your customers, business partners, and the general public are aware that you are on the Internet. The key is to integrate all your on-line activities into your regular marketing using the following rule of thumb:

Rule of Thumb

Include your Internet addresses wherever your telephone and fax numbers appear. Internet addresses include e-mail addresses, "mail robot addresses," and World Wide Web addresses.

With Internet addresses becoming as recognizable as telephone numbers and fax numbers, you should be including your World Wide Web addresses and e-mail addresses in all external communications, including newspaper and magazine ads and TV and radio commercials. You should also be listing your Internet addresses on business cards, company letterhead, packing orders, invoices, and all other company literature. The Internet is yet another way for the consumer to reach you, so it is important that you integrate *all your external communications* with your Internet presence.

KPMG, the public accounting and professional services firm, took out advertisements in the *Globe & Mail* and other newspapers shortly before the 1995 federal budget was released, announcing that its analysis of the budget would be available on its World Wide Web site. This was, in many ways, a watershed for the Internet in Canada, for it was the first time that the authors of this book have seen a major organization advertise its World Wide Web address so prominently.

KPMG reports that it had some 50,000 visits to its federal budget site over a one-week period following the ad.

KPMG is by no means the only company including a World Wide Web address in its ads. IBM, Xerox, Motorola, Godiva Chocolatier, and numerous other firms are now doing the same. Advertisements featuring World Wide Web addresses are starting to appear everywhere. The following ad for gourmet coffee appeared in an industry magazine called *CoffeeTalk*, which is targeted at coffee manufacturers, distributors, and retailers. The ad was created by J.P. Hogan and Company, an advertising and public relations firm in Knoxville, Tennessee. The ad includes both an e-mail address and a World Wide Web address.

Issue a Press release   Consider issuing a press release to let the local and national media know that you have launched a World Wide Web site. This may generate some additional publicity for your organization and your site. To give you an idea of what such a press release would look like, here is the media advisory that Bell Canada issued when it launched its World Wide Web site in early 1995:

Bell Establishes a Presence on the Internet

(OTTAWA - March 23, 1995) — Bell Canada has posted a new billboard on the Internet.

Recognizing the vitality and the exponential growth of the Internet in the past few years, Bell has established its own site on the World Wide Web (WWW).

Do you want to know all the latest news about Bell and the telecommunications industry? Are you interested in Bell's SmartTouch(TM) Services? Would you like to know what Bell is doing on the Information Highway? Through the use of audio messages, rendered graphics and text Bell will offer its customers access to:

News releases and informational updates;
Executive speeches;
Information on products and services for business and
    residence;
Updates on Bell's information highway initiatives;
Information about Bell Canada and other BCE
    companies;
Information on the telecommunications industry as a
    whole
Information about Bell sponsorships in various com-
    munities across Ontario and Québec; and
Other great sites on the WWW.

Making this site interactive, Bell will also give customers access to an e-mail forum where they can comment on Bell's site, ask questions about the company and its policies or get information on products and services.

Bell's site is also a doorway to several other locations on the Internet. Users browsing Bell's site will be able to access the sites of MCI (including Grammercy Press), Stentor, Ottawa's Museum of Science and Technology, the Ontario Museum Index and the Bell Centre for Creative Communications at Centennial College.

Bell will update its site regularly so that frequent visitors will always have something new to see. In coming months, Bell plans to add a lot more information such as the 1994 annual report, fact sheets, backgrounders and a catalogue of products that can be ordered on-line.

The address for Bell's new WWW site is: **http://www.bell.ca**.

Bell Canada, the largest Canadian telecommunications operating company, markets a full range of state-of-the-art products and services to more than seven million business and residence customers in Ontario and Québec.

Bell Canada is a member of Stentor — an alliance of Canada's major telecommunications companies.

The Evolution of World Wide Web Sites

To close this chapter, we offer the following comments, written by Dave Little, who works with Toronto-based e-Commerce Inc., a company that has been involved in the design of many sophisticated World Wide Web sites. It neatly summarizes the issues that organizations need to think about when they are constructing a World Wide Web site.

The Key Question is This: What Makes an Excellent Web Site?

As we have been using the Web for years, starting when there were literally 6 sites in existence, we can comment on how the Web has changed.

FIRST-GENERATION sites were produced by the technology crowd. The site message was almost always technical, befitting the needs of those early pioneers. Hypertext, as a navigation mechanism, was poorly implemented. The visual side was, well, attempted. All Web pages were static.

SECOND-GENERATION Web sites arrived in late 1993. Graphic artists are now a part of the implementation team. Importantly, the metaphor that is hypertext is now being moderately leveraged, often by the Web author and the graphic designer in tandem. Here we first see two-way communication mechanisms. Simple forms allow the user to feed information back to the Web server (we trust that the Web server is in turn passing this feedback on to real people!). All Web pages, save for form submission confirmation pages, are static. Second-generation sites become the *de facto* standard. Failing to measure up to the second-generation Web site mark is suicide.

THIRD-GENERATION Web sites distinctly change the game. Third-generation Web sites embody the current state-of-the-art in Web site development. Assume the development team includes graphic design talent. Assume a good understanding of hypertext as an information navigation and delivery tool. A new role is that of the information designer, contributing to the overall site architecture and function. But the key issue is interactivity. Building an interactive Web site means that both delivering your message and servicing the users' needs may be accomplished with personality and character. To do this requires a sound understanding of the Web architecture, programming expertise, vision, and creativity. We move from static Web pages into the domain of dynamically generated Web pages. We can now tie databases and other relevant back-end systems to the Web server. Yes, there will be some static Web pages, but delivering a reason for the user to come back, again, and again, dictates that the site be interactive, innovative, and constantly evolving. We are marrying creative technology with a limited but evolving medium. To deliver on your goals, think in terms of pushing the definition of a third-generation Web site.

Fourth-Generation World Wide Web Sites

We are going to go one step further than Mr. Little and suggest that your organization design a "fourth-generation" Web site. A fourth-generation Web site contains all the elements of a third-generation Web site, but the key difference is that it is not created by the information systems department in isolation. Earlier in this chapter we stressed the need for senior managers to get involved in the design and implementation of World Wide Web sites. A fourth-generation Web site is one that has been created with the support, funding, and attention of senior management. Clearly, it is this type of World Wide Web site that will enjoy the greatest degree of strategic success.

CHAPTER 11

Issues to Think About

> The best thing about the future, Dean Acheson once said, is that it comes only one day at a time. Unfortunately, this is no longer true. The future is crashing into the present with frightening speed. All the more reason for today's business leaders to be rooted in the future.
>
> Beyond the millennium:
> CEOs size up the future,
> *Chief Executive*, January/February 1995

Business is terrified about the Internet. It's no wonder. The media is full of negative stories about the Internet, so many sensible business executives have become literally terrified of what may happen if they get involved with it. Business needs a reality check when it comes to Internet issues. In this chapter we will examine the main issues that business needs to address on the Internet. We will tackle these issues from an objective and practical perspective.

First of all, if you are a business executive serious about the Internet, do not let the press deter you from implementing the Internet in your organization.

Many members of our national press cannot seem to figure out the Internet and the on-line world. The result is that they often play up the negative and sensational aspects of the Internet. Hence a plethora of articles has appeared across the country that focus on the Internet's dark side, that is, issues such as security problems ("cybercrime") and pornography. (The authors do acknowledge that there are some reporters who have provided an objective and balanced view of the Internet. These reporters should be commended for their efforts.)

For example, the authors of this book are regularly contacted by the press to talk about the Internet. Inevitably, one of the first questions is "isn't

INTERNET ISSUES

(1) Internet Security

Risks associated with dialup connections
- electronic mail is not secure unless encrypted;
- credit card orders are not secure unless encrypted;
- computer viruses are possible if downloading executable files.

Risks associated with dedicated connections
- all risks associated with dialup connections;
- unauthorized access to a company computer from the Internet.

Strategies to protect electronic mail transmissions
- use encryption;
- consider using an internal e-mail system;
- consider using a commercial e-mail service.

General Internet security strategies
- keep informed;
- create an Internet security manual;
- consider outsourcing.

(2) Electronic Commerce

Two important issues
- transaction security;
- electronic payment methods.

Three different methods of electronic payment
- credit card encryption using a World Wide Web browser;
- electronic cash systems;
- PIN-based systems.

(3) Intellectual Property
- be cognizant of the risks;
- consider encouraging the distribution and use of copyrighted and trademarked material;
- have a lawyer review your World Wide Web site;
- be vigilant.

(4) Other Issues
- consider posting a notice of limited liability;
- consider international Internet users;
- employee vs. employer e-mail ownership;
- employee productivity.

the Internet full of pornography?" It gets quite tiresome and indeed, frustrating. We are witnessing a knowledge revolution the likes of which the world has never seen, and all the media can do is hype the pornography issue.

It is time to deal with the Internet and the entire on-line services industry on a rational and practical level, without the hype, without the sensationalism, and certainly with a greater degree of maturity and responsibility in our national media. It should be clear by now that tens of millions of people sign onto the Internet every day to perform business activities. People use the Internet for marketing, selling, customer support, research, and communications. The Internet is a fundamental business tool used around the world, not the "completely dark place" that some media reports make it out to be.

The Internet does, however, present business with some rather thorny issues, mostly concerning computer security and intellectual property. In this chapter we will address some of the issues that a business executive will be faced with when developing an Internet strategy. These issues include

- ➤ security concerns and risks, especially credit card orders, computer viruses, the privacy of electronic mail, and the security of your own corporate network;

- ➤ electronic commerce;

- ➤ intellectual property;

- ➤ other issues, especially legal issues and employee productivity.

Internet Security Concerns

Internet security is perhaps the number one issue on the minds of businesses contemplating an Internet connection. No wonder: the media screams with headlines about security breaches on the Internet. Businesses are led to believe that as soon as they join the network, they will be deluged with thousands of hackers ready, willing, and able to steal their corporate crown jewels.

In a memorable item on the popular TV newsmagazine 60 Minutes, co-host Mike Wallace portrayed the Internet as a dangerous place for businesses.

> If you're going to cruise the information superhighway, like 30 million Americans are doing right now, you'd better be aware that cruising alongside you are intruders, hackers who can break into your computer and ferret out your credit records, your medical records, just about everything private that you wouldn't want to share with a stranger. Well, beyond that, they can also break into just about any corporation's computers and find out their most

> closely guarded business strategies and secrets. The
> busiest road on the information superhighway is called
> the Internet, the worldwide linkup of computers that be-
> long to corporations, government agencies, universities
> and folks like you and me. And just like us, their comput-
> ers, too, are being ripped off by the hackers.
>
> Mike Wallace
> "Highway Robbery"
> 60 Minutes, February 26, 1995

The *60 Minutes* story was not a balanced report. There was no coverage given to the many methods by which an organization can minimize the risk of an Internet break-in. There was no discussion about the fact that many thousands of organizations around the world have properly secured their Internet computers, no review of the thriving commercial Internet security industry, and no outline of the many emerging electronic commerce initiatives. Instead, we saw a typical, one-sided, alarmist report that the Internet was a high-risk place for your business to be. The fallout was severe, and business executives around the world recoiled in horror.

What are the Risks?

Any computer technology, including the Internet, introduces a level of risk. As with any computer security issue, if an organization pays attention and does the right things, it can minimize the risk to an acceptable degree. There are three types of security risks on the Internet:

➤ the risk of someone breaking into your computers through the Internet;

➤ the risk of someone intercepting electronic mail messages being sent through the Internet by your firm;

➤ the risk of infecting your firm's computers with a computer virus, if someone in your firm downloads an executable (i.e., a program that runs) file from the Internet.

The nature of the security risk on the Internet manifests itself in different ways, depending upon the type of access to the network:

➤ Organizations that have put in place a dialup or simple e-mail link to the Internet, without establishing a permanent TCP/IP connection, face little risk of someone breaking into their computers. Their main concern should be with computer viruses and the privacy of e-mail messages and credit card data being sent through the Internet.

> Organizations that provide a direct, permanent link from their corporate network to the Internet (i.e., a TCP/IP connection) also need to be concerned about computer viruses and the privacy of e-mail messages. However, these organizations face the additional risk of someone breaking into their computers from the Internet and must implement appropriate security measures to minimize this risk.

Dialup Connections to the Internet

Dialup users of the Internet do not have to fear that someone may break into their computer while they are connected to the Internet. Linking into the Internet through a modem, for example, does not mean that people will be able to access your PC and trash your files. It does not mean that you are exposing all the information on your PC to the outside world. Only organizations with dedicated Internet connections need to worry about someone breaking into their computers from the Internet.

As a dialup user, the risks that you face are different. Dialup users of the Internet face three security risks:

> electronic mail;

> credit card orders;

> computer viruses.

Each of these risks will be discussed below.

Risks Associated with Electronic Mail   CommerceNet, which we described in Chapter 2 ("a Silicon Valley-based initiative in which major computer companies such as IBM, Apple, and Hewlett Packard are coming together with major banks and commercial concerns, such as the Bank of America and MasterCard, to define the tools of future Internet-based networked commerce") describes the security of Internet messages in the following way:

WHY IS SECURITY AN ISSUE?

In the "real" world, where information is exchanged in physical form, there is a great deal of security infrastructure, built up over literally thousands of years, that we take for granted.

The postal service is a good example. For a nominal fee, you are able to send a message anywhere in the world. If you want that message to be private, you enclose it within an envelope. Tampering or changing the message would require breaking the seal on the envelope and committing a federal crime. If you wish to make sure that your

---

message was received, you ask for a return receipt. To make sure that the person who received the message was the one you intended him or her to be, you might check his or her signature. He or she might check yours.

Now imagine that someone has just constructed a brand-new postal service from scratch. The service operates at blinding speed, sorting and forwarding messages through various postal clearinghouses in seconds instead of days. But the new service has some drawbacks. Anyone can be a postmaster, and there is nothing to prevent a postmaster from making copies of the mail as it passes through his clearinghouse. Messages are written on postcards, and instead of signatures and return receipts, all message identification is written in identical block letters: "This message is from John at IBM." So the postcard-sorters can't help but see entire messages; there is little to prevent a phony message from being swapped for a genuine one; there is no guarantee that the persons on either end of the message exchange are the people on the address; and there is no means of verifying that a message was received.

Such a postal service exists today, and it's known as the Internet. By design, the Internet allows wiretapping, and it's estimated that 20% of the message traffic sent via the Internet is copied and stored somewhere (by someone other than sender and receiver) for later reference. Most messages are sent as plain block text…an intercepted message can be read by different software platforms.

When you transmit an e-mail message through the Internet, you should be aware that someone at a site which is involved in the transmission of your message could potentially read it or even change the contents. In general, the "site" administrators at both the originating and receiving ends have the ability to read a user's messages if they so desire. However, most site administrators will respect a user's right to privacy and believe that tampering with a private e-mail message is unethical.

There is always the possibility that your message can be intercepted and tampered with on its way to the destination site. This risk exists because of the way in which e-mail is routed through the Internet. An e-mail message being sent through the Internet might pass through several different Internet sites as it travels to the destination site. At each intermediate site, there may be people who have the tools and the knowledge to access your message. For example, someone could write a program that checks Internet messages for certain keywords as they pass through a site. An Internet message containing any of the keywords could then be copied and read.

It is also quite easy for anyone to forge a message on the Internet and make it look like it is being sent by someone else, although experienced Internet users can readily identify such forgeries. For example, in late 1994 a message was posted on the Internet that appeared to have come from the Premier of Ontario, Bob Rae. The message was quickly identified as a forgery, although the incident was widely publicized and received considerable media coverage.

The incident had one positive consequence. It revealed the public's lack of understanding about Internet security. Many assumed that an intruder had broken into the Premier's Internet computer and sent the message from there. For example, Mike Harris, the leader of the Progressive Conservative Party of Ontario, issued a press release as soon as he became aware of the incident. The press release exposed Mr. Harris' ignorance of how the Internet works:

> Checks with computer experts have confirmed that the sender either had special access to the Premier's office computers, broke into the system from another location, or skillfully re-configured their computer to expropriate the Premier's Internet address....At worst, this incident raises serious questions about the security of information stores in computers operated by the highest office in Ontario....
>
> Excerpt from News Release Issued by the Ontario Progressive Conservative Caucus December 8, 1994

Mr. Harris clearly failed to understand that *anyone* can forge a message on the Internet with minimal effort, and a person does not need to break into the Premier's Internet computer to create a message impersonating the Premier.

While there is little anyone can do to prevent people from posting forged messages on the Internet, there are steps that can be taken to protect the privacy of electronic mail messages. Any business executive planning an Internet strategy should consider the following precautions:

➤ Consider the use of an encryption program such as PGP (Pretty Good Privacy). Encryption "scrambles" the contents of an electronic mail message so that only the intended recipient can read it. If someone else intercepts an encrypted message, he/she will be unable to read it. PGP includes a digital signature feature that allows the sender of an e-mail message to electronically "sign" the message before it is transmitted. The digital signature allows the recipient of a message to verify that the signature is authentic and that it belongs with the associated text (it is possible for someone to substitute a different message with a signature).

> In cases where you might be sending sensitive documents through the Internet, consider establishing and using an internal, private e-mail network instead.

> If you need to send confidential documents to trading partners and business associates, you could consider using a commercial e-mail service, such as MCIMail or AT&T Mail, which provide secure e-mail services. Be prepared to pay heavily, however, since some of these systems charge upwards of $0.25 for every thousand characters that you send.

In summary, be cognizant of the Internet e-mail security issue, judge what is an acceptable level of risk with respect to the type of mail that you plan to use on the network, and act accordingly.

Risks Associated With Credit Card Orders   Many dialup users of the Internet will make use of the World Wide Web and may visit sites that allow purchases using credit cards. *If you buy something through a "non-secure" World Wide Web site, and provide your credit card number, you are at risk of an intruder obtaining your credit card number.* This is because the credit card information is generally transmitted to the retailer as an e-mail message. This means that all the risks associated with e-mail messages also apply to credit card orders, unless you are ordering from a "secure" site. If the Web site where you placed your order is not secure, a smart hacker could find the credit card number as it travels through the Internet.

This issue is really a short-term problem, since software to support encrypted credit card transactons is rapidly becoming available. More and more Internet retailers are providing users with secure transaction facilities that protect the privacy of credit card orders. We discuss this issue in greater depth in the section "Electronic Commerce" below.

Risks Associated With Computer Viruses   Dialup Internet users frequently download programs from the Internet. If you download an executable program from the Internet, you need to be careful that it does not contain a virus, a destructive program that can corrupt your computer files. To protect your computer against viruses, you should purchase a computer virus checker, or run the virus utility that came with your computer, and run all the programs you download through it. You can purchase a virus checker at most computer retail stores. You *cannot* catch a virus by using electronic mail on the Internet. The risk only occurs when you download an executable file from the Internet, or if someone actually sends you such a file through e-mail.

Dedicated Internet Connections

Organizations that want to establish information sites on the Internet or provide a large number of employees with full access to the network purchase a dedicated link to the Internet. Once this is done, anyone on the corporate network can access the Internet directly without having to use a modem, and the organization can establish its own information resources on the World Wide Web.

Organizations with dedicated Internet connections face all the risks that dialup users face (i.e., e-mail privacy, security of credit card transmissions, computer viruses). However, because one or more of their computers are permanently connected to the Internet, they face the additional risk of someone from the Internet gaining unauthorized access to their network.

There are several hardware and software tools that can be implemented to reduce the risk of unauthorized entry to your network. One of the most common tools is a "firewall," a computer that acts as a security guard for your internal corporate network. The firewall stands between your corporate network and the Internet and controls what goes in and out. Any organization linking its corporate network to the Internet should consider using a firewall. However, no computer technology, including the firewall, is 100% foolproof. *Firewalls can help minimize, but not eliminate, the risk of someone breaking into your computers from the Internet.*

If burglars want to break into your house, they will probably find a way in, regardless of how much money you have spent on sophisticated alarm systems and expensive security devices. Likewise, if a determined hacker wants to break into your network through the Internet, he will probably find a way. The sophistication of today's computer systems makes it impossible to identify every possible security weakness. Cyberspace fugitives are constantly uncovering new or little-known security holes. The only way to completely eliminate the security risk is to not connect to the Internet at all.

Throughout this book we have stressed the fact that the Internet gives your organization a strategic advantage. If you do not connect to the Internet, you place your organization at a *strategic disadvantage*. Not connecting to the Internet because you are afraid of the security risks is like not purchasing a house because someone may break in. The threat of a home break-in has not deterred millions of Canadians from buying a home. It is a risk that Canadians accept and have learned to minimize by purchasing alarm systems and other security devices. Internet-connected organizations must learn to accept the risks associated with a dedicated Internet connection and implement appropriate security devices to reduce the risks.

General Strategies for Internet Security

There are many things business can do to minimize Internet security risks to an acceptable degree.

Keep Informed

In addition to investing the necessary funds to properly secure their site, organizations must keep aware of current Internet security issues and newly discovered security weaknesses. There are organizations on the Internet that will keep your organization abreast of important matters related to Internet security. For example, the Computer Emergency Response Team at Carnegie Mellon University regularly issues security alerts to the Internet community (**http://www.sei.cmu.edu/SEI/programs/ cert.html**). CERT maintains a 24-hour telephone hotline for security matters and maintains a repository of security bulletins and security advice on its Internet site.

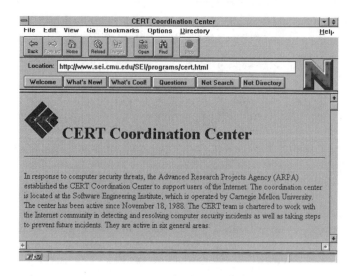

In response to computer security threats, the Advanced Research Projects Agency (ARPA) established the CERT Coordination Center to support users of the Internet. The coordination center is located at the Software Engineering Institute, which is operated by Carnegie Mellon University. The center has been active since November 18, 1988. The CERT team is chartered to work with the Internet community in detecting and resolving computer security incidents as well as taking steps to prevent future incidents. They are active in six general areas:

Create an Internet Security Manual

It is important that organizations create an Internet security manual. This manual should serve two functions:

> It should educate employees about Internet security issues. For example, it is important that employees be aware that messages sent through the Internet are not secure unless encrypted. Employees should also know that they should not send confidential documents through the Internet unless they are protected. Employees should be aware that any document sent through the Internet can easily be forwarded to other people and to public mailing lists. (While it is considered bad etiquette to forward a piece of private e-mail to someone else without the permission of the sender, it is done all the time.) Employees should also understand the issues associated with computer viruses, and what to do if they find one on their computer.

> It should set standards and policies for Internet security within an organization. For example, the policies should address issues such as employee passwords and the sharing of computer accounts. Many Internet break-ins occur because employees use passwords that are easy to guess, and intruders who are trying to break into a corporate network through the Internet will often try to gain access to employees' accounts.

Consider Outsourcing

Finally, it is important to note that an organization does not have to establish a dedicated Internet connection in order to create an Internet site, such as a World Wide Web site. As we explained in Chapter 9, organizations can choose to rent their Internet site from an Internet presence provider. This allows an organization to reap all the benefits associated with an Internet presence without having to incur the security risk of linking their company computers to the Internet.

Electronic Commerce

Tools to support the secure selling of goods and services are rapidly emerging on the Internet. Such tools are important and necessary; without secure tools for electronic commerce, consumers will be reluctant to enter into business relationships on-line, including purchasing goods and services.

What is Required?

Electronic commerce refers to on-line monetary transactions between a purchaser and a seller. Before electronic commerce can be widely accepted by the Internet community, two requirements must be in place:

➤ tools to ensure a secure, encrypted transaction between a purchaser and seller on the Internet;

➤ tools to provide for electronic, on-line payment.

Transaction Security

Transaction security is defined by the CommerceNet initiative on its World Wide Web site (**http://www.commerce.net**):

WHAT IS A "SECURE TRANSACTION"?

A secure transaction of information messages possesses the following characteristics:

- Confidentiality: others cannot eavesdrop on an exchange.
- Integrity: the messages received are identical to the messages sent.
- Authenticity: you are assured of the persons with whom you are making an exchange.
- Non-Repudiability: none of the involved parties can deny that the exchange took place.

An exchange of gifts in your home with a family member is a trivial example of a secure transaction: it is occurring in the privacy of your home, you can see that what is given is also received, you know with whom you are exchanging, and it can't be denied that exchange took place.

Such capabilities are rapidly emerging on the Internet. Two components of transaction security are examined below.

Encryption Software Netscape Communications, the company that makes the Netscape World Wide Web browser (the software that we have used throughout the book), sells commerce software that allows Internet merchants to accept orders securely from Netscape browser users. For example, if you are using the Netscape browser software to access the World Wide Web, you can make a secure purchase from any of the hundreds of Internet merchants that use the Netscape commerce software and provide your credit card number or other personal information with confidence that the information will not be accessed by someone else.

For example, consider Virtual Vineyards, a company that sells wine on the Internet. Virtual Vineyards uses the Netscape commerce software so they can accept secure credit card orders from Netscape browser users. When you access Virtual Vineyard's World Wide Web site using the Netscape browser, you are informed that you are entering a completely secure area.

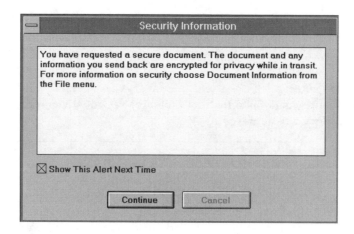

Once you have selected the "Continue" button, you are immediately taken to the Virtual Vineyards site (**http://www.virtualvin.com**). The Netscape browser lets you know that the area is secure by locking the "key" found in the bottom left-hand corner of the screen, as seen below. In unsecured sites the key is broken.

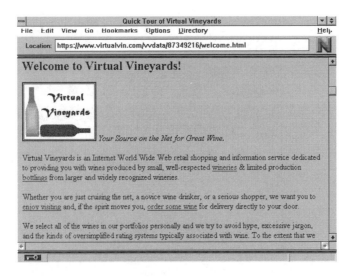

Because the area is secure, there is no risk of an intruder capturing a credit card number when a wine order is being placed using the Netscape browser. When an order is placed, the credit card number is encrypted (i.e., scrambled) so that it cannot be read by an intruder.

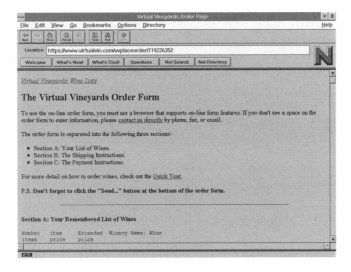

When you leave the Virtual Vineyards site for an insecure site, Netscape alerts you that you are entering an insecure area:

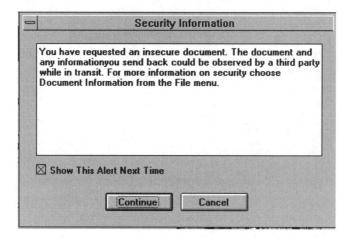

In this example we have focused on the Netscape browser and Netscape commerce software. Other vendors of World Wide Web browsers are also releasing secure versions of their browsers that will allow for the encrypted exchange of information, thus providing transaction security to their users.

Visitor Authentication   Many Internet sites authenticate the identity of visitors. They will restrict access to those who are valid, paying customers of the service or who are willing to provide certain information. Quote.Com, the company mentioned in Chapter 3, allows "visitors" to obtain five free stock quotes per day, but to obtain more you must become a full, paying customer (for U.S. $9.95 a month). If you try to access the service, you are asked for your user ID and password:

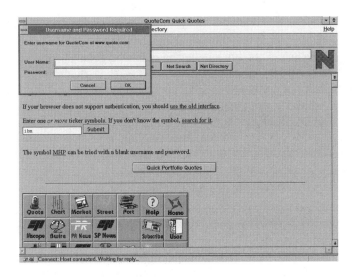

HotWired, an initiative of *WIRED Magazine*, allows only those who have filled out a questionnaire to become registered users of the service.

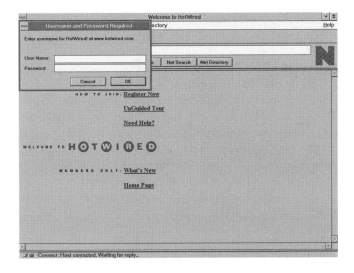

If you fail the authentication, HotWired conveniently displays a screen that allows you to register. Why does HotWired require users to register? Because when registering, individuals must provide demographic information, which *WIRED Magazine* then uses to build a profile of visitors, enabling it to sell advertising space.

Electronic Payment

The other side of electronic commerce concerns methods of providing on-line, electronic payment. While it is one thing to permit people to securely provide a credit card number through the Internet, it is another to ensure that the credit card is valid and that the user's limit has not been reached. There are many initiatives emerging on the Internet to support electronic payment; these involve credit card companies (Visa and MasterCard), banks (Bank of America and others), and finance companies (Wells Fargo and others). Keeping up with all the developments is a challenging task, and we provide some good information resources in Appendices A and B.

Currently, there are three evolving methods of electronic payment on the Internet:

➣ *Encrypted credit card purchases through a Web browser.* As mentioned above with the Virtual Vineyards example, this is already possible using the Netscape browser. The next step is to provide on-line authorization. At the time of writing tests were being conducted with credit card companies such as Visa and MasterCard to provide for automatic authorization of credit card purchases made through the Internet. By the time you read this, such standards may already exist.

➣ *Digital or electronic cash systems.* In this case, a company or individual can create an account with a company that is establishing its own unique global currency, a currency based not in any particular country, but established for use on the Internet. *The Economist* noted the trend to digital cash in the article "So Much for the Cashless Society," November 26, 1994. "Ideally, the ultimate e-cash will be a currency without a country (or a currency of all countries), infinitely exchangeable without the expense and inconvenience of conversion between local denominations."

DigiCash (**http://www.digicash.com**) is a good example of an evolving electronic cash system on the Internet. A company established in Amsterdam, DigiCash uses its own currency called "ecash." DigiCash notes that "ecash is electronic cash with all the benefits of conventional cash. It enables fast and anonymous payments over computer networks, just as if both parties shared the same room."

DigiCash plans to permit anyone to open an account in which "DigiCash credits" are deposited. The DigiCash credits can then be spent in sites around the Internet that accept DigiCash. Software that permits the use of DigiCash is supplied on Windows, Macintosh, and UNIX systems. In this way, DigiCash is defining its own global currency, far out of the reach of local financial regulators. An interesting concept, and one sure to cause more Internet-induced stress to governments and organizations!

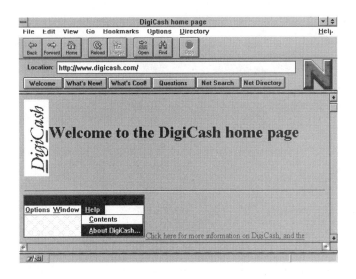

PIN-based systems. There are several initiatives on the Internet that make use of a PIN (personal identification number) system. Users provide their credit card number once over the telephone and are assigned a special PIN number, which they can use to purchase goods and services. As a security precaution, some PIN-based systems will contact the owner of the PIN number by electronic mail each time an on-line purchase is made using their PIN number. This is an additional safeguard to prevent unauthorized use of the PIN number. PIN systems do not need to use encryption, since credit card data are never transmitted over the Internet.

An example of an organization using a PIN system on the Internet is First Virtual Holdings (**http://www.fv.com**). Internet users can apply for a First Virtual account and then purchase "information" goods from Internet vendors that are part of the First Virtual network. First Virtual only supports information-type products (e.g., documents and reports) that can be obtained directly on the Internet, and not physical goods and services.

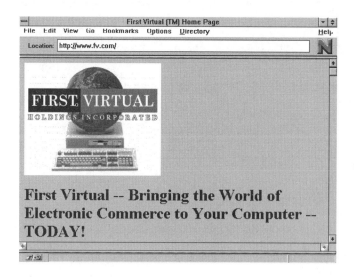

First Virtual -- Bringing the World of Electronic Commerce to Your Computer -- TODAY!

Intellectual Property

Intellectual property violations are common on the Internet. These violations refer to trademark and copyright infringements, such as the unauthorized distribution of a copyrighted document on the Internet. Any information that you might put on the Internet — documents, logos, pictures, graphics, sound files, video files — can be easily copied by Internet users and quickly distributed to others on the Internet. Moreover, it is easy for anyone to scan or key in a copyrighted paper document and circulate it around the Internet.

The nature of intellectual property infringements will become more serious over time as a result of new technological developments. For example, high-speed links to the Internet will soon be a reality: most cable companies in North America are testing "cable modems," devices that provide high-speed access to on-line services such as the Internet through the cable system. Cable modems can provide speeds hundreds of times faster than standard PC modems.

These emerging high-speed links to the network mean that it will be possible for anyone to e-mail the contents of a CD-ROM, compact disc, or even a video to friends. It will mean that people can establish World Wide Web sites containing movies, songs, or videos that others can download.

The problem is compounded by the fact that the Internet is an international system with no borders. National laws have become almost impossible to enforce especially when the violator is in another country. For example, consider a paperback book. There is nothing to prevent someone in China from inputting the book and then posting it on an Internet site in that country where the contents can be accessed by anyone in the world. When the culprit is in another country, the author has little legal recourse. Identifying the culprit is a monumental task in itself, given the global scope of the Internet and the ability for people to post documents "anonymously."

The Internet is a "photocopier" of mammoth proportions and will pose all kinds of challenges to traditional laws and concepts related to intellectual property. Some believe that it is futile to fight the Internet on this issue. *The Vancouver Sun* reported the thoughts of a journalist at *WIRED Magazine*, a publication that regularly reports on the Internet: "Let the copies breed. Whatever it is that we are constructing by connecting everything, we know the big thing will copy effortlessly. The I-way is a gigantic copy machine. It is a law of the digital realm: anything digital will be copied, and anything copied once will fill the universe."[1]

The article then goes on to observe how difficult it will be to control the flow of digital bits in the information age: "every effort to restrict copying is doomed to failure. Copy-protection schemes in software were abandoned because they didn't work. In the U.S. Supreme Court, home-tapers of satellite TV shows won the right to copy copyrighted material in their homes. Controlling copies is futile. This presents a problem for all holders of intellectual property who adhere to the notion of copyright — such as Hollywood moguls and authors. Copyright law as we know it will be dead in 50 years. A legal system that shifts its focus from the 'copy' to the 'use' must take its place, letting copies proliferate, and tracking only how and when an item is used. When an article is displayed to others for a fee, or quoted in another piece, a few pennies will then be deducted from the user's account."

In other words, many believe that since it is impossible to prevent the copying of digital information, a different approach needs to be taken. Yet even if the approach discussed in the article were used, how does one enforce appropriate use of copyrighted material? The Internet by its very nature makes it impossible to regulate any sort of fee-for-use scheme. For example, how do you collect a fee from someone in another country who is distributing material illegally?

Others do not share this view and believe that enforcement simply needs to be put in place. They use the recent potential trade war between the United States and China concerning the copying of software as an example in which international pressure can be brought to bear on any issue. The problem with the Internet, of course, is that it is not just a problem with one country, but a problem with all countries plugged into the network.

What are the solutions? No one is really sure. It is a very difficult issue to solve. Many do believe that the copyright laws of today, which were created without the concept of digital media in mind, need to be completely revamped to address the problems inherent in the information age.

---

[1] Road signs for traveling "the I-Way," *Vancouver Sun*, July 2, 1994.

> The concept of "copyrighting" could be lost on the infor-
> mation highway as the world moves closer to the free flow
> of information, U.S. experts said. "It's up in the air what's
> going to happen," said Dr. Lance Hoffman, an investigator
> for a National Science Foundation project on security and
> privacy. "We don't really have a regime to enforce (copy-
> right) law globally. We don't know what's going to hap-
> pen."…It's like stealing from the library, he said, but on a
> grand scale, with virtually no way to get caught…He said
> current copyright laws have worked because they applied
> to a physical world. In the electronic realm of cyberspace,
> current legislation is unenforceable."[2]

The law is trying to catch up, but many lawyers and others involved with intellectual property are really not quite sure what to do or where to start. Indicated
Hoffman, "'Maybe the whole nature of intellectual property has to be reexamined.'
Sharon Bywater, a telecommunications policy specialist with the U.S. government's
National Telecommunications and Information Administration, agreed — but said
finding regulations that will work in all cases is a tough call. 'And every time we
come up with something that would apply to all different sectors, we find it is just
about impossible to implement.'"[3]

In Canada the Canadian Information Highway Council, a federal body advising
the government on issues and strategies related to the "information highway," has
formed a special committee to deal with the issue, and a number of other groups
are looking into the matter in Canada and around the world. As a result, businesses
and producers of intellectual property might have to learn to think differently about
their rights in the wired world.

Strategies for Dealing with Intellectual Property Issues

> Be cognizant of the fact that virtually anything you put on the Internet
> could be copied and that there is little you can do about it. Build your
> Internet site accordingly with this knowledge in mind. Do not put mate-
> rial on your World Wide Web site that you do not want people to copy, un-
> less there is a valid business reason for doing so.

---

[2] Lawless cyber frontier, *The Toronto Sun*, June 5, 1994.

[3] Lawless cyber frontier, *The Toronto Sun*, June 5, 1994.

➤ Learn to think differently when it comes to intellectual property. Is there certain information that you can put on your World Wide Web site without causing you or your lawyers a lot of grief? Are the benefits obtained by putting the material on your Web site greater than the potential loss caused by copying? For example, one of the authors posts all his newspaper and magazine articles on the Internet, so that anyone can access them for free. Theoretically, these articles could be resold for a fee to other publications, yet by loading them onto the World Wide Web, they become part of the marketing draw for the author. People visit his on-line brochure, and in some cases establish a business relationship. Hence, publishing the articles on the Internet and suffering the potential risk of unauthorized copying is offset by the benefits obtained in doing so.

➤ Learn about the concept of "free" information and what it represents in this digital age. Many organizations now dealing with the Internet have learned its great paradox — success comes from making material available for free!

How can this be so? Examples abound in the software industry. Netscape Communications has built a successful software business by giving away "beta copies" of its software for free on the Internet. By doing so, it managed to quickly build such credibility on a global scale that many now purchase the software for the U.S. $39 fee. It is also enjoying success in selling its secure "server version" for fees of U.S. $1,250 to U.S. $5,000. Delrina Corporation, a Canadian company, is giving away versions of its WinComm Pro software on the Internet in the hope that many people will pay for the more sophisticated retail version. CA Associates gave away one million copies of its accounting software, hoping to establish a customer base to which it could then sell upgrades. The Toronto Dominion Bank is giving away copies of its business planning software on the Internet in order to build a relationship with potential customers.

In an interesting twist, an Ontario radio station has placed its logo on the Internet and encourages Internet users to copy and distribute it (**http://feldspar.com/Q92/Welcome.html**):

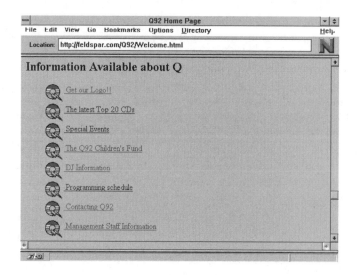

In all these examples, the companies have used the concept of "free" to establish a market for future sales. Companies must learn to think in such innovative ways when dealing with their own intellectual property. The whole concept of "free" in the software industry has proven itself to be a means of leveraging further sales, and anyone learning to do business on the Internet has to examine whether the concept of "free" will work with his/her core business and intellectual property.

Do what you can to make the Internet community aware that any materials you post are copyrighted and/or trademarked or are restricted from copying. Include copyright notices in any contributions you make to Internet mailing lists or discussion groups. Many will think twice about using your material without permission if a copyright notice is visible. For example, one of the authors of this book includes the following copyright notice on all articles that he places on the Internet:

> The attached article, by Jim Carroll (**jcarroll@jacc.com**) was originally written for the publication, xxxxxxx. This article, and other articles by Jim Carroll, can be found at the Web site **http://www.e-commerce.com/jacc.html**.
>
> This article is Copyright(c) 1995 J.A. Carroll Consulting, and may be freely distributed throughout the Internet, corporate e-mail systems or other systems via e-mail, as long as this header remains intact. This article may not be reprinted for publication in print or other media without permission of the author.

Many people throughout the global Internet will respect these restrictions.

Could someone take an article provided on the Internet and distribute it elsewhere without permission? Of course. But the same thing could be done with an article found in a magazine. The Internet increases the risk dramatically because it makes unauthorized copying and distribution easy to accomplish.

Have your legal counsel review your World Wide Web site and prepare the appropriate legal notices. For example, the Toronto Dominion Bank (**http://www.tdbank.ca/tdbank**) provides extensive trademark information on its World Wide Web site:

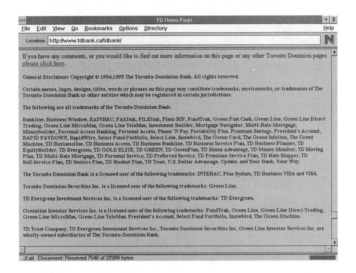

Lotus has included a legal notice on its World Wide Web site (**www.lotus.com**) which provides trademark information. The Lotus site goes one step further than the TD Bank site, however, for it outlines the terms and conditions whereby materials from the company's Web site *can* be copied by Internet users.

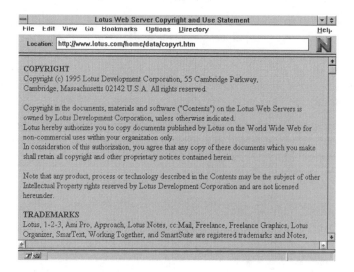

Other organizations, like Bell Canada (**http://www.bell.ca**), have taken a simpler approach and simply include a small copyright notice at the bottom of their World Wide Web pages.

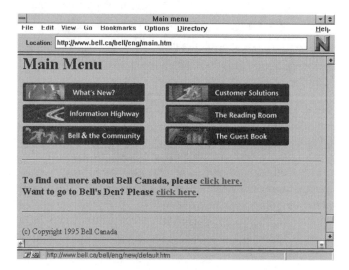

Check with your legal counsel to determine what approach is required in your specific situation. Will the display of copyright and trademark notices have an effect? It can't hurt. A few years ago retail stores discovered that if they placed a cardboard policeman in the entrance to a store, along with a warning about shoplifting, actual losses due to shoplifting decreased. The appeal to the human psyche worked. Maybe the same thing will work on the Internet.

> Be vigilant. Organizations will have to be on guard against unauthorized or abusive use of their intellectual property on the Internet, and must be prepared to act swiftly when encountering gross violations.

The Internet will cause a lot of grief for lawyers, governments, and producers of intellectual property. Attempts will be made to deal with the issue by revising copyright and trademark laws, but these efforts will likely have little impact. We are becoming a world of digital bits, and it is virtually impossible to control the flow of digital bits on the Internet. Business must act accordingly and must learn to think differently.

Other Issues

There are other issues to think about when getting involved with the Internet. Several of these issues are discussed below.

Consider Posting a Notice of Limited Liability

If your organization provides information on its World Wide Web site that Internet users may interpret as "official" or "authoritative," it is a good idea to place a limitation of liability on your site cautioning users that the information may be incorrect or out-of-date. For example, Qantas Airlines has placed such a notice on its Web site (**http://www.anzac.com/qantas/qantas.htm**). Qantas cautions: "Please note that this information is presented free of charge to you. It may be incomplete, it may be out of date, it may even be just plain wrong! You should verify all information contained here before acting on it with either a Qantas representative or with a professional travel agent. In return for allowing you open access to this material, we require your acceptance that we will not be liable for any actions you may take as a result of your receiving this information."

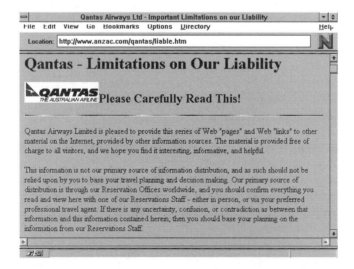

Do Not Forget that the Internet is International

If your organization has a presence in more than one country, and you establish a World Wide Web site, keep in mind that your site will receive visitors from all over the world. Some of the information on your Web site may not apply to specific countries. Goodyear Tire, for example, has addressed this tricky issue by including a legal notice on its World Wide Web site:

> Goodyear provides access to Goodyear international data and, therefore, may contain references or cross references to Goodyear products, programs and services that are not announced in your country. Such reference does not imply that Goodyear or a Goodyear subsidiary or distributor in your country intends to announce such products, programs or services. All actions resulting from a search of this data must be related to solutions using only products, programs and services announced by Goodyear or a Goodyear subsidiary or distributor in your country.
>
> Excerpt from the Goodyear Tire World Wide Web Site
> **http://www.goodyear.com**

Deal with the Privacy of e-mail

When an employee sends an electronic mail message through the Internet, privacy is not guaranteed unless the message is encrypted. But what about e-mail messages that are stored on an employee's office computer? When an organization provides its employees with access to the Internet, employees can use the company's internal e-mail system to communicate with people outside the organization. Therefore, an employee's internal electronic mailbox may contain copies of Internet messages that have been sent and received by the employee.

Many employees regard their Internet mail as private and personal, and they believe that an employer has no right to read it. Many employers, on the other hand, believe that any electronic mail that resides on a company computer is the property of the organization, and, therefore, they reserve the right to inspect an employee's electronic mailbox at will.

Differences in opinion with respect to the privacy of electronic mail in the workplace has led to many lawsuits. To minimize the risk of a costly lawsuit, it is important that organizations clearly define their position with respect to electronic mail and make employees aware of it. Organizations may wish to create an electronic mail policy and have their employees sign it. By doing this, there can be no question about an employee's interpretation of the company's policy on electronic mail privacy.

Deal with Employee Productivity

The Internet is a valuable tool, but using it can be time-consuming. Some Internet discussion groups easily generate dozens of messages a day. Reading them can quickly consume an hour or more of an employee's day. In addition to partaking in Internet discussion groups related to their work activities, employees often take time out of their work day to participate in discussion groups related to their hobbies and personal interests.

The Internet is bursting with so much knowledge and information and so many diversions that a five-minute research trip to the World Wide Web can quickly turn into a one-hour excursion. The Internet can be a huge productivity waster if employees do not manage their time on the network. To curtail abuse of the Internet at work, organizations may want to establish policies on non-work-related use of the Internet during work hours.

The Bottom Line

By now you know that the Internet will change business, and you are hopefully beginning to think about the opportunities and the challenges that it will present for you. The important thing to keep in mind is that while the Internet does present business with some challenging issues, the Internet community is quickly developing solutions and strategies for many of these issues.

In Appendix A we provide a list of some of the Internet sites that you can use to keep up-to-date on emerging Internet issues that we have reviewed in this chapter. Business executives responsible for Internet-related business strategy should become familiar with the state of these issues in order to proceed with their own Internet strategies and corporate Internet policies.

CHAPTER 12

The Future Internet

A 21st-century form of organization is gradually beginning to take shape. I call this new structure the "network organization...the network organizations of the future will be global, they will be connected electronically to people...Network organizations — which will be rich with information — will recognize that certain functions can be better done elsewhere. As a result, these companies will enter into joint ventures, partnerships, associations, informal cooperation agreements, consortiums and temporary deals that will stretch today's traditional definitions of where one company ends and another begins. By being open to these informal and formal links, network organizations will be able to gain access to the entire world."

Tomorrow's Company Won't Have Walls, *New York Times*, June 18, 1989

All of this talk about the "information superhighway" is more of a dream than reality, and will probably remain that way for this decade. The Internet is here and now, and is the earliest manifestation of the way business is going to work into the next century. Those companies not connected within 3 years will probably be in the same position as those companies who don't have a fax or telephone today — out of the loop, and soon out of business.

Darren Mallette, ab454@freenet.carleton.ca

*H*as your career or company been affected by the changes alluded to in the first quote above? Do you find yourself hearing more of your friends talk like Darren Mallette, a typical user of the Internet? Has the organization you work for or that you lead become a networked organization? Has it been downsizing, and is it now relying more on outside experts to get work done? Are joint ventures and partnerships becoming the rule of the day rather than the exception in your business and industry?

Are you a refugee of the corporate world? Did you decide to strike out on your own to become a consultant? Do you now hire yourself out to companies on a regular basis? Have you found many of your friends doing this?

THE FUTURE INTERNET

(1) The Internet is supporting the emergence of two important trends:
- the proliferation of the networked organization;
- an explosion in electronic, home-based publishing.

(2) The networked organization is an organization that has learned to support many of its activities with minimal staff and through the efficient use of telecommunications. Two characteristics of the networked organization are
- the end of the job and reliance on part-time workers;
- interorganizational partnering.

(3) The Internet supports the networked organization in two ways:
- it provides efficiencies in communications;
- it helps organizations find corporate partners.

(4) The Internet radically changes the current information paradigm, since it allows anyone to be a global publisher.

If you answered "yes" to any of these questions, then the twenty-first century style of "networked organization" is already affecting you, and the Internet will soon become (or is already) a fundamental part of your day-to-day working life. The reason? The Internet is taking on a central role in this new, wired business world.

In this book, we have examined many of the opportunities found within the Internet, and we hopefully have inspired you to explore its options. Yet, the ultimate impact of the Internet on the business world, far beyond its use as a tool to establish markets, support customers, re-engineer the delivery of services, or change the delivery of education, might be its impact on just what a business organization is. The ultimate impact of the Internet will be far more subtle, and far more profound, for it is the foundation of the "networked organization," perhaps one of the most significant business developments of all time.

The Networked Organization

What is a "networked organization"? Simply, it is an organization that has learned to support many of its activities through the efficient use of telecommunications and has learned to operate with minimal full-time staff as a result.

In such an organization people can be working anywhere at any time, since e-mail, fax, cellular phones, the Internet, and other technologies support efficient communications between different physical locations. People working for the organization do not necessarily have to be employees — they will work for the organization for the period of time that their particular skills are needed and will then disband.

Consultants and business gurus have been predicting the arrival of the networked organization for many years. A global networked organization implies efficient global communications. With the arrival of the global Internet, we now have a technology to support networked organizations.

Is the Networked Organization Real?

It is easy to ignore the concept of the networked organization and the changes that it will introduce. Perhaps things will not change. Perhaps it is just hype. Perhaps the form of business we have all become used to will continue uninterrupted in the future. Executive complacency — the belief that things will not change — is a dangerous attitude in business. Just ask the folks at IBM, Digital Equipment, or the many other organizations that have seen wrenching change in their industry in the last decade.

Lester M. Alberthal Jr., CEO of Electronic Data Systems, a global systems company, stated that "the pre-eminent challenge business leaders face today is how to anticipate the challenges of tomorrow — for their customers as well as for themselves

— and to develop strategies not only to meet those challenges, but to take full advantage of them. It is no longer sufficient simply to avoid complacency."[1]

Many do not know what the real impact of the Internet will be. But there are two signs in the economy that predict that true networked organizations are close at hand: the "end of the job," and an increase in interorganization partnering.

The End of the Job

One characteristic of the networked organization is the reliance on part-time help: organizations will buy expertise when a particular skill is needed, rather than having a particular skill available at all times in the form of employees. Jobs, it would seem, are an endangered species in our economy.

So said *Fortune Magazine*, in a much talked-about cover article ("The end of the job") on September 19, 1994. *Fortune* noted that "every morning's newspaper carries another story of new job losses. We hear the recession has been over for quite a while, but the percentage of workers who are jobless has not fallen as after previous recessions. The Clinton Administration is trying to create jobs, but critics claim some of its new taxes and regulations will destroy jobs. We are told the only way to protect our jobs is to increase our productivity, but then we discover that re-engineering, using self-managed teams, flattening our organizations, and turning routine work over to computers always make many jobs redundant. We used to read predictions that by 2000 everyone would work 30-hour weeks, and the rest would be leisure. But as we approach 2000 it seems more likely that half of us will be working 60-hour weeks and the rest of us will be unemployed. What's wrong?" It is true — business everywhere continues on its quest to re-engineer itself and to do more with less. Who is left to do the work? Smaller companies, with fewer staff.

The article went on to indicate that "what is disappearing is the very thing itself: the job. That much sought after, much maligned social entity, a job, is vanishing like a species that has outlived its evolutionary time."

Fortune was commenting on a trend that many people believe is under way in the economy: corporate loyalty, guarantees of employment, and other traditional aspects of the "job for life" are gone. Noted a human resources magazine recently "…many organizations cling to old assumptions about one of the most critical relationships of all: the implied contract between employer and employee. Until recently, loyalty was the cornerstone of that relationship. Employers promised job security and a steady progression up the hierarchy in return for the employee's fitting in, performing in prescribed ways and sticking around. Longevity was a sign of healthy employer–employee relations; turnover was a sign of dysfunction. None of these assumptions apply today. Organizations can no longer guarantee lifetime careers, even if they want to."[2]

---

[1] Beyond the millennium: CEOs size up the future, *Chief Executive*, January/February 1995.

[2] The 21st century employer-employee partnership, *HRMagazine*, January 1994.

What is happening to all these people? Many are pursuing new, independent careers, hiring themselves out to companies as consultants, or are forming small companies that make available specialized expertise. What is just now becoming apparent is that many people used their recession-induced career change of the early 1990s as an opportunity to do something new. With computer technology becoming so inexpensive, many found it practical to establish themselves as small, independent companies or consultants.

The Internet plays perfectly into the trend of the "end of the job," for not only does it permit people to communicate with the networked organization, but it provides them with powerful new capabilities needed to cope in this new, "jobless" economy. Noted *Fortune*: "tomorrow's organization certainly must turn a significant part of its work over to a contingent work force that can grow and shrink and reshape itself as its situation demands." We are, it would seem, becoming an economy of consultants, ready to work on particular projects for companies on a moment's notice.

The article from which the opening quote to this chapter was taken commented on a new style of organization that will emerge in our economy and also noted that "the hub of the network organization will be small, centralized and local. At the same time, it will be connected to an extended network that is big, decentralized and global. People from the network and from outside the company will join the group at the hub for periods of time and then leave it."

The "end of the job" has brought the project-oriented worker with it — a contingent workforce of people prepared to work for a company not as employees, but as independent entities.

Interorganization Partnering

The other trend in the economy is an increasing reliance on interorganization partnerships. Whether it is a business establishing joint ventures, the arrival of new industry consortiums, different levels of government working together, an increasing reliance on a growing number of small companies, or research projects between different groups around the world, interorganization partnerships are occurring on a large scale.

As the business world becomes more complex, the expertise required to complete company projects becomes more and more specialized. The result is that companies often do not have access to the particular talent they need to finish a particular job. In many cases, when they do not hire part-time specialized talent, they gain access to critical resources by partnering with another company. Many of the companies that organizations partner with are small, nimble, quick to respond, and quick to evolve, and many have been established in the last decade. This is a very significant trend in the economy, and one that will continue.

In an interview, John Naisbitt, author of several books on the future of the world, including *Megatrends*, noted that "...the world will be increasingly dominated by small and medium-sized companies; not only will that be the case, it already is the case. In the US today the companies in the Fortune 500 represent only

10 per cent of the economy, down from 20 per cent in 1970; but you would not get that impression by reading the press."[3]

Small business is driving growth in the economy, and in many cases, it is small business that is driving intercorporate partnership. The average one-person office and small business can use the Internet to publish information about its business activities, order goods from suppliers, monitor market trends, and send information to clients and customers. The Internet provides businesses with the ability to do all of this through a single computer connection. For this reason, the Internet is extremely relevant to small businesses.

The Internet opens the small business organization up to the world, and allows it to take a full and complete role in the emerging networked organization. This is perhaps the greatest benefit of the Internet, for through it, the era of the global village has truly arrived. Because of this trend, we will continue to see an explosion in the creation of small businesses throughout our global economy.

Efficiencies in Communications

These two trends are beacons that the day of the networked organization is quickly approaching. The networked organization will increasingly call upon the talents of "part-time experts" and corporate partners in order to get the job done. But for many organizations, learning how to do business *efficiently* with part-time experts and corporate partners is a brand new concept.

Communications between joint venture partners and part-time experts have generally occurred the old-fashioned way: paper letters are sent via courier, fax machines are overused, and paper mail is sent via Canada Post. Conference calls tie up the desk calendar pages of busy executives. Frequent meetings take place in order to encourage ongoing communications among "the team."

Old-fashioned communication methods work well to support old-fashioned business organizations. They do not work well in this new, hypercharged Internet-based world, where thoughts, ideas, and information can travel the globe at the speed of light. As more companies plug their communications systems into the Internet, the opportunity to work with "part-time experts" and corporate partners is growing, particularly since needed talent is accessible anywhere there is a telephone jack. More importantly, organizations are discovering that important knowledge resources, in the form of part-time experts and corporate partners, *can be found through the Internet.*

The Internet is leading to new forms of business relationships in which telecommunications plays a fundamental role in the support of the relationship. Part-time experts, business alliances, joint ventures, partnerships, and other cooperative efforts that use the Internet to support the "networked organization" stand a better chance of success because of the more rapid sharing of thoughts, knowledge, and

---

[3] Megatrends and global paradoxes, *Management Decision*, 1994.

information. Hence the Internet is helping to drive the move toward the arrival of the networked organization. And by doing so, it will help to change business in ways that we can only begin to imagine.

Everyone is a Publisher

The Internet represents another significant change that we have noted throughout this book. On the Internet everyone is a publisher, a journalist, an author, or a video producer. Everyone is a contributor of information.

Through the Internet the entire information paradigm of the last 200 years is undergoing a complete and radical shift. This is perhaps one of the most significant developments in recent human history. Today, news and information come from newspapers, magazines, television, and radio. What we see and hear in the media is often a small fraction of what flows across the news wires. The news we get is often heavily filtered with the bias of the particular news vendor. What we get as news is what other people think news should be.

The Internet rips this paradigm to shreds, for it provides all users in the world with their own Gutenberg printing press, and the means to contribute information to the world. News is now something different: it is the collective thought of a hundred million, living, breathing souls, each with his/her own unique perspective on life and the human condition. News comes unfiltered, naked, and pristine in its honesty and frankness.

During the Persian Gulf War, one of the authors of this book received Internet messages from a friend, huddled in a Tel Aviv apartment, who described his fear of dying. The messages described how he had carefully put his gas mask on and huddled in darkness listening to the missiles come in. This type of news has an immediacy and impact that just cannot be portrayed through traditional media sources.

This style of news is an everyday occurrence on the Internet, and in some cases, provides people with more immediate information concerning world events. It is often dramatic. With the siege of Sarajevo, many people managed to deliver live reports over the Internet in the early stages of the war, directly from their homes in the one-time Olympic ski village. It also happened with the infamous Karla Homolka case, where everyone on the Internet had access to the banned trial details. It happened with the California and Kobe earthquakes, where survivors delivered live disaster reports to the Internet community.

For Canada the Internet represents a significant shift in our entire national concept of information. Many believe this to be a good thing, given the growing hostility of Canadians toward the information elites, for example, the Canadian Radio and Telecommunications Commission (CRTC) and its mandate to attempt to control what Canadians can watch on TV.

Many people recognize that the Internet defies national laws, national borders, and national content rules. On the Internet information can come from anywhere via trillions of routes.

Much of the talk of the information superhighway focuses on the 500-channel universe that we will be able to access through our televisions. Yet, we will not have a 500 channel universe — we will have a 1,000,000-channel universe. Or a 100-million channel universe. Or maybe a 500-million channel universe! Why? Everyone, everywhere, can become a content producer in the next decade — *through the Internet*. Take the computer-based world as found through the Internet, combine it with advancements in video camera technology, add high-speed communication links to the home or office, mix in some digital editing and special effects, and anyone, anywhere will be able to produce his/her own show on the Internet. There is literally nothing to prevent the authors from establishing *The Canadian Internet Advantage Show* for distribution through their Web site (and maybe we will!).

The entire global information paradigm is in the midst of wrenching change as a result of the Internet. The Internet's most significant and profound contribution to business and society is that anyone on the Internet has the ability to publish and reach a large, worldwide audience. The Internet is an information revolution, the likes of which the world has never seen.

Where Will the Internet Take Us?

We opened Chapter 1 with the following observation, and it seems fitting to close this book with the same observation:

> The Internet is important, for one simple reason — it is the leading edge of a trend in which all the computers in the world are becoming wired together. The mere existence of such a trend gives pause for some thought. How will business be affected? Education? Government? Science? Our own personal lives?
>
> No one knows for sure what will happen, but one thing is certain — the impact on our world of a trend in which all computers globally become linked together will be dramatic.

In this book we have outlined the many opportunities that the Internet provides for businesses, government, educational institutions, not-for-profit organizations and the health care sector. With all the talk of the "information superhighway," it is easy for a business to lose focus and wait for the emergence of some high-speed network in the near future. It is easy to dismiss the Internet as a fad, a storm that will blow over next year. It is easy to think that the change evidenced within the Internet will not be that severe, and that our comfortable business world will continue much as it has in the past.

Many believed that the invention of the Gutenberg press would not have much of an impact on the world as it existed in the Middle Ages. Yet, the rapid spread of information that resulted led to the Renaissance, a European explosion of art, knowledge, and commerce of such degree that it drove the economic expansion of the world well into the twentieth century.

We would do well to remember the lessons taught to us by the printing press. We would do well, as business executives, to keep a careful eye on this thing called the Internet.

Selected Useful On-Line Resources

If you are a user of the Internet (or are destined to become one), you will find that there are many useful information resources available on the network that will help you keep track of Internet activities in business, government, education, not-for-profit organizations, and the health sector. We provide a listing of some of these on-line resources below.

In Chapter 1, we noted that any Internet user, anywhere in the world, can publish information on any topic, at any time. Most of the resources listed in this Appendix were prepared by Internet users and organizations on the Internet and the majority of these resources are distributed through the Internet as a public service, at no charge.

This Appendix is divided into two main sections

General Resources

➤ World Wide Web Directories

➤ Other Significant Directories

➤ World Wide Web Search Engines

➤ On-Line Newsletters and Publications

➤ USENET Search Mechanisms

Resources by Type

➤ Business

➤ Government

➤ Education

➤ Not-For-Profit Organizations

➤ Health Care.

General Resources

This section provides a summary of resources of use to any organization or individual who wants to discover information on the Internet or track issues related to the evolution of the Internet.

Directories of World Wide Web Sites

Central Index of Canadian World Wide Web Sites

World Wide Web: **http://www.csr.ists.ca/w3can/Welcome.html**

This index contains the Internet's most comprehensive directory of Canadian World Wide Web sites. Entries can be viewed by category type or geographical location. Categories include associations, businesses, colleges, universities, government, and schools.

City.Net

World Wide Web: **http://www.city.net**

City.Net provides an excellent geographical index to information on the Internet. It provides pointers to information resources on cities, towns, and countries around the world. It is especially useful for locating tourism and economic development activities on the Internet.

EINet Galaxy

World Wide Web: **http://galaxy.einet.net**

This is a searchable subject-oriented directory of Internet resources. Categories include arts and humanities, business and commerce, government, leisure and recreation, medicine, and science.

NCSA's What's New Index

World Wide Web: **http://gnn.com/gnn/wn/whats-new.html**

The What's New Index is the Internet's most popular directory of new World Wide Web sites. Several hundred new sites are announced on this site every week. Entries are organized alphabetically by week.

Open Market's Commercial Sites Index

World Wide Web: **http://www.directory.net**

The Commercial Sites Index is one of the best places to look for the World Wide Web addresses of commercial organizations. Thousands of organizations are listed, with hundreds of new organizations added every week.

Whole Internet Catalog

World Wide Web: **http://gnn.com/wic**

The Whole Internet Catalog lists hundreds of World Wide Web resources by subject category. Categories include arts and entertainment, business and finance, computers, education, government, health and medicine, recreation, science and technology, the social sciences, and travel.

World Wide Web Virtual Library

World Wide Web: **http://info.cern.ch/hypertext/DataSources/bySubject/Overview.html**

The World Wide Web Virtual Library contains dozens of subject-specific Web directories, covering everything from Aboriginal studies to medieval studies to whale watching.

Yahoo

World Wide Web: **http://www.yahoo.com**

Located at Stanford University, Yahoo is probably the closest thing that the Internet has to a "yellow pages." It is one of the most comprehensive and up-to-date subject-oriented World Wide Web indices on the network. Yahoo is useful because of its index structure. For example, you can quickly focus on specific industries such as arts and crafts, automotive, or financial services. Yahoo is a must for anyone serious about learning how to use the Internet.

Other Significant Directories

Clearinghouse for Subject-Oriented Internet Resource Guides

World Wide Web: **http://asa.ugl.lib.umich.edu/chhome.html**

This directory provides subject-specific guides to Internet resources. Over 70 guides are available, covering such subjects as agriculture, business, cancer, economics, film, history, journalism, and telecommunications. The clearinghouse is sponsored by the University of Michigan's University Library and School of Information and Library Studies.

World Wide Web Search Engines

Search engines are searchable databases of World Wide Web sites. Lycos and WebCrawler are two of the most popular search engines on the Internet.

Lycos

World Wide Web: **http://lycos.cs.cmu.edu**

Lycos is a search engine hosted by Carnegie Mellon University. The Lycos database can be searched by document title and content.

WebCrawler

World Wide Web: **http://webcrawler.cs.washington.edu/WebCrawler/
WebQuery.html**

WebCrawler is a search engine hosted by the University of Washington. The database
can be searched by document title and content.

On-Line Newsletters and Publications

There are many, many publications that you can subscribe to on the Internet that
report important Internet issues and announce new Internet resources. The following on-line publications are free and focus on issues related to the Internet, the information highway, electronic commerce, and other related issues.

Edupage

World Wide Web: **http://www.educom.edu/edupage.new** (current issue),
http://www.educom.edu/edupage.old/.index.html (back issues)

To subscribe: Send a message to **listproc@educom.edu** and in the body of
the message place the following command:
subscribe edupage YourFirstName YourLastName

Edupage promotes itself as a "a summary of news items on information technology." It is published three times a week by Educom, a Washington, D.C.-based con-
sortium of colleges and universities. Edupage provides concise summaries of articles
in the mainstream press about the Internet, the information highway, telecommunications, and other technology issues. It is an excellent source of news and information for anyone with an interest in current information technology trends.

In, Around, and Online

World Wide Web: **http://www.clark.net/pub/robert/home.html**

To subscribe: Send a message to **listserv@clark.net** and in the body of the
message place the following command:
subscribe online-l YourFirstName YourLastName. You can
also subscribe through the Web site listed above.

This publication promotes itself as "a weekly survey of events in the consumer on-
line services industry" and includes reports on industry initiatives related to electronic commerce, significant new Internet initiatives by major *Fortune* 500 companies,
and other Internet-related events. Very well written and up-to-date.

Cowles/SIMBA Media Daily: Internet Information

World Wide Web: **http://www.mecklerweb.com/simba/internet.htm**

A good daily source of information for what is going on in the on-line industry; similar to a news wire. Reports can be found on the evolution of electronic commerce
and other business activities on the Internet.

Netsurf

World Wide Web: **http://www.netsurf.com/nsd/index.html**

To subscribe: Send a message to **nsdigest-request@netsurf.com**. Include the following command in the body of the message: **subscribe nsdigest-text**

Netsurf is an upbeat, interesting newsletter summarizing new World Wide Web sites established on the Internet; a "guide to interesting news, places and resources on-line..." with "...short, crisp newsbytes, notices, and reviews designed to provide informative and entertaining snapshots of the vast wired world." A good way to keep in touch with new Internet initiatives and appreciate the diversity of the Internet.

USENET Search Mechanisms

One problem with the Internet is that it generates too much information. This is especially true with the area of the Internet known as USENET. USENET carries over 10,000 discussion groups covering thousands of different topics. To help deal with the problem of information overload, several services have been developed that permit Internet users to search USENET newsgroups for specific topics or issues. Two of the most prominent USENET search mechanisms are the Stanford NetNews filter and InfoSeek.

Stanford University NetNews Filter

World Wide Web: **http://sift.stanford.edu**

E-mail: **netnews@db.stanford.edu** (place the word **help** in the body of the message)

This allows you to set a search profile of items/topics you wish to track within USENET. On a regular basis you are sent, via e-mail, the first few lines of any USENET articles that match your search profile. You can quickly retrieve the full text of any item.

InfoSeek

World Wide Web: **http://www.infoseek.com**

InfoSeek is a commercial venture with a monthly fee of $9.95 per month plus per-transaction fees. InfoSeek keeps a four-week database of the contents of over 10,000 USENET newsgroups. Internet users can search the database by keyword. Other options include tracking of various computer and high-tech publications, World Wide Web pages, annual reports, and newswires.

Resources By Type

This section includes some specialized resources of interest to businesses, government organizations, educators, not-for-profit organizations, and health care workers.

Business Resources

Cool Site of the Day

World Wide Web: **http://www.infi.net/cool.html**

Each day, this site recognizes a World Wide Web resource as "cool." Web sites are chosen based on their content, style/presentation, innovation, and/or graphics. While not strictly a business resource, this site provides some excellent examples of World Wide Web design and layout. Several prominent business sites have been featured on the "Cool Site of the Day," including CBS Television and Sega.

Interesting Business Sites on the Web

World Wide Web: **http://www.rpi.edu/~okeefe/business.html**

This site contains examples of innovative and exciting uses of the World Wide Web by businesses. It is maintained by Bob O'Keefe at the School of Management, Rensselaer Polytechnic Institute in Troy, New York.

Internet Marketing List Archives

World Wide Web: **http://galaxy.einet.net/hypermail/inet-marketing**

To subscribe: Send a message to **listproc@einet.net** and place the following command in the body of the message: **subscribe inet-marketing FirstName LastName YourCompanyName**

Internet Marketing is an Internet mailing list "established to discuss appropriate marketing of services, ideas, and items to and on the Internet." It is an excellent source of information and discussion about marketing on the Internet. If you subscribe, be prepared for a lot of e-mail. An alternative to subscribing is to read/search the archives through the World Wide Web.

Thomas Ho's Favorite Electronic Commerce WWW Resources

World Wide Web: **http://www.engr.iupui.edu/~ho/interests/commmenu.html**

Thomas Ho is a Senior Fellow in the Department of Information Systems at the University of Singapore. He has prepared this extensive list of business-related Internet resources, which includes articles, business sites, electronic publishers, industry associations, Internet storefronts, and information highway initiatives. This site is one of the best summaries of business and commerce information culled from across the Internet.

NETTRAIN MAILING LIST

To subscribe: Send a message to **listserv@ubvm.cc.buffalo.edu** and place the following command on the first line of the body of the message: **subscribe nettrain-l FirstName LastName YourCompanyName**

Archives: **http://ubvm.cc.buffalo.edu/~listserv/NETTRAIN**

NETTRAIN is an Internet mailing list for the exchange of information, advice, and resources about training people to use the Internet. It is an excellent resource if you are involved in Internet training in your organization.

Government Resources

FedWorld

World Wide Web: **http://www.fedworld.gov**

FedWorld provides a comprehensive central access point for finding United States government information on the Internet. FedWorld provides access to dozens of U.S. government agencies and departments on the World Wide Web and organizes the entries into subject categories such as health care, energy, justice, manufacturing, and transportation.

Open Government Trial

World Wide Web: **http://debra.dgbt.doc.ca/opengov**

Sponsored by Industry Canada, the Open Government Trial is an excellent starting point for locating Canadian federal, provincial, and municipal government information on the Internet.

Educational Resources

Academy One

World Wide Web: **http://www.nptn.org**

Academy One is an international on-line educational resource for students, educators, parents and administrators of grades kindergarten through 12. This site provides access to Academy One projects and information. It contains a good index to Internet educational resources by category.

AskERIC

World Wide Web: **http://ericir.syr.edu/**

AskERIC provides access to lesson plans, archives of educational mailing lists, links to useful educational information resources on the World Wide Web, and summaries of electronic journals and other publications available through the Internet. AskERIC is recognized as one of the best educational sites on the Internet. It includes a search capability to quickly narrow in on the topic you are looking for.

Educational Resources Mailing List

To Subscribe: Send an e-mail message to **listserv@unb.ca** and include the following command on the first line of the body of the message: **subscribe EDRES-L YourFirstName YourLastName**

A mailing list for announcements, descriptions, and reviews of education-related Internet resources. An excellent resource for keeping track of new educational resources on the Internet.

Internet Educational Resources Guide

World Wide Web: **http://www.dcs.aber.ac.uk/~jjw0/index_ht.html**

A "launchpad" for educators who want to discover educational resources on the Internet. This site indexes World Wide Web sites, mailing lists, on-line magazines, and newsgroups of interest to educators. The guide was prepared as part of a final year project in the Department of Computer Science, University of Wales, in Aberystwyth, Wales. Highly recommended.

SchoolNet

World Wide Web: **http://schoolnet.carleton.ca**

SchoolNet is a federal, provincial, and territorial Internet initiative that helps schools get connected to the Internet. SchoolNet's Web site provides general information on the SchoolNet project as well as pointers to useful educational resources on the Internet.

Web 66 Registry of Schools with World Wide Web Sites

World Wide Web: **http://web66.coled.umn.edu/schools.html**

Web 66 is a directory of World Wide Web sites maintained by K-12 schools in Canada, the United States, and over 10 other countries. An excellent resource for understanding how schools worldwide are using the World Wide Web.

Not-for-Profit Organizations and Associations Resources

Activist Resources

World Wide Web: **http://www.cs.caltech.edu/~adam/LEAD/active_links.html**

An eclectic selection of resources for activists, from around the Internet.

EnviroWeb

World Wide Web: **http://envirolink.org/start_web.html**

A project of the EnviroLink Network, EnviroWeb provides information on dozens of environmental resources available on the Internet, including mailing lists and World Wide Web sites.

Institute for Global Communications

World Wide Web: **http://www.apc.org**

The Institute for Global Communications is a computer network serving individuals and organizations working toward peace, environmental protection, human rights, social and economic justice, sustainable and equitable development, health, and non-violent conflict resolution. IGC's Web site contains information on dozens of not-for-profit organizations and maintains links to newsletters, publications, World Wide Web sites, and other Internet resources produced for and by not-for-profit organizations. Some of the topics indexed include acid rain, endangered species, forests, health, labor issues, human rights, animal rights, and justice.

Internet Resources for Non-Profit Public Service Organizations

World Wide Web: **http://asa.ugl.lib.umich.edu/chdocs/nonprofits/nonprofits.html**

This directory was created "to help administrators and employees of non-profit, public service organizations easily locate relevant information on the Internet." It provides information on mailing lists, USENET newsgroups, and other Internet resources relevant to not-for-profit organizations.

Internet Resources for Not-for-Profits in Housing, Health, and Human Services

World Wide Web: **http://www.ai.mit.edu/people/ellens/Non/online.html**

This directory is maintained by Munn Heydorn of The First National Bank of Chicago. It includes pointers to World Wide Web sites, mailing lists, USENET groups, and other Internet resources of interest to not-for-profit organizations that work in the housing, health, and human services areas.

Phillip A. Walker's Table of Contents

World Wide Web: **http://www.clark.net/pub/pwalker/**

A general index to the Internet, including a comprehensive listing of not-for-profit resources on the Internet.

The Internet Non-Profit Centre

World Wide Web: **http://www.human.com:80/inc/**

The Internet Non-Profit Centre provides information on non-profit organizations, wise giving practices, and issues of concern to donors and volunteers.

Select Non-Profit Organizations on the Internet

World Wide Web: **http://www.ai.mit.edu/people/ellens/non.html**

Provides pointers to World Wide Web sites maintained by not-for-profit organizations. Also contains links to other collections of not-for-profit resources on the Internet.

USENET: **soc.org.nonprofit**

A USENET discussion group for not-for-profit organizations from around the world. This is a good place to seek advice and opinions on issues relevant to the not-for-profit sector.

Health Care Resources

HospitalWeb

World Wide Web: **http://dem0nmac.mgh.harvard.edu/hospitalweb.html**

The goal of this site is to "provide a simple and globally accessible way for patients, medical researchers, and physicians to get information on any hospital in the world". It provides a central index of hospitals with World Wide Web sites.

NetVet

World Wide Web: **http://netvet.wustl.edu**

This outstanding site provides a central index to veterinary and animal resources available on the Internet. It is maintained by Dr. Ken Boschert of Washington University, who is a veterinarian by profession.

World Wide Virtual Library — Medicine

World Wide Web: **http://golgi.harvard.edu/biopages/medicine.html**

A directory of Internet medical resources, the directory is organized by information provider and subject, including subjects such as anesthesiology, cosmetic surgery, dentistry, dermatology, nutrition, pathology, and pharmacy.

Useful Internet-Related Publications

Keeping up with the Internet can be a challenging task. To help you keep pace with the Internet's rapid growth and to keep abreast of new Internet resources, trends, and technologies, we recommend the following publications. Some publications will provide you with a sample issue if you ask. Publications in this Appendix are listed under five categories:

➤ Internet and education

➤ Internet security

➤ Internet and business

➤ general interest

➤ other Internet-related publications.

Internet and Education

Classroom Connect
Frequency: 9 issues per year
Format: Color newsletter
Available by postal subscription only

Classroom Connect has regular features on educational resources on the Internet and guidance on how to use the Internet in the classroom.

Classroom Connect
Wentworth Worldwide Media
1866 Colonial Village Lane
Lancaster, PA 17605-0488 U.S.A.

Voice: (717) 393-1000
            1-800-638-1639
Fax: (717) 393-5752
Internet: **connect@wentworth.com**
World Wide Web: **http://www.wentworth.com/wentworth**

Canadian subscriptions: US$49.00 per year
U.S. subscriptions: US$39.00 per year

Internet Security

Data Security Letter
Frequency: 11 Times a Year
Format: Paper (12–16 pages per issue)
Available by postal subscription only

Mission statement: The *Data Security Letter* provides data security professionals with a depth and breadth of computer security information, exploring fully topics that are touched on only superficially elsewhere, with an emphasis on ongoing research, recent trends, and their application to the needs of government and industry.

There are regular features on the Internet.

Data Security Letter
3060 Washington Road (Rt. 97)
Glenwood, MD 21738 U.S.A.

Voice: (301) 854-6889
Fax: (301) 854-5363
Internet: **dsl@tis.com**
World Wide Web: **http://www.tis.com**

Canadian and U.S.
  subscriptions (one year):   US$345.00 (businesses)
                                US$89.00   (individuals and educational organizations)
Other countries (one year):   US$370.00 (businesses)
                                US$114.00 (individuals and educational organizations)

Internet Security Monthly
Frequency: Monthly
Format: Paper
Available by postal subscription only

Internet Security Monthly serves as an international news bulletin for the protection of data communications on the information highway. Features include firewalls, UNIX security, cryptography, privacy, legislation, and contributions to the international debates on the security of the Internet and the integrity of data and messages.

Internet Security Monthly
Suite 400
1825 I Street Northwest
Washington, D.C. 20066 U.S.A.

Voice: (202) 775-4947
Fax: (202) 429-9574
Internet: **nso@delphi.com**

International subscriptions
  (including Canada) (one year): US$120.00

U.S. subscriptions (one year):   US$95.00

Internet and Business

Internet Business Advantage
Frequency: Monthly
Format: Newsletter
Available by postal subscription only

Internet Business Advantage is written for entrepreneurs and small to mid-size companies who want to learn how to do business on the Internet.

Internet Business Advantage
c/o Wentworth Worldwide Media
1866 Colonial Village Lane
P.O. Box 10488
Lancaster, PA 17605-0488 U.S.A.

Voice: 1-800-638-1639
Fax: (717) 393-5752
Internet: **success@wentworth.com**
World Wide Web: **http://www.wentworth.com**

Canadian and U.S. subscriptions (one year): US$67.00

Internet Business Report
Frequency: Monthly
Format: Paper
Available by postal subscription only

The *Internet Business Report* provides in-depth analysis and reporting on Internet issues that affect the business community. Issues are typically 8–12 pages in length.

Internet Business Report
c/o CMP Publications Inc.
600 Community Drive
Manhasset, New York 11030 U.S.A.

Voice: 1-800-340-6485 (subscriptions only)
Fax: (516) 733-6960 (subscriptions only)
Internet: **ibrsub@cmp.com** (subscriptions only)
World Wide Web: **http://techweb.cmp.com/techweb**

Canadian and U.S. subscriptions (one year):   US$279.00
Overseas subscriptions (one year):   US$379.00

The Internet Letter
Frequency: Monthly
Format: Paper
Available by postal mail or electronic mail

Mission Statement: *The Internet Letter* covers the businesses that use the Internet, the political forces that shape it, and the information that flows across it.

Jayne Levin, Editor
The Internet Letter
220 National Press Building
Washington, D.C. 20045 U.S.A.

Voice: (202) 638-6036
Fax: (202) 638-6019
Internet: **info@netweek.com**
World Wide Web: **http://www.infohaus.com/access/by-seller/Internet_Letter**

North American subscriptions (one year):   US$249.00
Outside North America (one year):   US$295.00

General Interest Internet Publications

Internet World
Frequency: Monthly
Format: Color glossy
Available at newsstands or by postal subscription

Each issue of *Internet World* contains articles, news, and tips for both new and experienced Internet users.

Internet World
20 Ketchum Street
Westport, Connecticut 06880 U.S.A.

Voice: 1-800-632-5537
             (203) 226-6967 (editorial)
             1-800-573-3062 (subscriptions)
Fax: (203) 454-5840
Internet: **iwedit@mecklermedia.com** (editorial)
World Wide Web: **http://www.mecklerweb.com**

Canadian subscriptions:
  One-year subscription: US$41.73
  Two-year subscription: US$73.83

U.S. subscriptions:
  One-year subscription: US$29.00
  Two-year subscription: US$49.00

NetGuide — The Guide to Online Services and the Internet
Frequency: Monthly
Format: Color glossy
Available at newsstands or by postal subscription

From *NetGuide's* Web site: *NetGuide* provides a comprehensive view of the commercial online world and the Internet. We take a critical look at online content through reviews of cybersites; furnish up-to-date listings of new places online, describe and evaluate the best Internet tools (software, hardware and peripheral computer equipment); apprise readers of the best techniques for accessing and using online resources; and publish informed opinion on issues relevant to the online experience. Our features cover the full depth and breadth of the net; people, trends, events, issues. NetGuide is accessible to all levels of readers, but focuses on providing information to those who are seriously committed to online activity in business and at home.

NetGuide
600 Community Drive
Manhasset, New York 11030 U.S.A.

Voice: (516) 562-5000
          1-800-829-0421 (subscriptions only)
Fax: (516) 562-7406
Internet: **netmail@netguide.cmp.com**
World Wide Web: **http://techweb.cmp.com/techweb**

Canadian subscriptions (one year):   US$32.97
U.S. subscriptions (one year):   US$22.97

OnTheInternet
Frequency: Bi-monthly
Format: Black & white magazine
Available by postal subscription

OnTheInternet is a general interest Internet publication which is free with membership in the Internet Society.

Internet Society
12020 Sunrise Valley Drive, Suite 270
Reston, VA 22091 U.S.A.

Voice: (703) 648-9888
Fax: (703) 648-9887
Internet: **isoc@isoc.org** (general information)
           membership@isoc.org (individual membership information)
           org-membership@isoc.org (organizational memberships)
World Wide Web: **http://www.isoc.org**

Individual membership: **US$35.00 per year**
Student membership: **US$25.00 per year**

Other Internet-Related Publications

INFORMATION HIGHWAYS
The Magazine for Consumers of Strategic Electronic Information
Frequency: Bi-monthly
Format: Color glossy
Available by postal subscription only

The purpose of *INFORMATION highways* is to provide a forum for the consumers, vendors, and publishers of electronic information services and products.

INFORMATION *highways*
c/o Database Canada Inc.
162 Joicey Blvd.
Toronto, Ontario M5M 2V2 Canada

Voice: (416) 488-7372
Fax: (416) 488-7078
Internet: **infohiwy@io.org**

Canadian subscriptions:
  One-year subscription: Cdn$98.00
  Two-year subscription: Cdn$175.00
Addresses outside Canada:
  One-year subscription: US$105.00
  Two-year subscription: US$189.00

INTERACTIVE AGE
Content, Technology and Communications for the Information Highway
Frequency: Bi-monthly
Format: Color glossy newspaper
Available by postal subscription only

INTERACTIVE AGE reports on developments concerning the information highway, with a heavy focus on Internet reporting, as well as cable TV and telephone ventures into the wired world.

INTERACTIVE AGE
Circulation Department
P.O. Box 1194
Skokie, IL 60076-8194 U.S.A.

Voice: (516) 562-5000
Internet: **ianewsub@interact.cmp.com**
World Wide Web: **http://techweb.cmp.com/ia**

Subscriptions: **Subscription is free, but this is a controlled circulation publication. To qualify, you must show that you have a purchasing influence concerning technology investment in your organization. To obtain a subscription form, send a message to** ianewsub@interact.cmp.com, **or visit their Web site at** http://techweb.cmp.com/ia/.

WIRED Magazine
Frequency: Monthly
Format: Color glossy
Available at newsstands or by postal subscription

WIRED is a colorful magazine covering the on-line and high-tech world, with regular features on the Internet.

WIRED *Magazine*
520 Third Street
Fourth Floor
San Francisco, California 94107 U.S.A.

Voice: (415) 222-6200
Fax: (415) 222-6209
Internet: **info@wired.com** (general questions)
           talk2subs@wired.com (subscriptions)
           editor@wired.com (editorial correspondence)
World Wide Web: **http://www.wired.com**

Canadian and Mexican subscriptions:
US$64.00 for one year, US$119.00 for two years (individuals)
US$103.00 for one year, US$191.00 for two years (institutions)

U.S. subscriptions:
US$39.95 for one year, US$71.00 for two years (individuals)
US$80.00 for one year, US$143.00 for two years (institutions)

Foreign subscriptions:
US$79.00 for one year, US$149.00 for two years (individuals)
US$110.00 for one year, US$210.00 for two years (institutions)

Directory of Canadian Internet Access Providers

This is a comprehensive directory of organizations that sell access to the Internet in Canada. This directory covers the entire spectrum of Internet access providers in Canada, from those offering only dialup Internet accounts to those offering high-speed dedicated Internet connections.

This directory is divided into three sections. The first section lists national Internet access providers. The second section is a province-by-province listing of local and regional Internet access providers in Canada. The third section lists U.S. companies that provide Internet access in Canada.

Each entry in this directory contains six pieces of information, in the following order:

(1)   the name of the access provider;

(2)   the city or town where the provider is based;

(3)   the Internet domain of the provider;

(4)   a list of cities and towns served by the provider;

(5)   a list of Internet services offered by the provider;

(6)   the address of the provider's World Wide Web site (optional, since some access providers do not have a Web site).

For item (5), there are eight possible Internet services that may be listed:

➤ Leased line. A leased line is used when an organization wants a dedicated, permanent high-speed connection to the Internet. A dedicated connection means that the organization is connected to the Internet around the clock.

- ISDN (Integrated Services Digital Network). ISDN is a special type of dedicated connection. ISDN can be used by organizations that want a dedicated, permanent high-speed connection to the Internet.

- SLIP/PPP. SLIP and PPP are types of dialup Internet accounts. A dialup account means that you dial into your access provider whenever you want to use the Internet. SLIP and PPP connections are the most powerful types of dialup Internet accounts, since your computer is directly connected to the Internet during your Internet session. SLIP/PPP accounts allow you to run programs such as Netscape, the software that we used throughout this book. Some providers only offer dedicated SLIP/PPP service, which means that they only offer permanent SLIP or PPP connections, not dialup SLIP or PPP accounts.

- Dedicated dialup. Dedicated dialup service provides an organization with an exclusive dialup telephone line that is not shared with any other organization. This type of service eliminates the possibility of busy signals, since the line is private.

- Interactive Accounts. Interactive accounts are a type of dialup Internet account. You log in to your access provider's computer and access Internet services from a menu or a command line on the remote computer. Interactive accounts are not as powerful as SLIP/PPP accounts, since your computer is not directly connected to the Internet during your Internet session. You are limited to the Internet services that are offered on the remote computer. The types of Internet services that are offered on interactive accounts vary from one access provider to another.

- Shell accounts. Shell accounts are a special type of interactive account (explained above). Shell accounts means that the provider will give you access to their UNIX shell, where you key in Internet commands from a command line.

- UUCP. UUCP accounts allow individuals and organizations to use Internet mail and discussion groups, but not any of the other popular Internet services such as the World Wide Web. With UUCP service you compose and read your messages off-line and call your access provider regularly to send and pick up messages. UUCP accounts have declined in popularity due to their limited funtionality.

- e-mail only. This means that the access provider only offers Internet electronic mail.

Prices are not listed in this directory. Contact the access providers directly for pricing information.

> If you are an Internet provider, and you would like to be listed in this directory, please send an e-mail message to the authors at **handbook@uunet.ca**.

Appendix C: Table of Contents

Many of the access providers listed in this directory are also Internet presence providers and can set up Web sites, mailing lists and mail reflectors for organizations. Check with each provider for details.

National Internet Providers

Advantis Canada (IBM Global Network)
Markham, Ontario
ibm.net

3500 Steeles Avenue East   Voice: 1-800-268-3100 (Canada-wide Toll-Free)
Markham, Ontario   Fax: (905) 316-6967
L3R 2Z1   Internet: connect@vnet.ibm.com

Service Area:	Toronto, Montréal, Victoria, Vancouver, Edmonton, Calgary, Regina, Winnipeg, London, Ottawa, Québec City, Halifax.
Services:	Leased Line, Dedicated Dial-up, SLIP/PPP.
World Wide Web:	http://www.ibm.net/adv/canada

AT&T Mail
Toronto, Ontario
attmail.com

Unitel Electronic Commerce Services   Voice: 1-800-567-4671 (Canada Toll-Free)
2005 Sheppard Avenue East, Suite 215
Toronto, Ontario
M2J 5B4

Service Area:	Where Datapac service is available.
Services:	E-mail only.

Cycor Communications Inc.
Charlottetown, Prince Edward Island
cycor.ca

Cycor Communications Inc.   Voice: 1-800-282-9267
P.O. Box 454   1-800-ATCYCOR
Charlottetown, Prince Edward Island   Fax: (705) 472-6765
C1A 7K7   Internet: sign.me.up@cycor.ca
                                             support@cycor.ca

Service Area:	Charlottetown, Halifax, Vancouver, Toronto, Montréal, Moncton, St. John's, Saskatoon, Winnipeg, Calgary, Ottawa. 16 additional sites scheduled for 1995.
Services:	Leased Line, Dedicated Dial-Up, SLIP/PPP.
World Wide Web:	http://www.cycor.ca

*f*ONOROLA i*internet
Ottawa, Ontario
fonorola.net, fonorola.ca, fonorola.com

250 Albert Street, Suite 205	Voice:	(604) 683-3666 (Vancouver)
Ottawa, Ontario		(403) 269-3666 (Calgary)
K1P 6M1		(416) 364-3666 (Toronto)
		(519) 642-3666 (London)
		(519) 741-3666 (Kitchener)
		(613) 780-2200 (Ottawa)
		(514) 954-3666 (Montréal)
		(716) 856-3666 (Buffalo)
	Fax:	(613) 232-4329
	Internet:	info@fonorola.net
		sales@fonorola.net

Service Area: British Columbia, Alberta, Manitoba, Ontario, Québec.

Services: Leased Line, ISDN, SLIP/PPP.

World Wide Web: http://www.fonorola.net

INSINC
Integrated Network Services Inc.
Vancouver, British Columbia
insinc.net

Suite 1740	Voice:	(604) 687-7575 (Vancouver)
P.O. Box 12095		(403) 269-3290 (Calgary)
555 West Hastings Street		(416) 499-2083 (Toronto)
Vancouver, British Columbia		(514) 354-2267 (Montréal)
V6B 4N5		1-800-563-4744 (Canada Toll-Free)
	Fax:	(604) 687-7121
	Internet:	ed.placenis@insinc.net (Edward Placenis)

Service Area: Canada-wide.

Services: Leased Line.

World Wide Web: http://www.insinc.net

MPACT Immedia Inc.
Montréal, Québec
immedia.ca, mpact.ca

1155, boul. René-Lévesque Ouest	Voice: (514) 397-9747
Suite 2250	1-800-361-7252
Montréal, Québec	Fax: (514) 398-0764
H3B 4T3	Internet: service@immedia.ca

Service Area:	Most Canadian cities are accessible locally (depends on public data network availability).
Services:	E-mail only.

PowerNet
Richmond Hill, Ontario
powerwindows.ca

404 Steeles Avenue West	Voice: (905) 889-1616
Unit 5	Fax: (905) 889-1199
Thornhill, Ontario	Internet: info@powerwindows.ca
L4J 6X3	

Service Area:	Canada-Wide.
Services:	Leased Line, Dedicated Dial-Up, SLIP/PPP, Interactive Accounts, UUCP.

UUNET Canada Inc.
Toronto, Ontario
uunet.ca

1 Yonge Street, Suite 1400	Voice: (416) 368-6621
Toronto, Ontario	1-800-INET-123
M5E 1J9	Fax: (416) 368-1350
	Internet: info@uunet.ca

Service Area:	British Columbia: Vancouver
	Alberta: Calgary, Edmonton
	Ontario: London, Kitchener, Ottawa, Toronto, Sudbury
	Québec: Montréal, Québec City
	Nova Scotia: Halifax
	PEI: Charlottetown
Services:	Leased Line, ISDN, Dedicated Dial-Up, SLIP/PPP, UUCP, Interactive Accounts.
World Wide Web:	http://www.uunet.ca

WEB
Toronto, Ontario
outreach@web.apc.org

c/o NirvCentre
401 Richmond Street West, Suite 104
Toronto, Ontario
M5V 3A8

Voice: (416) 596-0212
Fax: (416) 596-1374
Internet: support@web.apc.org

Service Area:	Toronto, Ottawa, Montréal, Vancouver, Thunder Bay, Guelph, North Bay, Kitchener-Waterloo.
Services:	SLIP/PPP, UUCP, Interactive Accounts.
World Wide Web:	http://spinne.web.apc.org

WorldLinx Telecommunications
Toronto, Ontario
worldlinx.com, resonet.com

BCE Place
181 Bay Street, Suite 350
P.O. Box 851
Toronto, Ontario
M5J 2T3

Voice: (416) 350-1000
        1-800-567-1811
Fax: (416) 350-1001
Internet: info@worldlinx.com

Service Area:	Local points-of-presence in over 300 locations across Canada.
Services:	Leased Line, ISDN, Dedicated Dial-Up, PPP, Interactive Accounts.
World Wide Web:	http://www.worldlinx.com

Yukon Territory

YukonNet
Whitehorse, Yukon
yknet.yk.ca

203A Main Street
Suite 5
Whitehorse, Yukon
Y1A 2B2

Voice: (403) 668-8735
Fax: (403) 668-8734
Internet: info@yknet.yk.ca

Service Area:	Whitehorse.
Services:	Leased Line, Dedicated Dial-Up, SLIP/PPP.
World Wide Web:	http://www.yknet.yk.ca

Northwest Territories

Network North Communications Limited
Yellowknife, Northwest Territories
netnorth.com

P.O. Box 2044	Voice: (403) 873-2059
Yellowknife, Northwest Territories	Fax: (403) 873-4996
X1A 2P5	Internet: patg@netnorth.com (Pat Guinan)

Service Area:	Yellowknife.
Services:	Leased Line, ISDN, Dedicated Dial-Up, SLIP, Interactive Accounts.
World Wide Web:	http://zeus.netnorth.com

NTnet Society
Yellowknife, Northwest Territories
ntnet.nt.ca

Box 1976	Voice: (403) 669-7284
Yellowknife, Northwest Territories	Fax: (403) 669-7286
X1A 2P5	Internet: info@ntnet.nt.ca

Service Area:	Yellowknife.
Services:	Leased Line, SLIP/PPP.

British Columbia

A&W Internet Inc.
Kelowna, British Columbia
awinc.com

Head Office:	
#21-1851 Kirscher Road	Voice: (604) 763-1176
Kelowna, British Columbia	Fax: (604) 860-1654
V1Y 4N7	Internet: info@awinc.com

Service Area:	British Columbia: Kelowna, Williams Lake, Penticton, Merritt, Nelson, Quesnel, Prince Rupert, Trail, Fort. St. John, Kamloops Alberta: Banff, Medicine Hat, Edmonton
Services:	Leased Line, ISDN, Dedicated Dial-Up, SLIP/PPP, Interactive Accounts, Shell Access.
World Wide Web:	http://www.awinc.com

Satellite Offices:

Kelowna, B.C.
A & W Internet Inc.
21-1851 Kirscher Road
Kelowna, British Columbia
V1Y 4N7

Voice: (604) 763-1176
Fax: (604) 860-1654
Contact: Wolfgang Hinners
         wolf@awinc.com

Williams Lake, B.C.
Stardate Internet
297A Borland St.
Williams Lake, British Columbia

Voice: (604) 392-7175
Fax: (604) 392-7175
Contact: Richard Sanders
         stardate@stardate.awinc.com

Penticton, B.C.
Ashnola Internet Management Ltd.
456 Main Street
Penticton, British Columbia
V2A 5C5

Voice: (604) 492-7672
Fax: (604) 492-4334
Contact: Gary Lutz
         glutz@aim.awinc.com

Merritt, B.C.
Valley Business & Computer Services Ltd.
Box 188
204-2090 Coutlee Ave
Merritt, British Columbia
V0K 2B0

Voice: (604) 378-9272
Fax: (604) 378-5221
Contact: Perry Martens
         pmartens@vbcs.awinc.com

Banff, Alberta
Bowest Computer Systems Ltd.
Box 1689
210 Bear Street
Banff, Alberta
T0L 0C0

Voice: (403) 762-5159
Fax: (403) 762-2052
Contact: Moe Prozny
         mprozny@bowest.awinc.com

Nelson, B.C.
PACIFIC ONRAMP
532 Baker Street
Nelson, British Columbia
V1L 4H9

Voice: (604) 352-9600
Fax: (604) 352-9585
Contact: John McInnes
         jmcinnes@onramp.awinc.com

Quesnel, B.C.
ABC Internet
248 Read Street
Quesnel, B.C. V2J 2M2

Voice: (604) 992-1230
Fax: (604) 992-3930
Contact: Sky Smaill
         ssmaill@abc.awinc.com

Medicine Hat, Alberta
Memory Lane Computer Electronics Ltd.
221 Kingsway Ave SE
Medicine Hat, Alberta
T1A 2Y2

Voice: (403) 526-2288
Fax: (403) 527-8780
Contact: Ken Short
         kshort@mlc.awinc.com

Prince Rupert, B.C.
Kaien Computer Solutions
297-1st Ave East
Prince Rupert, B.C. V8J 1A7

Voice: (604) 624-5424
Fax: (604) 627-1093
Contact: Robert Ingvallsen
          kaien@awinc.com

Trail, B.C.
PACIFIC ONRAMP
1265 Cedar Ave
Trail, British Columbia
V1R 4B9

Voice: (604) 364-2099
Fax: (604) 364-2296
Contact: John McInnes
          jmcinnes@awinc.com

Fort. St. John, B.C.
Computer World
9912-97th Ave
Fort St. John, British Columbia
V1J 6L8

Voice: (604) 787-7200
Fax: (604) 787-0702
Contact: Peter Lythall
          plythall@awinc.com

Edmonton, Alberta
Access Internet
9868 63rd Ave.
Edmonton, Alberta

Voice: (403) 944-0745
Contact: Brad Martinsen
          bmartins@awinc.com

Kamloops, B.C.
CommPass Internet Services Inc.
Kamloops, B.C.

Voice: (604) 851-2046
Contact: Tom Page
          tpage@awinc.com

BCnet
Vancouver, British Columbia
bc.net

BCnet Headquarters
515 West Hastings Street
Vancouver, British Columbia
V6B 5K3

Voice: (604) 291-5209
Fax: (604) 291-5022
Internet: info@BC.net

Service Area:	All of British Columbia.
Services:	Leased Line, ISDN, Dedicated Dial-Up, SLIP/PPP.

BCTEL Advanced Communications

Burnaby, British Columbia
bctel.net

Suite 2600	Voice: 1-800-268-3488 Toll-Free
4720 Kingsway	Fax: (604) 454-5199
Burnaby, British Columbia	Internet: info@bctel.net
V5H 4N2	

Service Area:	Nanaimo, Victoria, Vancouver, North Vancouver, Newton, Langley, Abbottsford, Kelowna, Vernon, Kamloops, Quesnel, 100 Mile House, Williams Lake, and Prince George.
Services:	Leased Line.
World Wide Web:	http://www.bctel.net

cafe.net

Vancouver, British Columbia
cafe.net

#709-700 West Pender	Voice: (604) 681-6365
Vancouver, British Columbia	Fax: (604) 687-3797
V6C 1G8	Internet: tipping@cafe.net (Matt Tipping)

Service Area:	Vancouver and Lower Mainland.
Services:	Leased Line, ISDN, Dedicated Dial-Up, SLIP/PPP, UUCP, Interactive Accounts, Shell Access.
World Wide Web:	http://www.cafe.net

Cyberstore Systems Inc.

Vancouver, British Columbia
cyberstore.ca, cyberstore.com, cyberstore.net

Suite 201 - 601 West Broadway	Voice: (604) 482-3400
Vancouver, British Columbia	Fax: (604) 482-3433
V3L 3C5	(604) 482-3444
	Internet: info@cyberstore.ca

Service Area:	Vancouver, Victoria, and Kelowna.
Services:	Leased Line, ISDN, Dedicated Dial-Up, SLIP/PPP, Interactive Accounts.
World Wide Web:	http://www.cyberstore.ca

Deep Cove Bulletin Board Systems Ltd.

White Rock, British Columbia
deepcove.com

#5 - 15273 24th Avenue	Voice: (604) 536-5855
White Rock, British Columbia	Fax: (604) 536-7418
V4A 2H9	Internet: wayne.duval@deepcove.com (Wayne Duval)

Service Area:	Vancouver, Richmond, Surrey, White Rock, West Vancouver, North Vancouver, Burnaby, Delta, Abbotsford, Cloverdale, Port Moody, Coquitlam, New Westminster, Langley, Maple Ridge, Matsqui.
Services:	SLIP/PPP, Interactive Accounts.
World Wide Web:	http://deepcove.com

Designed Information Systems Corporation (DISC)

Burnaby, British Columbia
aurora.net, aurora-net.com, disc-net.com

5065 Anola Drive	Voice: (604) 294-4357
Burnaby, British Columbia	Fax: (604) 294-0107
V5B 4V7	Internet: sales@aurora.net

Service Area:	Lower Mainland of British Columbia.
Services:	Leased Line, SLIP/PPP, UUCP, Interactive Accounts, Shell Access.
World Wide Web:	http://www.aurora.net

Digital Ark

Courtenay, British Columbia
ark.com

Irenyx Data Group Incorporated	Voice: (604) 334-1662
P.O. Box 3310, 3906 Island Highway	Internet: info@mars.ark.com
Courtenay, British Columbia	
V9N 5N5	

Service Area:	Courtenay, Comox, Cumberland.
Services:	Leased Line, Dedicated Dial-Up, SLIP, UUCP, Interactive Accounts.
World Wide Web:	http://www.ark.com

Helix Internet
Vancouver, British Columbia
helix.net

#902-900 West Hastings Street	Voice: (604) 689-8544
Vancouver, British Columbia	Fax: (604) 685-2554
V6C 1E6	Dialup: (604) 689-8577
	Internet: info@helix.net

Service Area:	British Columbia.
Services:	Leased Line, Dedicated Dial-Up, SLIP/PPP, Interactive Accounts, Shell Access.
World Wide Web:	http://www.helix.net

hip communications inc.
Vancouver, British Columbia
hip.com

#350-1122 Mainland Street	Voice: (604) 685-0123
Vancouver, British Columbia	Fax: (604) 654-9881
V6B 5L1	Internet: info@hip.com

Service Area:	Greater Vancouver area.
Services:	Leased Line, ISDN.
World Wide Web:	http://www.hip.com

ICE ONLINE
Burnaby, British Columbia
iceonline.com

Box 30606	Voice: (604) 298-4346
#201 Lougheed Hwy.	Fax: (604) 298-0246
Burnaby, British Columbia	Internet: info@iceonline.com
V5C 6J5	

Service Area:	Vancouver, Victoria.
Services:	Dedicated Dial-Up, SLIP/PPP, UUCP, Interactive Accounts, Shell Access.
World Wide Web:	http://www.iceonline.com

InfoMatch Communications Inc.
Burnaby, British Columbia
infomatch.com

#143-9632 Cameron Street	Voice: (604) 421-3230
Burnaby, British Columbia	Fax: (604) 421-3230
V3J 7N3	Internet: accounts@infomatch.com

Service Area: Vancouver, Burnaby.

Services: Dedicated Dial-Up, SLIP, Interactive Accounts, Shell Access.

World Wide Web: http://infomatch.com

Infoserve Technology Limited
Burnaby, British Columbia
infoserve.net

#203-6811 Sellers Avenue	Voice: (604) 482-8238
Burnaby, British Columbia	Fax: (604) 482-8248
V5J 4R2	Internet: sysop@unix.infoserve.net

Service Area: Vancouver Lower Mainland (Vancouver, North Vancouver, Burnaby, New Westminster, Surrey, Richmond, Coquitlam, Port Coquitlam, Langley, Aldergrove).

Services: Dedicated Dial-Up, SLIP/PPP, Interactive Accounts, Shell Access.

World Wide Web: http://www.infoserve.net

Internet Direct
Vancouver, British Columbia
direct.ca

#1628-555 West Hastings	Voice: (604) 691-1600
Vancouver, British Columbia	Fax: (604) 691-1605
V6B 4N6	Internet: info@direct.ca

Service Area: Lower Mainland of British Columbia.

Services: Leased Line, ISDN, Dedicated Dial-Up, SLIP/PPP, Interactive Accounts, Shell Access.

World Wide Web: http://www.direct.ca

The Internet Shop Inc.
Kamloops, British Columbia
netshop.bc.ca

1160 8th Street	Voice: (604) 376-3710
Kamloops, British Columbia	Fax: (604) 376-5931
	Internet: info@netshop.bc.ca

Service Area:	Kamloops, Barriere, Pritchard, Savona, Chase, Logan Lake, Westwold, Douglas Lake.
Services:	Leased Line, ISDN, Dedicated Dial-Up, SLIP/PPP, UUCP, Interactive Accounts, Shell Access.
World Wide Web:	http://www.netshop.bc.ca

Island Internet
Nanaimo, British Columbia
island.net

515b Campbell Street	Voice: (604) 753-1139
Nanaimo, British Columbia	Fax: (604) 753-8542
V9R 3G9	Internet: info@island.net

Service Area:	Nanaimo, Parksville, Qualicum Beach, Nanoose, Bowser, Chemainus, Crofton, Ladysmith, Cedar, Cassidy, Duncan, Lantzville.
Services:	Leased Line, Dedicated Dial-Up, SLIP/PPP, UUCP, Interactive Accounts, Shell Access.
World Wide Web:	http://www.island.net

ISLAND NET
Victoria, British Columbia
amtsgi.bc.ca, islandnet.com

P.O. Box 6201, Depot 1	Voice: (604) 727-6030
Victoria, British Columbia	Fax: (604) 383-6698
V8P 5L5	Internet: info@islandnet.com

Service Area:	Victoria, Shawnigan Lake, Cobble Hill, Colwood, Langford, Sooke, Metchosin, Nanaimo.
Services:	Dedicated Dial-Up, SLIP/PPP, UUCP, Interactive Accounts, Shell Access.
World Wide Web:	http://www.islandnet.com

MINDLINK! Communications Corporation
Langley, British Columbia
mindlink.net

#105 - 20381 62nd Avenue	Voice: (604) 534-5663
Langley, British Columbia	Fax: (604) 534-7473
V3A 5E6	Internet: info@mindlink.net

Service Area:	Lower Mainland of British Columbia: Abbotsford, Aldergrove, Beach Grove, Bowen Island, Bridgeview, Cloverdale, Coquitlam, Fort Langley, Haney, Ladner, Langley, Mission, Newton, Pitt Meadows, Port Coquitlam, Port Moody, Richmond, Vancouver (East, North, South, West), Whalley, White Rock, Whonnock. Outside the Lower Mainland: Prince George
Services:	Leased Line, Dedicated Dial-Up, SLIP/PPP, UUCP, Interactive Accounts, Shell Access.

World Wide Web: http://www.mindlink.net

North Okanagan Information Freeway Inc.
Vernon, British Columbia
noif.ncp.bc.ca

2179 11th Avenue	Voice: (604) 542-0112
Vernon, British Columbia	Fax: (604) 549-3751
V1T 8V7	Internet: rspraggs@noif.ncp.bc.ca (Robert Spraggs)

Service Area:	Vernon, Salmon Arm, Sicamous, Sorento, Armstrong, Enderby, Lumby, Winfield, Kelowna, Westbank, Oyama, and Summerland.
Services:	Leased Line, ISDN, Dedicated Dial-Up, SLIP/PPP, UUCP, Interactive Accounts, Shell Access.

World Wide Web: http://www.ncp.bc.ca

Okanagan Internet Junction
Vernon, British Columbia
junction.net

Suite 1, 4216 25th Avenue	Voice: (604) 549-1036
Vernon, British Columbia	Fax: (604) 542-4130
V1T 1P4	Internet: info@junction.net

Service Area:	Vernon, Lumby, Oyama, Armstrong, Enderby, Falkland.
Services:	Leased Line, Dedicated Dial-Up, SLIP/PPP, UUCP, Interactive Accounts, Shell Access.

World Wide Web: http://www.junction.net

Pacific Interconnect Enterprises Inc.
Victoria, British Columbia
pinc.com

4252 Commerce Circle	Voice:	(604) 953-2680
Victoria, British Columbia	Fax:	(604) 953-2659
V8Z 4M2	Internet:	info@dataflux.bc.ca
		info@interlink.bc.ca

Service Area:	Victoria.
Services:	Leased Line, Dedicated Dial-Up, SLIP/PPP, UUCP, Interactive Accounts, Shell Access.
World Wide Web:	http://www.pinc.com

Peace Region Internet Society
Dawson Creek, British Columbia
pris.bc.ca

10805-14th Street	Voice:	(604) 782-5128
Dawson Creek, British Columbia	Fax:	(604) 782-6069
V1G 4V6	Internet:	pris_info@pris.bc.ca

Service Area:	Dawson Creek, Fort St. John, Fort Nelson.
Services:	Dedicated Dial-Up, SLIP/PPP, Interactive Accounts.

Pro.Net Communications Inc.
Vancouver, British Columbia
pro.net, pronet.bc.ca

890 West Pender Street, Suite 410	Voice:	(604) 688-9282
Vancouver, British Columbia	Fax:	(604) 688-9229
V6C 1J9	Internet:	info@pro.net

Service Area:	Greater Vancouver area.
Services:	Leased Line, ISDN, Dedicated Dial-Up, SLIP/PPP.
World Wide Web:	http://www.pro.net

Sunshine Net Inc.
Grantham's Landing, British Columbia
sunshine.net

Box 44
Grantham's Landing, British Columbia
V0N 1X0

Voice: (604) 886-4120
Fax: (604) 886-4513
Internet: admin@sunshine.net

Service Area:	The Sunshine Coast of British Columbia from Port Mellon to Egmont. Includes Gibsons and Sechelt.
Services:	SLIP/PPP.

World Wide Web: http://www.sunshine.net/sunshine.html

Synaptic Communications
Prince George, British Columbia
netbistro.com

1363 4th Avenue
Prince George, British Columbia
V2L 3J6

Voice: (604) 563-8668
Fax: (604) 563-4280
Internet: info@vortex.netbistro.com

Service Area:	Prince George, Hixon, Red Rock, Salmon Valley.
Services:	Dedicated Dial-Up, SLIP/PPP, UUCP, Interactive Accounts, Shell Access.

World Wide Web: http://www.netbistro.com

UNIServe Online
Aldergrove, British Columbia
uniserve.com

27009 Fraser Highway
Aldergrove, British Columbia
V4W 3L6

Voice: (604) 856-6281
Fax: (604) 856-7796
Internet: netinfo@gumby.uniserve.com

Service Area:	North and West Vancouver, Greater Vancouver area, Delta, Langley, Aldergrove, Chilliwack, Sardis.
Services:	Leased Line, ISDN, Dedicated Dial-Up, SLIP/PPP, UUCP, Interactive Accounts, Shell Access.

World Wide Web: http://www.uniserve.com

Whistler Networks

Whistler, British Columbia
whistler.net, whistler.com, whistlernet.bc.ca

Suite 204
1200 Alpha Lake Road
Whistler, British Columbia
VON 1B0

Voice: (604) 932-0606
Fax: (604) 932-0600
Internet: info@whistler.net

Service Area:	Whistler, Pemberton.
Services:	Leased Line, Dedicated Dial-Up, SLIP/PPP, Interactive Accounts, Shell Access.
World Wide Web:	http://www.whistler.net

Wimsey Information Services Inc.

Burnaby, British Columbia
wimsey.com, wimsey.bc.ca, wis.net

8523 Commerce Court
Burnaby, British Columbia
V5A 4N3

Voice: (604) 257-1111
Fax: (604) 257-1110
Internet: info@wimsey.com

Service Area:	Greater Vancouver, Kelowna.
Services:	Leased Line, ISDN, Dedicated Dial-Up, SLIP/PPP, UUCP, Interactive Accounts, Shell Access.
World Wide Web:	http://www.wimsey.com

World Tel Internet Canada

Vancouver, British Columbia
worldtel.com

Suite 810 - 675 West Hastings Street
Vancouver, British Columbia
V6B 1N2

Voice: (604) 685-3877
Fax: (604) 687-0688
Internet: info@worldtel.com

Service Area:	Vancouver.
Services:	Leased Line, ISDN, Dedicated Dial-Up, SLIP/PPP, UUCP, Interactive Accounts, Shell Access.
World Wide Web:	http://www.worldtel.com

Alberta

A&W Internet Inc.
Kelowna, British Columbia
awinc.com

Head Office:
#21-1851 Kirscher Road
Kelowna, British Columbia
V1Y 4N7

Voice: (604) 763-1176
Fax: (604) 860-1654
Internet: info@awinc.com

Service Area: Banff, Medicine Hat, Edmonton

See Main Entry Under Province of British Columbia.

AGT Limited
Edmonton, Alberta
AGT.Alta.net

Section 20F
10020 - 100th Street
Edmonton, Alberta
T5J 0N5

Voice: (403) 310-2255 (only works in Alberta)
           (403) 310-3100 (only works in Alberta)
Fax: (403) 493-4277

Service Area: Calgary.

Services: Leased Line, ISDN, Dedicated Dial-Up, SLIP/PPP.

World Wide Web: http://www.agt.alta.net

Alberta SuperNet Inc.
Edmonton, Alberta
supernet.ab.ca

#325 Pacific Plaza
10909 Jasper Avenue
Edmonton, Alberta
T5J 3L9

Voice: (403) 441-3663
Fax: (403) 424-0743
Internet: info@supernet.ab.ca

Service Area: Edmonton, Red Deer, Calgary, Slave Lake.

Services: Leased Line, Dedicated Dial-Up, SLIP/PPP, UUCP, Interactive Accounts, Shell Access.

World Wide Web: http://www.supernet.ab.ca

ARnet

Edmonton, Alberta
arc.ab.ca

c/o Alberta Research Council
Box 8330
Edmonton, Alberta
T6H 5X2

Voice: (403) 450-5189
          (403) 450-5197
Fax: (403) 461-2651
Internet: ARnet@arc.ab.ca
          penno@arc.ab.ca (Ralph Penno)

Service Area:	Lethbridge, Calgary, Alberta, Athabasca
Services:	Leased Line, ISDN, Dedicated Dial-Up, Dedicated SLIP/PPP.
World Wide Web:	http://www.arc.ab.ca

CADVision Development Corp.

Calgary, Alberta
cadvision.com

Suite 1590
300 5th Avenue S.W.
Calgary, Alberta
T2P 3C4

Voice: (403) 777-1300
Fax: (403) 777-1319
Internet: info@cadvision.com

Service Area:	Calgary.
Services:	Leased Line, ISDN, Dedicated Dial-Up, PPP, UUCP, Interactive Accounts.
World Wide Web:	http://www.cadvision.com

Canada Connect Corporation

Calgary, Alberta
canuck.com

#201 1039 17th Ave. S.W.
Box 2621, Station M
Calgary, Alberta
T2P 3C1

Voice: (403) 777-2025
Fax: (403) 777-2026
Internet: info@canuck.com

Service Area:	Calgary.
Services:	Leased Line, ISDN, Dedicated Dial-Up, SLIP/PPP, UUCP, Interactive Accounts, Shell Access.
World Wide Web:	http://www.canuck.com

CCI Networks

Edmonton, Alberta
ccinet.ab.ca

Head Office:	
4130 - 95 Street	Voice: (403) 450-6787
Edmonton, Alberta	Fax: (403) 450-9143
T6E 6H5	Internet: info@ccinet.ab.ca

Service Area:	Calgary, Edmonton, Drayton Valley, Grand Prairie, Fort McMurray, Fort Vermilion, Red Deer, Wetaskiwin
Services:	Leased Line, ISDN, Dedicated Dial-Up, SLIP/PPP, UUCP
World Wide Web:	http://www.ccinet.ab.ca

Satellite Offices:

Edmonton
CCI Networks,
4130 - 95 Street   Voice: (403) 450-6787
Edmonton, Alberta   Fax: (403) 450-9143
T6E 6H5

Calgary
CCI Networks
#202, 1201 - 5th Street SW   Voice: (403) 237-7737
Calgary, Alberta   Fax: (403) 237-7734

Fort McMurray:
Altech Telecommunications
Bay 3, 10015 Centennial Dr.   Voice: (403) 743-1829
Fort McMurray, Alberta   Fax: (403) 791-7092
T9H 1Y2

Grande Prairie:
Custom Communications
10304 - 100 Street   Voice: (403) 538-2012
Grand Prairie, Alberta   Fax: (403) 539-5904
T8V 2M1

Red Deer:
Real Time Technologies Inc. (RTT)
6831 - 52 Avenue   Voice: (403) 357-5930
Red Deer, Alberta   Fax: (403) 357-5932
T4N 4L2

Wetaskiwin:
The Wetaskiwin Telephone Co.
5110 - 49 Street   Voice: (403) 352-6029
Wetaskiwin, Alberta   Fax: (403) 352-6034
T9A 1H7

Drayton Valley:
Town of Drayton Valley
Attn: Nesen Naidoo
5120 - 52 Street   Voice: (403) 542 5327 ext. 380
Drayton Valley, Alberta   Fax: (403) 542-5753
T0E 0M0

Fort Vermilion:
Fort Vermilion School Division
Attention: Perry Moulton
P.O. Bag #1   Voice: (403) 926-2537
Fort Vermilion, Alberta   Fax: (403) 926-2726
T0H 1N0

Cybersurf Internet Access (CIA)
Calgary, Alberta
cia.com

P.O. Box #81–Bay #5   Voice: (403) 777-2000
4404-12th Street N.E.   Fax: (403) 777-2003
Calgary, Alberta   Internet: info@cia.com
T2E 6K9

Service Area:	Calgary.
Services:	Leased Line, ISDN, Dedicated Dial-Up, UUCP, Interactive Accounts.

Debug Computer Services (The Magic BBS)
Calgary, Alberta
debug.ab.ca

Box 53096   Voice: (403) 248-5798
Marlborough Postal Outlet   Internet: root@debug.cuc.ab.ca
Calgary, Alberta
T2A 7P1

Service Area:	Calgary.
Services:	Dedicated Dial-Up, SLIP/PPP, UUCP, Interactive Accounts, Shell Access.

ED TEL

Edmonton, Alberta
eon.net, edtel.alta.net

Box 20500
44 Capital Boulevard
10044-108th Street
Edmonton, Alberta
T5J 2R4

Voice: (403) 423-INET (4638)
Fax: (403) 428-0917
Internet: helpdesk@planet.eon.net

Service Area:	Edmonton.
Services:	Leased Line, ISDN, SLIP/PPP.
World Wide Web:	http://www.edtel.alta.net

The Internet Companion

Edmonton, Alberta
tic.ab.ca

Box 72092, Ottewell PO
Edmonton, Alberta
T6B 3A7

Voice: (403) 474-3975
Fax: (403) 477-7063
Internet: info@tic.ab.ca

Service Area:	Edmonton.
Services:	Dedicated Dial-Up, SLIP/PPP, UUCP, Interactive Accounts, Shell Access.
World Wide Web:	http://www.tic.ab.ca

InterNode Networks

Calgary, Alberta
internode.net

112 Rivergreen Cr. S.E.
Calgary, Alberta
T2C 3V6

Voice: (403) 296-1190
Fax: (403) 279-9581
Internet: info@internode.net

Service Area:	Calgary.
Services:	Dedicated Dial-Up, SLIP/PPP, UUCP, Interactive Accounts, Shell Access.
World Wide Web:	http://www.internode.net

Lethbridge Internet Services

Lethbridge, Alberta
lis.ab.ca

815 - 3rd Ave. S.
Lethbridge, Alberta
T1J 0H8

Voice: (403) 381-4638
Fax: (403) 320-0484
Internet: info@lis.ab.ca

Service Area:	Lethbridge.
Services:	Leased Line, ISDN, Dedicated Dial-Up, SLIP/PPP, UUCP, Interactive Accounts.

World Wide Web: http://www.lis.ab.ca

Lexicom Ltd.

Calgary, Alberta
lexicom.ab.ca

#60-203 Lynnview Rd. S.E.
Calgary, Alberta
T2C 2C6

Voice: (403) 255-3615
Fax: (403) 258-1542
Internet: info@lexicom.ab.ca

Service Area:	Calgary.
Services:	Leased Line, ISDN, Dedicated Dial-Up, SLIP/PPP, UUCP, Interactive Accounts.

World Wide Web: http://www.lexicom.ab.ca

The Network Centre

Calgary, Alberta
tnc.com

11211 76th Avenue
Edmonton, Alberta
T6G 0K2

Voice: (403) 955-7166
Fax: (403) 944-0233
Internet: tncinfo@tnc.com

Service Area:	Edmonton, Calgary.
Services:	Leased Line, ISDN, Dedicated Dial-Up, SLIP/PPP.

World Wide Web: http://www.tnc.com

Nucleus Information Service
Calgary, Alberta
nucleus.com

1835B-10th Avenue S.W.	Voice: (403) 249-9009
Calgary, Alberta	Fax: (403) 249-5121
T3C 0K2	Internet: info@nucleus.com

Service Area:	Calgary.
Services:	Dedicated Dial-Up, SLIP/PPP, UUCP, Interactive Accounts, Shell Access.
World Wide Web:	http://www.nucleus.com

Telnet Canada Enterprises, Ltd.
Calgary, Alberta
tcel.com

Penthouse	Voice: (403) 245-1882
1812-4th Street S.W.	Fax: (403) 228-9702
Calgary, Alberta	Internet: info@tcel.com
T2S 1W1	

Service Area:	Calgary.
Services:	Leased Line, ISDN, Dedicated Dial-Up, SLIP/PPP, UUCP, Interactive Accounts, Shell Access.
World Wide Web:	http://www.tcel.com

TerrAffirmative
Grande Prairie, Alberta
terranet.ab.ca

10301-89th Street	Voice: (403) 539-6972
Grande Prairie, Alberta	Fax: (403) 539-6993
T8X 1G2	Internet: info@terranet.ab.ca

Service Area:	Grande Prairie and area.
Services:	Dedicated Dial-Up, SLIP/PPP, Interactive Accounts, Shell Access.
World Wide Web:	http://www.terranet.ab.ca

Vertex Communications Inc.
Calgary, Alberta
worldweb.com

100 Discovery Place	Voice: (403) 247-1391 (Calgary)
3553 31st St. N.W.	(403) 448-9337 (Edmonton)
Calgary, Alberta	Fax: (403) 282-1238 (Calgary)
T2L 2K7	Internet: sales@worldweb.com

Service Area: Calgary.

Services: Dedicated Dial-Up, SLIP/PPP, UUCP, Interactive Accounts, Shell Access.

World Wide Web: http://www.worldweb.com

WorldGate
Edmonton, Alberta
worldgate.edmonton.ab.ca,worldgate.com

16511 - 85th Avenue	Voice: (403) 481-7579
Edmonton, Alberta	Fax: (403) 444-7720
T5R 4A2	Internet: info@worldgate.edmonton.ab.ca

Service Area: Edmonton.

Services: Leased Line, Dedicated Dial-Up, SLIP/PPP, UUCP, Interactive Accounts, Shell Access.

World Wide Web: http://www.worldgate.com

Saskatchewan

HMT Internet Inc.
Yorkton, Saskatchewan
hmtnet.com

36-2nd Avenue	Voice: (306) 782-9150
Yorkton, Saskatchewan	Fax: (306) 786-6160
S3N 1G2	Internet: info@hmtnet.com

Service Area: Yorkton.

Services: Leased Line, Dedicated Dial-Up, SLIP/PPP, Interactive Accounts, Shell Access.

Saskatchewan Telecommunications (SASKTEL)

Regina, Saskatchewan
sasknet.sk.ca

2121 Saskatchewan Drive Regina, Saskatchewan S4P 3Y2	Voice: 1-800-644-9205 (Saskatchewan residents only) 1-800-SASKTEL (Canada-wide) Fax: (306) 347-0041 Internet: feedback@sasknet.sk.ca

Service Area: Entire province of Saskatchewan.

Services: Leased Line, ISDN, Dedicated Dial-Up, SLIP/PPP, Interactive Accounts, Shell Access.

World Wide Web: http://www.sasknet.sk.ca

UNIBASE Telecomm Ltd.

Regina, Saskatchewan
unibase.com

3002 Harding Street Regina, Saskatchewan S4V 0Y4	Voice: (306) 789-9007 Fax: (306) 761-1831 Internet: leigh@unibase.unibase.com (Leigh Calnek)

Service Area: Regina, Saskatoon, Prince Albert.

Services: Leased Line, Dedicated Dial-Up, SLIP/PPP, UUCP, Interactive Accounts, Shell Access.

World Wide Web: http://www.unibase.com

Western Business Machines/WBM Office Systems

Regina and Saskatoon, Saskatchewan
wbm.ca

424 McDonald Street Regina, Saskatchewan S4N 6E1 Voice: (306) 721-2560 Fax: (306) 721-2498 Internet: info@eagle.wbm.ca	601 2nd Avenue Saskatoon, Saskatchewan S7K 2C7 Voice: (306) 664-2686 Fax: (306) 664-8717 Internet: info@eagle.wbm.ca

Service Area: Regina and Saskatoon.

Services: Leased Line, Dedicated Dial-Up, SLIP/PPP.

World Wide Web: http://www.wbm.ca

Manitoba

Astra Network, Inc.
Winnipeg, Manitoba
man.net

2633 Portage Avenue	Voice: (204) 987-7050
Winnipeg, Manitoba	Fax: (204) 987-7058
R3J 0P7	Internet: info@man.net

Service Area: Winnipeg.

Services: Leased Line, ISDN, Dedicated Dial-Up, SLIP/PPP.

World Wide Web: http://www.man.net

Common Internet Inc.
Brandon, Manitoba
common.net

P.O. Box 20116	Voice: (204) 725-5750
Brandon, Manitoba	Fax: (204) 725-5751
R7A 6Y8	Internet: info@common.net

Service Area: Brandon

Services: SLIP/PPP, Interactive Accounts.

World Wide Web: http://www.common.net

Docker Services Limited
Brandon, Manitoba
docker.com

117 - 10th Street	Voice: (204) 727-7788
Brandon, Manitoba	Internet: mikem@docker.com (Michael Malazdrewicz)
R7A 4E7	

Service Area: Brandon.

Services: Leased Line, Dedicated Dial-Up, SLIP/PPP.

World Wide Web: http://www.docker.com

Escape Communications Corp.

Winnipeg, Manitoba
escape.ca

Suite 206 - 1383 Pembina Hwy   Voice: (204) 925-4290
Winnipeg, Manitoba   Fax: (204) 925-4291
Canada   Internet: info@escape.ca
R3T 2B9

Service Area:	Winnipeg
Services:	Leased Line, ISDN, SLIP/PPP.
World Wide Web:	http://www.escape.ca

Internet Solutions Inc.

Winnipeg, Manitoba
remcan.ca

310 Nairn Avenue   Voice: (204) 982-1060
2nd Floor, Bridgeport Building   Fax: (204) 663-8563
Winnipeg, Manitoba   Internet: info@mail.remcan.ca
R2L 0W9

Service Area:	Winnipeg.
Services:	Leased Line, Dedicated Dial-Up, SLIP/PPP.
World Wide Web:	http://www.remcan.ca

Kwanza InternetXpress

Winnipeg, Manitoba
kwanza.com

Unit #1   Voice: (204) 987-8380
1325 Markham Road   Fax: (204) 987-8382
Winnipeg, Manitoba   Internet: info@kwanza.com
Canada
R3T 4J6

Service Area:	Winnipeg
Services:	SLIP/PPP.
World Wide Web:	http://www.kwanza.com

Magic Online Services Winnipeg Inc.
Winnipeg, Manitoba
magic.mb.ca

1483 Pembina Hwy., #150	Voice:	(204) 949-7777
Winnipeg, Manitoba	Fax:	(204) 949-7790
R2T 2C6	Internet:	info@magic.mb.ca

Service Area:	Winnipeg.
Services:	Dedicated Dial-Up, SLIP/PPP, UUCP, Interactive Accounts, Shell Access.
World Wide Web:	http://www.magic.mb.ca

MBnet
Winnipeg, Manitoba
MBnet.MB.CA

c/o Computer Services	Voice:	(204) 474-7325
University of Manitoba	Fax:	(204) 275-5420
15 Gillson Street	Internet:	info@MBnet.MB.CA
Winnipeg, Manitoba		
R3T 2N2		

Service Area:	Winnipeg.
Services:	Leased Line, Dedicated Dial-Up, Dedicated SLIP/PPP.
World Wide Web:	http://www.mbnet.mb.ca

Ontario

Achilles Internet
Gloucester, Ontario
achilles.net

Dennis J. Hutton Associates Ltd.	Voice:	(613) 830-5426
1810 Thornecrest	Fax:	(613) 824-2342
Gloucester, Ontario	Internet:	office@dragon.achilles.net
K1C 6K7		

Service Area:	Gloucester, Ottawa, Nepean, Kanata, Alymer, Hull, Gatineau.
Services:	Leased Line, ISDN, Dedicated Dial-Up, SLIP/PPP, UUCP, Interactive Accounts.
World Wide Web:	http://www.achilles.net

Babillard Synapse Inc.
Gatineau, Québec
synapse.net

22 Beloeil	Voice:	(819) 561-1697
Gatineau, Québec	Fax:	(613) 564-2924
J8T 7G3	Internet:	daniel.coulombe@bbs.synapse.net

Service Area:	Ottawa, Hull, Aylmer, Kanata, Gloucester, Nepean, Cumberland.
Services:	Dedicated Dial-Up, SLIP/PPP, UUCP, Interactive Accounts.
World Wide Web:	http://www.synapse.net

Barrie Internet
Barrie, Ontario
barint.on.ca

Barrie Internet	Voice:	(705) 733-3630
5 James Street	Fax:	(705) 721-5767
Barrie, Ontario	Internet:	info@barint.on.ca
L4N 6M5		

Service Area:	Barrie and Surrounding Region
Services:	Leased Line, Dedicated Dial-Up, SLIP/PPP.
World Wide Web:	http://barint.on.ca

CIMtegration Inc.
Toronto, Ontario
cimtegration.com

2727 Steeles Avenue West, Suite 300	Voice:	(416) 665-3566
North York, Ontario	Fax:	(416) 665-8285
M3J 3G9	Internet:	info@cimtegration.com

Service Area:	Toronto and surrounding area.
Services:	Leased Line, ISDN, Dedicated Dial-Up, PPP, UUCP, Interactive Accounts, Shell Access.
World Wide Web:	http://www.cimtegration.com

Communications Inter-Accès

Montréal, Québec
interax.net

5475 Pare, Suite 104	Voice:	(514) 367-0002
Montréal, Québec	Fax:	(514) 368-3529
H4P 1R4	Internet:	info@interax.net

See main entry under Province of Québec.

ComputerLink Online Inc./Internet Direct Inc.

Etobicoke, Ontario
cml.com, idirect.com

5150 Dundas Street West, #306	Voice:	(416) 233-7150
Etobicoke, Ontario	Fax:	(416) 233-6790
M9A 1C3	Internet:	sysop@cml.com
		info@cml.com

Service Area:	Metropolitan Toronto. Oshawa/Whitby (ComputerLink).
Services:	Leased Line, Dedicated Dial-Up, SLIP/PPP, UUCP, Interactive Accounts, Shell Access.
World Wide Web:	http://idirect.com

CRS Online

Etobicoke, Ontario
canrem.com

24-12 Steinway Blvd.	Voice:	(416) 213-6000
Etobicoke, Ontario		1-800-563-2529
M9W 6M5	Fax:	(416) 213-6038
	Internet:	info@canrem.com

Service Area:	Hamilton, Stoney Creek, Dundas, Lynden, Brantford, Burlington, Milton, Caledon East, Orangeville, Hespeler, Guelph, Kitchener-Waterloo, Brampton, Georgetown, Toronto and surrounding areas, Aurora, Newmarket, Barrie, Moonstone, Orillia, Midland, Ajax, Oshawa, Bowmanville.
Services:	Interactive Accounts.

Daac Systems
Aurora, Ontario
daacsys.com, dcsnet.com

Suite 115
14845-6 Yonge Street
Aurora, Ontario
L4G 6H8

Voice: (905) 841-4147
Fax: (905) 841-7490
Internet: info@daacsys.com

Service Area:	Toronto and surrounding area.
Services:	Dedicated Dial-Up, UUCP.

Fleximation Systems Inc.
Mississauga, Ontario
flexnet.com, flexnet.ca

1495 Bonhill Road
Units 1 and 2
Mississauga, Ontario
L5T 1M2

Voice: (905) 795-0300
              1-800-263-8733
Fax: (905) 795-0310
Internet: admin@flexnet.com

Service Area:	Vancouver, Calgary, Winnipeg, Guelph/Cambridge, Toronto and Greater Toronto area, Mississauga, Markham, Pickering, Orangeville, Caledon East, Caledon, Aurora, Castlemore, Oakville, Brampton, Woodbridge, Bolton, Kleinburg, Palgrave.
Services:	Leased Line, ISDN, Dedicated Dial-Up, SLIP/PPP, UUCP.
World Wide Web:	http://www.flexnet.com

Focus Technologies
Mississauga, Ontario
ftn.net, ftn.ca

5380 Timberlea Blvd.
Mississauga, Ontario
L4W 2S6

Voice: (905) 602-6266
              1-800-FTN-INET
Fax: (905) 602-6272
Internet: info@ftn.net

Service Area:	Throughout Ontario.
Services:	Leased Line, Dedicated Dial-Up, SLIP/PPP, UUCP, Interactive Accounts, Shell Access.
World Wide Web:	http://www.ftn.net

Foxnet Communications

Thunder Bay, Ontario
foxnet.net

28 South Cumberland Street	Voice: (807) 343-0225
Thunder Bay, Ontario	Fax: (807) 343-0223
P7B 2T2	Internet: info@mail.foxnet.net

Service Area:	Thunder Bay, Kakabeka Falls.
Services:	Leased Line, Dedicated Dial-Up, SLIP/PPP, UUCP.
World Wide Web:	http://www.foxnet.net

Global-X-Change Communications Inc.

Ottawa, Ontario
globalx.net

709-170 Laurier Avenue West	Voice: (613) 235-6865
Ottawa, Ontario	Fax: (613) 232-5285
K1P 5V5	Internet: info@globalx.net

Service Area:	Ottawa, Kanata, Nepean, Gloucester, Cumberland, Hull, Aylmer, Gatineau, Wakefield, Kemptville, Osgoode, Stittsville, Rockcliffe Park, Orleans.
Services:	Leased Line, Dedicated Dial-Up, SLIP/PPP.
World Wide Web:	http://www.globalx.net

HookUp Communications

Oakville, Ontario
hookup.net

1075 North Service Road West	Voice: 1-800-363-0400 Toll-Free Canada-Wide
Suite 207	Direct Dial: (905) 847-8000
Oakville, Ontario, Canada	Fax: (905) 847-8420
L6M 2G2	Internet: info@hookup.net

Service Area:	56 Kbps dedicated access across Canada. Local dial-up access in much of the 519, 416, 905, and 613 area codes.
Services:	Leased Line, ISDN, Dedicated Dial-Up, SLIP/PPP, UUCP, Interactive Accounts, Shell Access.
World Wide Web:	http://www.hookup.net

ICOM Internet Services

Hamilton, Ontario
icom.ca

7 May Street	Voice: (905) 522-1220
Suite 201	Fax: (905) 546-1996
Hamilton, Ontario	Internet: sales@icom.ca
L8R 1J6	support@icom.ca

Service Area: Hamilton

Services: Leased Line, ISDN, Dedicated Dial-Up, SLIP/PPP.

World Wide Web: http://www.icom.ca

InaSec Inc.

Ottawa, Ontario
inasec.ca

29 Beechwood Avenue	Voice: (613) 746-3200
Suite 320	Fax: (613) 747-2046
Ottawa, Ontario	Internet: mike@inasec.ca (Michel Paradis)
K1M 2M1	

Service Area: Ottawa.

Services: Dedicated Dial-Up, SLIP/PPP, UUCP, Interactive Accounts, Shell Access.

World Wide Web: http://www.inasec.ca

InfoRamp Inc.

Toronto, Ontario
inforamp.net

134 Adelaide Street East	Voice: (416) 363-9100
Suite 207	Fax: (416) 363-3551
Toronto, Ontario	Internet: staff@inforamp.net
M5C 1K9	

Service Area: Toronto and surrounding area.

Services: Leased Line, ISDN, Dedicated Dial-Up, SLIP/PPP, UUCP, Interactive Accounts, Shell Access.

World Wide Web: http://www.inforamp.net

INFOWEB/MAGI Data Consulting Incorporated
Ottawa, Ontario
magi.com

20 Colonnade Road	Voice: (613) 225-3354
Nepean, Ontario	Fax: (613) 225-2880
K2E 7M6	Internet: info@magi.com

Service Area: National Capital Region and surrounding cities.

Services: Leased Line, Dedicated Dial-Up, SLIP/PPP, UUCP, Interactive Accounts, Shell Access.

World Wide Web: http://www.magi.com

Inter-Com Information Services Ltd.
London, Ontario
icis.on.ca

1464 Adelaide Street North	Voice: (519) 679-1620
London, Ontario	Fax: (519) 679-1583
N5X 1K4	Internet: info@icis.on.ca

Service Area: London.

Services: Leased Line, ISDN, Dedicated Dial-Up, SLIP/PPP, UUCP.

World Wide Web: http://www.icis.on.ca

Interlog Internet Services
Toronto, Ontario
interlog.com

1235 Bay Street	Voice: (416) 975-2655
Suite 400	Fax: (416) 975-2655
Toronto, Ontario	Internet: internet@interlog.com
M5R 3K4	

Service Area: Metropolitan Toronto.

Services: Leased Line, ISDN, Dedicated Dial-Up, SLIP/PPP, Interactive Accounts, Shell Access.

World Wide Web: http://www.interlog.com

Internet Access Inc.
Ottawa, Ontario
ottawa.net

1916 Merivale Road	Voice: (613) 225-5595
Suite 202	Fax: (613) 722-2778
Nepean, Ontario	Internet: info@ottawa.net
K2G 1E8	

Service Area:	Ottawa, Nepean, Gloucester, Kanata, Orleans, Kemptville, Hull, Gatineau, Rockland.
Services:	Leased Line, ISDN, Dedicated Dial-Up, SLIP/PPP, UUCP, Interactive Accounts, Shell Access.
World Wide Web:	http://www.ottawa.net
	http://www.shop.net

Internet Connect Niagara
St. Catharines, Ontario
niagara.com

25 Church Street	Voice: (905) 988-9909 (Sales)
St. Catharines, Ontario	(905) 988-1700 (Technical Support)
L2R 3B1	Fax: (905) 988-1090
	Internet: sales@niagara.com
	info@niagara.com

Service Area:	St. Catharines, Thorold, Welland, Niagara Falls, Niagara-on-the-Lake, Pelham, Port Robinson, Wellandport, Vineland, Beamsville.
Services:	Leased Line, ISDN, Dedicated Dial-Up, SLIP/PPP, UUCP, Interactive Accounts, Shell Access.
World Wide Web:	http://www.niagara.com

Internex Online
Toronto, Ontario
io.org

1 Yonge Street	Voice: (416) 363-8676
Suite 1801	Fax: (416) 369-0515
Toronto, Ontario	Internet: support@io.org
M5E 1W7	

Service Area:	Toronto.
Services:	SLIP/PPP, Interactive Accounts, Shell Access.
World Wide Web:	http://www.io.org

Kingston Online Services

Kingston, Ontario
kosone.com

303 Bagot, #309
LaSalle Mews
Kingston, Ontario
K7K 5W7

Voice: (613) 549-8667
Fax: (613) 549-0642
Internet: info@limestone.kosone.com

Service Area:	Kingston, Gananoque, Napanee, Verona, Lansdowne, Odessa, Harrowsmith, Seeley's Bay, Howe's Island, Bath, Deseronto, Wolfe Island, Sydenham, Inverary, Wilton, and Yarker.
Services:	Leased Line, Dedicated Dial-Up, PPP, UUCP, Interactive Accounts, Shell Access.
World Wide Web:	http://limestone.kosone.com

Magic Online Services Toronto Inc.

Toronto, Ontario
magic.ca

260 Richmond Street West, Suite 206
Toronto, Ontario
M5V 1W5

Voice: (416) 591-6490
Fax: (416) 591-6409
Internet: info@magic.ca

Service Area:	Toronto.
Services:	Leased Line, ISDN, Dedicated Dial-Up, SLIP/PPP, Interactive Accounts, Shell Access.
World Wide Web:	http://www.magic.ca

Metrix Interlink Corporation

Montréal, Québec
interlink.net, rezonet.net, interlink.ca

500 boul. René-Lévesque Ouest
Suite 1004
Montréal, Québec
H2Z 1W7

Voice: (514) 875-0010
Fax: (514) 875-5735
Internet: info@interlink.net

Service Area:	Toronto.

See main entry under Province of Québec.

MapleNet Technologies Inc.
North York, Ontario
maple.net

Suite 500	Voice: (416) 756-2000
150 Consumers Road	Fax: (416) 756-2088
North York, Ontario	Internet: info@maple.net
M2J 1P9	

Service Area:	Toronto and Surrounding Area.
	Port Elgin, Owen Sound, Kincardine.
Services:	Leased Line, ISDN, Dedicated Dial-Up, SLIP/PPP, Shell Access.
World Wide Web:	http://www.maple.net

MGL Systems Computer Technologies Inc.
Guelph, Ontario
mgl.ca

RR #1	Voice: (519) 651-2713
Guelph, Ontario	Fax: (519) 836-1309
N1H 6H7	Internet: info@mgl.ca

Service Area:	Guelph, Kitchener-Waterloo, Cambridge.
Services:	Leased Line, Dedicated Dial-Up, SLIP/PPP, UUCP, Interactive Accounts, Shell Access.
World Wide Web:	http://www.mgl.ca

Mindemoya Computing
Sudbury, Ontario
mcd.on.ca

P.O. Box 21013	Voice: (705) 523-0243
1935 Paris Street	Internet: info@mcd.on.ca
Sudbury, Ontario	
P3E 6G6	

Service Area:	Sudbury.
Services:	SLIP/PPP, UUCP, Interactive Accounts, Shell Access.
World Wide Web:	http://www.mcd.on.ca

NetAccess Systems Inc.
Hamilton, Ontario
netaccess.on.ca

Suite E   Voice: (905) 524-2544
231 Main Street West   Fax: (905) 524-3010
Hamilton, Ontario   Internet: info@netaccess.on.ca
L8P 1J4

Service Area:	Greater Hamilton-Burlington area.
Services:	Leased Line, ISDN, Dedicated Dial-Up, SLIP/PPP, UUCP, Interactive Accounts, Shell Access.

World Wide Web: http://netaccess.on.ca

net.ROVER Inc.
Toronto, Ontario
netrover.com

215 Carlingview Drive   Voice: (416) 213-8686
Suite 202   Fax: (416) 213-8684
Toronto, Ontario   Internet: info@netrover.com
M9W 5X8

Service Area:	Toronto.
Services:	Leased Line, ISDN, Dedicated Dial-Up, SLIP/PPP, UUCP, Interactive Accounts, Shell Access.

Nova Scotia Technology Network Inc. (NSTN)
Dartmouth, Nova Scotia
nstn.ca

201 Brownlow Avenue   Voice: (902) 481-NSTN (6786)
Dartmouth, Nova Scotia   1-800-336-4445 (Toll-Free Canada-Wide)
B3B 1W2   Fax: (902) 468-3679
                               Internet: info@nstn.ca (Automated)
                                         sales@nstn.ca (Sales/Marketing Team)

Service Area:	Ottawa and Toronto

See main entry under Province of Nova Scotia.

ONet Networking

Toronto, Ontario
onet.on.ca

4 Bancroft Avenue, BC101	Voice: (416) 978-4589
Toronto, Ontario	Fax: (416) 978-6620
M5S 1C1	Internet: info@onet.on.ca

Service Area: Barrie, Belleville, Brockville, Chalk River, Deep River, Kingston, Kitchener-Waterloo, North Bay, Oakville, Ottawa, Guelph, Hamilton, London, Peterborough, St. Catharines, Sarnia, Sault Ste. Marie, Sudbury, Toronto, Thunder Bay, Welland, and Windsor.

Services: Leased Line, Dedicated Dial-Up, SLIP/PPP.

World Wide Web: http://onet.on.ca/onet/index.html

Online Computer Distribution

Peterborough, Ontario
oncomdis.on.ca

194 Charlotte Street	Voice: (705) 749-9225
Peterborough, Ontario	Fax: (705) 749-9226
K9J 2T8	Internet: pstewart@oncomdis.on.ca (Paul Stewart)

Service Area: Peterborough.

Services: Leased Line, Dedicated Dial-Up, Interactive Accounts.

World Wide Web: http://www.oncomdis.on.ca

Online Systems of Canada

London, Ontario
onlinesys.com

383 Richmond Street	Voice: (416) 642-0731
Suite 900	Fax: (416) 642-0733
London, Ontario	Internet: support@onlinesys.com
N6A 3C4	

Service Area: London, St. Thomas, Woodstock, Sarnia, Stratford, Ingersoll, Strathroy, Exeter.

Services: SLIP/PPP, UUCP, Interactive Accounts, Shell Access.

ONLink
North Bay, Ontario
onlink.net

ONLINK	Voice: (705) 495-2951
Ontario Northland Systems	1-800-667-0053
555 Oak Street East	Fax: (705) 472-6765
North Bay, Ontario	Internet: info@onlink.net
P1B 8L3	

Service Area: North Bay, Timmins, New Liskeard.

Services: Leased Line, SLIP/PPP.

World Wide Web: http://www.onlink.net

ONRAMP Network Services Inc.
Markham, Ontario
onramp.ca

570 Hood Road	Voice: (905) 470-4064
Markham, Ontario	Fax: (905) 477-4808
L3R 4G7	Internet: info@onramp.ca

Service Area: Toronto, Oakville, Aurora, Markham, Pickering.

Services: ISDN, Dedicated Dial-Up, SLIP/PPP.

World Wide Web: http://www.onramp.ca

Passport Online
Toronto, Ontario
passport.ca

173 Dufferin Street	Voice: (416) 516-1616
Suite 302	Fax: (416) 516-1690
Toronto, Ontario	Internet: info@passport.ca
M6K 3H7	

Service Area: Toronto.

Services: Leased Line, ISDN, Dedicated Dial-Up, SLIP/PPP, Interactive Accounts.

World Wide Web: http://www.passport.ca

RESUDOX Online Services
Nepean, Ontario
resudox.net

P.O. Box 33067	Voice: (613) 567-6925
Nepean, Ontario	Fax: (613) 567-8289
K2C 3Y9	Internet: admin@resudox.net

Service Area: Ottawa, Orleans, Nepean, Kanata, Hull, Gloucester.

Services: Dedicated Dial-Up, SLIP/PPP, UUCP, Interactive Accounts, Shell Access.

World Wide Web: http://www.resudox.net

Sentex Communications Corporation
Guelph, Ontario
sentex.net

727 Speedvale Avenue West	Voice: (519) 822-9970
Unit #6	Fax: (519) 822-4775
Guelph, Ontario	Internet: info@sentex.net
N1K 1E6	

Service Area: Kitchener, Waterloo, Cambridge, Guelph, Toronto.

Services: Leased Line, ISDN, Dedicated Dial-Up, SLIP/PPP, UUCP, Interactive Accounts, Shell Access.

World Wide Web: http://www.sentex.net

Soonet Corp.
Sault Ste. Marie, Ontario
soonet.ca

477 Queen Street East	Voice: (705) 253-4700
Sault Ste. Marie, Ontario	Fax: (705) 253-4705
P6A 1Z5	Internet: service@soonet.ca

Service Area: Sault Ste. Marie, Echo Bay, Heyden, Bruce Mines, Deborah, St. Josephs Island.

Services: Dedicated Dial-Up, SLIP/PPP, UUCP, Interactive Accounts, Shell Access.

World Wide Web: http://www.soonet.ca

TerraPort Online Inc.
North York, Ontario
terraport.net

191 Ravel Road
North York, Ontario
M2H 1T1

Voice: (416) 492-3050
Fax: (416) 492-3255
Internet: info@terraport.net

Service Area:	Toronto and Surrounding Area.
Services:	Leased Line, ISDN, Dedicated Dial-Up, SLIP/PPP.
World Wide Web:	http://www.terraport.net

The-Wire
Toronto, Ontario
the-wire.com

12 Sheppard Street
Suite 421
Toronto, Ontario
M5H 3A1

Voice: (416) 214-WIRE (9473)
Fax: (416) 862-WIRE (9473)
Internet: sysadm@the-wire.com

Service Area:	Metropolitan Toronto.
Services:	Dedicated Dial-Up, SLIP/PPP, Interactive Accounts, Shell Access.
World Wide Web:	http://www.the-wire.com

The Usual Suspects
London, Ontario
suspects.com

430 Loverage Street
London, Ontario
N5W 4T7

Voice: (519) 451-4288
Internet: info@suspects.com

Service Area:	London.
Services:	SLIP/PPP, Interactive Accounts, Shell Access.
World Wide Web:	http://www.suspects.com

UUISIS

Nepean, Ontario
uuisis.isis.org

81 Tartan Drive
Nepean, Ontario
K2J 3V6

Voice: (613) 825-5324
Internet: rjbeeth@uuisis.isis.org (Rick Beetham)

Service Area:	Ontario: Gloucester, Kanata, Nepean, Ottawa, Orleans, Vanier. Québec: Hull, Gatineau, Aylmer.
Services:	Dedicated Dial-Up, UUCP, Interactive Accounts.

UUNorth International Inc.

Willowdale, Ontario
north.net

3555 Don Mills Road
Unit 6-304
Willowdale, Ontario
M2H 3N3

Voice: (416) 225-8649
Fax: (416) 225-0525
Internet: info@uunorth.north.net

Service Area:	Toronto.
Services:	Leased Line, ISDN, Dedicated Dial-Up, SLIP/PPP, UUCP, Interactive Accounts.

World Wide Web: http://www.north.net

Vaxxine Computer Systems Inc.

Jordan Station, Ontario
vaxxine.com

4520 Jordan Road
Jordan Station, Ontario
L0R 1S0

Voice: (905) 562-3500
Fax: (905) 562-3515
Internet: admin@vaxxine.com

Service Area:	Grimsby, Beamsville, St. Catharines, Niagara Falls, Welland.
Services:	Leased Line, Dedicated Dial-Up, SLIP/PPP, UUCP, Interactive Accounts, Shell Access.

World Wide Web: http://alpha.vaxxine.com

WINCOM
Windsor, Ontario
wincom.net

4510 Rhodes Drive
Unit 903
Windsor, Ontario
N8W 5K5

Voice: (519) 945-9462
Fax: (519) 944-6610
Internet: info@wincom.net

Service Area:	Windsor, Pleasant Park, McGregor, Emeryville, Belle River, Kingsville, Lasalle, Tecumseh, Amherstburg, Maidstone, Essex, Stoney Point, Leamington, Harrow.
Services:	Leased Line, Dedicated Dial-Up, SLIP/PPP, UUCP, Interactive Accounts, Shell Access.

World Wide Web: http://www.wincom.net

WorldCHAT™
Burlington, Ontario
wchat.on.ca

3018 New Street
Burlington, Ontario
L8P 3B5

Voice: (905) 637-9111
Fax: (905) 637-0140
Internet: info@wchat.on.ca

Service Area:	Metro Toronto, Mississauga, Scarborough, North York, Milton, Oakville, Burlington, Hamilton, Dundas, Ancaster, Stoney Creek, Grimsby, Caledonia, Hagersville.
Services:	Dedicated Dial-Up, SLIP/PPP, UUCP, Interactive Accounts, Shell Access.

World Wide Web: http://www.wchat.on.ca

WorldLink Internet Services Inc.
Ottawa, Ontario
worldlink.ca

600 - 99 Bank Street
Ottawa, Ontario
K1P 6B9

Voice: (613) 233-7100
Fax: (613) 233-9527
Internet: info@worldlink.ca

Service Area:	Almonte, Aylmer, Carleton Place, Carp, Chelsea, Constance Bay, Cumberland, Embrun, Gatineau, Gloucester, Hull, Jockvale, Kanata/Stittsville, Low, Luskville, Manotick, Metcalfe, Navan, North Gower, Orleans, Osgoode, Ottawa, Perkins, Quyon, Richmond, Rockland, Russell, St. Pierre de Wakefield, Wakefield.
Services:	Dedicated Dial-Up, SLIP/PPP, UUCP, Interactive Accounts, Shell Access.

World Wide Web: http://www.worldlink.ca

Québec

Accès Public LLC
Québec City, Québec
llc.org

CP 11
Station B
Québec City, Québec
G1K 7A1

Voice: (418) 692-4711
Fax: (418) 656-8212
Internet: info@llc.org

Service Area:	Greater Québec City area.
Services:	Dedicated Dial-Up, SLIP/PPP, UUCP, Interactive Accounts, Shell Access.
World Wide Web:	http://www.llc.org

CiteNet Telecom Inc.
Montréal, Québec
citenet.net, citenet.com, citenet.ca

4890 Eymard
Montréal, Québec
H1S 1C5

Voice: (514) 721-1351
Internet: info@citenet.net

Service Area:	Montréal.
Services:	Leased Line, ISDN, Dedicated Dial-Up, SLIP/PPP, UUCP, Interactive Accounts, Shell Access.
World Wide Web:	http://www.citenet.net

Communications Accessibles Montréal Inc.
Montréal, Québec
cam.org

2055 Peel, Suite 825
Montréal, Québec
H3A 1V4

Voice: (514) 288-2581
Fax: (514) 288-3401
Internet: info@cam.org

Service Area:	Montréal, Laval, South Shore.
Services:	Dedicated Dial-Up, SLIP/PPP, UUCP, Interactive Accounts, Shell Access.
World Wide Web:	http://www.cam.org

Communications Inter-Accès

Montréal, Québec
interax.net

5475 Pare, Suite 104	Voice: (514) 367-0002
Montréal, Québec	Fax: (514) 368-3529
H4P 1R4	Internet: info@interax.net

Service Area: Montréal, Toronto and Québec City.

Services: Leased Line, ISDN, Dedicated Dial-Up, SLIP/PPP, UUCP.

World Wide Web: http://www.interax.net

Communications Vir

Montréal, Québec
vir.com, montreal.com

C.P. 628, Succursale Victoria	Voice: (514) 933-8886
Montréal, Québec	Fax: (514) 630-9047
H3Z 2Y7	Internet: info@vir.com

Service Area: Greater Montréal area.

Services: Dedicated Dial-Up, SLIP/PPP, Interactive Accounts, Shell Access.

World Wide Web: http://www.vir.com/index.html

FMMO Publications Informatiques

Sherbrooke, Québec
fmmo.ca

289 King Street West	Voice: (819) 565-3666
Sherbrooke, Québec	Fax: (819) 565-4195
J1H 1R2	Internet: info@fmmo.ca

Service Area: Sherbrooke, Lennoxville, Fleurimont, Rock-Forest, Magog, Ascot, Bromptonville, Windsor, Richmond, Coaticook, Compton.

Services: Leased Line, ISDN, Dedicated Dial-Up, SLIP/PPP, UUCP, Interactive Accounts, Shell Access.

World Wide Web: http://www.fmmo.ca

Information Technology Integration
Boisbriand, Québec
iti.qc.ca

2816 Beriot	Voice: (514) 437-6169
Boisbriand, Québec	Fax: (514) 437-6169
J7E 4H4	Internet: lavalle@ey.ca (Mario Lavallee)

Service Area:	Montréal, and St-Jérôme.
Services:	Leased Line, Dedicated Dial-Up, SLIP/PPP, Interactive Accounts, Shell Access.

INFOPUQ
Sainte-Foy, Québec
infopuq.uquebec.ca

Université du Québec	Voice: (418) 657-4422
2875, boulevard Laurier	Fax: (418) 657-2132
Sainte-Foy, Québec	Internet: infopuq@uquebec.ca
G1V 2M3	

Service Area:	Chicoutimi, Hull, Montréal, Québec City, Rimouski, Rouyn-Noranda, Trois-Rivières.
Services:	Interactive Accounts.

Internet Saguenay Lac St-Jean Inc.
Chicoutimi, Québec
saglac.qc.ca

930 Jacques Cartier East	Voice: (418) 543-7777
Chicoutimi, Québec	Fax: (418) 678-1129
G7H 2A9	Internet: info@saglac.qc.ca

Service Area:	Chicoutimi and area.
Services:	Leased Line, Dedicated Dial-Up, PPP.
World Wide Web:	http://saglac.qc.ca

Internet Trois-Rivières

Trois-Rivières, Québec
itr.qc.ca

Internet Trois-Rivières
400, rue Williams
Trois-Rivières, Québec
G9A 3J2

Voice: (819) 379-UNIX
Fax: (819) 379-0343

Service Area:	Trois-Rivières
Services:	Dedicated Dial-Up, SLIP/PPP.
World Wide Web:	http://www.itr.qc.ca

Lanternette Communications

Montréal, Québec
lanternette.com

4670 Ste-Catherine West, #100
Westmount, Québec
H3Z 1S5

Voice: (514) 934-5017
Fax: (514) 939-3594
Internet: info@lanternette.com

Service Area:	Montréal.
Services:	Leased Line, Dedicated Dial-Up, SLIP/PPP.
World Wide Web:	http://www.lanternette.com

Login

Montréal, Québec
login.net

8626, rue de Marseille
Montréal, Québec

Voice: (514) 493-8866
Fax: (514) 626-1700
Internet: info@login.net

Service Area:	Montréal.
Services:	Leased Line, ISDN, Dedicated Dial-Up, SLIP/PPP, UUCP, Interactive Accounts, Shell Access.
World Wide Web:	http://newmarket.com

Magnett Internet Gateway

Montréal, Québec

magnet.ca

1425 René-Lévesque Ouest
Suite 1105
Montréal, Québec
H4C 2G9

Voice: (514) 861-8622
Fax: (514) 861-8640
Internet: info@magnet.ca

Service Area:	Montréal
Services:	SLIP/PPP.

Metrix Interlink Corporation

Montréal, Québec

interlink.net, rezonet.net, interlink.ca

500, boul. René-Lévesque Ouest
Suite #1004
Montréal, Québec
H2Z 1W7

Voice: (514) 875-0010
Fax: (514) 875-5735
Internet: info@interlink.net

Service Area:	Montréal, Toronto, Québec City.
Services:	Leased Line, Dedicated Dial-Up, SLIP/PPP, UUCP, Interactive Accounts, Shell Access.
World Wide Web:	http://www.interlink.net

PubNIX Montréal

Côte St-Luc, Québec

pubnix.qc.ca, pubnix.net

P.O. Box 147
Côte St-Luc, Québec
H4V 2Y3

Voice: (514) 948-2492
Internet: info@pubnix.net

Service Area:	Greater Montréal area.
Services:	Dedicated Dial-Up, SLIP/PPP, UUCP, Interactive Accounts, Shell Access.
World Wide Web:	http://www.pubnix.qc.ca

Réseau Internet Québec Inc.
Levis, Québec
riq.qc.ca

47 Verdun	Voice: (418) 837-9210
Levis, Québec	Fax: (418) 837-6083
G6V 6J2	Internet: info@riq.qc.ca

Service Area:	Québec City.
Services:	Leased Line, ISDN, Dedicated Dial-Up, SLIP/PPP, UUCP.
World Wide Web:	http://www.riq.qc.ca

RISQ (Réseau Interordinateurs Scientifique Québécois)
Montréal, Québec
risq.net

Attention: Centre d'information du RISQ	Voice: (514) 398-1234
1801 McGill College Avenue, Suite 800	Fax: (514) 398-1244
Montréal, Québec	Internet: cirisq@risq.net
H3A 2N4	

Service Area:	Montréal, Québec City, Sherbrooke, Chicoutimi, Hull, and Trois-Rivières.
Services:	Leased Line, Dedicated Dial-Up, Dedicated SLIP/PPP.
World Wide Web:	http://www.risq.net

Vircom Inc.
Laval, Québec
vircom.com, gamemaster.qc.ca

1600 Blvd. Le Corbusier	Voice: (514) 990-2532
P.O. Box 58009	Internet: glador@vircom.com
Laval, Québec	
H7S 2M4	

Service Area:	Montréal.
Services:	Dedicated Dial-Up, SLIP/PPP, Interactive Accounts.
World Wide Web:	http://www.vircom.com

Nova Scotia

Internet Services and Information Systems Inc. (ISIS)
Halifax, Nova Scotia
isisnet.com

Suite 1501
Maritime Centre
1505 Barrington Street
Halifax, Nova Scotia

Voice: (902) 429-4747
Fax: (902) 429-9003
Internet: info@isisnet.com

Service Area:	Halifax/Dartmouth Metropolitan area, including Sackville and Bedford.
Services:	Leased Line, Dedicated Dial-Up, SLIP/PPP, UUCP, Interactive Accounts, Shell Access.

World Wide Web: http://www.isisnet.com

Nova Scotia Technology Network Inc. (NSTN)
Dartmouth, Nova Scotia
nstn.ca

201 Brownlow Avenue
Dartmouth, Nova Scotia
B3B 1W2

Voice: (902) 481-NSTN (6786)
            1-800-336-4445 (Toll-Free Canada-Wide)
Fax: (902) 468-3679
Internet: info@nstn.ca (Automated)
           sales@nstn.ca (Sales/Marketing Team)

Service Area:	Nova Scotia: Amherst, Truro, Halifax, Bridgewater, Yarmouth, Kentville, Greenwood, Sydney. New Brunswick: Moncton, Dieppe, Riverview, Salisbury. Ontario: Toronto, Ottawa.
Services:	Leased Line, ISDN, Dedicated Dial-Up, SLIP/PPP, UUCP.

World Wide Web: http://www.nstn.ca

New Brunswick

Maritime Internet Services
Saint John, New Brunswick
mi.net

28 King Street
P.O. Box 6477
Partown Place
Saint John, New Brunswick
E2L 4R9

Voice: (506) 652-3624
Fax: (506) 652-5451
Internet: info@mi.net

Service Area:	Saint John, New Brunswick.
Services:	Leased Line, Dedicated Dial-Up, SLIP/PPP, UUCP, Interactive Accounts.
World Wide Web:	http://www.mi.net

NBNet
Saint John, New Brunswick
nbnet.nb.ca

New Brunswick Telephone Company Ltd. (NBTel)
One Brunswick Square
P.O. Box 1430
Saint John, New Brunswick
E2L 4K2

Voice: 1-800-561-4459 (New Brunswick)
          (506) 458-1690
Internet: info@nbnet.nb.ca

Service Area:	All of New Brunswick.
Services:	Leased Line, Dedicated Dial-Up, SLIP/PPP.
World Wide Web:	http://www.nbnet.nb.ca

Nova Scotia Technology Network Inc. (NSTN)
Dartmouth, Nova Scotia
nstn.ca

201 Brownlow Avenue
Dartmouth, Nova Scotia
B3B 1W2

Voice: (902) 481-NSTN (6786)
          1-800-336-4445 (Toll-Free Canada-Wide)
Fax: (902) 468-3679
Internet: info@nstn.ca (Automated)
          sales@nstn.ca (Sales/Marketing Team)

Service Area:	Moncton, Dieppe, Riverview, Salisbury

See main entry under Province of Nova Scotia.

Prince Edward Island

Island Services Network
Charlottetown, Prince Edward Island
isn.net

129 Kent Street	Voice:	(902) 892-4ISN (4476)
Charlottetown, Prince Edward Island	Fax:	(902) 892-DATA (3282)
C1A 1N4	Internet:	sales@isn.net

Service Area: Charlottetown.

Services: Leased Line, Dedicated Dial-Up, SLIP/PPP, UUCP.

World Wide Web: http://www.isn.net

PEINet Inc.
Charlottetown, Prince Edward Island
peinet.pe.ca

P.O. Box 3126	Voice:	(902) 892-PEINet (7346)
Charlottetown, Prince Edward Island	Fax:	(902) 368-2446
C1A 7N9		

Service Area: Complete local access across Prince Edward Island.

Services: Leased Line, Dedicated Dial-Up, SLIP/PPP, Interactive Accounts, Shell Access.

World Wide Web: http://www.peinet.pe.ca

Raven Information Systems
Charlottetown, Prince Edward Island
raven.net

P.O. Box 2906	Voice:	(902) 894-4946
Charlottetown, Prince Edward Island	Internet:	Dale_Poole@raven.net
C1A 8C5		

Service Area: Prince Edward Island.

Services: UUCP, Interactive Accounts (e-mail and USENET only).

Newfoundland

Compusult Limited
Mount Pearl, Newfoundland
compusult.nf.ca

40 Bannister Street	Voice: (709) 745-7914
Mount Pearl, Newfoundland	Fax: (709) 745-7927
A1N 1W1	Internet: info@compusult.nf.ca

Service Area: St. John's and Mount Pearl.

Services: Leased Line, Dedicated Dial-Up, SLIP/PPP, UUCP, Interactive Accounts, Shell Access.

World Wide Web: http://www.compusult.nf.ca

The Enterprise Network Inc.
St. John's, Newfoundland
entnet.nf.ca

P.O. Box 13670	Voice: 1-800-563-5008
Station "A"	Fax: (709) 729-7039
St. John's, Newfoundland	Internet: Customer_Service@porthole.entnet.nf.ca
A1B 4G1	

Service Area: St. John's, Clarenville, St. Alban's, Stephenville, Baie Verte, Forteau. 1-800 service is available elsewhere in the province.

Services: Interactive Accounts.

NLnet (Newfoundland Regional Network)
St. John's, Newfoundland
nlnet.nf.ca

c/o Department of Computing and Communications	Voice: (709) 737-4555
Memorial University of Newfoundland	Fax: (709) 737-3514
St. John's, Newfoundland	Internet: support@nlnet.nf.ca
A1C 5S7	

Service Area: St. John's, Clarenville, Corner Brook, Grand Falls, Windsor, Labrador City, Stephenville, Burin and Gander.

Services: Leased Line, Dedicated Dial-Up, SLIP/PPP, Interactive Accounts, Shell Access.

World Wide Web: http://www.nlnet.nf.ca

STEM~Net
St. John's, Newfoundland
stemnet.nf.ca

Memorial University of Newfoundland	Voice: (709) 737-8836
E-5038, G.A. Hickman Building	Fax: (709) 737-2179
St. John's, Newfoundland	Internet: staff@calvin.stemnet.nf.ca
A1B 3X8	

Service Area:	Labrador City, Stephenville, Corner Brook, Gander, St. John's, Grand Falls, Windsor, Marystown, Clarenville.
Services:	SLIP/PPP, Interactive Accounts, Shell Access. (Note: services are restricted to qualified Newfoundland educators.)
World Wide Web:	http://info.stemnet.nf.ca

U.S.-Based Providers

America Online Inc.
Vienna, Virginia
aol.com

8619 Westwood Center Drive	Voice: 1-800-827-6364 (Canada Toll-Free)
Vienna, Virginia 22182-2285	Corporate Headquarters: (703) 448-8700

Service Area:	Burnaby (B.C.), Calgary, Dundas (Ontario), Edmonton, Halifax, Hull, Kitchener, London, Ottawa, Toronto, Vancouver, Winnipeg and Windsor.
Services:	Interactive Accounts.

ANS
Elmsford, NY
info@ans.net

1875 Campus Commons Drive, Suite 220	Voice: 1-800-456-8267 or (703) 758-7700
Reston, VA 22091-1552	Fax: (703) 758-7717
	Corporate Headquarters: (914) 789-5300

Service Area:	Primarily in the U.S.; also internationally via agreements with organizations based in the country of origin.
Services:	Leased Line, Dedicated SLIP/PPP.
World Wide Web:	http://www.ans.net

BIX

Cambridge, Massachusetts
bix.com

Delphi Internet Services
1030 Massachusetts Avenue
Cambridge, Massachusetts 02138

Voice: (617) 354-4137
Corporate Headquarters: (617) 491-3342
Fax: (617) 491-6642
Internet: info@bix.com

Service Area:	Burnaby (B.C.), Calgary, Dundas (Ontario), Edmonton, Halifax, Hull, Kitchener, London, Ottawa, Toronto, Vancouver, Winnipeg and Windsor.
Services:	Interactive Accounts.

CompuServe Incorporated

Columbus, Ohio
compuserve.com

5000 Arlington Center Blvd.
Columbus, Ohio 43220

Voice: 1-800-848-8199 Canada Toll-Free
Corporate Headquarters: (614) 457-8600
Fax: (614) 457-0348 (Corporate Office)

Service Area:	There are local access numbers in the following Canadian cities: Calgary, Edmonton, Halifax, London, Montréal, Ottawa, Regina, Québec City, Saskatoon, Toronto, Vancouver, Winnipeg. CompuServe is rapidly adding new local access numbers in Canada. Call CompuServe to determine if there is a local access number in your community.
Services:	Interactive Accounts.
World Wide Web:	http://www.compuserve.com

DELPHI

Cambridge, Massachusetts
delphi.com

Delphi Internet Services
1030 Massachusetts Avenue
Cambridge, Massachusetts 02138

Voice: (617) 491-3393 or 1-800-695-4005 (Toll-Free)
Corporate Headquarters: (617) 491-3342
Fax: (617) 491-6642
Internet: askdelphi@delphi.com

Service Area:	Burnaby (B.C.), Calgary, Dundas (Ontario), Edmonton, Halifax, Hull, Kitchener, London, Ottawa, Toronto, Vancouver, Winnipeg and Windsor.
Services:	Interactive Accounts.
World Wide Web:	http://www.delphi.com

eWorld (Apple Computer Inc.)
Cupertino, California and Markham, Ontario
eworld.com

20525 Mariani Avenue
Cupertino, California 95014

Voice: 1-800-775-4556 Toll-Free

Service Area:	Burnaby (B.C.), Vancouver, Calgary, Edmonton, Winnipeg, Dundas (Ontario), Kitchener, London, Ottawa, Toronto, Windsor, Montréal, Québec City, Halifax.
Services:	Interactive Accounts.
World Wide Web:	http://www.eworld.com

GEnie
Rockville, Maryland
genie.geis.com

GE Information Services
P.O. Box 6403
Rockville, Maryland 20850-1785

Voice: 1-800-638-9636 Canada Toll-Free
Fax: (301) 251-6421

Service Area:	Calgary, Edmonton, Halifax, Hamilton, Kitchener, London, Mississauga, Montréal, Ottawa, Québec City, Toronto, Vancouver, Victoria, Winnipeg.
Services:	Interactive Accounts.
World Wide Web:	http://www.ge.com/geis/index.html

HoloNet
Berkeley, California
holonet.net

Information Access Technologies Inc.
46 Shattuck Square, Suite 11
Berkeley, California, 94704

Voice: (510) 704-0160
Fax: (510) 704-8019
Internet: info@iat.mailer.net or support@holonet.net

Service Area:	Calgary, Edmonton, Halifax, London, Montréal, Ottawa, Regina, Québec City, Saskatoon, Toronto, Vancouver, Winnipeg.
Services:	Dedicated Dial-Up, SLIP/PPP, UUCP, Interactive Accounts.
World Wide Web:	http://www.holonet.net

MCI Mail
Washington, D.C.
mcimail.com

1133 19th Street
Washington, D.C. 20036

Voice: 1-800-444-6245 (Canada Toll-Free)
Direct Dial: (202) 833-8484
Fax: (202) 416-5858
Internet: 3393527@mcimail.com (MCI Mail Customer Support)

Service Area:	Local access numbers across Canada.
Services:	E-mail only.

NovaLink Interactive Networks
Westborough, Massachusetts
novalink.com

200 Friberg Parkway - Suite 4003
Westborough, Massachusetts 01581

Voice: 1-800-274-2814 Canada Toll-Free
Fax: (508) 836-4766
Internet: info@novalink.com

Service Area:	Calgary, Edmonton, Halifax, London, Montréal, Ottawa, Regina, Québec City, Saskatoon, Toronto, Vancouver, Winnipeg.
Services:	Dedicated Dial-Up, SLIP, Interactive Accounts, Shell Access.
World Wide Web:	http://www.novalink.com

Prodigy
White Plains, New York
prodigy.com

445 Hamilton Avenue
White Plains, New York 10601

Voice: 1-800-PRODIGY (1-800-776-3449) Toll-Free

Service Area:	Local dial-up numbers in 20 Canadian cities. Call Prodigy to determine if there is a local access number near you.
Services:	Interactive Accounts.
World Wide Web:	http://www.astranet.com

The WELL
Sausalito, California
well.com, well.sf.ca.us

1750 Bridgeway
Sausalito, California 94965-1900

Voice: (415) 332-4335
Fax: (415) 332-4927
Internet: info@well.com

Service Area:	Calgary, Edmonton, Halifax, London, Montréal, Ottawa, Regina, Québec City, Saskatoon, Toronto, Vancouver, Winnipeg.
Services:	Interactive Accounts.
World Wide Web:	http://www.well.com

Index